BMW
SIX CYLINDER COUPES & SALOONS
Gold Portfolio
1969-1976

Compiled by
R.M.Clarke

ISBN 1 85520 4371

 BROOKLANDS BOOKS LTD.
P.O. BOX 146, COBHAM,
SURREY, KT11 1LG. UK

Printed in Hong Kong

Brooklands Books

MOTORING

BROOKLANDS ROAD TEST SERIES

Abarth Gold Portfolio 1950-1971
AC Ace & Aceca 1953-1983
Alfa Romeo Giulietta Gold Portfolio 1954-1965
Alfa Romeo Giulia Coupés 1963-1976
Alfa Romeo Giulia Coupés Gold Port. 1963-1976
Alfa Romeo Spider 1966-1990
Alfa Romeo Spider Gold Portfolio 1966-1991
Alfa Romeo Alfasud 1972-1984
Alfa Romeo Alfetta Gold Portfolio 1972-1987
Alfa Romeo Alfetta GTV6 1980-1986
Allard Gold Portfolio 1937-1959
Alvis Gold Portfolio 1919-1967
AMX & Javelin Muscle Portfolio 1968-1974
Armstrong Siddeley Gold Portfolio 1945-1960
Aston Martin Gold Portfolio 1948-1971
Aston Martin Gold Portfolio 1972-1985
Aston Martin Gold Portfolio 1985-1995
Audi Quattro Gold Portfolio 1980-1991
Austin A30 & A35 1951-1962
Austin Healey 100 & 100/6 Gold Portfolio 1952-1959
Austin Healey 3000 Gold Portfolio 1959-1967
Austin Healey Sprite Gold Portfolio 1958-1971
Barracuda Muscle Portfolio 1964-1974
BMW 1600 Collection No.1 1966-1981
BMW 2002 Gold Portfolio 1968-1976
BMW 6 Cylinder Coupés & Saloons Gold P. 1969-1976
BMW 316, 318, 320 (4 cyl.) Gold Port. 1975-1990
BMW 320, 323, 325 (6 cyl.) Gold Port. 1977-1990
BMW M Series Gold Portfolio 1976-1997
BMW 5 Series Gold Portfolio 1981-1987
BMW 6 Series Gold Portfolio 1976-1989
Bricklin Gold Portfolio 1974-1975
Bristol Cars Gold Portfolio 1946-1992
Buick Automobiles 1947-1960
Buick Muscle Cars 1965-1970
Cadillac Allanté 1986-1993
Cadillac Automobiles 1949-1959
Cadillac Automobiles 1960-1969
Caprice 1965-1976 Limited Edition
Charger Muscle Portfolio 1966-1974
Checker Limited Edition
Chevrolet 1955-1957
Impala & SS Muscle Portfolio 1958-1972
Chevrolet Corvair 1959-1969
Chevy II & Nova SS Muscle Portfolio 1962-1974
El Camino & SS Muscle Portfolio 1959-1987
Chevelle & SS Muscle Portfolio 1964-1972
Chevrolet Muscle Cars 1966-1971
Chevy Blazer 1969-1981
Chevrolet Corvette Gold Portfolio 1953-1962
Chevrolet Corvette Sting Ray Gold Port. 1963-1967
Chevrolet Corvette Gold Portfolio 1968-1977
High Performance Corvettes 1983-1989
Camaro Muscle Portfolio 1967-1973
Chevrolet Camaro & Z-28 1973-1981
High Performance Camaros 1982-1988
Chrysler 300 Gold Portfolio 1955-1970
Imperial 1955-1970 Limited Edition
Chrysler Valiant 1960-1962
Citroen Traction Avant Gold Portfolio 1934-1957
Citroen 2CV Gold Portfolio 1948-1989
Citroen DS & ID 1955-1975
Citroen DS & ID Gold Portfolio 1955-1975
Citroen SM 1970-1975
Cobras & Replicas 1962-1983
Shelby Cobra Gold Portfolio 1962-1969
Cobras & Cobra Replicas Gold Portfolio 1962-1989
Crosley & Crosley Specials Limited Edition
Cunningham Automobiles 1951-1955
Daimler SP250 Sports & V-8 250 Saloon Gold P. 1959-1969
Datsun Roadsters 1962-1971
Datsun 240Z & 260Z Gold Portfolio 1970-1978
Datsun 280Z & ZX 1975-1983
DeLorean Gold Portfolio 1977-1995
Dodge Muscle Cars 1967-1970
Dodge Viper on the Road
ERA Gold Portfolio 1934-1994
Excalibur Collection No.1 1952-1981
Facel Vega 1954-1964
Ferrari 1947-1957 Limited Edition
Ferrari 1958-1963 Limited Edition
Ferrari Dino 1965-1974
Ferrari Dino 308 & Mondial Gold Portfolio 1974-1985
Ferrari 328 348 Mondial Gold Portfolio 1986-1994
Fiat 500 Gold Portfolio 1936-1972
Fiat 600 & 850 Gold Portfolio 1955-1972
Fiat Pininfarina 124 & 2000 Spider 1968-1985
Fiat X1/9 Gold Portfolio1973-1989
Fiat Abarth Performance Portfolio 1972-1987
Ford Consul, Zephyr, Zodiac Mk. I & II 1950-1962
Ford Zephyr, Zodiac, Executive Mk. III & IV 1962-1971
Ford Cortina 1600E & GT 1967-1970
High Performance Capris Gold Portfolio 1969-1987
Capri Muscle Portfolio 1974-1987
High Performance Fiestas 1979-1991
High Performance Escorts Mk. I 1968-1974
High Performance Escorts Mk. II 1975-1980
High Performance Escorts 1980-1985
High Performance Escorts 1985-1990
High Perf. Sierras & Merkurs Gold Portfolio 1983-1990
Ford Automobiles 1949-1959
Ford Fairlane 1955-1970
Ford Ranchero 1957-1959
Edsel 1957-1960 Limited Edition
Ford Thunderbird 1955-1957
Ford Thunderbird 1958-1963
Ford GT40 Gold Portfolio 1964-1987
Ford Bronco 1966-1977
Ford Bronco 1978-1988
Goggomobil Limited Edition
Holden 1948-1962
Honda CRX 1983-1987
Hudson 1946-1957 Limited Edition
International Scout Gold Portfolio 1961-1980
Isetta Gold Portfolio 1953-1964
ISO & Bizzarrini Gold Portfolio 1962-1974
Kaiser - Frazer 1946-1955 Limited Edition
Jaguar and SS Gold Portfolio 1931-1951
Jaguar C-Type & D-Type Gold Portfolio 1951-1960
Jaguar XK120, 140, 150 Gold Portfolio 1948-1960
Jaguar Mk. VII, VIII, IX, X, 420 Gold Port. 1950-1970
Jaguar Mk. 1 & Mk. 2 Gold Portfolio 1959-1969
Jaguar E-Type Gold Portfolio 1961-1971
Jaguar E-Type V-12 1971-1975
Jaguar S-Type & 420 Limited Edition
Jaguar XJ12, XJ5.3, V12 Gold Portfolio 1972-1990
Jaguar XJ6 Series I & II Gold Portfolio 1968-1979
Jaguar XJ6 Series III Perf. Portfolio 1979-1986
Jaguar XJ6 Gold Portfolio 1986-1994
Jaguar XJS Gold Portfolio 1975-1988
Jaguar XJS Gold Portfolio 1988-1995
Jaguar XK8 Limited Edition
Jeep CJ5 & CJ6 1960-1976
Jeep CJ5 & CJ7 1976-1986
Jensen Interceptor Gold Portfolio 1966-1986
Jensen Healey 1972-1976
Lagonda Gold Portfolio 1919-1964
Lancia Aurelia & Flaminia Gold Portfolio 1950-1970
Lancia Fulvia Gold Portfolio 1963-1976
Lancia Beta Gold Portfolio 1972-1984
Lancia Delta Gold Portfolio 1979-1994
Lancia Stratos 1972-1985
Land Rover Series I 1948-1958
Land Rover Series II & IIa 1958-1971
Land Rover Series III 1971-1985
Land Rover 90 110 Defender Gold Portfolio 1983-1994
Land Rover Discovery 1989-1994
Land Rover Story Part One 1948-1971
Lincoln Gold Portfolio 1949-1960
Lincoln Continental 1961-1969
Lincoln Continental 1969-1976
Lotus Sports Racers Gold Portfolio 1953-1965
Lotus Seven Gold Portfolio 1957-1973
Lotus Caterham Seven Gold Portfolio 1974-1995
Lotus Elan Gold Portfolio 1962-1974
Lotus Elan Collection No. 2 1963-1972
Lotus Elan & SE 1989-1992
Lotus Europa Gold Portfolio 1966-1975
Lotus Elite & Eclat 1974-1982
Lotus Turbo Esprit 1980-1986
Marcos Coupés & Spyders Gold Portfolio 1960-1997
Maserati 1965-1970
Matra 1965-1983 Limited Edition
Mazda Miata MX-5 Performance Portfolio 1989-1996
Mazda RX-7 Gold Portfolio 1978-1991
McLaren F1 Sportscar Limited Edition
Mercedes 190 & 300 SL 1954-1963
Mercedes G-Wagen 1981-1994
Mercedes S & 600 1965-1972
Mercedes S Class 1972-1979
Mercedes 230 • 250 • 280SL Gold Portfolio 1963-1971
Mercedes SLs & SLCs Gold Portfolio 1971-1989
Mercedes SLs Performance Portfolio 1989-1994
Mercury Muscle Cars 1966-1971
Messerschmitt Gold Portfolio 1954-1964
MG Gold Portfolio 1929-1939
MG TA & TC Gold Portfolio 1936-1949
MG TD & TF Gold Portfolio 1949-1955
MGA & Twin Cam Gold Portfolio 1955-1962
MG Midget Gold Portfolio 1961-1979
MGB Roadsters 1962-1980
MGB MGC & V8 Gold Portfolio 1962-1980
MGB GT 1965-1980
MGC & MGB GT V8 Limited Edition
MG Y-Type & Magnette ZA/ZB Limited Edition
Mini Gold Portfolio 1959-1969
Mini Gold Portfolio 1969-1980
Mini Gold Portfolio 1981-1997
High Performance Minis Gold Portfolio 1960-1973
Mini Cooper Gold Portfolio 1961-1971
Mini Moke Gold Portfolio 1964-1994
Morgan Three-Wheeler Gold Portfolio 1910-1952
Morgan Plus 4 & Four 4 Gold Portfolio 1936-1967
Morgan Cars Gold Portfolio 1968-1989
Morris Minor Collection No. 1 1948-1980
Shelby Mustang Muscle Portfolio 1965-1970
High Performance Mustang IIs 1974-1978
High Performance Mustangs 1982-1988
Nash & Nash-Healey 1949-1957 Limited Edition
Nash-Austin Metropolitan Gold Portfolio 1954-1962
Oldsmobile Automobiles 1955-1963
Oldsmobile Toronado 1966-1978
Opel GT Gold Portfolio 1968-1973
Opel Manta 1970-1975 Limited Edition
Packard Gold Portfolio 1946-1958
Pantera Gold Portfolio 1970-1989
Panther Gold Portfolio 1972-1990
Pontiac Tempest & GTO 1961-1965
Firebird & Trans-Am Muscle Portfolio 1973-1981
High Performance Firebirds 1982-1988
Pontiac Fiero 1984-1988
Porsche 356 Gold Portfolio 1953-1965
Porsche 912 Limited Edition
Porsche 911 1965-1969
Porsche 911 1970-1972
Porsche 911 1973-1977
Porsche 911 SC & Turbo Gold Portfolio 1978-1983
Porsche 911 Carrera & Turbo Gold Port. 1984-1989
Porsche 911 Gold Portfolio 1990-1997
Porsche 924 Gold Portfolio 1975-1988
Porsche 928 Performance Portfolio 1977-1994
Porsche 944 Gold Portfolio 1981-1991
Porsche 968 Limited Edition
Range Rover Gold Portfolio 1970-1985
Range Rover Gold Portfolio 1986-1995
Reliant Scimitar 1964-1986
Renault Alpine Gold Portfolio 1958-1994
Riley Gold Portfolio 1924-1939
R. R. Silver Cloud & Bentley 'S' Series Gold P.1955-1965
Rolls Royce Silver Shadow Gold Portfolio 1965-1980
Rolls Royce & Bentley Gold Portfolio 1980-1989
Rolls Royce & Bentley Limited Edition 1990-1997
Rover P4 1949-1959
Rover P4 1955-1964
Rover 3 & 3.5 Litre Gold Portfolio 1958-1973
Rover 2000 & 2200 1963-1977
Rover 3500 & Vitesse 1976-1986
Saab Sonett Collection No.1 1966-1974
Saab Turbo 1976-1983
Studebaker Gold Portfolio 1947-1966
Studebaker Hawks & Larks 1956-1963
Avanti 1962-1990
Sunbeam Tiger & Alpine Gold Portfolio 1959-1967
Toyota Land Cruiser Gold Portfolio 1956-1987
Toyota Land Cruiser 1988-1997
Triumph Dolomite Sprint Limited Edition
Triumph TR2 & TR3 Gold Portfolio 1952-1961
Triumph TR4, TR5, TR250 1961-1968
Triumph TR6 Gold Portfolio 1969-1976
Triumph TR7 & TR8 Gold Portfolio 1975-1982
Triumph Herald 1959-1971
Triumph Vitesse 1962-1971
Triumph Spitfire Gold Portfolio 1962-1980
Triumph 2000, 2.5, 2500 1963-1977
Triumph GT6 Gold Portfolio 1966-1974
Triumph Stag Gold Portfolio 1970-1977
TVR Gold Portfolio 1959-1986
TVR Performance Portfolio 1986-1994
VW Beetle Gold Portfolio 1935-1967
VW Beetle Gold Portfolio 1968-1991
VW Beetle Collection No.1 1970-1982
VW Karmann Ghia 1955-1982
VW Bus, Camper, Van 1954-1967
VW Bus, Camper, Van 1968-1979
VW Bus, Camper, Van 1979-1989
VW Scirocco 1974-1981
VW Golf GTI 1976-1986
Volvo PV444 & PV544 1945-1965
Volvo Amazon-120 Gold Portfolio 1956-1970
Volvo 1800 Gold Portfolio 1960-1973
Volvo 140 & 160 Series Gold Portfolio 1966-1975
Westfield Limited Edition

Forty Years of Selling Volvo

BROOKLANDS ROAD & TRACK SERIES

Road & Track on Alfa Romeo 1964-1970
Road & Track on Alfa Romeo 1971-1976
Road & Track on Aston Martin 1962-1990
R & T on Auburn Cord and Duesenburg 1952-84
Road & Track on Audi & Auto Union 1952-1980
Road & Track on Audi & Auto Union 1980-1986
Road & Track on Austin Healey 1953-1970
Road & Track on BMW Cars 1966-1974
Road & Track on BMW Cars 1975-1978
Road & Track on BMW Cars 1979-1983
R & T on Cobra, Shelby & Ford GT40 1962-1992
Road & Track on Corvette 1953-1967p
Road & Track on Corvette 1968-1982
Road & Track on Corvette 1982-1986
Road & Track on Corvette 1986-1990
Road & Track on Ferrari 1975-1981
Road & Track on Ferrari 1981-1984
Road & Track on Ferrari 1984-1988
Road & Track on Fiat Sports Cars 1968-1987
Road & Track on Jaguar 1950-1960
Road & Track on Jaguar 1961-1968
Road & Track on Jaguar 1968-1974
Road & Track on Jaguar 1974-1982
Road & Track on Jaguar 1983-1989
Road & Track on Lamborghini 1964-1985
Road & Track on Lotus 1972-1983
R & T on Mazda RX-7 & MX-5 Miata 1986-1991
Road & Track on Mercedes 1952-1962
Road & Track on Mercedes 1963-1970
Road & Track on Mercedes 1971-1979
Road & Track on Mercedes 1980-1987
Road & Track on MG Sports Cars 1949-1961
Road & Track on MG Sports Cars 1962-1980
R & T on Nissan 300-ZX & Turbo 1984-1989
Road & Track on Pontiac 1960-1983
Road & Track on Porsche 1951-1967
Road & Track on Porsche 1968-1971
Road & Track on Porsche 1972-1975
Road & Track on Porsche 1975-1978
Road & Track on Porsche 1979-1982
Road & Track on Porsche 1985-1988
R & T on Rolls Royce & Bentley 1950-1965
R & T on Rolls Royce & Bentley 1966-1984
Road & Track on Saab 1972-1992
R & T on Toyota Sports & GT Cars 1966-1984
R & T on Triumph Sports Cars 1953-1967
R & T on Triumph Sports Cars 1967-1974
R & T on Triumph Sports Cars 1974-1982
Road & Track on Volkswagen 1951-1968
Road & Track on Volkswagen 1968-1978
Road & Track on Volkswagen 1978-1985
Road & Track on Volvo 1957-1974
Road & Track on Volvo 1977-1994
R & T - Henry Manney at Large & Abroad
R & T - Peter Egan's "Side Glances"
R & T - Peter Egan "At Large"

BROOKLANDS CAR AND DRIVER SERIES

Car and Driver on BMW 1955-1977
Car and Driver on Corvette 1978-1982
Car and Driver on Corvette 1983-1988
C and D on Datsun Z 1600 & 2000 1966-1984
Car and Driver on Ferrari 1955-1962
Car and Driver on Ferrari 1963-1975
Car and Driver on Ferrari 1976-1983
Car and Driver on Mopar 1956-1967
Car and Driver on Mopar 1968-1975
Car and Driver on Mustang 1964-1972
Car and Driver on Pontiac 1961-1975
Car and Driver on Porsche 1955-1962
Car and Driver on Porsche 1963-1970
Car and Driver on Porsche 1970-1976
Car and Driver on Porsche 1977-1981
Car and Driver on Porsche 1982-1986
Car and Driver on Volvo 1955-1986

BROOKLANDS PRACTICAL CLASSICS SERIES

PC on Austin A40 Restoration
PC on Land Rover Restoration
PC on Metalworking in Restoration
PC on Midget/Sprite Restoration
PC on MGB Restoration
PC on Sunbeam Rapier Restoration
PC on Triumph Herald/Vitesse
PC on Spitfire Restoration

BROOKLANDS HOT ROD 'MUSCLECAR & HI-PO ENGINES' SERIES

Chevy 265 & 283
Chevy 302 & 327
Chevy 348 & 409
Chevy 350 & 400
Chevy 396 & 427
Chevy 454 thru 512
Chrysler Hemi
Chrysler 273, 318, 340 & 360
Chrysler 361, 383, 400, 413, 426, 440
Ford 289, 302, Boss 302 & 351W
Ford 351C & Boss 351
Ford Big Block

BROOKLANDS RESTORATION SERIES

Auto Restoration Tips & Techniques
Basic Bodywork Tips & Techniques
Classic Camaro Restoration
Chevrolet High Performance Tips & Techniques
Chevy Engine Swapping Tips & Techniques
Chevy-GMC Pickup Repair
Chrysler Engine Swapping Tips & Techniques
Engine Swapping Tips & Techniques
Ford Pickup Repair
Land Rover Restoration Tips & Techniques
MG 'T' Series Restoration Guide
MGA Restoration Guide
Mustang Restoration Tips & Techniques

MOTORCYCLING

BROOKLANDS ROAD TEST SERIES

AJS & Matchless Gold Portfolio 1945-1966
BSA Twins A7 & A10 Gold Portfolio 1946-1962
BSA Twins A50 & A65 Gold Portfolio 1962-1973
BMW Motorcycles Gold Portfolio 1950-1971
BMW Motorcycles Gold Portfolio 1971-1976
Ducati Gold Portfolio 1960-1974
Ducati Gold Portfolio 1974-1978
Ducati Gold Portfolio 1978-1982
Laverda Gold Portfolio 1967-1977
Moto Guzzi Gold Portfolio 1949-1973
Norton Commando Gold Portfolio 1968-1977
Triumph Bonneville Gold Portfolio 1959-1983
Vincent Gold Portfolio 1945-1980

BROOKLANDS CYCLE WORLD SERIES

Cycle World on BMW 1974-1980
Cycle World on BMW 1981-1986
Cycle World on Ducati 1982-1991
Cycle World on Harley-Davidson 1962-1968
Cycle World on Harley-Davidson 1978-1983
Cycle World on Harley-Davidson 1983-1987
Cycle World on Harley-Davidson 1987-1990
Cycle World on Harley-Davidson 1990-1992
Cycle World on Honda 1962-1967
Cycle World on Honda 1968-1971
Cycle World on Honda 1971-1974
Cycle World on Husqvarna 1966-1976
Cycle World on Husqvarna 1977-1984
Cycle World on Kawasaki 1966-1971
Cycle World on Kawasaki Off-Road Bikes 1972-1979
Cycle World on Kawasaki Street Bikes 1972-1976
Cycle World on Norton 1962-1971
Cycle World on Suzuki 1962-1970
Cycle World on Suzuki Off-Road Bikes 1971-1976
Cycle World on Suzuki Street Bikes 1971-1976
Cycle World on Triumph 1967-1972
Cycle World on Yamaha 1962-1969
Cycle World on Yamaha Off-Road Bikes 1970-1974
Cycle World on Yamaha Street Bikes 1970-1974

MILITARY

BROOKLANDS MILITARY VEHICLES SERIES

Allied Military Vehicles No.2 1941-1946
Complete WW2 Military Jeep Manual
Dodge Military Vehicles No.1 1940-1945
Hail To The Jeep
Military & Civilian Amphibians 1940-1990
Off Road Jeeps: Civ. & Mil. 1944-1971
US Military Vehicles 1941-1945
US Army Military Vehicles WW2-TM9-2800
VW Kubelwagen Military Portfolio 1940-1990
WW 2 Jeep Military Portfolio 1941-1945

RACING

Le Mans - The Jaguar Years - 1949-1957
Le Mans - The Ferrari Years - 1958-1965
Le Mans - The Ford & Matra Years - 1966-1974
Le Mans - The Porsche Years - 1975-1982

7117

CONTENTS

ACKNOWLEDGEMENTS

As interest increases in modern BMWS, so the older classic models are becoming more and more appreciated. This is why, when the print run of our earlier Road Test volume on the six-cylinder coupés was exhausted, we decided not to go for a simple reprint but rather for an enlarged volume in our Gold Portfolio series. This new book covers not only the coupés - long accepted as classics - but also the contemporary big saloons with which they shared so much.

Regular readers of Brooklands books will know that our Gold Portfolio and other road test volumes make available printed material which has become hard to find. In putting these books together, we depend on the generosity and understanding of those who originally published the material, and for the present volume, our sincere thanks go to the owners of *Autocar, Autosport, Car, Car and Driver, Car South Africa, Classic and Sportscar, Competition Car International, Competition Car, Modern Motor, Motor, Motor Sport, Motor Trend, Popular Classics, Road & Track, Road Test, Sports Car Graphic, Sports Car World, Track and Traffic, Wheels* and *World Car Guide.*

R.M. Clarke

Nineteen sixty-eight was a milestone year for BMW. Not only was it the year when production exceeded 500 cars a day for the first time ever, but it was also the year when two brand-new six-cylinder ranges were introduced at the Frankfurt Show. They were the E3 saloons and the E9 coupés, and they shared the new iron-block, alloy-head M52 engine, latterly known to BMW fans as the "Big Six".

The saloons picked up several features which the Neue Klasse models had introduced seven years earlier. Although their body shells were new, they shared the big glass area, crisp lines and forward-sloping front panel of the smaller saloons, adding to this a neat twin-headlamp installation. Like the Neue Klasse, they also had all-round independent suspension, with MacPherson struts at the front and semi-trailing arms at the rear.

The new saloons came in 2500 and 2800 forms, and were priced to do battle with Mercedes' 250 and 250SE models. The new coupés, meanwhile, came in 2800CS guise to take on Stuttgart's ageing but newly re-engined 280SE coupés. The BMWs looked fresh, even though they were actually re-engined and facelifted editions of the earlier 2000 and 2000CS four-cylinder coupés. Their wheelbases had been stretched by three inches ahead of the passenger cabin to accommodate the new engine, and a new four-lamp nose gave them a family resemblance to the new E3 saloons whose revised front suspension they also took on.

Both saloons and coupes were another big hit for BMW, despite high prices. From 1971, both ranges benefited from a new 3-litre engine which came in carburettor or higher-powered fuel-injection forms. In addition, the low-volume "homologation special" 3.0CSL coupé arrived, and went on to confirm the company's growing reputation on the race tracks. The CSL picked up a collection of aerodynamic addenda in late 1972 to take on its now-legendary "Batmobile" appearance, and the racing versions were further developed with two even larger engines.

Meanwhile, a smaller-engined (2.5CS) coupe arrived in 1974 to meet depressed demand for big-engined cars after the first Oil Crisis. That year had already seen the introduction of a long-wheelbase saloon aimed at the long-wheelbase versions of Mercedes' S-Class cars. As befitted the flagship model, it had a new 3.3-litre engine, although smaller-engined editions were introduced later. Towards the end of 1976, the 3.3-litre model was uprated with fuel injection to become the 3.3Li.

Coupé production ended in 1975 after 29,569 of all types had been built, and saloon production ended two years later. There had been 207,377 examples on the standard wheelbase, and a further 12,656 long-wheelbase cars.

James Taylor

ROAD & TRACK
R&T
ROAD TEST

NEW MODEL ANALYSIS AND ROAD & TRACK ROAD TEST
BMW 2500 & 2800
Testing the basic model of the new BMW prestige line

THE BMW 2500 completely lacks that slightly pompous, unapproachable air of a comparable Mercedes sedan—with which it is obviously designed to compete—looking instead squat (though it isn't really low), a bit fat (it isn't) and rather aggressive with its noticeably wide wheels. It's not a strikingly modern styling exercise but it is nevertheless quite modern in concept. The front end says BMW with its center section, but the lip above it that extends into and along the body side is definitely Corvair in origin, and the low beltline, with attending large glass areas, is made possible by a canted engine.

Inside the 2500 the driver quickly realizes benefits of the low hood and windowsills. The seats are chair-high (when Chrysler advertised chair-high seats in 1949, who would have thought we could have them with cars as low as 56 in. overall?), have a great longitudinal adjustment range and recline fully; their adjustable headrests don't unduly obstruct rearward vision. There is outstanding vision all around; no front vent windows, and the rear roof pillars are of reasonable thickness. Only windshield wipers that are too short detract from the view outward.

Controls, and logical placement thereof, are a part of the BMW personality. A pullup handbrake is located between the two front seats and carries anchors for out-of-use seatbelt buckles; all controls are near at hand, especially those for the wipers and lighting which are stalks on the steering column—though BMW misses one point by putting the wiper *speed* control on the dash. Heater controls are logical once you've sorted them out but aren't lighted for night use. The instruments are neat and white-on-black, but need more intermediate marks between their main numerical divisions; we prefer having an oil pressure gauge, though BMW engineers do not. The steering wheel position and angle are satisfactory and the shift lever is both close and short—all the essentials of good control are to be found in this seating package.

The all-new 6-cyl engine is a jewel. At low speeds it combines a sporting exhaust note (very much like that of the Pontiac six) with a modest amount of BMW cam-drive whine

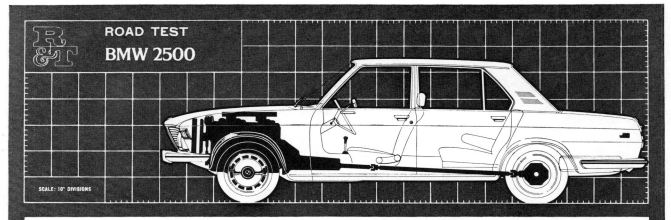

ROAD TEST
BMW 2500

SCALE: 10" DIVISIONS

PRICE

Basic list................$5284
As tested................$5619

ENGINE

Type..........6 cyl inline, sohc
Bore x stroke, mm.....86.0 x 71.6
  Equivalent in.......3.39 x 2.82
Displacement, cc/cu in...2494/152
Compression ratio..........9.0:1
Bhp @ rpm.........170 @ 6000
  Equivalent mph...........117
Torque @ rpm, lb-ft...176 @ 3700
  Equivalent mph............70
Carburetion.two Solex 35/40 INAT
Type fuel required.......premium

DRIVE TRAIN

Clutch diameter, in..........9.4
Gear ratios: 4th (1.00).....3.64:1
  3rd (1.38).............4.92:1
  2nd (2.12).............7.62:1
  1st (3.85)............13.01:1
Final drive ratio..........3.64:1

CHASSIS & BODY

Body/frame...........unit steel
Brake type: disc, 10.7-in. dia front
  & rear; drum handbrake; vacuum
  assist
  Swept area, sq in.........493
Wheels...........steel disc, 14 x 6
Tires.....Michelin XAS 175 HR-14
Steering.....worm & roller, power
  Overall ratio...........18.9:1
  Turns, lock-to-lock........3.9
  Turning circle, ft.........35.2
Front suspension: MacPherson
  struts, lower A-arms, coil
  springs, tube shocks
Rear suspension: semi-trailing
  arms, coil springs, tube shocks

MAINTENANCE

Engine oil capacity, qt........6.1
Every 4000 mi. chg eng oil & filter,
  chk or chg air cleaner, minor op'l
  check
Every 8000 mi: cln fuel filter,
  tighten belts, lube carb linkage,
  torque cyl head, tune engine,
  chg plugs, rotate tires, major op'l
  check
Tire pressures, psi........29/27
Warranty, mo/mi.....12/12,000

ACCOMMODATION

Seating capacity, persons.......5
Seat width, front/rear.2 x 23.0/55.0
Head room, front/rear...38.0/37.0
Seat back adjustment, deg.....85
Driver comfort rating (scale of 100):
  Driver 69 in. tall...........100
  Driver 72 in. tall...........90
  Driver 75 in. tall...........70

INSTRUMENTATION

Instruments: 140-mph speedo,
  8000-rpm tach, 99,999 odo, 999.9
  trip odo, water temp, fuel level
Warning lights: oil press, generator, brake system, fuel level,
  high beam, directionals, hazard
  flasher, window heater

EQUIPMENT

Standard: radial tires, power disc
  brakes
Optional: automatic transmission
  ($340), power steering ($190),
  AM/FM radio ($145), air con-
  ditioning

GENERAL

Curb weight, lb............3005
Test weight................3350
Weight distribution (with
  driver), front/rear, %....55/45
Wheelbase, in..............106.0
Track, front/rear......56.9/57.6
Overall length..............185.0
  Width....................68.9
  Height...................56.1
Ground clearance, in.........5.5
Overhang, front/rear....34.7/44.3
Usable trunk space, cu ft.....14.6
Fuel tank capacity, gal......19.8

CALCULATED DATA

Lb/hp (test wt)..............19.7
Mph/1000 rpm (4th gear).....18.9
Engine revs/mi (60 mph)....3180
Engine speed @ 70 mph....3710
Piston travel, ft/mi.........1495
Cu ft/ton mi................83.2
R&T wear index..............47
R&T steering index.........1.38
Brake swept area sq in/ton....294

ROAD TEST RESULTS

ACCELERATION

Time to distance, sec:
0–100 ft....................3.8
0–250 ft....................6.4
0–500 ft....................9.5
0–750 ft...................12.0
0–1000 ft..................14.4
0–1320 ft (¼ mi).........17.3
Speed at end of ¼ mi, mph....81
Time to speed, sec:
0–30 mph....................3.7
0–40 mph....................5.6
0–50 mph....................7.3
0–60 mph...................10.0
0–70 mph...................13.1
0–80 mph...................17.0
0–100 mph..................30.7
Passing exposure time, sec:
  To pass car going 50 mph....6.0

FUEL CONSUMPTION

Normal driving, mph.........20.9
Cruising range, mi..........414

SPEEDS IN GEARS

4th gear (6050 rpm), mph.....118
3rd (6200)..................87
2nd (6200)..................57
1st (6200)..................31

BRAKES

Panic stop from 80 mph:
  Deceleration, % g..........77
  Control..............very good
Fade test: percent of increase in
  pedal effort required to main-
  tain 50%-g deceleration rate in
  six stops from 60 mph.......nil
Parking: hold 30% grade.....yes
Overall brake rating.....very good

SPEEDOMETER ERROR

30 mph indicated......actual 29.1
40 mph....................39.3
60 mph....................57.6
80 mph....................76.0
100 mph...................94.6
Odometer, 10.0 mi....actual 9.88

ACCELERATION & COASTING

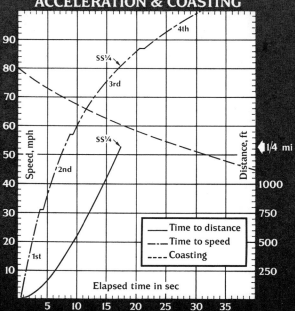

BMW 2500

400 in average driving—over 20 mpg is most impressive in a luxury sedan with this kind of performance.

In through-the-gears acceleration the 2500 is as impressive to the clocks as it is to the ear, producing quarter-mile times that any self-respecting Detroit engineer would say can't be done with 2.5 liters, 3000 lb and tractability. And, like all BMWs, the 2500 is designed to run all day at its maximum speed—which turns out to be 118 mph. We spent considerable time at over 100 mph in the 2500, easily enough to be firm in the knowledge that it's a car designed to be driven fast in comfort and safety. It seems to get into its stride only *above* the usual legal speeds in America.

The 2500's manual transmission is a departure from previous BMWs; its Borg-Warner synchromesh (4-cyl cars use Porsche synchro) is lighter and more "notchy" than the action we're used to in BMWs. We have no strong preference; both are satisfactory, though we appreciate the B-W advantage of being able to shift directly from neutral to 1st without a crunch. There was a high-pitched squeal from the throwout bearing of the test car, but otherwise the diaphragm clutch worked smoothly and positively.

In smooth-road cruising at moderate or high speeds the 2500 is an exceptionally quiet car; perhaps the low road noise and astonishingly low wind noise are what make the engine whir so noticeable. Some whine from the Michelin XAS tires is also heard at speed; but these tires return great dividends in wet-road adhesion, as we found out when trying to trip up the car in the rain. It almost can't be done. Floods in California brought out the need for good ventilation, and the 2500 didn't let us down here either; besides adequate heat output there is a fair supply of fresh air from the dash vents; two sets of extractor vents (one cleverly concealed at the trunklid's leading edge) get stale air out but not as well as we anticipated.

BMW's power steering is light and quick but disappointingly lacking in road feel. We haven't yet driven a 2500 with unassisted steering but suspect that the model's lack of caster (see the analysis above) is mostly responsible. Otherwise the car's handling is exemplary: there's lots of cornering power (even more is available with the optional D70-14 tires) and a just-right balance of generally neutral handling with slight power-off oversteer. Rough surfaces bring out the expected BMW suspension suppleness and utter lack of body flexing or rattling—we're afraid chassis like this make us hypercritical of more ordinary efforts. Two problems typical of BMW's semi-trailing rear suspension remain in the 2500—wheel patter on brutal clutch engagement and inside wheel lifting on hard cornering—neither of which is a serious problem. The wheel patter occurs only in acceleration tests, and the lifting puts a relatively innocent limit on the cornering activities.

Braking is nearly as impressive as handling; correct proportioning allows a deceleration rate of 0.77 g on dry pavement with excellent directional control, and our standard fade test failed to produce a trace of fade though there was some pulling to the left. In everyday use the 2500's brakes are smooth, usually free of squeal and neither under- nor over-assisted by the vacuum unit.

Though the paintwork wasn't outstanding on our early production example, all other details gave evidence of painstaking craftsmanship—an engine compartment that will delight the eye, a trunk compartment pretty enough to live in and a total absence of ill fits or phony-looking materials.

In all, the 2500 is a sedan to delight the keen and well-heeled driver. Typically German in its combination of design for fast driving and maneuverability with a low displacement, high-output engine, it also bears an unmistakable BMW personality which has been unavailable heretofore in such a spacious, luxurious car. It costs a lot, but that's the price you pay for top quality; and there is no doubt that its performance is faster, more sporting and longer-legged than that of its nearest competitor.

and practically no other underhood noise; as the revs climb toward its redline of 6200 rpm it takes on a snarl delightfully like that of a Porsche 911. At low speeds it belies its modest 2.5-liter displacement with surprisingly generous torque and flexibility, but out on the freeway it sounds much too busy in spite of the easygoing 3.54:1 final drive. Most of this obtrusive hum comes from the exhaust, a little from underhood. Our test car was somewhat reluctant to keep running when it wasn't fully warmed up in spite of its advanced automatic choke design and reluctant to stop running when it was warmed up; and we had trouble with the complex vacuum-operated dashpot that keeps the throttle from closing too abruptly (for emission control). Though the tank capacity is less than 20 gal, the 2500's cruising range is comfortably above 300 miles even in the hardest driving and actually tops

1969 Cars

Big Bee-Ems

BMW move into the larger-car market

IN GERMANY the typical BMW is significantly cheaper than the cheapest Mercedes and in any case appeals to a more sporting kind of buyer, but the Bavarian company have now set their quartered circular badge in direct opposition to the three-pointed star by their announcement of a pair of new models, called the 2500 and the 2800, powered by different versions of a new six-cylinder engine and equipped with larger and restyled bodies compared to the 1800 and 2000. A third new model is the 2800 coupé, basically the 2000 CS coupé fitted with the new 2800 engine.

The new bodyshell retains the characteristic BMW front grille but elsewhere has been completely restyled with a sloping bonnet line, a lower waist and an appearance which is generally cleaner and more modern than that of the 1800/2000 range which it will augment, not replace. It is 5½in. longer in wheelbase (7in. longer overall) while track and overall width are around 5 in. and 4 in. greater respectively giving ample space for five people with luggage capacity to match. The new cars will be available in Britain next year but prices have not yet been decided.

Engine

Although the new six-cylinder engine shares neither bore nor stroke dimensions with any of its smaller four-cylinder brothers, it is of the same general layout, with a single overhead camshaft operating inclined valves through rockers. The fully balanced crankshaft runs in seven main bearings and is fitted with a torsional vibration damper. A developed cylinder head is fitted, using a form of combustion chamber described as "triple hemispherical" which is designed to provide extra space around the sparking plug. This is claimed to be so efficient that the American exhaust emission control regulations can be met without auxiliary air injection, though the low pollution level is no doubt helped by the fact that the carburetters are both electrically and cooling-water heated to ensure complete vaporization at all times. The second chokes of the two twin-choke instruments are automatically opened by manifold depression, while cold-starting enrichment is automatic also. A novel feature of the installation is a thermostat on the input side of the water pump which regulates the flow in response to the temperature of the cooled water returned from the radiator—which depends mainly on the ambient temperature—and on the temperature of the heated water from the cylinder head which depends mainly on engine load.

In 2.5-litre form, the bore is 86 mm., stroke 71.6 mm. and capacity 2,494 c.c. Maximum power from a 9.0:1 compression ratio is 150 (net b.h.p. at 6,000 r.p.m.) and maximum torque is 155.4 lb.ft. at 3,700 r.p.m. By comparison the four-cylinder 2000TI engine of 1,990 c.c. develops 120 b.h.p. at 5,500 r.p.m. For the bigger 2800 unit the stroke is increased to 80 mm raising the capacity to 2,788 c.c. and the maximum power (with the same compression ratio) to 170 (net) b.h.p. at 6,000 r.p.m.

A four speed floor-shift manual ZF gearbox with Borg-Warner synchromesh is the standard fitting, driving through a divided propeller shaft via a fixed final drive unit to half-shafts each of which have two sealed-for-life, constant-velocity joints. The final drive ratio is 3.64:1 for the 2500 and 3.54:1 for the 2800; top speeds for the two cars are claimed to be 118 and 124 m.p.h. Automatic transmission is optional.

Running gear

The new cars have the MacPherson strut front suspension and semi-trailing arms rear suspension used on all other BMWs but at the front the struts have been angled backwards to increase the negative camber of the outside wheel when the front wheels are on lock. To understand how this occurs, imagine the strut angled so far back as to become horizontal (when the system wouldn't work, of course), any "steering" angle of the front wheels would then become wholly a camber angle, so tilting the struts rearward introduces a camber change with lock. The excessive castor angle which such an arrangement implies is eliminated by moving the bottom ball joint back from the strut axis. An additional advantage of the rearward angled struts is that the upper mounting points which take the suspension loads can be moved closer to the strong scuttle bulkhead. Longitudinal compliance has been built into the rear suspension which now has high-mounted springs, the tops of which are about level with the top of the rear seat backrest. On the 2500 the spring struts can optionally be replaced by the self levelling Boge Nivomat units which are a standard fitting on the 2800.

Interior

An important feature of the new interior is the full fresh-air ventilation system with a central grille and two swivelling vents on the facia and extraction slots in the rear pillars and around the rear window. For quick warm-up there is permanent hot water circulation through the heater matrix.

Following the strong-centre-and-crushable-ends design of the body structure, the interior is provided with many safety features, including a collapsible steering column, child-proof rear door locks, extensive padding, a snap-off holder for the front ashtray and yielding plastic material for all knobs, window winders, etc.

With front seats adjustable for rake and reach, a rev-counter as well as a speedometer for both the 2500 and 2800 models, and several compartments, pockets and shelves for odds and ends the cars are lavishly equipped. A heated backlight is optional on the 2500, standard on the 2800. **M**

Typical BMW lines, lengthened and lowered, produce a very pleasing, unsensational result.

General layout of the single overhead camshaft in-line six. Note the deep water-jacketing around the combustion chambers and valves.

The thermostat of the cooling system is mounted on the intake side of the water pump and responds to the temperature of the cooled water from the radiator as well as the heated water from the cylinder head.

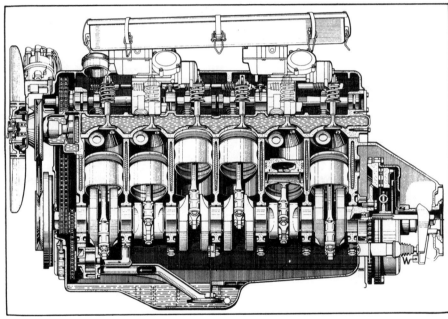

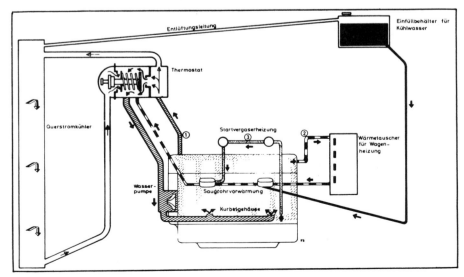

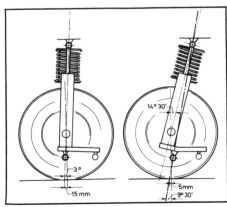

As explained in the text, tilting the MacPherson struts rearwards increases negative camber on the outside wheel when it is turned by the steering; the resultant increased castor is eliminated by moving the bottom swivel joint backwards.

BMW'S 2500

From Jerry Sloniger in Europe.

THIS BMW beast called the 2500 has such a great engine you sort of forget how fine the rest of the car can be too. Their mill pulls from 1500 rpm in top, takes a ton and a half of deluxe five-seater to near-as-not 120, comes on with a whisper and returns better than 18 mpg at European road speeds.

> AT-A-GLANCE: exceptionally smooth . . . suited to the sporting gentry . . . devastatingly quick for 2.5 litres . . . "among the finest passenger vehicles going" . . . or how to out-Mercedes Mercedes.

What more? Well, it's about as easy a car to do the ton in as any I know and among the finest passenger vehicles going when you want to cover plenty of two-lane road at a high average speed.

The only machines to mention in the same breath are new Mercedes — direct homeland competition for the Bavarians though they don't care to make a point of that. It boils down to the nitty gritty that BMW is the only Teuton with the rep needed if you want to match bumpers with DB. And Munich was canny enough to pick its own ground — the sporting set.

Mind you this full-fledged test machine we enjoyed for nearly 1600 swingin' miles was nothing like the

Only a modicum of understeer and as little lean under hard cornering as any luxury sedan going — the BMW is for rich people who still remember that driving can be fun.

animal of my first test. Without being quoted BMW boys admit they civilised them for production. Rather than the mettle of a race horse at the gate the car is not a thoroughbred pacer eating sugar from a small child's hand.

Despite this we're still talking about the same automobile. Apart from rear leg room: I missed on that, calling it too thin on first acquaintance. No excuse except that the driver's seat was so much fun I underrated rear comfort. A fairly sporting suspension eases the 2500 out of your limousine class but there is certainly enough room.

Relativity comes in here. The 2500, which is capable of dusting off most sport cars, may be softer than its prototype cousin but is tauter and quicker to respond than most of the world's sedans. It would stick beyond reason with moderate understeer and lean (assuming proper rubber) treating linked S-bends with contempt.

My tyre qualification comes up because main mileage was covered on Continental radials. These squealed like your maiden aunt at a love-in on dry roads and displayed all the adhesion of well-lubricated drag slicks on polished marbles when it rained.

The 2.5 litre BMW comes without power steering, a $150 option on a car costing roughly $3900 at home. Except when parking this is just dandy. You can turn the biggish machine with considerable overhang in 36 feet but it takes muscle. Underway road feel is just right.

Brakes are equally positive but unassuming. A soft pedal with progressive travel calls up four discs which haul a BMW 2500 down from ton-up speeds *right now*. And there is no lock-up from odd corners. In the wet a boot load helps though.

The shift is another departure for BMW who dropped one of the finest sedan boxes going (Porsche syncro) in favor of a ZF which is

BMW 2500 looks lower and sportier than its contemporaries from any angle. Note no front quarter vents and rear pillar extractors.

The cockpit is sporting-simple, perhaps too stark for the luxury class but drivers will love it every bit.

Twin carbs and an overhead cam — one of the most elastic sedan engines I know, yet it swings.

BMW's 2500

even more precise, truer into every notch and the epitomy of positive feel. All this comes at the expense of perhaps fractionally slower shifts at the outside.

Along with such outstanding action the engine is so elastic you forget to down-shift around town. Two takes the car to 60, three to 96 for passing and sub 10-second 0-60 runs are routine. The engine comes on with a smoothness to make rotary pistons redundant.

The combination of silky acceleration and modest thirst at max rpm is pure engineering. Based on their fours the single-ohc six with two carbs, seven mains and twelve crank weights, goes even further into thermodynamics.

Just over 155 lbs/ft of torque at 3700 rpm speak for themselves, louder and clearer even than 150 DIN hp. With a red line of 6200 the BMW will pull 7000 without a murmur. Well, okay; with a sporting purr of a murmur.

Still I kind of wish they had spent half as much time on color-keyed thinking. An anaemic greenish white paint called Florida, matt black dash, fish-belly head-liner and manure-brown door panels ask too much of even the color-blindest theoretical engineer you know.

Otherwise the interior plan is mostly fine. Two aviation-calibre dials handle speed and rpm with smaller faces for temperature and fuel. But too damn many idiot lights use space which could hold a couple of combo dials. Bit schizo that: sporting instrumentation courtesy of their baby-bomb sedan

Typical simplicity — a grab handle, cum armrest, cum hidden door latch. No frills. Maximum safety.

racers but "not too many" for the sedate-sedan snob.

Underneath this dash is sloped and padded into drop-down bins, a big one for the passenger and small glove (sic) box for the driver which also hides fuses, bonnet handle and odometer reset. Then they divide the dash-top tray so small articles can't slither. Munich has consequent thinkers, however color-unconscious they may be.

Drivers of average build will have trouble placing the corners at first due to aerodynamic rounding off and despite slathers of glass. (If you want the rear pane heated it costs about $25 extra, one of the better bargains on modern wheels.) Rear corners in particular are shy about their whereabouts — vast boot on 105 inch wheelbase you see — but the luggage capacity is nice.

Touring as such comes on strong with a tank holding just shy of 16.5 gallons though the dial only reads to 13 and a bit. This scares you into a pump long before you must park a dry BMW and hitch in. On the other hand old hands will tend to feel "there's plenty more after empty", and get caught twice as often as need be.

In short you get great handling, uncannily quiet engine as advanced as any recipe in modern motordom and ultimate driver control over environment — superb balance all around. And even with all this Munich can over-engineer the ergonomics.

Better that than a wandering lump, of course. Never mind the modest lean toward a Germanic limousine syndrome, this BMW 2500 is one car no owner short of the fully embalmed could bear to let his chauffeur drive.   #

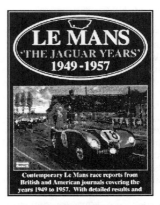

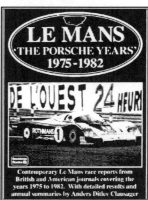

BMW road impressions:

The 2800CS

By DAVID PHIPPS

WHILE in Geneva recently I was able to borrow a BMW 2800CS coupé for a few hours, and it proved to be a much nicer car than the 2000CS which it so closely resembles. Apart from the change from four to six cylinders (and 120 to 170 bhp), the 2800 also has revised suspension, power steering and a restyled interior with beautiful cloth-trimmed seats, the end product being far more suitable for long-distance driving than the majority of so-called Grand Touring cars.

First impressions were of the beautifully precise gearshift and ultra-light steering, without which it would never have been possible to get into or out of parking spaces. On the Lausanne autoroute the car ran absolutely straight and true at over 120 mph—at which speed it was also impressively quiet—and on the twisty road up to St Cergue its Continental radials refused to break traction even in second gear. The smoothness and quietness of the engine tended to make the car feel less

accelerative than it really was, but 0-60 mph took only 9 secs, and a standing-start quarter-mile was covered in just over 16 secs. Acceleration was also very good in the higher speed ranges, allowing cruising speed to be regained very quickly after traffic hold-ups. My only reservation concerned the brakes, which started to smell in the early stages of the descent from St Cergue and would probably need harder linings if they were to be used regularly in this manner.

The most obvious external differences between the 2800 and the 2000 lie in the styling of the headlamps and grille, the 2800 being a great deal simpler and cleaner. The six-cylinder engine fits in very neatly and seems to have no adverse effects on either weight distribution or handling—thanks partly to the new front suspension as used on the 2500/2800 saloons. This features MacPherson struts angled backwards to increase the negative camber of the outside wheels during

cornering, and the consequent increase in castor has been eliminated by re-locating the bottom swivel joint. Rear suspension is by semi-trailing arms and coil springs, with anti-roll bars at both front and rear.

The engine follows customary BMW practice with a chain-driven overhead camshaft operating inclined valves in what are described as triple-hemispherical combustion chambers—the latter having been designed to meet American pollution regulations without the need for an air pump. Further assistance in this department is provided by both electrical and water heating of the two twin-choke Solex carburetters, which also incorporate an automatic cold starting device. Bore and stroke are 86 x 80 mm, giving a capacity of 2788 cc, and with a compression ratio of 9:1 the maximum output is 170 bhp (DIN) at 6000 rpm. The gearbox, with its ultra-light shift, is by ZF, and automatic transmission is available as an optional extra.

The interior equipment is all of very good quality, and provided the front seats are not pushed too far back there is adequate room for two adults in the rear compartment. There is a very comprehensive heating and ventilation system, and an electrically-heated rear window is a standard fitting. All in all this is a very desirable car, and far more practical than the majority of limited-production high performance coupés.

The 2800CS has the same body shape as the four-cylinder 2000CS, but with a much more attractive four-headlamp frontal treatment (left). A leather-rim wheel, central console and beautifully-trimmed cloth seats distinguish the interior (right).

Autotest

BMW 2500
(2,494 c.c.)

AT-A-GLANCE: New German six-cylinder. Outstanding performance and refinement; excellent finish and high standard of comfort. Superb engine and gearbox combination, smooth ride, very good handling and stability. An example in its class.

MANUFACTURER
Bayerische Motoren Werke A.G., 8 München 13, Lercheroner Strasse 76, West Germany.

UK CONCESSIONAIRES
BMW Concessionaires Ltd., Victoria Road, Portslade, Sussex.

PRICES
Basic	£2,264	0	0
Purchase Tax	£693	11	10
Total (in GB)	£2,957	11	10

EXTRAS (inc. P.T.)
Power steering*	£99	4	5
Automatic transmission	£198	8	10
Limited-slip differential	£75	1	0

*Fitted to test car

PRICE AS TESTED	£3,056	16	3

PERFORMANCE SUMMARY
Mean maximum speed	121 mph
Standing start ¼-mile	17.2 sec
0—60 mph	9.3 sec
30—70 mph through gears	9.9 sec
Typical fuel consumption	22 mpg
Miles per tankful	365

IF DESIGN could be taught by example we would campaign all the British manufacturers of luxury cars to investigate the BMW six-cylinder range. Seldom have we tested a new model with so much good about it and which impressed us so easily. From simple details like the instrument panel and seat material to fundamentals like the exemplary engine-transmission train combination, this is a superbly satisfying car to own and drive.

Announced almost inconspicuously a year ago, the six-cylinder BMWs are a logical development of the highly successful 1600/1800/2000 family. The 2500 engine is virtually the same as that of the 1600 with two extra cylinders added and the same kind of single overhead camshaft working opposed valves through rockers. It has two progressive choke Solex carburettors and develops 150 bhp (DIN) at 6,000 rpm. This is 30 bhp more than that of the 2000 TI, which is a much more highly tuned four.

For some reason the choice of bore and stroke (84 x 71mm) in the 1600 resulted in a particularly smooth-running unit. The 2500 (86 x 71.6mm) has the added benefit of being perfectly in balance like all sixes, and its smoothness is uncanny, even for a six. Starting is always immediate, hot or cold, and an automatic choke takes care of idling speed and mixture strength during warming up so perfectly that the driver notices no difference between hot and cold running. Full power seems to be available always, at a touch of the throttle.

Idling is even and steady at around 750 rpm, and there is a red line on the rev counter between 6,200 and 7,000 on a scale continuing to 8,000 rpm. During performance testing we used 6,500 as a limit on the dead accurate rev counter, and this gave nicely

spaced maxima in the gears of 34, 62 and 93 mph. There is a tremendous eagerness in the way the needle spins around the dial, with a strong pull of even torque and a pleasant whine from the camshaft drive.

According to factory curves, the 2500 engine develops over 145lb.ft. of torque all the way from 2,000 to 5,200 rpm, with a peak of 155 at 3,750. This is borne out by the top gear acceleration figures which are within a 2.4 sec spread for each 20 mph increment all the way from 20 mph to 90 mph.

There can be no doubt that our test car, a left-hand-drive demonstrator, was developing all its claimed power and perhaps a mite more. It certainly felt extremely lively and we improved on the manufacturer's claims for both top speed and acceleration. With exactly the same reading in both directions on a still day we clocked a maximum of 121 mph, 3 mph better than expected. On acceleration through the gears we recorded a mean of 9.3sec for 0 to 60 mph compared with a claim of 10.4.

Cold figures only tell a part of the story, and this saloon is really indecently fast for its size, image and appearance. Even today, a 0 to 60 mph time of less than 10 sec is very good by

sports car standards, and only a few years ago it was considered quick for the Sunbeam Tiger and Lotus-Cortina. In absolute terms it can accelerate faster than a Jaguar XJ6 4.2, a Mercedes 600, the Reliant Scimitar 3-litre and every four-seater we have tested, disregarding big American cars which have engines well over twice the size.

One's enthusiasm only starts with the engine though, the rest of the car being equally impressive. It is unusual for a manufacturer of a good gearbox to do anything but stick to what he knows works well. BMW have gone several steps ahead of all their competitors and their own previous design with the four-speed unit fitted to the new cars. Compared with the 2000 Tilux we tested recently and the 2002 we have been running as a staff car for 30,000 miles, the 2500 box is much lighter to use, has shorter lever movements and feels even more positive. Like the engine, it is an example to all other manufacturers of just how a manual box should feel; the driver finds he cannot use it

enough, such is his satisfaction derived from its sweet, clickety-click action. There is light spring loading across the gate towards the top-third plane.

Like all the controls, the clutch is extremely positive with a nice progressive action. It has a longish movement (just under 6in.) and must be fully floored for the gearbox to work at its best. Pedals are much better positioned than on any previous right-hand-drive BMW.

Brakes (divided circuits with twin vacuum servos, discs all round) have lots of initial bite

ACCELERATION

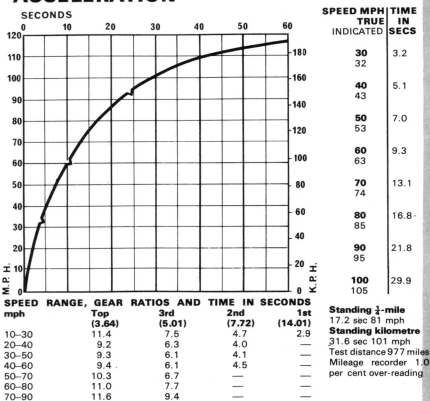

SECONDS

SPEED MPH TRUE INDICATED	TIME IN SECS
30 32	3.2
40 43	5.1
50 53	7.0
60 63	9.3
70 74	13.1
80 85	16.8
90 95	21.8
100 105	29.9

SPEED RANGE, GEAR RATIOS AND TIME IN SECONDS

mph	Top (3.64)	3rd (5.01)	2nd (7.72)	1st (14.01)
10–30	11.4	7.5	4.7	2.9
20–40	9.2	6.3	4.0	—
30–50	9.3	6.1	4.1	—
40–60	9.4	6.1	4.5	—
50–70	10.3	6.7	—	—
60–80	11.0	7.7	—	—
70–90	11.6	9.4	—	—
80–100	14.8	—	—	—

Standing ¼-mile
17.2 sec 81 mph
Standing kilometre
31.6 sec 101 mph
Test distance 977 miles
Mileage recorder 1.0
per cent over-reading

PERFORMANCE

MAXIMUM SPEEDS

Gear	mph	kph	rpm
Top (mean)	121	194	6,150
(best)	121	194	6,150
3rd	93	150	6,500
2nd	62	100	6,500
1st	34	55	6,500

BRAKES

(from 70 mph in neutral)
Pedal load for 0.5g stops in lb

1	28–20		6	23
2	25		7	23–26
3	28		8	25–28
4	25		9	25–30
5	25		10	25–32

RESPONSE (from 30 mph in neutral)

Load	g	Distance
20lb	0.42	72ft
40lb	0.72	42ft
60lb	0.80	38ft
80lb	0.85	35.4ft
Handbrake	0.27	
Max. Gradient	1 in 3	

CLUTCH

Pedal 35lb and 5.75in.
MOTORWAY CRUISING
Indicated speed at 70 mph . . . . 74 mph
Engine (rpm at 70 mph) . . . . . . 3,550 rpm
.(mean piston speed) . . . . 1,980 ft/min
Fuel (mpg at 70 mph) . . . . 26.0 mpg
Passing (50–70 mph) . . . . 6.1 sec

COMPARISONS

MAXIMUM SPEED MPH

BMW 2500	. . . .	(£3,058)	**121**
Jaguar XJ6 4.2 auto	. . . . .	(£2,623)	120
Mercedes 250 auto	. . . .	(£3,075)	108
Triumph 2.5 PI	. . . . . .	(£1,480)	106
Austin 3-litre auto	. . . . . .	(£1,696)	99

0–60 MPH, SEC

BMW 2500	. . . .	**9.3**
Jaguar XJ6 4·2 auto	. . . .	10.1
Triumph 2.5 PI	. . . .	10.4
Mercedes 250 auto	. . . .	12.7
Austin 3-litre auto	. . . .	14.8

STANDING ¼-MILE, SEC

BMW 2500	. . . .	**17.2**
Triumph 2.5 PI	. . . .	17.4
Jaguar XJ6 4.2 auto	. . . .	17.5
Mercedes 250 auto	. . . .	19.0
Austin 3-litre auto	. . . .	20.3

OVERALL MPG

BMW 2500	. . . .	**21.8**
Triumph 2.5 PI	. . . .	21.6
Mercedes 250 auto	. . . .	17.3
Jaguar XJ6 4.2 auto	. . . .	15.2
Austin 3-litre auto	. . . .	14.9

GEARING (with 175-14in. tyres)

Top	. . . . . .	19.7 mph per 1,000 rpm
3rd	. . . . . .	14.3 mph per 1,000 rpm
2nd	. . . . . .	9.3 mph per 1,000 rpm
1st	. . . . . .	5.1 mph per 1,000 rpm

TEST CONDITIONS: Cloudy. Wind: 0–5 mph. Temperature: 15 deg. C. (59 deg. F.). Barometer 29.7 in Hg. Humidity: 60 per cent. Surfaces: dry concrete and asphalt.

WEIGHT: Kerb weight 26.2 cwt. (2,938lb—1,335kg) (with oil, water and half full fuel tank). Distribution, per cent F, 56.6; R, 43.4. Laden as tested: 29.9 cwt (3,346lb—1,521kg).

TURNING CIRCLES: Between kerbs, L, 33 ft 2 in.; R, 32 ft 5 in. Between walls, L, 35 ft 2 in.; R, 34 ft 5 in. steering wheel turns, lock to lock 4.1.

Figures taken at 12,400 miles by our own staff at the Motor Industry Research Association proving ground at Nuneaton and on the Continent.

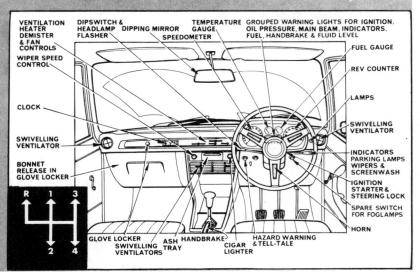

CONSUMPTION

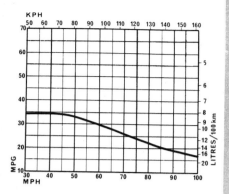

FUEL

(At constant speeds—mpg)

30 mph	34.8
40 mph	34.8
50 mph	32.8
60 mph	29.4
70 mph	26.0
80 mph	22.5
90 mph	19.4
100 mph	16.8

Typical mpg 22 (12.8 litres/100km)
Calculated (DIN) mpg 23.7 (11.9 litres/100km)
Overall mpg 21.8 (13.0 litres/100km)
Grade of fuel   Premium, 4-star (min. 97 RM)

OIL

Miles per pint (SAE 20W/50   . . . negligible

SPECIFICATION
FRONT ENGINE, REAR WHEEL DRIVE

ENGINE

Cylinders . . .	6, in line
Main bearings .	7
Cooling system .	Water, pump, fan and thermostat
Bore	86.0mm (3.39in.)
Stroke	71.6mm (2.82in.)
Displacement .	2,494 c.c. 152.2 cu.in.)
Valve gear . . .	Single overhead camshaft
Compression ratio	9.0-to-1 Min. octane rating: 97RM
Carburettors . .	Two Solex 35/40 INAT
Fuel pump . . .	Pierburg mechanical
Oil filter . . .	Full flow, replaceable element
Max. power . .	150 bhp (DIN) at 6,000 rpm
Max. torque . .	155.4 lb.ft. (DIN) at 3,700 rpm

TRANSMISSION

Clutch	Fichtel and Sachs diaphragm spring
Gearbox	Four-speed all-synchromesh
Gear ratios . .	Top 1.0
	Third 1.375
	Second 2.12
	First 3.85
	Reverse 4.13
Final drive . . .	Hypoid bevel, 3.64-to-1

CHASSIS and BODY

Construction . .	Integral, with steel body

SUSPENSION

Front	Independent, MacPherson struts, lower links, coil springs, telescopic dampers
Rear	Independent, semi-trailing arms, coil springs, telescopic dampers

STEERING

Type	Worm and roller, power-assisted on test car
Wheel dia. . . .	16.5 in.

BRAKES

Make and type .	ATE, discs front and rear
Servo	ATE vacuum
Dimensions . .	F. 10.7in. dia.; R. 10.7in. dia.
Swept area . .	F. 213 sq.in.: R. 213 sq.in. Total 426 sq.in. (292 sq.in./ton laden)

WHEELS

Type	Pressed steel disc, fire stud fixing. 6.0in. wide rim
Tyres—make . .	Various, Dunlop on test car
—type . .	SP Sport radial ply tubed
—size . .	175—14in.

EQUIPMENT

Battery	12 Volt 55 Ah
Alternator . . .	Bosch 44 amp a.c.
Headlamps. . .	Hella tungsten-halogen 220/110 watt (total)
Reversing lamp .	Standard
Electric fuses . .	10
Screen wipers .	2-speed, self-parking
Screen washer .	Standard, electric
Interior heater .	Standard, air-mixing type
Heated backlight	Extra
Safety belts . .	Standard in front, anchorages built in at rear
Interior trim . .	Cloth seats pvc headlining
Floor covering .	Carpet
Jack	Pillar type
Jacking points .	2 each side
Windscreen . .	Toughened
Underbody protection . .	Rubber underseal at wheel arches; wax compound elsewhere

MAINTENANCE

Fuel tank . . .	16.5 Imp. gallons (low level warning lamp) (75 litres)
Cooling system .	21.1 pints (including heater)
Engine sump . .	8.8 pints (5 litres) SAE 20W/50. Change oil ever 4,000 miles. Change filter element every 4,000 miles.
Gearbox	2.1 pints SAE 80. Change oil every 16,000 miles
Final drive . . .	3.2 pints SAE 90. No change needed
Grease	No points
Tyre pressures .	F. 27: R. 26 psi (normal driving) F. 30: R. 31 psi (full load)
Max. payload. .	1,035lb (470kg)

PERFORMANCE DATA

Top gear mph per 1,000 rpm	19.7
Mean piston speed at max. power . . .	3,340 ft/min
Bhp per ton laden	101

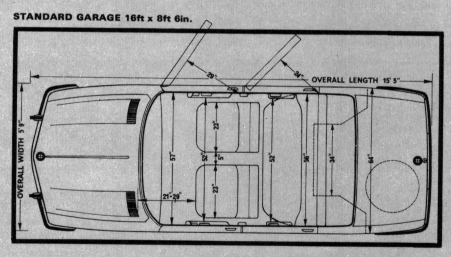

STANDARD GARAGE 16ft x 8ft 6in.

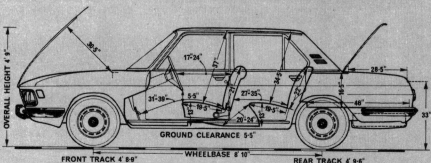

SCALE 0.3in. to 1ft
Cushions uncompressed

and stop the car reassuringly. Most check braking requires only 15–20lb effort on the pedal, and resistance to fade was first class with no more effort being needed after 10 stops from 70 mph than at the beginning. Ultimate braking was a little lacking, no better than 0.9g being recorded, but this is more a function of tyres and surface conditions. Radials are standard, the test car being on Continentals.

There have been major revisions to the normal BMW front suspension for the new cars, the independent semi-trailing arm rear end staying much the same. At the front the Mac-Pherson struts are tilted back at 14½ deg to feed suspension loads into a stiffer part of the body and front wheel castor and offset have been rearranged to give a particularly light and shock-free steering. Our test car had the optional power-assistance for ZF worm and roller box. We found both systems gave rise to some criticism, each with different symptoms probably stemming from the same cause. On the power-assisted car the steering felt too sensitive around the straight-ahead position, calling for concentration to follow a smooth line when cornering. Without power assistance initial wheel movements were too dead and the response was much slower. A slight difference in ratio is quoted, the power-assisted car needing only 4 turns from lock to lock compared with 4½ on the non-assisted version.

The BMW is a tremendously stable car right up to maximum speed. It cruises easily at 100 mph with just over 5,000 showing on the rev counter. At high speed there is very little wind noise and the engine is most unobtrusive.

Handling is best described as typically BMW, only better. The whole car feels lower than the four-cylinder models and seems to hug the road at all four corners better with less roll when

flicking it through bends fast. There is slightly more understeer and less of a tail-end twitch at the limit. Without power assistance the steering felt a fraction too slow when cornering fast, a criticism which did not apply to the assisted mechanism. The low-profile radials on 6in. rims add security to fundamentally safe cornering. Thinking this was just like other BMWs we regularly surprised ourselves at the extra cornering power in hand.

The ride too is an improvement and very smooth. Radial-ply thump is well insulated and there is a general feeling of soft agility on bumps which absorbs disturbances well without float or excessive pitching. An option on this model is self-levelling rear suspension. We tried it on the 2800 which has it as standard and found it worked effectively. With five extra spare wheels and tyres in the boot (about 200lb) the car rode level and handled just as it did unladen.

Seats are softly upholstered and covered in nylon cord cloth which is much more pleasant to sit on than pvc or leather and does not get hot and sticky when the car is parked in the sun. In front of the driver is a single instrument cluster with all the dials under a one-piece curved glass. On the left is a large diameter speedometer (which overreads throughout by 6 per cent) matched by an equally large rev counter on the right. Between these two are the fuel gauge and temperature gauge with a row of warning tell-tales below. Switches are well placed around the wheel rim in easy reach, the wipers being started and stopped by pushing on the end of the indicator stalk. Particularly neat are the three individually coloured push buttons under the edge of the facia which pop out and light up when in use. They control the four-way hazard warning flashers, the heated rear window and the fog lamps (when fitted).

Heating and ventilation is effective, with hot and cold air blending controlled by a sliding quadrant, a three-speed booster fan and high capacity cold air ducts feeding swivelling nozzles at each end of the facia and a central

louvred letter box fitted with swivelling vanes. Extraction of stale air is through slots to external rear quarter grilles and outlets in the boot lid hinge.

Provision for storing oddments in the car is generous and varied. There is a reasonable glove locker in front of the passenger and a deep trough under the screen rail with ribs to prevent loose objects sliding about. In the centre of the car under the heater console is an open bin big enough to take a lady's handbag, and in each front door trim panel there is an expanding map pocket. On the right-hand panel inside the boot there is a double compartment tray which takes a gallon can or a camera bag if required.

The seats are at a comfortable height from the floor and the low waistline makes visibility very good indeed. The driver can see the fallaway line of the bonnet ahead and his corner views are uncluttered by front quarterlights. At the rear the whole of the boot lid can be seen as an indication of the extremities when reversing.

It is obvious from first acquaintance that the 2500 BMW has been carefully thought out from stem to stern. One British manufacturer started to cost the construction and fittings, shuddered with admiration and gave up. As we said at the beginning, few cars have impressed us so much and few cars are so good in so many of their dynamic features.

Praise of this kind would be open to dispute if we were to judge the range on one example. In fact, we drove a 2800 coupe to the Geneva Motor Show and back in March, tested a 2500 for performance in this country and collected a 2800 saloon for long-term assessment from Munich at the end of July. They were all equally as good as each other, and our long-term car has already covered 2,000 miles in only four weeks. Most of the time we sit restlessly in the office looking for an excuse to drive it—and that's how much anybody who knows what driving is all about will enjoy a six-cylinder BMW. ●

Top left: There is little apart from the figures on the boot lid to distinguish the 2500 from the 2800. Both models have a rubber insert in the wrap-round bumpers. Bottom left: Cloth seats with front headrests are extremely well shaped and the instruments are all behind a single curved glass. Above: Two twin-choke carburettors are hidden under the air cleaner and the accessories are all well laid out

MOTOR TESTED

High price, high rewards

A car for affluent enthusiasts; superb engine and gearbox; very fast; surprisingly light and agile to drive; very comfortable and well planned interior.

ELSEWHERE in this issue you can read how the big BMWs have created a new market of their own in Germany rather than invaded the Mercedes field. Having now driven two of these outstanding cars—an automatic 2500 and a manual 2800— for nearly 3,000 miles, we can understand why. Although they cost and even look much like some of Mercedes' middleweights, they are in fact rather different in character and clearly intended to appeal to a different sort of customer. Their success stems from the imaginative cross-pollination of luxury carriage and sports saloon, a marriage best expressed on the one hand by outstandingly comfortable and well planned living quarters, and on the other by tenacious roadholding and a wonderful engine and gearbox.

Despite their excellent road behaviour, though, it would be wrong to imagine that these big BMWs feel quite so sportingly agile as some of the smaller ones. The accent is on light and easy control and stability rather than super-responsiveness. Any losses in handling, moreover, are countered by gains in comfort and accommodation. The inside is roomy enough to cosset five adults in sumptuously furnished and finished surrounding—comfort that is underlined by the excellence of the seats, a commanding driving position, a splendid view out through deep windows, fingertip switchgear control, instruments of copy-book clarity, an efficient new ventilation system, and the provision in nearly every spare corner of a pocket or compartment for odds and ends, not to mention a capacious boot. A host of new safety features—new, that is, to BMW—has also been incorporated.

Clearly, these cars have been designed not just for anyone with money but for affluent enthusiasts in particular. They reflect

status without flamboyance; they are roomy but not unnecessarily big; they handle well without a roly-poly ride; and they perform at express speeds without consuming unreasonable quantities of petrol. Even the automatic 2500, on which the bulk of this report is based, has a top speed approaching 120 m.p.h. and an easy cruising gait of well above 100 m.p.h., underlining its capabilities as a five seater GT car. The manual 2800 (see page 61) is even faster.

Unfortunately, the price of such sporting affluence is high—£3,073 for the automatic 2500, £3,244 for the manual 2800 which has self-levelling rear suspension and a limited slip differential as standard equipment. The £2,475 Jaguar 4.2 XJ6, bogey of all lush Continental imports and in our view still bettered by none on overall merit, accentuates the burden of import duty and, perhaps, the fact that Jaguar can still teach the world something about costing.

Acknowledging the Jaguar's peerless position, though, more than one driver here expressed a preference for the big BMW "because it's more fun to drive". Which serves to show that objective assessment has little meaning when you can afford to indulge your personal whims!

Performance and economy

Tagging an extra two cylinders on to an outstanding o.h.c. "four" could hardly fail to produce a really superb engine. Triple hemispherical combustion chambers are said to induce such efficient and smooth ignition that there is no sharp internal pressure rise—often the cause of harshness and high bearing loads. The claim is supported by the engine's exceptional smoothness. Moreover, combustion is so complete that no auxiliary air injection is needed to satisfy American exhaust emission regulations—another measure of the engine's efficiency.

PRICE: £2,264 plus £693 11s. 10d. purchase tax equals £2,957 11s. 10d. Automatic transmission £198 8s. 10d extra. Price as tested £3,155 19s. 8d.

BMW 2500

Judging by the car's performance, the catalogued 150 (net) b.h.p. at 6,000 r.p.m. seems almost a modest claim. The automatic chokes of the two twin-choke Zenith carburetters are primed with a stab on the throttle after which the engine starts instantly from cold. Without a brief warm-up period, though', it would often stall when you first engaged gear. Apart from this initial momentary hestitation, the engine is faultless in its behaviour and performance. Once warm, it idles smoothly and gently on all six cylinders, it blips like a racing engine, spins without any rough periods up to the red-lined limit of 6,200 r.p.m. and delivers bags of torque all the way with creamy smoothness and a crisp and expensive hum.

The automatic transmission of the 2500 inevitably takes the edge off the acceleration which is notable not so much for its initial kick as the way it goes on and on with little let up at really high speeds. Clearly, this is a car that has been bred for

every road condition, from Alpine pass to Autobahn, where it will cruise at 110 m.p.h. BMW claim a top speed of 118 m.p.h. which, given a long run in on a flat road, we see no reason to dispute since the car was building up to over 115 m.p.h. on parts of the MIRA track before tyre scrub on the banking slowed it down a little.

According to our flow meter, the automatic 2500 was thirstier than the manual 2800 at any speed. Although fuel economy is not a strong point, with a consumption range between 17.5 and 23.5 m.p.g. it is by no means unreasonable for such a fast five seater. With a 16.5-gallon fuel tank, you could go for up to 380 miles between fill-ups though long-distance work at high speed will reduce the range to little more than 250 miles. The handbook specifies the best petrol, incidentally.

Transmission

The BMW concessionaires anticipate selling more automatics than manuals in the new big-car range. The 3-speed ZF automatic transmission fitted to the 2500, an expensive extra costing £198 more than the standard four-speed manual box, is controlled by

Performance

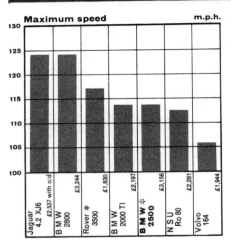

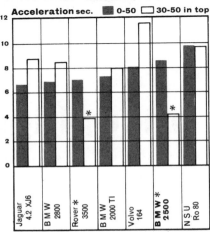

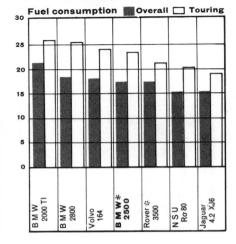

✻ Automatic transmission:— 30-50 in 'kick-down'

Performance tests carried out by Motor's staff at the Motor Industry Research Association proving ground, Lindley.

Test Data: World copyright reserved; no unauthorised reproduction in whole or in part.

Conditions
Weather: Good, wind 0-5 m.p.h.
Temperature: 74-86°F.
Barometer: 29.6 in. Hg.
Surface: Dry asphalt.
Fuel: Premium 98 octane (RM) 4-star rating.

Maximum Speeds

	m.p.h.	k.p.h.
Mean lap banked circuit	113.5	183
Best one-way ¼-mile	115.5	186
2nd gear } auto change at {	75	121
1st gear } 5,500 r.p.m. {	40	64

"Maxmile" speed: (Timed quarter mile after 1 mile accelerating from rest)
Mean 107.1
Best 110.0

Acceleration Times

m.p.h.	sec.
0-30	4.3
0-40	6.2
0-50	8.6
0-60	11.9
0-70	15.3
0-80	19.8
0-90	26.5
0-100	35.0
Standing quarter mile	18.6
Standing kilometer	33.7

Kickdown m.p.h.	sec.
20-40	3.6
30-50	4.2
40-60	5.7

	sec.
50-70	6.7
60-80	7.9
70-90	11.2
80-100	15.2

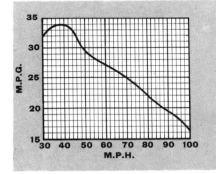

Fuel Consumption
Touring (consumption midway between 30 m.p.h. and maximum less 5% allowance for acceleration).
.... 23.5 m.p.g.
Overall .... 17.5 m.p.g.
(=16.2 litres/100km)
Total test distance .... 1,010 miles

Brakes
Pedal pressure, deceleration and equivalent stopping distance from 30 m.p.h.

lb.	g.	ft.
25	0.33	91
50	0.68	44
75	0.88	34
85	0.95	31.5
Handbrake	0.30	100

Fade Test
20 stops at ½g deceleration at 1 min. intervals from a speed midway between 40 m.p.h. and maximum speed (=77 m.p.h.)

	lb.
Pedal force at beginning	35
Pedal force at 10th stop	40
Pedal force at 20th stop	40

Steering
Turning circle between kerbs: ft.
Left 29.5
Right 30.2
Turns of steering wheel from lock to lock .. 4.3
Steering wheel deflection for 50ft. diameter circle .... 1.3 turns

Speedometer

Indicated	10	20	30	40	50	60	70
True	10	20	30	40	49	59	68
Indicated	80	90	100				
True	78	88	98				

Distance recorder .... accurate

Weight
Kerb weight (unladen with fuel for approximately 50 miles) .... 26.5 cwt.
Front/rear distribution 55/45
Weight laden as tested .... 30.2 cwt.

Parkability
Gap needed to clear 6ft. wide obstruction in front.

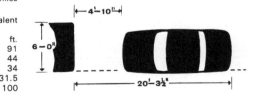

a small knitting-needle lever, topped by a rather mean knob, which moves easily in a fore-and-aft slot on the transmission tunnel. From a right-hand drive position, the lever must be pushed away from you, a little awkwardly, to overcome the detent holds which can be easily over-ridden unless you are delicate. It is much easier to operate the lever cleanly from the left seat, as originally intended. The indicator window is cleverly incorporated in the instrument panel, where a light shines behind the appropriate P, R, O (for neutral), A, 2, 1 setting; when the side lights are switched on, the tell-tale is automatically dimmed to prevent night-time glare.

In its behaviour and smoothness, this is an outstandingly good automatic. The gearchanges are generally very smooth, if not quite imperceptible, the change-up speeds nicely related to throttle pressure, and kickdown response very good: on a light throttle, the 1-2, 2-3 changes practically merge together with the engine speed remaining virtually constant. At the other extreme, full throttle will let the engine run to 5,500 r.p.m. in first and second—40 and 75 m.p.h. respectively—before the next ratio slurs in reasonably smoothly. Surprisingly, you gain nothing in

acceleration by holding the lower ratios manually to the rev limit of 6,200 r.p.m.; retaining second on a twisty road, though, gives tremendously spirited one-gear performance up to around 85 m.p.h.

Handling and brakes

Fundamentally, the 2500/2800 series has the same all-independent suspension as that of the smaller BMWs, MacPherson struts at the front, semi-trailing arms at the back—a combination pioneered on the 1500 in 1962 and since widely adopted elsewhere. There are important refinements, though, particularly at the front. The angled struts and inclined pivots are so arranged that castor action—one cause of heavy steering—has been reduced to a value that just allows the steering to self centre, but no more. The geometry also introduces some negative camber to the outside front wheel on the turn, increasing its cornering power by reducing understeer—an excess of which will make the steering unresponsive. Thirdly, it prevents the nose of the car dipping much under braking—just as inclined wishbones can produce anti-dive characteristics.

There is a rubber insert in the substantial bumpers which wrap round all four corners.

The four quartz-halogen headlights, embedded in a familiar BMW frontage, can be quickly adjusted with thumb screws. The great depth of the front screen shows well here, too.

The central cubby provides support for ventilation grilles that can be angled left-right, up-down. They share a common volume control. The indicator window for the small gear selector is incorporated in the crisp instrument panel (right).

The front seats can be fully reclined and the headrests are adjustable for height. There is room for three adults in the back with the central arm rest up: legroom is quite good. (See above and below)

BMW 2500

It all works, too. The steering is remarkably light and accurate, if not all that quick, right down to walking speeds. Presumably it is then only the drag of the big tyres that makes parking quite heavy. On dry roads, the cornering powers are very high, even on bumpy surfaces, so you can hustle the car along an unfamiliar road with the assurance that there is always plenty of grip in reserve. Really vicious cornering, especially on a test track, reveals that the steering becomes a bit vague and indecisive on the limit, as though the front end were about to break away: on the road you almost invariably corner well below the sort of speeds that induces this sudden curious lack of feel which probably stems from the minimal castor and understeer. Similarly, it was on the test track rather than the road that we discovered a tendency for fuel surge to cut the engine and induce a mild and quite controllable tendency for the car to tighten its line in mid corner, even to drift the tail wide. Not surprisingly, too much power on a wet corner will slide the back wheels, too, while a trailing throttle approach can make the front end run wide as understeer sets in.

Good though they are in road manners, it would be wrong to imply that these big BMWs have quite the same responsive agility as some of the smaller ones. Despite quite firm suspension, they roll a little more—albeit still not very much—and generally feel a little softer. Less of a sports saloon, more a sporting carriage —which is presumably just what BMW had in mind.

On paper, the brakes have everything. Discs all round, servo assistance, a pressure limiting device to prevent the rear wheels locking prematurely, and twin circuits feeding two pairs of cylinders on each front disc. If one circuit fails, four-wheel braking at 75% full power is retained; if the other one goes, you are still left with 60%. Our standard fade test on the 2500 had a negligible effect so we subjected the faster 2800 to a less scientific but more punishing routine, braking hard from 110-120 m.p.h. several times on each lap of the MIRA road circuit. After three laps, smoke and heat haze were pouring from the wheels yet the brakes retained full efficiency throughout. We didn't record a maximum stop on the 2800; that on the 2500 (which has narrower tyres) was 0.95g before all the wheels locked. We suspect there was some servo lag on this car because gentle braking was a little snatchy and unprogressive. The front discs also squealed loudly sometimes.

The handbrake, which operates on separate drums on the rear discs, would hold the car on a 1-in-3 hill after a heavy two-fisted pull on the central lever. Quite a hard tug was necessary even to prevent the car creeping in gear.

Comfort and controls

Although by no means unresilient, the suspension is perhaps firmer than you might expect for a luxurious saloon. Certainly the car doesn't glide over bumps with the same smoothness as, say, a Jaguar XJ6, but what movement there is feels well controlled by firm damping. Perhaps many customers, graduating to these BMWs from more sporting machinery, might prefer it this way. At any rate, you are still cossetted in great comfort, even without a boulevard ride. The large front seats, anatomical-

continued

The spare wheel and tools are housed beneath the false floor of the very large boot which swallowed 12.3 cu. ft. of our test luggage.

BMW 2500 AUTO   AUG 1969 ELS

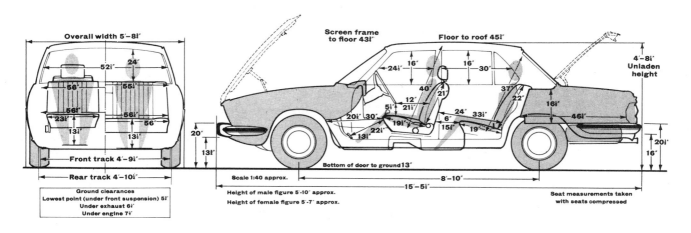

o.h.c. six-cylinder engine, rear-wheel drive, all-independent suspension.

Engine

Block material	Cast iron
Head material	Light alloy
Cylinders	6 in line
Cooling system	Water
Bore and stroke	
86 mm. (3.386 in.) 71.6 mm. (2.819 in.)	
Cubic capacity	2,494 c.c. (152.2 cu. in.)
Main bearings	Seven
Valves	o.h.c.
Compression ratio	9.0:1
Carburetters . . . Two Zenith 35/40 INAT two-stage	
	with automatic chokes
Fuel pump	Solex PE mechanical
Oil filter	Full flow
Max. power (DIN) . . . . 150 b.h.p. at 6,000 r.p.m.	
(SAE) . . . . 170 b.h.p. at 6,000 r.p.m.	
Max. torque (DIN) . . . 155.5 lb.ft. at 3,700 r.p.m.	

Transmission

Clutch	Fitchel and Sachs s.d.p. with
	diaphragm spring
Internal gearbox ratios	
Top gear	1.0:1
2nd gear	1.52:1
1st gear	2.56:1
Reverse	2.0:1
Final drive	Hypoid bevel 3.64:1
M.p.h. at 1,000 r.p.m. in:—	
Top gear	19.7
2nd gear	12.9
1st gear . . . . , . .	7.7

Chassis and body

Construction	Unitary body chassis

Brakes

Type	ATE discs all round; twin circuits and
	servo assistance; pressure limiting rear
	valve.
Dimensions . .	10.7 in. discs, front and back.

Suspension and steering

Front	Independent by inclined MacPherson
	struts and coil springs.
Rear	Independent by semi-trailing arms and
	coil springs; anti-roll bar. Boge Nivomat
	self-levelling dampers extra.

Shock absorbers:	
Front:	Telescopic
Rear:	Telescopic
Steering type . .	ZF-Gemmer worm and roller
Tyres	175 HR 14 or DR 70 HR 14
Wheels	Steel disc 6J x 14 well-based rims

Coachwork and equipment

Starting handle	No
Tool kit contents	One screwdriver, 2 spanners,
	plug spanner, wheel brace,
	pliers.
Jack	Pillar screw with winding
	handle.
Jacking points	Four, under body sill.
Battery	12 volt negative earth
	55 amp hrs capacity
Number of electrical fuses	10
Headlamps.	Four 5.4in. quartz iodine.
Indicators	Self cancelling flashers
Reversing lamp	Yes
Screen wipers	2-speed, self-parking
Screen washers	Electric pump
Sun visors	2
Locks:	
With key 1	Everything
With key 2	Front doors, ignition/starter
Interior heater	Fresh air 8 Kw unit as
	standard
Upholstery	Plastic or cloth
Floor covering	Carpet
Alternative body styles . .	None
Maximum load	3913lb.
Maximum roof rack load .	165lb.

Major extras available. Power assisted steering, limited slip differential, automatic transmission, self-levelling rear dampers, sliding roof.

Maintenance

Fuel tank capacity	16.5 galls
Sump	8.8. pints SAE 10W/50
Gearbox	2.1 pints ATF
Rear axle	2.6 pints
Steering gear	0.81 pints ATF
Coolant	21.1 (2 drain taps)
Chassis lubrication . . .	None
Minimum service interval .	4,000 miles
Ignition timing	
Contact breaker gap . .	0.015 in.

Sparking plug gap . . .	0.024 in.
Sparking plug type . .	Bosch W175T2
Tappet clearances (cold). .	Inlet 0.012 in.; Exhaust
	0.012 in.
Valve timing:	
inlet opens.	6° b.t.d.c.
inlet closes.	50° a.b.d.c.
exhaust opens.	50° b.b.d.c.
exhaust closes	6° a.t.d.c.
Rear wheel toe-in	0.04 in.
Front wheel toe-in	0.04 in.
Camber angle	0° ±30′
Castor angle	9° 30′ ±30′
King pin inclination . . .	6° 20′
Tyre pressures:	
Front:	29 p.s.i.
Rear:	27 p.s.i.

SAFETY CHECK LIST

Steering Assembly	
Steering box position	Behind front of engine
Steering column collapsible	Yes
Steering wheel boss padded	Yes
Steering wheel dished	Yes
Instrument Panel	
Projecting switches	None dangerously
Sharp cowls	No
Padding	Shin pads and facia
	top roll
Windscreen and Visibility	
Screen type	Laminated
Pillars padded	Slightly
Standard driving mirrors	One inside, one on
	driver's door
Interior mirror framed	Yes
Interior mirror collapsible	Yes
Sun visors	Two
Seats and Harness	
Attachment to floor	By bolted down slides
Do they tip forward?	No
Head rest attachment points	Yes—plus headrests
Back of front seats	Firm padding
Safety Harness	Lap and diagonal
Harness anchors at back	Yes
Doors	
Projecting handles	Yes—but flexible
Anti-burst latches	Yes
Child-proof locks	Yes

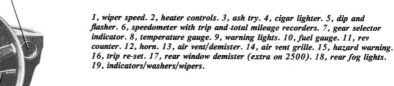

1, wiper speed. 2, heater controls. 3, ash try. 4, cigar lighter. 5, dip and flasher. 6, speedometer with trip and total mileage recorders. 7, gear selector indicator. 8, temperature gauge. 9, warning lights. 10, fuel gauge. 11, rev counter. 12, horn. 13, air vent/demister. 14, air vent grille. 15, hazard warning. 16, trip re-set. 17, rear window demister (extra on 2500). 18, rear fog lights. 19, indicators/washers/wipers.

BMW 2500

ly shaped for support, rather than softly padded to blend to your shape, provide a very comfortable and commanding driving position behind the big wood-rimmed steering wheel. A handy side lever releases the seats which have ample rearward adjustment for tall drivers and sloping runners to elevate short ones who need to sit close to the wheel. The knurled twist knob for adjusting the squab angle is slow and awkward to turn, though, especially if the seat is well back. The squab can be laid flat to make a bed of sorts. Heel and toe exercises on the 2800 were very easy as the pedals are much better placed and angled than in any previous BMW we have driven.

With the central armrest folded up, there is ample room for three adults in the back though rear legroom could only be called generous if the front seats were not on the last stop: the runners are so long that this is an unlikely setting. As no sacrifices have been made in accommodation for the sake of a low profile, there is plenty of headroom, front and back.

The low waistline, sit-up seats and deep windows make the inside particularly airy and the view out very good. There are no bad blind spots and all four corners can be seen easily from the driver's seat, though you must make allowances for the V-shaped front bumper when parking. Although the wipers are set for left-hand drive, they cover most of the glass on the right and don't seem to lift off at speed (the driver's has an aerofoil to keep it down). We also particularly liked the three-nozzle washers. There are two mirrors—a framed, dipping one inside mounted on a snap-off stalk for safety, and another on the driver's door, as in most German cars; both give a good view aft. The squashy sun visors can be swivelled sideways on rather stiff and flimsy looking plastic hinges.

The lights on both cars we tried were so badly adjusted that we couldn't judge them fairly. It was only just before handing the second one back that we discovered they have simple thumb-screw adjusters at the back with which the beams can be re-aligned in a matter of seconds. Judging by the intensity of the pool of light ahead, we suspect that the lamps are excellent when properly trimmed.

Interior ventilation, conspicuously lacking on most other BMWs, is excellent on these cars. A large swinging "chip grille" in the centre of the facia, with adjustable vertical vanes, admits air to the cabin at ambient temperature. Driver and front seat passengers have independent control over the distribution of air but not its volume which, with the noisy fan on full boost, is nearing hurricane strength. Without it, ram pressure alone gives only a meagre flow. Swivelling vents at each end of the facia can be used for supplementary cooling or, in cold wet weather, for demisting the side windows. With separate controls for temperature, volume and distribution, the powerful heater/demister is also quite versatile, though there are no separate outlets for the back seat passengers.

By £3,000 standards, we wouldn't call the automatic 2500 conspicuously quiet, though it certainly isn't noisy, either. Wind roar is about average and at 70 m.p.h. begins to dominate the efficient hum of the engine. Road noise is a little better isolated, thumps and tyre roar being well muffled.

Fittings and furniture

In finish, decor and detail design, the interior layout is superb. The instruments are masterfully simple and clear, the big white-on-black speedometer and rev counter being angled inwards to avoid any parallax error. Several drivers voted the instruments the best they had seen, despite the absence of an oil pressure gauge and ammeter: warning lights are provided instead in a neat central cluster which includes tell-tales for the handbrake and low fuel. The fuel gauge on both cars we tried, incidentally, often gave a misleading idea of what was left in the tank.

Beneath the instrument nacelle are three coloured push buttons for the hazard warning (red), optional rear window demister (yellow) and fog light (green). Fingertip inserts in the three steering wheel spokes sound the horn and the right-hand column stalk operates the washers (pull), wipers (push in) and indicators. We wait, in vain it seems, for British manufacturers to copy this excellent Continental system. The other stalk flashes and dips the headlights; although it has a logical up-for-main-beam movement, we would prefer a centre-return switch so that you don't have to think in a heated moment which way to move the lever.

Stowage space is generous and well planned. There is a trough atop the padded facia where cigarettes can be kept: ridges prevent them from sliding about. There is also a flop-down compartment on the passenger's side (which conceals the stiff bonnet release and inaccessible fuse box), a handy console cave in the centre, and door/seat squab map pockets. The boot is very large in floor area, not quite so generous in depth as the spare wheel is housed beneath the carpeted floor. There is also a two-compartment oddments box on one side (useful, say, for carrying bottles).

All three passengers have a roof-top grab handle and the front seats are fitted with head rests—more to prevent whip-lash injury than to provide pillows for relaxation. The inertia reel seat belts were comfortable to wear.

As an alternative to the plastic upholstery in the 2500 we tried, you can have velvety cloth furnishings; smart but impractical if you have children or livestock. Well fitted loop-pile carpet covers the floor and the plastic headlining is washable. Other equipment includes an electric clock, three ash trays, a cigar lighter, coat hooks, and arm rests that double as door pulls.

Servicing and accessibility

Servicing—including an engine oil and filter change—is needed every 4,000 miles. The full routine, followed by detailed notes on each job, is outlined in the excellent 100-page handbook that is packed with useful technical information, as well as instructions.

Accident damage should be easier and cheaper to repair as all the wings are bolted on and simple to replace. The body is also very well protected by wrap-round bumpers with full-width rubber inserts and rubber over-riders. Stainless steel trim is used extensively on the car, too.

Accessibility under the front hinged bonnet is good: the distributor, coil, washer bottle, battery, oil and radiator filters, and dipstick (a piece of flimsy wire) are all within easy reach. Generally, everything looks beautifully made and assembled.

1, radiator filler. 2, battery. 3, washer reservoir. 4, washer pump. 5, oil filler. 6, distributor. The massive double-pancake air cleaner masks much of the impressive looking engine.

MAKE: BMW MODEL 2500 automatic. MAKERS: Bayerische Motoren Werke AG, Munich, West Germany. CONCESSION-AIRES: BMW Concessionaires (Great Britain) Ltd., 142 Holland Pk. Ave., W.11.

Road Test:

The Six-Cylinder BMW 2800

An Extremely Fast and Accelerative Medium-Capacity Saloon which is Near-Perfect in Almost All Respects

A combination of horizontal and vertical grilles characterises the impressive frontal aspect of the high-performance BMW 2800.

AFTER reviving their fortunes with a range of extremely good o.h.c. four-cylinder motor cars, the Bayerische Motoren Werke AG of Munich tantalised us at last year's Motor Show with a six-cylinder version of these earlier models. At the time I ventured to wonder whether the six-cylinder BMW might not be a softened-up affair aimed at a different, luxury-loving public. I had to wait a long time before I was able to drive a BMW Six but, having done so, I can say that not only are these latest BMWs—the 2500 and the 2800—far from being what I had hoped they were not but that they are about as near-perfect on almost all counts as any sporting saloon motor-car can be.

Here is a car that even in 2500 form will exceed 120 m.p.h., clock an impressive and useful 17.2 sec. for a s.s. ¼-mile, exceed our legal top speed by over 20 m.p.h. in *third* gear, is as satisfactory to drive as former BMWs, which is saying a great deal, is as beautifully made and appointed as they, and which you can buy in this imports-protected country for under £3,000. I would have liked to have been able to tell you how much more performance the 2800 extracts from its extra 294 c.c. and additional 20 b.h.p. I am unable to do this because the publicity people messed me about over delivery dates, leaving insufficient time for fifth-wheeling, especially as, having driven the car down from London to the country late one night, I had to drive it back the next day because the bonnet resolutely refused to open (and for photography and the adding of oil you need to open it). The self-supporting lid had to be wrenched open and the catches lowered by altering their mountings. (The bonnet release is in the glove locker on the n/s of this r.h.d. car; it pulls down the light lid and secures it.) So you must just bear with me if I say the performance is adequate—very adequate indeed!

It would need a driver of some skill, and lucky with the traffic, habitually to take the BMW to its rev.-limit, which ranges between 6,200 and 7,000 r.p.m. To do this implies accelerating better than some fast sports-cars and getting 100 or so m.p.h. in 3rd gear. For those who need such performance, it is there. But the BMW offers so much more. It is comfortable, safe, delightful to drive, and a prestige purchase which offers the sort of high-quality finish and equipment for which German cars are noted.

It follows the current German interior pattern of a floor gear-lever mounted somewhat far back with stowage space before it, a central hand-brake behind that, a drop parcels-well in the facia, a rather wide transmission tunnel necessitating placing the left foot under the clutch pedal, stalk-controlled screen-wipers and washers, and rubber-capped bumpers. This means a very conveniently laid out driving compartment, added to which the BMW has controls which function impeccably. If you regard the BMW Six as an extension of the great four-cylinder BMWs with almost unbelievable performance but none of the splendid driving qualities impaired, you have a good idea of what motoring in one of the finest cars to emerge last year is like. In speed, acceleration and economy the BMW 2800 is not merely the equal, it is the superior of cars of considerably greater swept volume. The 86 × 80 mm. 2,788-c.c. single overhead camshaft engine produces 170 (D.I.N.) b.h.p. at 6,000 r.p.m. on a 9-to-1 c.r., which is enough to take the mickey out of many fabulous automobiles! I suppose you could call this BMW an XJ6-consumer, except that Jaguar say they do not sell cars to enthusiastic drivers, and the German car is very much an enthusiast's motor-car. . . .

There is the typically-BMW steering, firm rather than light, free from vices apart from the faintest trace of feed-back, and sure and positive in action. There is the suspension, firm but not frenzied, giving a comfortable ride without letting the wheels lose contact with the road. There is the handling, enabling corners to be taken as by a sports-car, with a high sense of security. The longer engine, giving a rather heavy front-end feel, has not promoted oversteer, the cornering remaining nicely neutral, the car's tail following the line through fast bends. There is the light clutch, the delightful gear-change, the rigid short lever under the left hand going from one position to the other with a smooth click, and the light progressive brakes.

These qualities combine to create a motor-car in which the very considerable performance can be used, or in this country a good proportion of it, in safety, with a high degree of enjoyment and without flamboyance. Open up and the engine accelerates, after some initial momentary snatch, with the smoothness of the legendary turbine, on and on up the rev. range, so that normally the driver will change up long before the big tachometer, the needle of which moves in top gear in the same plane as that of the matching speedometer, gets near the red marking. Inaudible when idling, the engine emits a hard purposeful sound around 5,000 r.p.m. Drive briskly on busy roads and confidence is bred from the quick accurate steering, the roll-free suspension, and those deceptively powerful all-disc servo brakes. You sit high on extremely accommodating seats upholstered in cloth (but nylon, not Bedford) like those of a top-bracket limousine from a more gracious age (if I prefer leather, it is a personal fad), after shutting doors which close with a dull high-quality "clonk". Detachable head-rests can be plugged into the front-seat squabs. The view of the road ahead is enhanced by the low mounting of the wood-rimmed steering wheel and on the Continent there would be every incentive to let the speed of the 2800 go to its 124-m.p.h. maximum.

You sit naturally to drive the BMW, as in a saloon you should, with the instrument binnacle immediately before you, Vdo 8,000-r.p.m. tachometer and 140-m.p.h. speedometer supplemented by small, simply-marked dials recording water heat and fuel contents. Behind the glass, the larger dials are angled for effective vision. An easily-reached knob on the right brings in the lamps; turning it dims out the instrument lighting. Below these two small dials there is a series of triple warning-light slots, labelled GENER., OIL, BEAM, FLASHER, FUEL, BRAKE, the respective colours being red, orange, blue (and rather too bright), green, white and red. The steering-wheel spokes depress to sound the horn; other knobs, on the top of the central console, look after hazard warning and wipers speed adjustment. Stalks to right and left of the steering column control, respectively, turn indicators, parking lamps, washers and wipers, and headlamps dipping and flashing.

The console contains a drawer-type ash-tray, ventilation grille with adjustable vents, the radio, if fitted, and generous open stowage space. The facia, with its discreet strip of wood trim, carries the heater quadrant levers, a small Vdo Kienzle clock more easily read by passenger than driver, and the press-button which drops the illuminated but unlockable parcels well. There are swivelling fresh-air vents at its extremities, but they do not pass as much air as the central inlets. The rear window can be heated and the driver of a l.h.d. BMW apparently has a drop stowage well similar to that before the front-seat occupant, although this did not figure on the test car. In addition there are pockets (which had split along the bottom) in the front doors, pockets on the backs of the adjustable front-seat squabs, and a deep shelf behind the windscreen, apart from the usual rear shelf.

The décor of the red BMW was beautifully done—black trim on the doors, with their shaped grips and sill interior locks, heavy grey carpets on the floor. Two keys are provided, very substantial, the master key operating all locks, including ignition/steering, and looking as if it belonged to a small safe. The essence of the BMW's instruments is easily read messages without detailed calibration, from upright white needles (speedometer and tachometer have clear figures in multiples of ten), and many warning lights arranged, however, so that the impression of a mobile fruit machine is avoided. The speedometer incorporates decimal trip and total mileometers. A rather ineffective anti-dazzle mirror and a good anti-dazzle driver's exterior mirror were fitted, together with the expected vizors, coat-hooks, grabs, etc. Items such as the ignition cutting the headlamps beam when it is switched off and rotating grips on the window-winders add to the air of high-quality which the impeccably-appointed interior imparts.

Very few items marred the pleasure of driving this remarkable motor-car. In sunlight the speaker-grille on the screen side of the instrument binnacle reflected in the windscreen glass. The Phoenix Senator 6/4-ply rayon radial tubed DR70HR14 low-profile tyres howled when resisting oversteer on sharp corners and yelped from the inside rear wheel if the power was brought in with verve for a fast getaway. There was that bother with the bonnet, and occasional brake-screech. Reverse gear, outboard of bottom gear, could be engaged inadvertently if one was so clumsy as to override its spring-loading. Otherwise, from the nice action of its lift-up external door handles to the extreme joy of driving the BMW 2800 as a car of this performance ability and controllability should be driven, I have nothing but praise for the best BMW yet.

The Munich manufacturer is no stranger to six-cylinder power units,

TOP : Extremely easy-to-read instruments and a low set wheel controlling impeccable steering can be seen in this view of the BMW 2800's interior.

CENTRE : Where the performance comes from—the well-buried single overhead camshaft engine of the biggest BMW.

BOTTOM : Personifying the character of the BMW 2800 is this neat and comprehensive tool-kit in the luggage boot. The size of the latter can be gauged by the Eversure Fillacan, which can be seen by the o/s wheel arch.

for pre-war BMWs used them, up to the well-remembered 328 sports car. The present 2500/2800 engines is in effect the 1600 with the benefit of two more cylinders. It has the alloy head and iron block, seven main bearings for the forged steel crankshaft and it is inclined at 30°. The single o.h. camshaft is chain-driven and valve seats and guides are shrunk in the head.

The valve rockers are of light alloy. The valve timing is: inlet opens 6° b.t.d.c., closes 54° a.b.d.c.; exhaust opens 54° b.b.d.c., closes 6° a.t.d.c., with clearances of 0.010 to 0.012 in., cold. Lubrication is by an Eaton rotor pump with full-flow filter, and carburation is by twin Zenith 35/40 two-stage carburetters with 117.5 main jets.

The running gear follows BMW practice with coil-spring struts front and back, in conjunction with lower wishbones and trailing links at the front and semi-trailing arms for the independent rear suspension which functions so well. Front suspension travel is 7.1 in., rear suspension travel 7.9 in., and the layout of the front struts has been revised. ZF-Gemmer hour-glass worm-and-roller steering is used, the ratio being 16.4 at the box and 18.9 overall, which translates into just over four turns, lock-to-lock, of the three-spoke steering wheel. The column has two universal joints and is collapsible in a crash. The brake discs have a diameter of 272 mm., the front ones actuated by four 40 mm. dia. pistons, the rear ones by two such pistons, with the hand-brake working on the rear discs. The all-steel body has a 21.2 cu. ft. capacity luggage boot, rather shallow, with a flat floor and a useful stowage box for a petrol can, etc. The fuel tank is said to hold 16½ gallons but the range suggests nearer 10 gallons. The filler cap is unsecured, unusual on a German car and is concealed behind the rear number plate.

The outputs claimed for this fine oversquare BMW power unit are 170 (D.I.N.) or 192 (S.A.E.) b.h.p., equal to 61 b.h.p. per litre at 6,000 r.p.m., with maximum torque, 173.6 lb. ft., developed at 3,700 r.p.m. Piston speed at 6,000 r.p.m. is 3,150 ft./min. and the claimed power/weight ratio is 128.6 b.h.p. per ton at the kerb, tank full, dropping to 99.5 b.h.p. per ton fully laden with typical passengers and luggage.

To appreciate just how much performance this luxury BMW Six gives, it will out-accelerate cars like the 4.2-litre Jaguar XJ6 and 6.3-litre Mercedes-Benz 600. The makers quote figures of 0-60 m.p.h. in under 10 sec. and 0-100 m.p.h. in 25 sec., and there is reason to believe that these can be bettered and that a s.s. ¼-mile can be achieved in under 17 sec.—impressive indeed, from a four-door, five-seater 2.8-litre saloon. (As I have explained, the demand for demonstrations prevented us from taking our own performance figures.) The handbook also gives the maxima in the gears as 34, 60, 90 and 124 m.p.h. at 6,000 r.p.m., and I was able to get nearly 110 m.p.h. indicated at 5,000 r.p.m. The axle ratio in the hypoid back axle with ZF limited-slip differential is 3.45 to 1, the other gear ratios being 4.9, 7.17 and 13.2 to 1. Incidentally, it is available with power steering and an automatic gearbox for those more interested in luxury than in the pleasure of driving.

Because of the changed test dates I was obliged to cause the BMW the indignity of using the congested A30 and A303 roads, instead of the more deserted going to which I am accustomed. However, even under these depressing circumstances it was great fun, and got along exceedingly well, cruising at !!! m.p.h. whenever the traffic permitted. On this journey I was able to ascertain that the fuel tank takes the car 216 miles before the low fuel level warning light begins to twinkle, 231 miles before this warning says "Fill up!" In fact, the absolute range, in some very mixed driving, proved to be 265 miles, which is fair enough for a saloon, some of whose occupants will be expected to wish to vacate the car before this, although inadequate for a genuine GT machine. A fuel consumption check, using 5-star petrol, returned an excellent 24.8 m.p.g. As for oil, the consumption was approximately 1,000 m.p.p.

The impeccable handling qualities of the car made light of what would otherwise have been some tedious motoring. Outside Torquay we paused at a large establishment which advertised "light lunches", only to be told that all they were prepared to offer, at 2.15 p.m., were hot pies. They appear to be keener on selling music than meals. Pressing on, I had a bright idea. Our homeward route took us past Exeter Airport and here, I thought, we would find the sort of meal we required. Sure enough, the big advertisement for the Airport restaurant announced that it was open to the public. Although we were merely driving a BMW and not buying a seat in a Bristol Freighter, I thought this might apply. But no—it was 3 p.m. and no cooked food was to be had. Remembering the many excellent meals I have enjoyed, at all manner of odd hours, at small aerodromes on the other side of the Channel, my sympathy goes out to anyone who has to get airborne from Exeter. Moreover, judging from the blind T-road from which they have to join the A30, I imagine that, having survived the hazards of aviation and probable starvation, they are likely to die while attempting to drive away.

It was nice to see a vintage solid-tyred Leyland platform lorry outside the premises of Hine Bros. near the Dorset border, bearing their insignia, but I was surprised to find that a fair was partially closing and encroaching on the roads of Crewkerne, for we have been disallowed motor racing (which is also a circus or fair) on public roads these past 44 years!

However, back to the BMW 2800, at speed it becomes very hushed, apart from subdued wind noise around the front door pillars. It makes light of congested traffic and proved equally effective along the winding country lanes by which I am able to get home after leaving the A30 at Dummer Down. It really is a splendid all-round car. I recall trying the first of the new line in BMWs, the 1500, in Germany and thinking how very refined it was. Later, more powerful versions never quite seemed to match up in this respect, although being exceedingly good cars. The 2800 has the refinement of the 1500, more "character" than the four-cylinder models, and must be regarded as one of the World's great cars.

If you have the sort of money the Concessionaires in this country charge for the BMW 2800, try it and you will almost certainly buy it. The price is £3,245 including p.t. and Import duty.—W. B.

Road Test

BMW 2800 CS

CAR AT A GLANCE: Hardtop body by Karmann. . . Full compliance with all U.S. regulations. . 125 mph top, effortless 100 mph cruise. . . Radials, 4-speed ZF box, 4-wheel discs and power ZF steering all standard.

by Sloniger

A BMW 2800 CS is either the silkiest big sports car swinger I know or the meanest 2+2 luxury GT coupe going. Or both. Particularly both.

This admittedly teutonic type package contains 6000 bucks worth of dynamite in a velvet glove. It's certain membership in that exclusive 125 mph club, yet the dues are a modest 15 miles to the gallon. It's zero to 60 is less than nine, without forgetting 20 to 125, all in fourth gear.

Slashing through, past or around mundane traffic poles like a bludgeon with fine-honed edges, the 2800 CS purrs so softly you might forget to shift into top. After all, second gear could earn you a ticket in any city and third will push 3000 pounds of sybaritic style over 100 without touching the red line.

Say the big BMW coupe is an automobile of superlatives and you've said

Lighting would be revised to sealed beams on U.S. bound 2800's and some states wouldn't allow the road lamps. Hopefully European glass makers will adopt the imbedded antenna.

almost all. Such statistics are beyond faulting, even though the buyer with sufficient scratch to live happily forevermore in BMW-land must still be prepared for niggles. These, though, mostly concern the wrappings.

Karmann, body builder to German motordom with a real Charles Atlas complex, had a problem of course. Pillarless hardtops are tricky to keep rigid. They handled that fine, but at the

expense of vast doors so heavy it takes two doormen to extract you. This is even when they open to right angles.

Next, the side windows won't crank clear out of sight. And while the glass does seal, it also whistles to distraction. Knobs for the wind wings require two hefty hands each, but are sited where only a couple of fingers can pertain. Then, for some reason BMW provides electricity for the rear quarter panes but powered side windows are an option.

The elegantly readable dash with round tach and speedo (10% at 100 is shamelessly fast) leaves almost all other functions to maybe-lights. These are flanked by a shelf with dividers to prevent slithering and the console bin has non-skip strips as well. But the two drop-down bins were always stuck and a two-hand operation. Carpets snap into place but the driver's fouled my pedals.

Things like that could blow the old mind if it were my six grand (German price including sliding roof) on the line.

Finally the moment comes to apply their symmetrical, universally programmed key-like lock to its slot — once you get it to work the heavy door locks, that is. You've made a walk-around noting matt grill and dinky side vents which BMW sedan sixes lack, the stock rear fog lamp and nearly invisible heating wires in the rear window, alloy wheels and the fact that no more than two can really go first class in this vehicle.

So you fire up, slot into first: and nothing else could possibly matter.

The piston engine still lives, dad. That is, provided it's made by BMW. Who needs rotaries, turbines or refrigerated steam? None could be smoother than a seven-bearing, single-OHC six, never mind its muscle. This engine produces 190 SAE hp so effortlessly it is indecent.

The torque (173.6 lbs./ft.) peaks at 3700 rpm but the band is flat enough to pull like a road runner from 2500 and pick up cleanly in top from 1500. In part, this comes from a bore of 86 mm and stroke (enlarged from the 2500) of 80 mm. Near-square engines often come on strong and early. Not all wind over 6000 without the slightest fuss, though.

Gear speeds work out to 35-65-100-125 while a classic 0-60 takes 8.9 seconds. More impressive, the CS goes from zero to 100 in 24 seconds. Most impressive, it will pull from 25 to 100 in top in barely over half a minute. And this is a 3045-lb. car at the curb, yet so like a Saturn launch when you tromp hard that I looked up the weight twice in disbelief.

All this power (two gears would serve a lazy driver) feeds through their ZF box with stub lever crying out to be used for the fun of it. Every notch takes hold like closing the front door at Fort Knox. None of this slippery-knife-in-butter-but-what-gear-do-I-have-now syndrome.

There is one caution. The car must be driven or left to its own devices. If

Natural habitat of the BMW 2800CS is the Alps. Car understeers slightly, then with warning breaks into a throttle controllable drift, that is, if your dad owns the tire factory.

you do choose to shift, note a small resistance built into the gate when moving from the III/IV plane left to the I/II side of their pattern. There is then a little larger resistance when going farther left to the R plane (up past I). Banging the lever across only takes you right on past the forward gears.

Their large, thin-rim, leather-covered steering wheel with matt spokes (set a touch high) is connected to boosted steering which it handles with four turns lock-to-lock. On a compact 100-inch wheelbase this gives 35-foot U-turns and playfully easy town maneuvers with enough road feel to ignore gusty cross winds when cruising near 120.

More to the point, it makes life easy in linked S-bends more often than not full of perambulating peasants. A small

Karmann went a little over-board to achieve rigidity in the hardtop body. Doors are excessively heavy and somehow not enough room was provided to fully sink the windows.

Strangely, despite the appearance of full instrumentation, most functions are watched over by warning lights. Sloniger rates stub ZF gate as superb.

break in oncoming traffic and you can pass inside or out, ignore tightening radii, and leave the queue without turning a hair — yours or theirs. There's no indecent exhaust rap and no wild skids. Simply give a wave and be gone.

Descending one face of the Alps we did finally manage to induce brake fade, though never total loss, and even then it came about largely because I didn't bother to shift down. With so much third-gear torque, who uses second? In five minutes the binders were back at work.

Hardly a small car overall at 178 inches by European standards, the BMW doesn't feel bulky in tight places because you can see the corners. Held by shoulder-hugger, near-bucket seats and hooked to light, positive steering we hardly noticed when the shocks began to fade. The car still handled rings around all but that one pure-bred, teeth-shaking GT you are sure to meet each day.

Perhaps this feeling was so strong because the effortless engine makes it unnecessary to shove and fight for small holes. You wait regally for a safe spot and sail into the sunset, unruffled.

Pushed really hard — since you asked — the BMW has mild initial understeer and rather more sudden transition to a wild drift angle than you first expect. All Munich bombs seem to appreciate cornering extravagantly tail-out at the limits, on throttle steering alone. Once you accept a road view through the side window as normal they can be held there indefinitely.

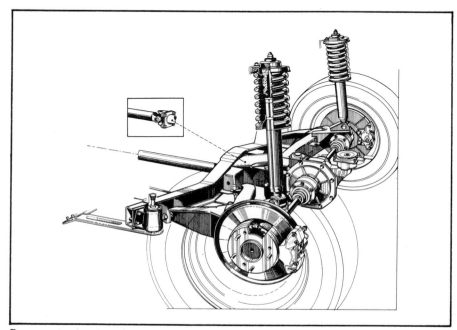

Rear suspension is coil too, with inclined rubber mounted trailing arms. The axle type is known as Niveaumat *or System Boge, and has a standard 50% locking differential.*

Canted sohc six puts out an honest 170 DIN (190 SAE) hp, and smoothly too, with seven main bearings. Note accessible distributor location at upper right.

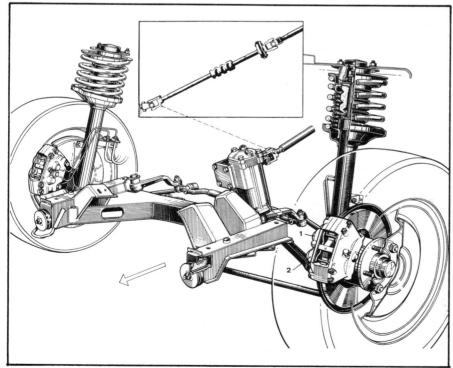

2800CS front suspension is by McPherson strut and rubber mounted.
Inset shows collapsible feature of the steering column; the gears are by ZF.

Few with the resources to buy a BMW CS to begin with would count pennies at the corner filling station but that amazingly good 14.5 mpg (including one 190-mile stretch in two hours and much full-bore mountain work) has other meanings. You only get 14.6 gallons to play with which is a mistake when two people are contemplating the modern grand tour. I gather larger tanks are coming soon.

A large if flat trunk carries all the extras and basics two need for Grand Hotel arrivals in appropriate style. Since the back is only comfortable for adults around town anyway, that proved sufficient.

Eagerly nubile onlookers may not fall all over themselves drooling at the heavy-set styling of a BMW 2800 CS — it does seem to come on best as a car for matinee idols with one Oscar already on the shelf — but they couldn't help admiring your casual competence once underway.

This coupe makes the most ham-footed driver among us look like Fangio setting lap records on his least frenetic day. ●

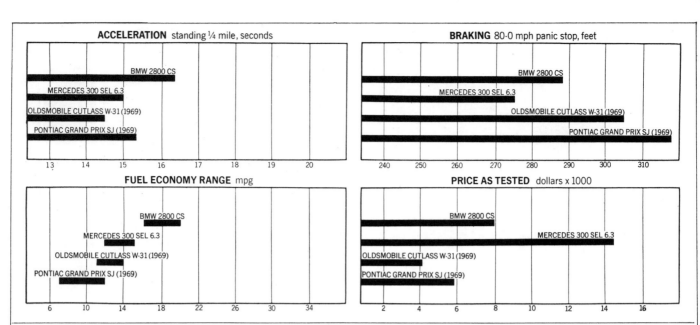

ACCELERATION standing ¼ mile, seconds

- BMW 2800 CS
- MERCEDES 300 SEL 6.3
- OLDSMOBILE CUTLASS W-31 (1969)
- PONTIAC GRAND PRIX SJ (1969)

13 14 15 16 17 18 19 20

BRAKING 80-0 mph panic stop, feet

- BMW 2800 CS
- MERCEDES 300 SEL 6.3
- OLDSMOBILE CUTLASS W-31 (1969)
- PONTIAC GRAND PRIX SJ (1969)

240 250 260 270 280 290 300 310

FUEL ECONOMY RANGE mpg

- BMW 2800 CS
- MERCEDES 300 SEL 6.3
- OLDSMOBILE CUTLASS W-31 (1969)
- PONTIAC GRAND PRIX SJ (1969)

6 10 14 18 22 26 30 34

PRICE AS TESTED dollars x 1000

- BMW 2800 CS
- MERCEDES 300 SEL 6.3
- OLDSMOBILE CUTLASS W-31 (1969)
- PONTIAC GRAND PRIX SJ (1969)

2 4 6 8 10 12 14 16

BMW 2800 CS

Importer: Hoffman Motors Corporation
375 Park Avenue
New York, N.Y.

Vehicle Type: Front-engine, rear-wheel-drive, 4-passenger coupe

Price as tested: $7965.00
(Manufacturer's suggested retail price, including all options listed below, Federal excise tax, dealer preparation and delivery charges, does not include state and local taxes, license or freight charges)

Options on test car: Base car, $7,480.00; leather upholstery, $310.00; tinted glass, $75.00; dealer preparation, $100.00

ENGINE
Type: 6-in-line, air-cooled, cast iron block and aluminum head, 7 main bearings
Bore x stroke...3.39 x 3.15 in, 86.0 x 80.0 mm
Displacement...............170.1 cu in, 2788 cc
Compression ratio...................9.0 to one
Carburetion......2 x 2-bbl Zenith 35/40 INAT
Valve gear..Chain driven single overhead cam
Power (SAE)............192 bhp @ 6000 rpm
Torque (SAE)............174 lb-ft @ 3700 rpm
Specific power output...........1.12 bhp/cu in, 68.9 bhp/liter
Max recommended engine speed...6200 rpm

DRIVE TRAIN
Transmission.............4-speed, all-synchro
Final drive ratio.....................3.45 to one

Gear Ratio		Mph/1000 rpm	Max. test speed
I	3.85	5.5	34 mph (6200 rpm)
II	2.08	9.7	60 mph (6200 rpm)
III	1.38	15.0	93 mph (6200 rpm)
IV	1.00	20.7	103 mph (5000 rpm)

DIMENSIONS AND CAPACITIES
Wheelbase...............................103.3 in
Track, F/R.......................56.9/55.2 in
Length................................183.5 in
Width..................................65.7 in
Height.................................53.9 in
Ground clearance........................5.5 in
Curb weight...........................3025 lbs
Weight distribution, F/R.........55.0/45.0%
Battery capacity...........12 volts, 55 amp/hr
Alternator capacity..................420 watts
Fuel capacity.........................14.5 gal
Oil capacity...........................5.3 qts
Water capacity........................12.7 qts

SUSPENSION
F: Ind., MacPherson strut, coil springs, antisway bar
R: Ind., semi-trailing arms, coil springs, antisway bar

STEERING
Type........Recirculating ball, power assisted
Turns lock-to-lock...........................4.0
Turning circle curb-to-curb............33.4 ft

BRAKES
F:..........10.7-in solid disc, power assisted
R: 9.84 x 1.58-in cast iron drum, power assisted

WHEELS AND TIRES
Wheel size.........................14 x 6.0-in
Wheel type............Cast light alloy, 5-bolt
Tire make and size.........Phoenix Senator DR70 HR 14
Tire type.........Rayon, radial ply, tube type
Test inflation pressures, F/R........27/26 psi

PERFORMANCE
Zero to	Seconds
30 mph	2.6
40 mph	3.2
50 mph	6.0
60 mph	8.3
70 mph	11.0
80 mph	14.2
90 mph	17.7
100 mph	22.7

Standing ¼-mile......16.3 sec @ 86.2 mph
Top speed (observed).................128 mph
80-0 mph....................288 ft (0.74 G)
Fuel mileage.....16-20 mpg on premium fuel
Cruising range...................232-290 mi

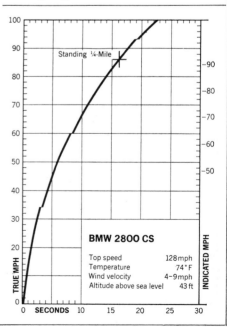

BMW 2800 CS

Top speed	128mph
Temperature	74°F
Wind velocity	4-9mph
Altitude above sea level	43 ft

Standing ¼-Mile

TRUE MPH / INDICATED MPH / SECONDS

BMW 2800 CS

BMW stays alive by offering automotive gems that a modest number of enthusiasts can't resist, despite the premium rise

The whole point is that you can light your cigarette with a Zippo. Alfred Dunhill makes brilliant lighters but you don't *need* one. Selectively fit mechanisms and gold-filled cases are spoken of with reverence but when you get right down to the hard core of truth those purebred qualities won't make your cigarette any more fiery or produce any more smoke than if you had touched it off with a clacking old stainless steel Zippo. No. You certainly don't need a Dunhill.

You don't need St. Emillion for lunch either. You can drink Gallo. Gallo may come off like vintage Kool-Aid in the presence of a truly great wine but if you've never tasted anything better you probably won't find any devastating deficiencies.

You don't need a BMW 2800 CS either. By any standard in the world it rates as a truly great automobile—an automobile that yields enormous dividends in driving pleasure—but you don't need it. More than that, considering the test car's $7965 price tag, you may not even be tempted—but that has no bearing on the BMW's virtues. It is an aristocratic motor car.

And, as aristocrats are selective in their endeavors, so is the BMW. It doesn't pretend to be an automotive be-all-and-end-all. Since it's a 2 + 2 it's hardly what you would choose for a school bus. With only 192 horsepower it falls easy prey to any number of Detroit super cars with their locomotive-size engines. Visually, it suggests nothing more than contemporary BMW—a flavor for which we've developed a strong taste, but nothing that will win converts to the fold. No, the 2800 CS is a non-participant in the field of automotive utility and falls in a universe high above the basic lusts of the immature car addict. And for the record, it makes no pretenses to do otherwise.

Instead, the 2800 CS is its maker's image of a surpassingly good personal automobile. Its makers are German engineers, which gives them credentials as good as anybody's to do the job, but more important, they are car enthusiasts of undisguised zeal. They dodge VWs on the autobahns at speeds that would get you thrown in jail in the U.S. and they never resist the opportunity for a few laps around Hockenheim or the Nürburgring. They are very simply men who like to drive, the quicker the better, and are in the

fortunate enough position to build their own cars. You may doubt the extent of their involvement with cars—dismiss it as a journalist's euphoric dream—but there is one hard, cold, economic fact that you cannot put aside. And this fact is the key that prompts BMW to build cars to a standard of excellence that Detroit can't match. You see, BMW is a small company. Its total production last year was about equal to the number of Grand Prixs that Pontiac stamped out and only 40% of the volume that Ford enjoys with the Mustang alone. This modest crop is the absolute seam-stretching limit of the factory's capability. Each year production facilities expand but the demand expands even faster and waiting lists grow longer and longer. At the same time BMW's management wisely acknowledges that it can't compete on equal terms with even the larger manufacturers in Germany (Volkswagen and Opel), let alone Detroit. Instead, it ducks the competition by building specialty cars that appeal to a relatively small volume of enthusiasts who are, in turn, willing to pay the premium prices that BMW requires to stay in business. Detroit has tried to do the same thing but its costs are too high, and when it raises the price the volume drops so low as to be hardly worth the trouble. The Shelby Mustang is a perfect example. In 1969 the Shelby's base price ranged between $4434 and $5027, depending upon the model, which is roughly $1000 over a similarly equipped Mach 1. Only 3150 cars were sold—a pit-

tance compared to the 300,000 car volume for the standard Mustang. And remember, even at the Shelby's inflated price Ford still wasn't able to build an exceptional automobile. It takes more money than that. Probably for $8000, the price of a Continental (and incidentally the price of BMW 2800 CS), Ford could make a magnificent Mustang, but if the Shelby is any example you could count the $8000-Mustang customers on your fingers. We all know that Yankee technology can't be bothered for such trifles when it has millions of garages to fill and so the continuation of the system is assured—Detroit turning out solid bread-and-butter cars by the millions and BMW staying alive by offering a collection of automotive gems that a modest number of enthusiasts can't resist, despite the price.

The entire BMW formula for success is predicated on the fact that you don't *need* one of their cars—you buy it because you can't resist. Drive it and you are hooked That is what happens with the 2800 CS. You slide into the driver's seat, a high, leather-covered easy chair, and you move it fore and aft until you find the right spot. And while you're adjusting the backrest angle to suit your driving posture you look around, just to check out the controls you have to work with. The large-diameter steering wheel reclines at a flat angle, much like that of a Ferrari. It's more than just a steering wheel—it's an object to be coveted in itself. Three black spokes taper out from a round, padded center to a hefty wood rim that has the grain structure and satin finish of a classic piece of furniture and at the same time the hardness of steel. The instrument panel is purely functional. All of the gauges are combined into four round dials directly before you and all of the levers, knobs and switches required to exact the most from the 2800 CS are either below the dials or on the console. The rest of the dash —which on Detroit cars serves as a playground for the stylists—is devoted to a finely detailed, wood-lined package shelf. All of which is to say that the 2800 CS is not a pullman car nor a midway thrill ride but a car for driving, and it looks that way.

A flat black key, with dimples rather than grooves and notches, fits into the ignition switch on the right side of the column. A half turn switches on more than just the en-

The BMW 2800 CS chooses to be a non-participant on the field of automotive utility and lives in a universe high above the basic lusts of the immature car addict. Unabashedly it is its maker's image of a surpassingly good personal automobile

gine—it starts a subtle feeling, like an electric current, that flows into your body from the steering wheel, the shift lever and the pedals. It flows in through your ears and through your eyes. You're under the BMW's spell now and it's a strong-willed man indeed who can resist.

You can hear the engine but it doesn't sound like an engine. It whirrs, like a motor, and the most delicate movement of your foot on the accelerator immediately causes the whir to change in pitch and the tachometer needle to rise or fall on its scale. You press the clutch pedal—it feels power assisted. The wood-knobed gearshift lever almost anticipates your intentions. The throws are lighter than anything you've ever driven, totally free of friction, and yet have a definite detent action that gently pulls the lever that last fraction of an inch into place. And the steering—you don't even suspect that it's power assisted. What greater compliment could there be? You might be ready to sign the check after only a trip around the block, but don't hurry. Live with the 2800 CS for a few days. Take it out on the expressway. At 70 mph there is no wind noise and the engine makes only a gentle purr. The single sound you are really conscious of is tire noise—a kind of frying sound—that is not transmitted through the car's structure but rather through the air so that in effect it is the same sound you would hear if you were standing along the road as the BMW went by. But $8000-Detroit cars are hard to fault on the open road too, so

try an undulating blacktop or a frost-heaved country lane. Here is where the BMW shows the depth of its poise. In fact, all of the expensive German cars—BMW, Mercedes and Porsche—are happy on poorly surfaced roads. The 2800 CS has fully independent suspension—MacPherson in front, semi-trailing arms in the rear—but there is more to it than that. The secret is that, as soon as you get off the autobahns, Germany is bumpy and the guys who tune the BMW's suspension would be derelict in their duties if they didn't make their cars perform well on their own roads. But never mind the reason. It is the result that you're driving and it works.

You might say BMW engineers developed a competent suspension system out of necessity, but it is the precision intricacies of engines that they enjoy and you don't have to drive the 2800 CS long to affirm the fact. Its engine is grossly extravagant by Detroit standards—you certainly don't need a powerplant built like a Rolex—but that is the appeal of a BMW. Take a look under the hood. Aluminum everywhere. A pair of aluminum, 3-branch intake manifolds curve into the aluminum SOHC cylinder head—a head whose combustion chambers are each formed by three partially overlapping hemispheres; an intake valve in one, an exhaust valve in one and a spark plug in the third. The short stroke crank turns on seven main bearings just above a cast aluminum oil pan. Its six cylinders displace 170 cubic inches and with a 9.0-to-one compression

ratio pump out 192 horsepower at 6000 rpm. You can turn it to 6200 before you touch the redline. When your everyday engines generate more than one horsepower per cubic inch they tend to be nervous and jerky but not the BMW. It idles with barely a murmur at 600 rpm. It is assembled to such close tolerances that it's free of offensive mechanical noises and it is muffled to an extent that would embarrass a Rolls-Royce. What's more, it moves the car smartly. The 2800 CS will leave any Mercedes, except the big V-8, in the dust, it will be moving faster at the end of a quarter mile than any of the carbureted Porsches and it is like the wind compared to a Cadillac or an Imperial. Still, at 16.3 seconds and 86.2 mph in the quarter it's hardly what you would call omnipotent—scrappy is more like it—and you had better exercise discretion if you enjoy running for pink slips on Woodward Avenue.

You'll fare a whole lot better if you confine your competitive urges to twisting back roads where cubic inches don't call the shots. Flailing within the limits of sanity on public roads is a serene occupation and only when you go all out on a road course do you discover that the BMW is a basically understeering car. You will also discover that, even though 55% of the weight rests on the front wheels, the BMW likes to swing its tail wide in abrupt transients—very much in Porsche fashion. Curiously, in left turns the suspension is more capable than the two Zenith carburetors. They invariably flood out when you are really pushing and you end up coasting from the apex on out until you are fully straightened away. Shades of Carter AFBs.

But thankfully carburetors have nothing to do with braking. That operation is taken care of by discs in front and drums at the rear with the entire system aided by a vacuum booster. The system is beautifully modulated so that lock-up of the fronts and rears occurs at precisely the same instant and the pedal is so sensitive that you can avoid or induce lock-up as you see fit. The latter attribute was particularly important during the braking test because the tires (Phoenix Senators, if that means anything to you) lost a significant portion of their decelerative force when they started to slide. The result is that, even though the thought of a more controllable braking system stretches our imagination, the 288 feet (0.74G) required to stop the BMW from 80 mph is not a very meritorious achievement and we have put the evil eye on the tires.

The 2800 CS is a driver's car and by this time you should have no doubts. Still, the wise old men at BMW have gone farther—just to make sure you don't get cold feet when you see the price tag. They know the coupe drives like an $8000 car but they've made it *look* like an $8000 car so that you'll never have to defend your choice against skeptics, infidels and the guy across the back fence who thinks you should have bought an Eldorado for that kind of money. Lift the hood and let them look underneath. Their jaws drop. They thought all engines were covered with blue paint. Let them sit inside. The windows are trimmed in chrome and they've never seen chrome so bright. And let them look at the wood on the instrument panel and side trim—a fine cabinet-maker's veneer overlayed on a special thin-layer plywood like die modelers use because it never warps or cracks. Your guests are remembering the 3M wood in their cars. Let them look around on the outside and discover the rubber-padded bumpers and the rubberized paint under the bumpers where the fenders begin to curve under the car. Let *them* worry about rock chips *you* don't have to.

And now for the grand finale. Pop open the trunk for them. It's finished like the inside of a Samsonite 3-suiter. The spare tire is out of the way under the floor. When they've almost recovered, loosen the

chrome-plated wing screw that retains what looks like a trap door on the underside of the trunk lid. Down swings a foam-lined *hors d'oeuvres* tray, bearing not canapes but every tool you might need in case of a road side misfortune: chrome-plated wrenches, screwdrivers, pliers, a spark plug wrench that grips onto the plug and spare light bulbs, fuses and spark plugs. There is no dissention in your group now and they are all feeling a little embarrassed as they remember their 2-door hardtop Timex which cost almost as much as your BMW.

Something that your Detroit-buying friends won't understand at all is that all of this effort has not been lavished on a box car-size package but rather on a machine the size of a Corvette. The BMW is a bit taller and about 3 inches narrower than a Sting Ray but it will park in the same slot— no small advantage in this ever burgeoning world. And despite its compact dimensions, the coupe's interior is comparable to a Mus-

tang. Rear headroom is short for the U.S. Government Bureau of Standards 6-footer and you have to push the front seats ahead somewhat for leg room—but you have to do that on far bigger cars too.

A road test of a car as virtuous as the BMW 2800 CS becomes a discussion of a machine's idiosyncrasies rather than a critical review because there simply isn't that much to criticize. We aren't sold on the tires, and the emission control system which does away with engine braking above 1800 rpm (the point below which everything goes back to normal) isn't to our liking but that is a pretty short list of faults. If all cars were like the 2800 CS then Consumer Reports would be out of the automobile rating business.

No, it's simply enough said. You don't *need* a BMW 2800 CS. Unless you need excellence, competence and a car that's near impossible to match anywhere in the automotive world.

Some people think the Mercedes is the best car in the world.

By Eric Dahlquist

Directly ahead, the road dropped away in a gentle reverse S, almost disappearing into the early morning mist that hung over the green plain like a thick, damp cobweb. Off to the left, you could see the vague hugeness of Chiemsee, the lake's water taking the first rays of the sun and giving glints of light that cut through the thin fog so it seemed almost that you were in a capsule plunging back to twilight-darkened earth from the laser-brilliance of deep outer space.

It is in our mind as a beautiful still-life flashed on the screen of memory, the way you show a 35mm slide to your friends the winter after the trip. But only one frame. A one-sixtieth second exposure. The amount of time you need to glance up from the highway at 220 kilometers-per-hour indicated (approx. 130 mph) and not lose control, for the race will be won or lost here — even your life. It is the most mortal of all German combat — Mercedes vs. BMW.

We came upon him about thirty kilometers outside of Munich on the autobahn that takes you to Austria — the connection to Salzburg. It was 7:30 in the morning and even at a steady 190 kms (117), you only had to blink your lights occasionally to move people from the fast lane because the twin concrete ribbons were deserted. He was just another white Mercedes ahead, going approximately 20 kms slower, and as he caught the momentary glare from our BMW 2800's quad headlights and dual driving lights, the closing rate began to decrease — and then vanish. It was the same startling effect as the sharp report of a .30-06 on an easily running deer.

The Mercedes, a 300 SL stick, had the advantage on immediate acceleration, gradually pulling away until about 205 indicated, where the 2800 automatic seemed to couple-up and foot by foot began to eat into the space between. After each speed zone or construction area it was always the same. In the mid-range, the 300 would slowly pull ahead and on top we would slowly pull back, particularly on the curves. And now it looked like it would finally be settled on this long, downhill run, like skiers going flat-out until the end. But, somehow it wasn't — slower traffic, construction, reduced speed zones — the judgement was postponed until we could get home, borrow a pair of cars, and decide which make was the better, if that's at all possible. Why you would try isn't even clear in our minds, except that Mercedes and BMW are grappling for the

Timeless as the Black Forest it stands in, the unpretentious Mercedes still rules the German luxury market as well as much of the rest of the civilized world.

German, yes, even the European prestige market and we'd like to know who's ahead.

While in Europe we had been exposed to a 280 SEL Mercedes automatic and a 2800 BMW automatic, but at different times and places. Getting either of these machines should present no problem in the States, except that it was late in the season, and both companies sell every car they make, so the supply was short. Mercedes, the larger importer, came up with exactly what we wanted, a well-broken in SEL with 24,000 miles on it. The BMW people didn't have a 2800 Automatic so they substituted a 4-speed, which they said was, if anything, slightly better in performance than their automatic version.

Really, the only thing you have to say about a Mercedes is that it is, and let it go at that. Most people in this country have been no nearer one than a dealer's window and yet conditioning since childhood causes them to know that it is the best car in the world, or at least tied with Rolls Royce. Having the companies' founders, Daimler-Benz, build the world's first two automobiles hasn't hurt anything over the years.

On a $7600 (base $6992) car, you expect everything to fit right and the doors to slam with the authority of a food locker, and you are not disap-

pointed. The fact that our American 280 had the equivalent of a year's running on it and still felt as precise and solid as the brand new one we drove in Germany, underscores better than any amount of historic-tradition prattle, how well the thing is put together. And if you still weren't convinced, all you have to do is ask someone who's been to Germany and ridden in the still rock-tight 10 year old M-B taxis.

Mercedes sedans all exhibit the quasi-box look of a '63 Valiant and that's just fine with them because it's the best way they've found to package people. The "L" in SEL means that the car has a four-inch longer wheelbase than the normal 280 SE, but it should stand for "limo," the back seat area is that large. And that's weird because at 112.2 and 196.8 inches respectively, the wheelbase and overall length nearly match the Buick Special, yet the interior space is greater than the 225 Electra or even, clap your ears, a Caddy four-door. And that's a direct dimension-by-dimension comparison. Headroom, legroom, hiproom, everything.

The front seat in a 280 doesn't just go fore and aft about a yard — an additional provision offers elevational changes as well. Not only that, but the seat tracks feel like they belong on a *continued on page 38*

continued on page 38

But not BMW.

But, a challenger looms on the horizon, the near horizon. Built in BMW's Upper Bavarian watch factory, the 2800 series will not be denied for very long.

BMW is the Pontiac of Europe. You can tell immediately, if you're driving a Mercedes. At every autobahn on-ramp some kid in a 2002 ti comes roaring out to gun you down. Ditto at traffic lights. Ditto on twisty mountain roads. Ditto everywhere.

Now, if it were just the irritating buzzing of some pesky Kamikazi mosquito, Mercedes would care less. Unfortunately for them, BMW (Bayerische Motoren Werke) happens to be outselling some of their lines model for model. But that isn't even the really important thing. With their smartly tailored, quick, small cars, first the 1500, then 1600, and especially the 2002 series, BMW has a broader base of appeal and is getting to the young, intelligent, high-paid swingers in Germany, precisely the people you want moving up in your line. Coupled with the general erosion of the Mercedes performance image and the "glorified truck" proposition, the tri-star seems, to hear BMW insurgents tell it, on the verge of eclipse.

Almost overnight, the 2002 blitzed a reputation about the same as the GTO had in the 'States in 1965 — invincible in its class. Well, then, the logical progression would be a bigger car with the same sort of characteristics — nimble response, good brakes and, above all, fast. All of which the new 2500-2800

sedan is. It also happens to be a good deal better than anything else BMW builds and that's why Mercedes is starting to hustle.

The 2500-2800's basic body shape is much more aerodynamic than the M-B stuff, yet not quite in the Torino's slippery state, since BMW thinks it prudent to provide excellent visibility for machinery capable of a least 125 mph. With a 185-inch overall length on a 106-inch wheelbase, the 2500-2800 has less room than the 280 SEL stretched M-B, yet it's not supposed to. BMW's primary target is the Mercedes 250 sedan and here they have all bases covered. What they have done, is aim at the 250 market with a car eligible to run heads up with the new Mercedes 3.5 V8.

BMW's interiors have noticeably warmer, plusher feelings than Mercedes, at least the ones we were in, by virtue of the nylon fabric, and choice leathers. Looking at it another way, the four-dial instrument nacelle (speedometer, tachometer, temperature, fuel), with its precisely lettered white on black numerals, gives the same impression as a Maserati. BMW has its own version of a substantial steering wheel, but theirs will attract more attention because it looks like it's out of a race car. Both M-B and BMW instrument groupings are easy to see, BMW's has the

better design, M-B an oil gauge instead of a light. Color gaugemanship a draw.

As far as detail quality goes on these machines, and it goes a long way, BMW is not what you would call wanting, yet it falls just shy of the Mercedes standard. As one German put it, "It's the difference between buying a car that lasts six years and one that has a planned life expectancy of ten, before major things start happening. You probably won't own the BMW long enough to worry about it."

A few kilometers in the BMW on a snakey, bumpy, Bavarian road tells you that they have leaped ahead in the handling race. Basically, it's a McPherson-strut deal in front, but with a few BMW tricks thrown in, like superior anti-dive characteristics. In back there is full independence and a good unsprung weight reduction by rubber mounting the differential on the frame; semi- trailing arms position the outer axles. Optional, is something called a Boge Nivomat unit with automatic level control for constant wheel camber despite load. All of which means it's a sedan that will corner the pants off most sports cars.

BMW wins again in the drag race sweepstakes, although the 3.5 M-B V8 will blunt this thrust somewhat. Six for six, the more recently conceived Bavarian power factory with its triple-hemisphere, combustion chambers, seven main bearings, turbine-smoothness and watch-like precision is so efficient that it passed the U.S. 1969 emission standards with no modifications. One of the SOHC's more interesting innovations is a pair of twin-Solex dual throat carburetors with split butterflies so that you have the QuadraJet effect — air velocity operated secondaries. There are absolutely no flat spots in the rev band and one wonders how response can ever be improved, even with the Kugelfischer mechanical fuel injection that is surely around the next corner.

Eighteen cubic inches doesn't sound like a lot when you're conditioned to things like 454 Chevys. In a BMW it's a bunch. The 2500, 152.2-cubic-inch, 170-hp version of the engine knocks off 0-60s around the 10.4 second range with standing quarters at 17.5. The 2800, 170.1 cubic inches and 192 horsepower does the same distances in 9.2 and 16.8 seconds, respectively. Our Mercedes 280 SEL, of course, is nearly in the Datsun range by comparison. Even the 3.5 V8 coupe we tried at the Hockenheim Press Day was hardly faster.

continued on page 39

MERCEDES vs. BMW

"Maybe what you should really think about is the rather disquieting idea that these

Mercedes continued

narrow-gauge railroad. Of course, all adjustments are manual. A German's concept of automobile involvement just doesn't include power seats. Electric windows you can justify because the driver can't physically operate all of them himself while moving, but seats are a no-no. There's a chance if Detroit's manual seats worked as well, including infinitely variable seatbacks, we might feel the same way.

You sit well back in the car with your arms in the straight-out position. The steering wheel is large and made from the same kind of last-forever hard rubber you used to find in '47 Packards. Through the top of it, the instrument cluster is directly in the line of vision — two round dials, one for the speedometer and the other for temperature, fuel, oil pressure, generator (although the car has an alternator), fuel tank reservoir, and emergency. All very straight forward and precisely marked.

The inside of a Mercedes is not opulent in the sense of a Cadillac Fleetwood, it is rich. The dash has its quota of wood trim and there is some on the doors as well, but it is real walnut, not what some chemist thinks walnut should look like. Even the trunk, which in our luxury cruisers has lately come under the same sort of carpeting mania as the Barris customs of the '50s, is not much more frivolous than a Chevy II. But then, because we tend to put more luggage than people in trunks these days, maybe it's all right to just have a big, square flat surface that holds lots of real suitcases.

During the development of their 1954 Grand Prix cars, M-B learned that a low pivot-point (i.e., low roll-center) would provide superior handling with a simple swing axle. Presto, it appears on all their cars for the next fourteen years, the low series, "new generation" models finally going to independent in '68. Low-series machines, however, don't make your reputation in the luxury car biz and what went in '54 doesn't go in '69. All of which the Stuttgarters know and won't be able to change for a few years because (a) the Mercedes technological revolution comes in slow, steady progression and (b) all their cars are back-ordered a year, so why should they?

Besides all that, the old, low-pivot is not all that bad — not as good as the BMW 2800 perhaps, but not down to American standards. The car has a certain amount of predesigned understeer which you can easily negate with the throttle and overrun any of our luxury slugs; in fact, almost any of our machines, period. Certainly, the one thing an American driver finds pleasure in is possessing relatively the same cornering force in the rough as well as the smooth. The truth of the matter is that U.S. tire innovators Firestone and Goodyear,

with their trick eight-inch-wide-ovals are making our cars look better in the curves than they really are. You know as soon as the road surface gets a little uneven and the car ricochets from one bump to the next.

Perhaps Mercedes' best asset is also its worst handicap. The general nature of the 280's cruising ride is rock smooth in the nature of those great old, steady, heavy cars of the past. Down in the lower reaches of the speed spectrum, the car takes items like raised tar strips like an F-100 pickup. And herein lies the problem. Mercedes critics maintain that the factory has not kept abreast of suspension progress and is producing glorified trucks with inflated price tags.

More important, the 180 horsepower, 2.8 liter (169.5 cubic inch) six is overburdened in its work of pulling a 3200 pound car around. Producing a 10.52 second 0-60 time and a 17.35 quarter mile shows there is some merit in at least the underpower thesis. The machine will cruise all day flat out, but car for car, the BMW 2800 will outrun it, if for no other reason than it is 200 pounds lighter. That is why M-B introduced the new 3.5-liter V8 for the 280 and 300 at the Frankfurt show; it gives

them a fender on BMW and sustains the "fastest-production-sedan-image" of the 6.3 with a little lower top speed (130 vs. 137 mph) at considerably less money ($10,000 vs. $14,000).

After the Chaparral's Nurburgring victory in '67, a funny thing happened at Mercedes — their automatic transmission sales jumped 60 percent. Up to that point, the German drivers' basic mistrust of someone other than himself making gear selection caused it to be almost solely an American option. At that, the engineers have kept the gear changes as swift and abrupt as B & M racing until, so there remains some feeling of a manual — probably a little too much for the typical American buyer. For some reason or other, Mercedes has seen fit to provide a very small brake pedal in their automatics, centered directly behind the steering wheel so you seem to always be moving one or the other of your legs at odd angles to get the car stopped. While we're on the subject, the 280 SEL's braking distance was a not-too-short-not-too-long 140 feet from 60 mph. The thing about it is that the four wheel discs will stop it all day long from 60 in 140 feet, without fade or the-back-and-coming-around. **/MT**

You know, it's a funny thing. Bulk for sheer bulk, a Caddy four door just blows a poor old 280 SEL into the weeds. Stunned by such mass, the passenger enters to find that size does not equate with room, that the SEL actually wins in the space race. Not surprisingly, then, it also beats the BMW. Acceleration is another thing. The Mercedes six just isn't as snappy as it should be.

130-mph vehicles have only a Maverick-sized engine."

BMW continued

The way we boil it down is like this: the magic of the Mercedes name is still there and so is the quality. BMWs of the same range and description are generally faster and have measurably better handling, although the average buyer, especially the American buyer, probably will never notice it. Both cars are extremely comfortable for long, high-speed trips, although the BMW seems to have a very slight edge with softer seats and springs. Given equal care, the Mercedes will probably last slightly longer, but it's in a range that first owners will probably never miss.

Mort Sahl measures the desireability of any car from the inside out — the view from the drivers seat is what counts because you live there. If BMW has a hard advantage, it is here, where you live — and for a reason they nor their competitors probably don't fully understand. It all happened so very long ago.

The BMW is made in Bavaria and Bavaria is predominately Catholic. Mercedes' home is Stuttgart. Stuttgart is predominately Calvinist. This all wouldn't mean much except that when it comes to designing in luxury, the Bavarian psyche is not hung up with

any of those old fears that overindulgence is, by its nature, evil, which is, if you remember from your Western Civilization class, part of the up-tight, Prussian, Calvinist, schtick. So, possibly Mercedes is a prisoner of its geography; they might not ever be able to match opulence with BMW tit for tat. But then, again.

The question, of course, is which one is best just to drive. We'd have to opt for the 2800 BMW because of its sporting flavor. As an all round family car, the choice wouldn't be so easy, especially if you had some kids. The SEL's playroom interior and vinyl upholstery would be important. Maybe such considerations aren't even relevant. Maybe what you should really think about is the rather disquieting idea that these 130-mph vehicles have only a Maverick-sized engine.

The one absolute truth we discovered after living with the Mercedes and the BMW in Germany and America, is that instead of buying a $4500 US car every two years, you're money and pleasure ahead to lengthen your trade-in periods and buy the best there is. Right now that happens to be Mercedes and BMW, but not necessarily in that order. **/MT**

MERCEDES

Type	SOHC Six
Bore & Stroke	3.41 x 3.1
Displacement	169.5 cu. ins.
Max. horsepower	180 @ 5750
Max. torque	193 @ 4500
Compression Ratio	9.5:1
Carburetion	Bosch injection
Transmission	4-speed auto.
Final Drive Ratio	3.89:1
Steering Type	ZF Power
Turning Diameter	
(Curb-to-curb-ft.)	39.6
Tire Size	7.35H-14
Brakes	4-wheel power discs
Front Suspension	double wishbones with coil springs
Rear Suspension: single-joint swing axle	
Body/Frame	
Construction	unit steel body
Acceleration 0-60 mph	10.52 sec.
Standing start ¼-mile	17.35 @ 76 mph
Wheelbase	112.2 ins.
Overall Length	196.8 ins.
Width	72.6 ins.
Height	55.9 ins.
Front Track	58.3 ins.
Rear Track	58.5 ins.
Curb Weight	3200 lbs.

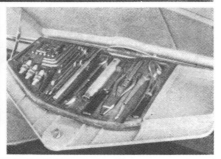

2800 BMWs don't match inside area with 280 SELs or Caddys, but do admirably well with an M-B 250 — it's natural foe. Powerplant is very modern, moving the car like a V8. Fold down tool tray in trunk is what makes BMWs luxurious.

BMW

Type	SOHC Six
Bore & Stroke	3.386 x 3.150
Displacement	170.1 cu. ins.
Max. horsepower	192 @ 6000
Max. torque	173.6 @ 3700
Compression Ratio	9.0:1
Carburetion	Dual Solex
Transmission	4-speed std.
Final Drive Ratio	3.54:1
Steering Type	ZF worm-roller
Steering Ratio	18.9:1
Turning Diameter	
(Curb-to-curb-ft)	35.2 ft.
Tire Size	DR70 x 14
Brakes	4-wheel power discs
Front Suspension	strut-type with shock-coils
Rear Suspension	fully indep.
Body/Frame	
Construction	unit steel body
Acceleration 0-60 mph	9.2 sec.
Standing Start ¼-mile	16.8 @ 84 mph
Wheelbase	106 ins.
Overall Length	185 ins.
Width	68.9 ins.
Height	57.1 ins.
Front Track	56.9 ins.
Rear Track	57.6 ins.
Curb Weight	2954 lbs.

BMW 2800CS

PRICE
Base $7665
As tested $8847
With options . . . . .Leather upholstery,
sliding roof, Baikal paint, tinted glass,
increase in DM exchange ($442)

ENGINE
Type . . . . .In-line 6, water-cooled,
iron block, aluminum head
Displacement . . . . . . .170.1 cu. in. (2788 cc)
Horsepower . . . . .192 hp @ 6000 rpm
Torque . . . . .174 lbs.-ft. @ 3700 rpm
Bore & stroke . . . . .3.39 in. x 3.15 in.
(86mm x 80mm)
Compression ratio . . . . .9.0 to 1
Valve actuation . . . . .Ohc, chain driven,
rocker followers
Induction system . . . .Dual Solex 35/40 INAT
Exhaust system . . . . . .Iron headers, 6 into 2
Electrical system . . . . .12-volt alternator,
point distributor
Fuel . . . . .Premium
Recommended redline 6200

DRIVE TRAIN
Clutch . . . . .Dry disc, hydraulic

Transmission	Gear Ratio	Overall Ratio
1st Synchro	3.85	13.28
2nd Synchro	2.08	7.18
3rd Synchro	1.38	4.76
4th Synchro	1.00	3.45

Differential . . . . .Hypoid bevel, 3.45 ratio

CHASSIS
Frame . . . . .Unit construction,
front engine, rear drive
Front suspension . . . . . . .MacPherson strut,
coil springs, anti-roll bar
Rear suspension . . . .Ind., semi-trailing arms,
coil springs, anti-roll bar
Steering . .Recirculating ball, power assisted,
4.0 turns,
turning circle 33.4 feet
Brakes. .Power assist, dual hydraulic circuit,
10.7-in. dia. front discs,
9.8-in. dia. rear drums
Wheels . . . . .14-in. dia.; 6-in. wide
Tires . . . . .Michelin XAS 175 x 14,
pressures F/R: 27/28 (rec.), 32/32 (test)

BODY
Type . . . . .Unit steel, 2-door, 4-passenger
Seats . . . . .Front buckets, rear buckets
Windows . . . . . . .2 power 2 manual, 2 vents
Luggage space . . . . . . .Rear trunk, 15 cu. ft.
Instruments. .150 mph speedo, 8000 rpm tach
Gauges: .temp, fuel
Lights: . . . . .amp, oil, fuel, temp

WEIGHTS AND MEASURES
Weight . . . . .3055 lbs. (curb), 3210 lbs. (test)
Weight distribution F/R 55%/45%
Wheelbase .103.3 in.
Track F/R . . . . .56.9 in./55.2 in.
Height . . . . .53.9 in.
Width . . . . .65.7 in.
Length . . . . .183.5 in.
Ground clearance . . . . .5.5 in.
Oil capacity .5.3 qt.
Fuel capacity . . . . .18.2 gal.
Coolant capacity . . . . .12.7 qt.

MISCELLANEOUS
Weight/power ratio
(curb/advertised) . . . . . . .15.90 lbs. per hp
Advertised hp/cu. in. 1.12
Speed per 1000 rpm (top gear) . . .20.8 moh
Warranty . . . . .12 months/12,000 miles

AERODYNAMIC FORCES AT 100 MPH

CORNERING CONDITIONS

PERFORMANCE
Acceleration . . . . .0-30 (3.4 sec.), 0-60 (8.7 sec.), 0-100 (25.2 sec.)
0-quarter mile (17.6 sec., 85.6 mph)

Top speed . . . . .129 mph (est.) at 6200 rpm (rpm limited)

Braking . . . . .Distance from 60 mph: 163 ft. (0.74 g av.)
Number of stops to fade: Not attainable
Stability: Excellent
Maximum pitch angle: 1.2°

Handling . . . . .Maximum lateral: 0.74 g right, N.A. left
Skidpad understeer: 5.1° right, 5.1° left
Maximum roll angle: 6.0°
Reaction to throttle, full: More understeer; off: Less understeer

Speedometer	30.0	40.0	50.0	60.0	70.0	80.0	90.0	100.0
Actual mph	27.5	37.0	45.5	55.0	64.0	74.0	82.5	91.5

Mileage . . . . .Average: 20.0 mpg
Miles on car: 1200 to 3200

Aerodynamic forces at 100 mph:
Drag . . . . .310 lbs. (includes tire drag)
Lift F/R . . . . .255 lbs./−25 lbs.

TEST EXPLANATIONS
Fade test is successive maximum g stops from 60 mph each minute until wheels cannot be locked. Understeer is front minus rear tire slip angle at maximum lateral on 200-ft. dia. Digitek skidpad. Autoscan chassis dynamometer supplied by Humble Oil.

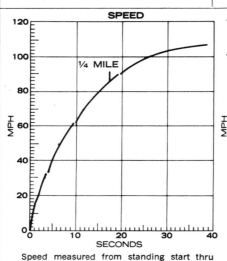

SPEED

Speed measured from standing start thru ¼ mile to maximum shown. Shift points indicated by line breaks.

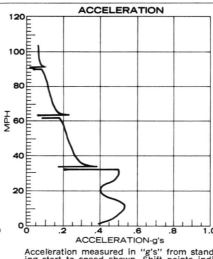

ACCELERATION

Acceleration measured in "g's" from standing start to speed shown. Shift points indicated by "spikes" on graph.

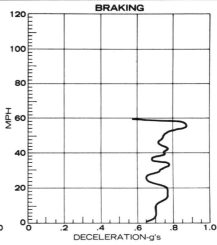

BRAKING

Brakes applied at 60 mph with maximum force, but using pedal "feathering" technique to prevent wheel lockup.

Judgment At San Clemente

**What chance does a *Wunder Kinder Auto* like the
BMW 2800CS have when pitted against America's
award-winning annual classics / by T. C. Browne**

SCG ROAD TEST

WHEN YOUR BASIC PATRIOTIC AMERICAN ROAD-TESTER approaches a four-wheeled motor vehicle that sits on a wheelbase of 103 inches, weighs about 3000 pounds, delivers less than 200 horsepower and is offered for general United States consumption at around $9000, he is likely to wonder how they can expect to get so much money for so little car. If the vehicle is offered by a factory based elsewhere than in America's Heartland (and, with the more popular domestic products selling near $1.00 per pound, it surely will be), he is also certain to wonder how well the implement will perform under what all red-blooded Americans like to think of as "our local driving conditions," whether "local" means Needles, California or Bad Axe, Michigan. With these dark reservations lurking just below the surface of our carefully contrived One World facade, SCG went forth to examine the latest and dearest from Bavaria, the BMW 2800CS.

In addition to the usual Van Valkenburgh star-chamber investigations at the Digitek skidpad in Mira Loma and the ¼-mile drag strip at Orange County International Raceway, we put in 1500 miles of sometimes wine-stimulated cornering, braking, and full-chat studies on the twisting Alpine Passes and speed-limitless Autobahnen/Autostrade of Germany, Austria, Italy, France and Switzerland (in our continuing explorations of the vineyards of Europe), as well as an additional 1800 miles of temperate, legal-limits-at-all-times assaults on the freeways of California and Nevada, to say nothing of one harrowing trip into the deepest abscesses of the Sunset Strip on Saturday night. Emboldened by having survived these reckless adventures and still seeking the car's hidden flaw, we flung caution to the Santa Ana (our local version of the *mistral*) and entered that uptight cradle of crew-cut patriotism— San Clemente. And thereby hangs the odd part of the tale.

It was the kind of sunny euphoric Sunday noon that has been attracting middle and middle-aged Americans to southern California ever since the

JUDGMENT AT SAN CLEMENTE

golden spike was rammed home and carpetbags came into widespread use. As we approached Howard Johnson's, home of the plasticized Sunday Chicken Dinner, to beard the local conservative population in its den, so to speak, we were astonished to discover what appeared to be a sort of informal used-car lot, complete with browsers and 11 of Detroit's finest, carefully aligned and with all the hoods opened. Since the cars were '70 models, it seemed unlikely that the lot-boy was recharging *all* the batteries, so we paused to investigate. The nearest human carried a clipboard and a striking resemblance to Sam Hanks. It *was* Sam Hanks! And there was Wally Parks (NHRA), Roy Richter (SEMA), Eric Dahlquist, Dick Day, Bill Sanders, Tom Uhler and Dick Wells (all from *Motor Trend*), Bob and Claudia Thomas (Ontario Motor Speedway), Mike Jones, A.B. Shuman, Cliff Wynne, John Lamn and Chuck Pendergast — as glittering an array of prominent motoring journalists and senior members of the Automotive D.A.R. as you're likely ever to find in one spot, now that the Mobil Economy Run has finally gone to the great A&W Root Beer stand in the sky. And what do you suppose they were doing with the Maverick, Hornet, Challenger, Barracuda (now called "Cuda," which sounds like something you might order in a taco parlor — "Gimme a chili-cuda with onions to go"), two Monte Carlos, *four* Torinos *and* a Lincoln? Let me tell you, motorsports fans and athletic supporters: They were picking, among other things, your 1970 CAR OF THE YEAR! Yessir, car buffs — and you can read all about it in the February issue of *Motor Trend* Magazine, on sale now!

This shocking coincidence derailed the pleasant train of thoughts about *Weisswurst mit Senf, Oktoberfeste,* past and future, and jerked us home to reality. As a consequence, I ordered the pecan waffle, since it was only ten cents more than the regular polystyrene version. And, although southern Californians invariably know upon what freeway they are traveling, it is often hard to sort out the towns along the way. So, I asked the waitress the name of the community upon whose precipice this palace of culinary delights was perched, and she proudly announced, "San Clemente — home of the President." I said, "Oh, I thought He was from Whittier." She: "Well, I mean the summer white house." I: "Then, what do you call the place in Key Biscayne?" She: "Oh, that's a private thing." Unable to comprehend this sort of local-booster logic, I sank back into ponders on less kinky enigmae like Cars-of-the-Year vs. masterpieces of the BMW 2800CS genre and all that. And, we are prepared to offer you some conclusions: The car so closely approaches functional perfection that finding something to criticize is virtually impossible. As a result, writing a story about the BMW 2800CS is quite difficult without resorting to undignified puffery more suited to Cars-of-the-Year which — you may be certain — will be "all-new" next year. The BMW 2800CS won't be all-new next year. Or the year after. And, therefore, might turn out to be the Car-of-the-Decade. Which no one, to the best of our knowledge, offers awards for. The BMW 2800CS, for reasons of price, size, performance and national origin, will necessarily be compared most often with a 2800-cc Mercedes, one version or another. We discussed this with Heidi, our consultant on Affairs Germanic, who, although Viennese, thinks in *Hoch Deutsch* and, being neither Prussian nor Bavarian, takes, so to speak, the long view. Her summation was that trying to pair off a BMW against a Mercedes would be like comparing Mozart's "Marriage of Figaro" with Wagner's "The Valkyrie." Which is not putting too fine a point on it.

The BMW surely has all the keen Old World quality to which we have lately become unaccustomed *except* when dealing with Mercedes and perhaps a few others whose names have, for the moment, somehow escaped me. You know — leather that really is, plating that doesn't look like it was put on over wicker with a whisk broom, paintwork into which no gnats have ever dove to their deaths. Honest, round instruments with honest, black faces, exotic wood paneling that may have come from a tree, a windscreen you can see out of and ashtrays you can use — the trick spoiler on the wiper arm that holds the blade on the glass at 100 mph. And that 4-speed gearbox — oh my, yes! It really does think for you. You sort of reach for it, it sees your hand approaching, gets frightened and slips into the ratio you had in mind. Well, almost. "But," you cry out, "for nine Gs, it *oughta* have all that good stuff!" "Right!" we reply — "but how many cars at the price do?" Now that that's settled, what does the 2800CS offer you that a similar size/price M-B won't? Well, that depends. Certainly not greater status. Like, if you mounted the three-pointed star on your skate-board, you'd zap the neighbors, right? No, it's a little more subtle than that. If the Merc is super-strong, over-engineered, stolid, conservative, self-assured and built to last through the next NATO maneuvers, the BMW is lightfooted, agile, friendly, aquarian and — as Van Valkenburgh puts it — "has the function of a sports car if not the image." The thinking man's GT car, if you like.

Now, about the flaws. We did find two: The outside mirrors are mounted so far astern as to require excessive head pivoting; and we couldn't measure lateral acceleration in the left-hand mode (see data panel) because the engine expired for want of fuel each time we tried.

At the end of the most exhaustive (well, celebrating the grape harvest during the "Fete de Vendanges" in Neuchatel is exhausting) series of tests on two continents to which SCG has ever subjected a car, it has become subtly apparent that the BMW 2800CS may just be the best for both worlds. And now, we are questioning how the *Wunder Kinder* of Munich can produce so much car for so *little* money. ⊕

GORDON CHITTENDEN PHOTOS

BMW 2800 CS

Beautiful, fast, stable, comfortable, quiet but—maybe too expensive?

THE BMW 2800 CS is a remarkable mating of an older chassis and body with a brand new engine. The 4-cyl, 135-bhp 2000 CS we tested three years ago was sophisticated and luxurious but underpowered and frankly a disappointing car for its over-$5000 price. Putting the 2788-cc, 192-bhp six into this car has resulted in all the expected performance improvements plus a new standard of sophistication and understated luxury for 6-cyl cars.

Performance aside, we always thought the 2000 CS had one of the most attractive basic bodies of any car in the world—unfortunately capped off with singularly awkward front-end styling. For the 2800 CS, BMW engineers and stylists kept the original unit body, added 3 in. to the wheelbase ahead of the windshield to accommodate the longer engine and designed an entirely new, absolutely satisfactory front end. Just how well this was done can be appreciated from the detail sketches in the accompanying R&T Styling Analysis on pages 48 - 49. These drawings tell the story

better than words but we'd like to say here that the changes —not the least of them being the adoption of wider, larger-diameter tires and the resulting larger wheel arches—has given the car a crisp, aggressive appearance. It looks *right*.

The interior looks right, too. There is not a trace of ostentation, but everything is there, tastefully and simply done. The front seats are superbly designed—fully supporting, upholstered in leather and adjustable through 75 degrees. The rear seats are equally good (though lacking a bit of the headroom and more than a little legroom), with a fold-down center armrest. The instrument panel, with large, properly round and easily readable gauges in front of the driver, is devoid of any decoration except for the handsome, full-width wood veneer. Also running full width is a most practical shelf for incidental items, with a padded edge and wood dividers every few inches to keep things from rolling about. In addition to this shelf there are snap-flush map pockets in each door; a useful shelf in front of the gearshift lever, under

43

BMW 2800 CS

the heating/ventilation unit; and *two* underdash storage compartments, a large one in front of the passenger and a smaller one to the left of the steering column. The latter compartment contains the hood release lever and the trip odometer reset knob, but—surprisingly for an expensive car—neither compartment is lockable. Nor is the fuel filler cap.

The steering wheel is large and well positioned, with a wood rim. The rim is elegant but not quite as pleasing in the hands as the leather-covered rim of a 2800 CS we tried in Germany last summer (shown in the color photos). That wheel also had its horn button in the center, replaced on our test car by three buttons, one in each spoke. The column has two control stalks, the left one for high beam and the much appreciated headlight flasher, the right one for the directional signals, windshield wiper switch and washers. The three functions of this lever took some getting used to but seemed right thereafter. The gearshift lever has a wood knob and a nice, zippered, leather boot. On the console around the gearshift are the electric window switches, the windshield wiper speed control and the cigarette lighter. The test car had electric lifts for the rear quarter windows only; the optional electric front lifts, tried in Germany, are slow but relieve the laborious cranking required with the manual system. All the controls are carefully placed where they are functionally correct, in contrast to the flight-deck array of switches on some GT cars. There is no BMW identification anywhere in the interior—you don't need to be reminded what car you are driving. But the BMW badge appears eight times on the exterior—others are being informed! Vision in every direction is excellent, unobscured by the headrests in their down positions.

Driven moderately, the 2800 CS is smooth and very, very quiet. At cruising speeds the only sound is the steady hum of the steel-belted Michelin XAS tires. The big BMW engine, fully described in the New Model Analysis and Road Test of the sedans in the May 1969 issue, is without a doubt the most efficient and sophisticated inline six in the world. It is powerful and responsive, yet remarkably easy on gasoline and meeting government emission regulations on carburetors with no added-on devices. Almost soundlessly willing at part-throttle, with amazingly low tappet noise, it has the most beautifully subdued snarl imaginable when opened up. Getting off in a hurry is accompanied by traditional BMW wheel patter—not objectionable but one of the few things about the car that is not ultra-refined. Accelerating suddenly from low engine speeds in the intermediate gears gave a momentary hesitation on our test car; the blame for this is laid to leather seals around the accelerator pump pistons which need more miles to seat correctly.

Gearing seems just right (the CS has a 3.45:1 final drive ratio, compared to the 2500's 3.64), permitting corrected speeds of 32, 61 and 91 mph in the first three gears and an observed corrected maximum of 126 mph. The speedometer was 8 percent optimistic—unacceptable, we think, in a car that makes such a strong appeal to alert, knowledgeable

COMPARISON DATA

	BMW 2800 CS	Mercedes 280 SL	Jaguar E-Type	Porsche 911E
List price	$8107	$7654	$6250	$7995
Curb weight, lb	2990	3120	3018	2361
0-60 mph, sec	9.3	9.9	8.0	8.4
Standing ¼-mi	17.4	17.1	15.7	16.0
Speed at end, mph	82	80	86	83
Panic stop from 80 mph, % g	80	90	84	84
Fade in 6 stops from 60 mph, %	48.0	nil	nil	nil
R&T wear index	50	60	55	39
R&T steering index	1.38	1.07	1.04	1.01
Fuel economy, mpg	19.0	17.5	15.9	18.4

drivers. The shifting action is very smooth, especially into 1st and reverse, often awkward on other transmissions. Making really quick changes we experienced an occasional snick as we beat the synchros. Handling is very good in all conditions, not as phenomenal as a Porsche 911 but exceptional for a luxurious 4-passenger car. Typically BMW, the inside rear wheel lifts in hard cornering. The Michelin radials squealed at the slightest provocation, but since the Semperits on the car driven in Germany did the same, it may well be a suspension characteristic. The optional D70-14 radials might help.

The power steering is very nearly as good as that of Mercedes, which is to say, tops. It feels just a bit light initially at high speeds but continued use of the car builds complete confidence; there is just enough feel to ensure accuracy. At lower speeds, the CS is really maneuverable. The brakes, unsatisfactory in our fade test, are discs in front and drums in back—a carryover from the older 2000 CS, as is the narrow rear track, which despite the wider wheels is still 2.4 in. less than that of the 2500/2800 sedans. According to specifications, the 2800 CS also has the small, 14.5-gal tank of the 2000 CS, but our test car and subsequent examples have a bigger, 18.5-gal tank—fortunately for the cruising range. Averaging 19 mpg over a variety of conditions which included some very hard driving, the 2800 CS is exceptionally efficient for a 2.8-liter, 3000-lb car.

Assembly quality and detailing are first rate and largely responsible for the car's tight, insulated character. The ride is very soft; under the hard driving conditions that the power and adhesion encourage, this results in a distinct but not disturbing bobbing motion over irregular surfaces—a minimal effect from fully independent suspension that combines ride and roadholding so well. Passengers are rarely aware of the level at which the driver is pressing on. At high speeds a poorly fitting vent window produced quite a bit of wind noise but since the other one was silent it was a matter of individual fit rather than design. There is surprisingly little noise from the unframed but rubber-edged mating of the main side windows just behind the driver's and front passenger's ears. Ventilation from the console system is excellent, with a satisfactory range of air supplied by the blower.

The BMW engine compartment is as well finished as the exterior of some cars, with a beautifully cast cam cover and rather tidy plumbing, including a radiator top tank on the left of the engine ahead of the firewall. Other than for inspection and photographic purposes, we had only one occasion to open the nicely counterbalanced hood—when the bellcrank on the accelerator linkage came adrift one night; fortunately it snapped back into place easily. The trunk is long, wide and well carpeted but not particularly deep, not quite accommodating full grocery sacks upright. The *pièce de resistance,* characteristic of the whole car, is the super-complete tool kit in a fold-down tray which fits neatly, out of the way but easy to get at, in the underside of the trunk lid. Contained therein: 3 double open-end wrenches, 4 double box-end wrenches, 3 Allen wrenches, pliers, channel-locks, regular screwdriver, Phillips screwdriver, plug socket wrench, a set of feeler gauges, 3 spark plugs, 3 bulbs and 6 fuses. Also, two special tools we couldn't identify, apparently for BMW-class adjustments!

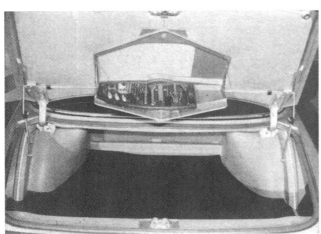

BMW 2800 CS

So far, so good: a car that in every facet of its appearance and performance (with the exception of lacking brute, unusable acceleration) awed and made covetous every member of the staff and everyone else who saw or rode in it. A car that simply conquered all road conditions with polished authority, a car as much for enthusiastic hard driving as for sedate, comfortable cruising. *But*—it costs over $8000 basic, over $8500 as equipped and close to $9000 with tax and license. It was already unattainable by mere mortals, before the re-evaluation of the German Deutschmark, at $7600. And the price can be boosted above $10,000 through a combination of options not fitted to our test car: automatic transmission, air conditioning, manual or electric sunroof, tinted glass, radio and electric front window lifts. Perhaps when one gets beyond, say, $7500 a few additional hundreds are not particularly crucial, but an American customer begins to balk at prices approaching $10,000 for an under-200-bhp, 6-cyl car. The answer to this, of course, is that the BMW is a far more stable, balanced, totally usable car than any other we can think of, and there is nothing remotely approaching the 2800 CS for significantly less. One has to look to the top-of-the-line Mercedes-Benz models, or to the Ferrari/Lamborghini class, to find more car. So anyone with $9000 to spend must find the 2800 CS close to irresistible.

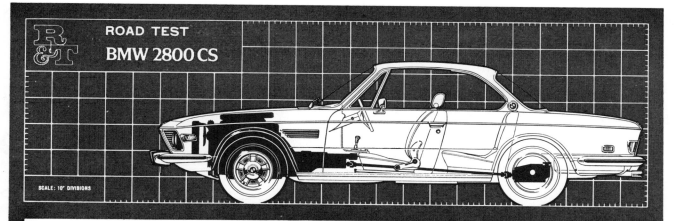

ROAD TEST
BMW 2800 CS

SCALE: 10" DIVISIONS

PRICE

List price, east coast....... $8022
List price, west coast...... $8107
Price as tested............ $8517
  Price as tested includes leather upholstery ($310), metallic paint ($100)

IMPORTER

Hoffman Motors Corp.
375 Park Ave., New York, N.Y.

ENGINE

Type............6 cyl inline, sohc
Bore x stroke, mm.....86.0 x 80.0
  Equivalent in.......3.39 x 3.15
Displacement, cc/cu in..2788/170
Compression ratio..........9.0:1
Bhp @ rpm...........192 @ 6000
  Equivalent mph...........126
Torque @ rpm...174 lb-ft @ 3700
  Equivalent mph............74
Carburetion.two Solex 35/40 INAT
Type fuel required......premium
Emission control....engine mods

DRIVE TRAIN

Transmission.....4-speed manual,
Gear ratios: 4th (1.00).....3.45:1
  3rd (1.38)..............4.75:1
  2nd (2.12)..............7.31:1
  1st (3.85)............13.28:1
Final drive ratio..........3.45:1

CHASSIS & BODY

Body/frame..........unit steel
Brake type: 10.7-in. disc front, 9.8-in. drum rear, power assisted; handbrake on rear drums
  Swept area, sq in.........394
Wheels........alloy disc, 14 x 6J
Tires...Michelin 175 HR 14 XAS
Steering type..ZF-Gemmer worm & roller, power assisted
  Overall ratio............18.9:1
  Turns, lock-to-lock........4.0
  Turning circle, ft........34.5
Front suspension: MacPherson struts, lower A-arms, coil springs, tube shocks, anti-roll bar
Rear suspension: semi-trailing arms, coil springs, tube shocks, anti-roll bar

ACCOMMODATION

Seating capacity, persons.......4
Seat width,
  front/rear....2 x 22.5/2 x 20.5
Head room, front/rear...36.5/36.0
Seat back adjustment, degrees..75
Driver comfort rating (scale of 100):
  Driver 69 in. tall...........90
  Driver 72 in. tall...........75
  Driver 75 in. tall...........70

INSTRUMENTATION

Instruments: 150-mph speedo, main & trip odo, 8000-rpm tach, water temp, fuel level, clock
Warning lights: oil pressure, alternator, fuel reserve, directionals, high beam, handbrake, rear window heater, emergency flashers

MAINTENANCE

Service intervals, mi:
  Oil change................4000
  Filter change.............4000
  Chassis lube.............none
  Minor tuneup...........4000
  Major tuneup..........8,000
Warranty, mo/mi.......12/12,000

GENERAL

Curb weight, lb............2990
Test weight................3325
Weight distribution (with driver), front/rear, %....56/44
Wheelbase, in. 103.3
Track, front/rear......56.9/55.2
Overall length.............183.5
  Width....................64.9
  Height...................53.9
Ground clearance............5.9
Overhang, front/rear....38.2/42.0
Usable trunk space, cu ft....14.5
Fuel tank capacity, U.S. gal...18.5

CALCULATED DATA

Lb/bhp (test weight)........17.3
Mph/1000 rpm (4th gear)....19.5
Engine revs/mi (60 mph)....3080
Engine speed @ 70 mph....3550
Piston travel, ft/mi.........1620
Cu ft/ton mi...............90.8
R&T wear index.............50
R&T steering index.........1.88
Brake swept area sq in/ton....227

ROAD TEST RESULTS

ACCELERATION

Time to distance, sec:
0–100 ft...................3.7
0–250 ft...................6.6
0–500 ft...................9.8
0–750 ft..................12.4
0–1000 ft.................14.8
0–1320 ft (¼ mi)........17.4
Speed at end of ¼ mi, mph....82
Time to speed, sec:
0–30 mph...................3.6
0–40 mph...................5.7
0–50 mph...................7.4
0–60 mph...................9.3
0–70 mph..................12.7
0–80 mph..................16.4
0–100 mph................28.8
Passing exposure time, sec:
  To pass car going 50 mph....5.9

FUEL CONSUMPTION

Normal driving, mpg..........19
Cruising range, mi..........350

SPEEDS IN GEARS

4th gear (6000 rpm).........126
  3rd (6200)................91
  2nd (6200)................61
  1st (6200)................32

BRAKES

Panic stop from 80 mph:
  Deceleration rate, % g......80
  Stopping distance, ft......352
  Control..............very good
Fade test: percent increase in pedal effort to maintain 50%-g deceleration rate in 6 stops from 60 mph.................48
Parking: Hold 30% grade?.....yes
Overall brake rating........good

SPEEDOMETER ERROR

30 mph indicated is actually..26.0
40 mph....................36.0
60 mph....................55.0
70 mph....................64.0
80 mph....................74.0
100 mph...................93.0
Odometer, 10.0 mi.........9.10

ACCELERATION & COASTING

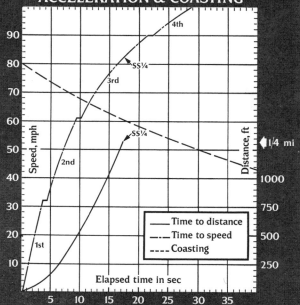

— Time to distance
—·— Time to speed
---- Coasting

Elapsed time in sec

47

THE RE DESIGNED AND CLEANED-UP DASHBOARD.

R & T STYLING ANALYSIS
BMW 2800 CS

ACCENTUATION OF HORIZONTAL LINES

WIDER LIP MOLDINGS

RUBBER MOLDINGS ON FRONT & REAR BUMPER.

BLACK ROCKER PANEL WITH CHROME-MOLDINGS → VISUAL REDUCTION OF BODY HEIGHT.

MAG WHEELS

NO POCKET ON THE 2800 DOOR — BUT MUCH NICER AND BETTER SEATS.

SAME REAR END ON 2000 & 2800 EXCEPT BUMPER: RUBBER-MOLDINGS FITTED ON 2800 CS.

BMW 2800

LONG-TERM REPORT

**12,000 miles with
prestige German saloon**

By Geoffrey P. Howard

Above: A few miles out of Munich and the total distance recorder shows all noughts at a true 73 mph

Right: Luxury interior with cloth upholstery and lots of clever details. There is a spring-loaded pocket in each front door, a glove locker and a central open "bin"

FIRST impressions can be fickle. Lots of cars with yards of showroom appeal dull off in use and become quite mundane with continued acquaintance, and a driver can become so familiar with his car that any shortcomings pass unnoticed as they develop. My feelings on the 24 July 1969 remain as fresh as if it were yesterday, largely because I relived them all over again last week when I re-acquainted myself with the same car after a considerable lapse away from it.

As regular readers will know there has been a BMW of one kind or another in use as an *Autocar* staff car for several years now. From a manual 1800 we moved to an automatic 2000 and then to one of the first 2002s in which we covered a very reliable 30,000 miles. Last July Mike Scarlett and Stuart Bladon went on a trip to Munich to pick up and bring home our new six-cylinder saloon. We had requested a 2500 manual car with power steering.

It was a blistering hot summer's day when they arrived back in the office, cheerful, perspiring and cluttered with the impedimenta of the job. With a nonchalance that comes only after years of self-control, Mike muttered "Oh, by the way, your car has an extra 300 c.c." Composure went by the board as I scrambled down to the car park to find the first right-hand drive 2800 in deep regal red, with grey cord

upholstery and no power steering.

"Impressed" is a king-sized understatement of how half the office, it seemed, reacted to a detail examination of our new toy. It was a beautiful piece of engineering from end to end, with quite the best laid out cockpit I have come across and an incredible tool kit hidden in the boot lid lining.

If the 2800 impressed in the car park, it positively sparkled on the road. The in-line six-cylinder engine is incredibly smooth all the way from a 750 rpm idle to the red mark at 6,200 rpm . . . and beyond. The running-in instructions were as generous as one would expect and Mike had taken a hasty picture on the *autobahn* outside Munich as the total mileage recorder passed all the zeros from its 99,978 (minus 22 in effect, to allow for factory testing) starting figure. Note that he is below 4,000 rpm and indicating just short of 80 mph, all within the manufacturer's recommended limits; not bad for a brand new car.

The trip back was made in remarkably good time and the car was in fine fettle after the 700-mile journey on which it averaged 24.6 mpg. It went straight to MLG at Chiswick for the first service and for seat belts to be fitted. The only complaints were a peculiar induction whistle on idling which had developed in Belgium, and

the beginnings of a rattle from the gearbox when idling in neutral. The whistle persisted for some time and then disappeared, while the rattle got slowly worse, especially when the transmission was really warm.

At the first glance one aspect of the detail trim had jarred my aesthetic senses. Decorative grille panels on the top of the bonnet lid were a garish chrome-plated plastic, while similar grilles for the air extractors on the rear quarter panels were sprayed in body colour. All four were easily removed and I sprayed them with a can of Bradville matt black aerosol, dramatically improving the effect to my eye at least.

There was no trouble at all during the early part of the car's life (although we were keeping a watchful ear on the gearbox) until one day in September when I was on a trip to Brighton. Just as I entered the busy part of the western town shopping area a most alarming scraping noise started up in the left front hub. Everyone stopped to stare at the noise which was at the same pitch, but louder, as an exhaust system dragging in the road. A hasty check showed nothing adrift so I crept noisily to the local BMW distributors, Seven Dials Motors, arriving just as the workshop was breaking for lunch.

Without introducing myself I put them to the test and they came up trumps. Im-

really no worse either. BMW warranties in the UK last six months or 6,000 miles, whichever is the first to be reached, but even after this limit they will consider claims on their circumstances. This is general policy and indicates no special favour to us; the gearbox had blatantly been noisy from scratch, and we could have insisted on earlier rectification.

A strip down showed that there was a faulty thrust race and some adjustment to the selectors was also carried out. When refitted it was much quieter but stiff and notchy for a couple of thousand miles until it freed off.

At about this time we decided to try tyres other than the Continental radials on which the car had been supplied. These were the latest 70-series profile and appeared to be well up to the performance capabilities of the car, but they suffered badly from a lack of wet road grip particularly in London. Michelin could not supply 70-series XAS so we accepted normal 185-section which is the size fitted to the BMW 2500.

Early on in the BMW's life I had raised the front tyre pressures 2 psi above standard to give quicker steering response and reduce some of the inherent understeer. With the XAS the steering was even better still and the whole problem of wet road adhesion was licked immediately. When the Continentals came off the car at 8,500 miles the front ones were 35 per cent worn and the rears 53 per cent worn. The Michelins showed wear rates of 20 per cent and 30 per cent respectively for an equivalent mileage.

Just as we reached the 12,000-mile mark a strange ticking noise began under the floor at prop-shaft speed. We rushed the car back to MLG who found a bolt in the rubber coupling had sheared in half and worked through to foul the gearbox tailshaft. It was caught in the nick of time before any damage was caused.

That really amounts to the total mechanical record for the car to date. Initially we had slight trouble with door catches which were soon sorted out with lubricant and attention to the striker plate positions. During performance testing a blackbird took off the track towards the car and we collected it slap in the middle of the pressed alloy radiator grille at about 110 mph. This was replaced at our expense as was the bright metal rubbing strip over the nearside rear wheel arch, which I grazed on a parked van when I misjudged the width in a narrow backstreet.

For quite some time early on we suffered from a flatspot on sharp right-hand corners and plug fouling in heavy traffic. These two faults were not connected for a long time until MLG stripped the carburettors and found a small piece of fluff in one of the needle valves which had been upsetting the level in that float chamber. After this the carburation was always absolutely clean at all times.

At the time when the measurements were taken for this 12,000-mile report a close examination was made throughout the car in detail. The exterior paintwork and bright metal have stood up to what has been a very severe winter extremely well indeed. The car only needs a quick wash to come up as shiny as when new and the chrome is free from pock-marks and rust.

Inside, the upholstery is about ready for a shampoo, the dark grey velvet cord ribs having lost their sheen on the wearing surfaces of the front seats. The carpets,

which do not lift out for brushing, should now be unscrewed and given a good beating. Other than this and a knob which has dropped off one of the heater control levers, the car is as perfect as the day it left the factory. We shall now go on to at least 20,000 miles and report again later in the year.

At the beginning of this article I described my feeling when first taking over the car and mentioned reliving them again. Although I ran the car almost exclusively for the first 8,000 miles, it then passed into more general staff use in order that the mileage would be clocked up faster in readiness for this report. In about eight weeks a further 4,000 miles was recorded and it was after this lapse that I came back to the car to refresh myself of its characteristics.

COST and LIFE of EXPENDABLE ITEMS

Item	Life in Miles	Cost per 10,000 Miles		
		£	s	d
One gallon of 4-star fuel, average cost today 6s 6d	21.2	154	0	0
One pint of top-up oil, average cost today 3s 6d ..	2,000		17	6
Front disc brake pads (set of 4)	10,000	8	10	0
Rear brake linings (set of 4)	20,000	4	19	0
tyres (front pair)	24,000	9	16	0
tyres (rear pair)	17,000	13	16	0
Service (main interval and actual costs incurred)	4,000	35	9	1
Total		227	7	7
Approx. standing charges per year:				
Depreciation		300	0	0
*Insurance		38	3	0
Tax		25	0	0
Total		590	10	7

Approx. cost per mile = 1s 2d
*Cornhill quotation including 65 per cent no claims bonus with a £50 excess and cover restricted to approved drivers only.

PERFORMANCE CHECK

Maximum speeds

Gear	mph 2500	2800	kph 2500	2800	rpm 2500	2800
Top (mean)	121	124	194	200	6,150	5,950
(best)	121	124	194	200	6,150	5,950
3rd	93	91	150	146	6,500	6,100
2nd	62	62	100	100	6,500	6,100
1st	34	33	55	53	6,500	6,100

Standing ¼-mile,   2500: 17.2 sec   81 mph
                     2800: 16.4 sec   83 mph
Standing kilometre   2500: 31.6 sec   101 mph
                     2800: 30.3 sec   104 mph

Acceleration, 2500: 3.2 5.1 7.0 9.3 13.1 16.8 21.8 29.9
Time in sec. 2800: 3.2 5.0 6.8 8.9 12.3 15.8 20.0 27.8 38.5

0 ————————————————————
True speed mph   30 40 50 60 70 80 90 100 110 120
Indicated speed
mph, 2500:   32 43 53 63 74 85 95 105
Indicated speed
mph, 2800:   30 41 52 64 75 86 97 108 118 129

Speed range, Gear Ratios and Time in seconds

Mph	Top 2500	2800	3rd 2500	2800	2nd 2500	2800	1st 2500	2800
	(3.64)	(3.45)	(5.01)	(4.74)	(7.72)	(7.31)	(14.01)	(13.29)
10-30	11.4	10.3	7.5	7.0	4.7	4.5	2.9	3.1
20-40	9.2	9.0	6.3	5.8	4.0	3.8	—	—
30-50	9.3	8.8	6.1	5.8	4.1	3.6	—	—
40-60	9.4	9.1	6.1	5.9	4.5	4.2	—	—
50-70	10.3	9.5	6.7	6.4	—	—	—	—
60-80	11.0	10.0	7.7	7.2	—	—	—	—
70-90	11.6	11.9	9.4	9.0	—	—	—	—
80-100	14.8	14.9	—	—	—	—	—	—
90-110	—	18.5	—	—	—	—	—	—

Fuel Consumption
Overall mpg, 2500: 21.8 mpg (13.0 litres/100km)
              2800: 21.4 mpg (13.3 litres/100km)

NOTE: "2500" denotes performance figures for BMW 2500 tested in AUTOCAR of 28 August, 1969.

mediate inspection revealed that one of the retaining bolts for the disc dust shield had worked loose, dropped out and become jammed in the lip of the sheet metal shield, being rubbed by the edge of the disc as the wheel turned. It took a little while to find a replacement bolt of the right size, but I was on my way again soon after lunch with a receipt for £1 10s. in my pocket.

The next item in the car's programme was to measure the performance at MIRA which we did at a mileage of just over 8,500. It was during these tests that I began to sense the engine becoming slightly rough on the overrun. By the time we had returned to London there was quite a definite resonance in what was up until then a perfectly smooth unit. I thought no more of it until Mike Scarlett reported he had abandoned the car on M1 with the crankshaft nose pulley adrift. This incorporates a torsional damper and had obviously been coming loose for some time. The car was collected by MLG and repaired under warranty. A check with their service manager and the concessionaires at Brighton showed that this was a unique happening and no similar faults had been reported.

By the time the 8,000-mile service came up it was decided to take the gearbox out and examine it for the source of the unusual tapping which was no better, though

BMW 2800
Long-term Report

An account of our second 12,000 miles with this delightful car

By David Thomas

WITH its odometer climbing towards the 15,000-mile mark at the start of my term of "ownership", the BMW was still a most desirable car. Other than some minor abrasions and scratches, the paintwork was in excellent order. The brightware had also survived well, only the boot-lid escutcheon showing signs of corrosion. The plush interior looked good, although much of the stitching on the velvet-cord front seat upholstery had worn away and there were signs of fraying around the headrest fixings.

Performance was fully up to scratch, but the engine idled somewhat erratically and had a marked tendency to run-on when hot. The gearchange was still excellent, synchromesh being virtually unbeatable and the lever movement exceptionally light and smooth. The box, however, seemed a trifle noisy at low speeds in a high gear, an impression I'd already gained during an earlier drive in this car. Brake squeal was a real problem, being embarrassingly loud at times. Otherwise the brakes behaved well.

Another niggling fault was noisy wiper action, while wheel-balance also left something to be desired. So, with just over 16,000 miles on the clock, the car was delivered to MLG at Chiswick for servicing and attention to these faults. The bill came to just over £37, including £13 10s labour charges. Among the items renewed were brake pads (because of the squeal), oil and air filters, the contact breaker assembly and a set of sparking plugs.

Idling was now silky-smooth, but there was still a trace of running-on. Later cars have electro-magnetic throttle stops which positively cut off the fuel supply, thus completely eliminating this problem. No action had been taken concerning gearbox noise, as MLG did not consider it abnormal.

Immediately prior to the service, fuel consumption had averaged 20.4 mpg. Now, driven in exactly the same fashion, the BMW was returning 25.4 mpg. For a large and decidedly brisk saloon, this is outstandingly good.

When a Grundig WK 4501 four-wave-band radio and matching AC 220 cassette

Far left: Cibié lamps give excellent lighting. Left: Fuel filler cap lives behind the hinged number plate. Above: Instrument layout is among the best we have seen

BMW 2800

Long-term Report . . .

player-cum-recorder were offered for appraisal, the BMW seemed the logical car to use. Atkinson Batteries, Pembridge Villas, W11 quickly and neatly installed this equipment. Unlike the four-cylinder BMWs, the front wing crowns are not integral with the bonnet, aerial installation thus being considerably simpler. Only one speaker was used, this being located in the space provided in the upper part of the instrument binnacle. In general, the performance justified the sizeable price tags (£59 5s 10d for the radio, £48 10s 7d for the player-recorder). My only real criticism was a tendency for the resiliently mounted cassette player to vibrate badly over some road surfaces. On one occasion this resulted in a mass of tangled tape. All my efforts at removal were in vain until the tape was cut.

Highlight of my spell of "ownership" was a holiday trip to Grado on Italy's Adriatic coast. The outward journey, through Belgium, Germany and Austria, then through the Felbertauerntunnel into Italy, was made in company with a somewhat tired Mini. The necessarily sedate (for the BMW) pace resulted in truly remarkable fuel economy. Over 380 miles were covered before the first refill, the BMW returning around 28 mpg for this stage. Some brisk driving in Italy and on the solo return trip brought the overall average down to 25.9 mpg, still an astonishingly good figure for a car of this type.

Even in this over-crowded corner of England, the BMW is a joy to drive. It performs very well indeed, is particularly comfortable and quiet, handles superbly and has brakes to match its performance. More difficult to define, but just as important, is that rare compactness and agility which so many of its rivals lack. Somehow, its size is never an embarrassment. Even in non-powered form, the steering is light and response quick. First-class visibility enables the car to be placed to a nicety. If ever a saloon deserved the tag "sporting", the BMW 2800 is it.

On long Continental trips, it is just as impressive. Straight-line stability on motorways is excellent. Mechanical noise is confined to a satisfying hum from the ultra-smooth power unit. Wind noise, although present, is certainly not excessive. One or two of the staff think it a trifle undergeared for motorway use, but performance figures prove otherwise. Away from the beaten track, the all-independent suspension (self-levelling at the rear) is a match for the worst surfaces. Thanks to the limited slip differential, traction is never a problem. On mountain passes, its agility pays handsome dividends. First-class ventilation and heating, plus cloth upholstery, mean maximum comfort whatever the weather.

In all, over 2,500 miles were covered on the return trip to Grado. No oil was consumed and the only spot of bother was a popped-off screen-washer pipe. On the outward trip, exceptionally heavy rain was encountered on the German autobahnen and also when crossing the Dolomites. On both occasions, the brakes tended to become water-logged. The appreciable delay before they "bit" certainly had to be

allowed for. Contrary to my expectations, the brakes thrived in the hot Italian sunshine. There was always a lot of pad dust on the front wheel trim rings, but fade was never a problem. Moreover, there wasn't a trace of squeal, although it staged a comeback as soon as we returned to cooler climes. Pad wear during this period must have been appreciable, as the reservoir level dropped enough to operate the warning light. I hesitate to condemn the low-level switch as over-sensitive, but not a great deal of ATE blue fluid was necessary to restore the correct level. Incidentally, BMW recommend that the fluid be renewed yearly, a task that was skipped on the test car. A look at the costs table will show that pads had to be renewed at 8,000-mile intervals, which isn't too good by modern standards. Later cars, it seems, use a different friction material. This is claimed to eliminate squeal and may well have better wearing qualities.

Back home again, I noticed that the car was squatting appreciably at the rear. This had no detrimental effect on its road behaviour when lightly laden—if anything, handling was even better than usual. Nevertheless, something was obviously amiss. The 20,000-mile service was also overdue and some other items needed attention. Once again, the work was entrusted to MLG. This time, the brake squeal was all but cured. Shims were interposed between the pistons and the pad backing plates, their function being to move the centre of pressure in such a way as to reduce the brake factor. The rear suspension defect was traced to dirt in the Boge struts. Also attended to was a defective reversing lamp (traced to a loose wire) and a stiff left-hand front window regulator. Including the routine service, the bill came to a modest £12 1s 8d.

One of the penalties of having a car of this type is that it is in great demand for long trips. Colleagues used it for a variety of reasons, but worthy of mention is Ray Hutton's journey to Hockenheim for the German Grand Prix. He spoke highly of the car, which averaged 23.0 mpg for the whole of the trip. Soon afterwards, it was used by Stuart Bladon to cover the Marathon at the Nürburgring. Stuart already shared my enthusiasm for the model, the trip merely confirming his earlier impressions. Despite being cruised at three-figure speeds for considerable periods, it returned an average of 23.2 mpg.

Unfortunately, I was destined to lose the car before having an opportunity of checking performance. Clearly, it was still going extremely well and may easily have bettered the original times. Bodily, there had been no visible deterioration and there were no signs of impending trouble. In fact, with over 23,000 miles on the clock, it felt as good as it ever did.

Two items mentioned in the previous report (*Autocar*, 16 April 1970) deserve special mention. One is the long-wearing properties of the Michelin XAS tyres fitted at 8,500 miles. Measurement of tread depth after a further 15,000 miles suggested a useful life of 25,000 miles for the fronts and 30,000 miles for the rears. This is remarkably good, especially in view of the fact that the car had been driven quite hard for much of the time.

Less palatable is the depreciation involved. Our earlier report suggested an annual figure of £300 (no trade guides were available at the time). It now seems that £650 is a more realistic amount.

Without a shadow of doubt, the BMW 2800 ranks as one of Europe's great cars. Although still rare in Britain, the number to be seen on the roads of Europe confirms that there are many who feel this way. □

COST and LIFE of EXPENDABLE ITEMS

Item	Life in Miles	Cost per 10,000 Miles		
		£	s.	d.
One gallon of 5-star fuel, average cost today 6s. 10d.	23.6	144	14	0
One pint of top-up oil, average cost today 3s. 6d.	Neg. cons.			
Front disc brake pads (set of 4)	8,000*	10	13	0
Rear disc brake pads (set of 4)	8,000*	8	2	6
Michelin XAS tyres (front pair)	25,000	11	5	6
Michelin XAS tyres (rear pair)	30,000	9	8	0
Service (main interval and actual costs incurred)	4,000	49	5	11
Total		233	8	11

Approx standing charges per year:			
Depreciation	650	0	0
†Insurance	38	13	0
Tax	25	0	0
Total	947	1	11

Approx cost per mile=22.7d.

* Although actual life slightly better, pad renewal would normally form part of routine service.

† Cornhill quotation, including 65 per cent no-claim bonus.
Cover restricted to approved drivers, with £50 excess on accidental damage.

This shot was taken on one of the many tracks surrounding the Nürburgring

IT IS TOO EASY TO DIS-miss the 2800CS as a belated attempt by BMW to cash in on a market hitherto dominated by Daimler Benz with the big 280 and 300 Coupé and Convertible. But there have always been BMW coupés. What about the beautiful 327 of 1937, close-coupled sister of the immortal 328 and direct progenitor of the almost equally graceful post-war Bristol 400? And what of the even more sought-after V8 507 Touring Sport of 1955, brainchild of the same Baron Albrecht Goertz who reappeared last year at Turin with a knife-edged Porsche pro-totype? Then there were the Bertone BMWs, all V8s, and the much smaller, much earlier 315 series of the 1930s. Clearly, the 2800CS stands heir to a sporting heritage, a tradition of grace and power. What, then, went wrong?

For *something* did. The coupé's more prosaic and much less ex-pensive stable companion, the 2800 saloon, shares with the Jaguar XJ6 the distinction of being, in our opinion, quite the finest motor car of its type in the world. This luxury version, its handbuilt body the work of Karmann, the indepen-dent German coachbuilder, its mechanical components derived directly from the volume-produced model, its specification even more

exotic, ought by all that's logical to be even better. Yet how often is this really so? How many coupés genuinely outshine their humbler cousins? Romeos who know their Alfas will tell you that the boxy Giulia Super saloon is worth two of any derivative coupé in the range. Lancia fans have often preferred the long-wheelbase cars to their superficially more sporting sisters. And few critics have found anything nicer to say about the costly two-door Mercs than they have already said about the utilitarian four-door models at several thousand pounds less ...

Our story starts, really, in 1965, when the 2000CS Coupé appeared as a conscious revival of the 327. It was the first model since the abortive three-door 600 that BMW had styled themselves, and it used as much as possible of the press-work from the existing staple, the 1500/1600/1800/2000, as well as all of the mechanical elements. It was not, however, a particularly at-tractive car to look at and it was disappointing to drive. We re-member taking one across to the Amsterdam show in 1967 and being horrified at the degree of wind noise caused by the pillarless, disappearing side windows. Struc-tural flexibility caused handling problems, too, we recall. The spring rates seemed ill-adjusted to the model's weight, and there were

minor gripes about the control layout and the lack of room in the back. Despite its compactness and reduced frontal area the coupé didn't go any faster than its pro-genitors (one reason may have been

that it was heavier), and it c a great deal more.

When the time came to produ a coupé version of the extrem successful 2800, thus sticking another thorn in the side of p

THE COST£IEST BMW

WHAT WENT WRONG? ASKS DOUG BLAIN

ld Uncle Merc (there has been no ve lost between the two firms nce BMW almost succumbed, illy nilly, to a takeover bid from B's truck division in 1959), the en of Munich obviously found it ifficult to resist the temptation recoup some of their losses on he earlier CS model. One must ve them due credit, too. They ent about the transformation oroughly, particularly from the yling point of view, so that many herwise well-informed enthuasts remain unaware that the rrent 2800CS is merely an enrged and updated version of the ur-cylinder car.

From outside, the most obvious ange is the complete replacement f the original ungainly front with set of pressings very like the ones at form the sharp end of the g saloon. Big mag wheels are other easy-to-spot alteration, e kind you can have as an option any 2800. Inside, the original ooden parcels tray with its neat strument cluster remains, though e instruments themselves are of urse new. So are the very comrtable front seats, which, like e pathetic perches behind, are xuriously upholstered in real ather. But those frameless side ndows are still there—electrily operated, naturally, whereas iginally this was an option.

The temptation, after one has got this far, is to assume that the rest—ie, the mechanical bit—is pure 2800. The engine and transmission certainly are, and so is the final drive. A glance at the front suspension reveals the familiar rearward-raked Macpherson struts of the big BMW saloons, and the steering (power assisted, alas, as standard) is also a transplant from the 2800 options list—or at least a partial one.

Now we find ourselves on difficult ground. For the foundation of the 2800CS is still the punt-like sheet steel chassis of the 10year-old 2000, and a close look shows what a lot of hacking and chopping is required to fit the suspension units and subframe from the bigger car to the front, thereby incidentally lengthening the wheelbase and widening the track substantially. The raked struts are housed in welded-in domes at the tops of the wheel arches, and there is evidence of much manipulation beneath to accommodate the other links and the anti-roll bar fixings and at the same time provide the spectacular degree of compliance for which the 2800 is noted. At the rear, however, things obviously haven't been so easy, and as far as we can make out BMW appear to have left the old 2000 semi-trailing A-arm setup more or less intact, even to the outer sliding pot joints and the drum brakes.

Not surprisingly, the result of all this ingenious but hardly dignified cutting and pasting is that the coupé, judged by the standards which its price suggests, feels a bit of a curate's egg to drive. Our test coincided with a longish period spent in custody of its four-door sibling, which as it happened was a well-used old nail of a press demonstrator. We really grew to love that car. It was loose and rattly mechanically, just like a well-run-in racer, and as tight as a drum in the suspension and body departments. It would float over atrocious surfaces, rocket through traffic, hurtle up the motorway at an indicated 120-plus, all laden to the gunwales, and completely free from extraneous sound apart from the muffled song of that marvellous sohc straight six.

The engine in the coupé is exactly the same, of course, and because the ensemble is almost a hundredweight lighter it goes even harder up to a top speed two or three mph higher. But there the similarity ends. Its different dimensions, different driving position and different outlook give the CS a totally different character, so that although it is smaller it immediately feels, to us at any rate, less chuckable. The body flexibility of the 2000 has been pretty well eliminated but the standard power steering, though excellent of its type, is not nearly as good as the extraordinarily light manual setup which makes the power option unnecessary on the saloon. And the ride—well, suffice to say it's pretty ordinary. One hears the bumps and one feels them. Not to excess, of course, but the fact that they are apparent is sufficient condemnation. The car patters and wiggles instead of floating over the rough patches, and the tail is that much more easily put out by an unexpected pothole. At the same time the hybrid's roadholding, despite reduced body roll, definitely lacks the tenacity that distinguishes its stablemate—especially in the wet, when it pays to be really wary with the right foot, at any rate on the standard German radials.

One would forgive all of this, dismissing the coupé as merely a rather ordinary prestige symbol, if it were not for the wind noise. This, at £5000 plus, is in our opinion inexcusable, starting as it does at about 50mph and increasing steadily as the glasses bow out and the gaps between them widen. In a car of this sort, even if one doesn't want to go hurtling through country lanes at boy-racer speeds, one does at least have a right to expect that the hi-fi be audible.

A brave try, BMW. But unworthy of the great Bayerischen Motoren Werke.

BMW 2800

FEW motorists have R6 500 available for buying a car, but those who are that fortunate would be well advised to consider the BMW 2800 sedan before taking the plunge.

Recently introduced in South African assembly, the BMW 2800 is in the super-car category and is one of the most enchanting cars we have ever driven. It is supremely comfortable and well-equipped in the style of Europe's top-flight cars, is capable of devastating performance, yet drives and handles with ease and grace.

With the classical BMW styling, it has no surplus bulk and mass, and conforms to the strictest safety requirements. It gives the impression that no expense has been spared to make this a first-class car.

INTERIOR EQUIPMENT

The driving position is comfortable and commanding, and sports-style without being ostentatious. Steering wheel and gearshift are finished in polished wood, and the instrumentation includes large dial-type speedometer and rev-counter and supplementary gauges, though surprisingly, no oil pressure gauge is provided.

At centre, a console with radio space and parcel shelf sweeps down to between the seats, and the single criticism is that the foot pedals are rather close-spaced — though this gave us no trouble on the road.

There is an oddments tray on the fascia top, and the very fine seats have built-in headrests. Storage space is completed by a drop glove-box,

and pockets in the doors and behind the seats. Trim, finish and equipment are of high standard and in good taste, with no flashiness.

SMOOTH ENGINE

The six-cylinder engine is a typical, robust-looking BMW unit with overhead camshaft with enclosed drive, under a bonnet which is front-hinged: a useful safety feature on a high-performance car. It is surmounted by a vast, twin-element aircleaner feeding two twin-choke carburettors, with a silenced air intake.

An advantage in an expensive car like this one is that the engine is a fully-balanced unit, with seven main bearings and 12 balance weights for smooth operation.

Underbonnet and firewall have full sound-deadening panels, so that only a whisper of mechanical sound reaches the interior of the car — the engine is barely audible at cruising speeds.

TOOL LOCKER

An exclusive feature on this car, deserving special mention, is the built-in tool locker under the luggage trunk lid.

This is a magnificent unit which always excites attention: it is equipped with a full range of everyday tools and special tools for this car, together with a spare set of spark plugs, spare fuses, spare bulbs, and other detailed items which might be required for maintenance or emergencies. At the turn of a hand screw, it drops down out of the raised trunk lid, and is padded to prevent rattles.

The trunk itself is roomy and trimmed throughout, with 0.6 m^3 of clear space.

PERFORMANCE FACTORS

In a dignified manner, the 2800 is a top-performance model. Its net power output is 122 kilowatts (about

164 bhp), and the engine revs smoothly to 6 000 rpm.

Transmission is four-speed, through a delightfully-smooth close-ratio gearbox which enables it to go to nearly 100 km/h in 2nd, and 150 km/h in 3rd. It is gently over-geared, peaking at just over 200 km/h in top — though it would not pull this speed on a level road.

A limited-slip differential with 25 per cent locking action transmits the power to the rear wheels, and big radial-ply super-speed tyres take care of traction.

PERFORMANCE

Owners would be unlikely to use their cars like this, but they might be interested to know that the car will tear away from rest with a bit of tail-wagging, and smoking tyres leaving twin black stripes on the roadway, to reach 100 km/h in 9·3 seconds, and 120 in 13·5 seconds.

Its maximum speed potential on a level road is 193 km/h — or a shade over 120 mph — and this car is built to be responsive and secure at high speeds. It is exceptionally steady at cruising speeds, and is little affected by side winds.

Another sterling safety feature is the ability to overtake swiftly at cruising speeds in the long-range third gear. The gearbox itself is very smooth and quick, and at 4·2 turns lock-to-lock, the steering is responsive and accurate.

FUEL ECONOMY

Having four carburettor chokes feeding the combustion chambers does not necessarily mean that a car must be heavy on petrol. At fixed speeds, it usually means improved economy, with only two chokes operating and the second stages in reserve.

Combustion efficiency is also vital: and the BMW 2800 has efficient hemispherical combustion chambers with

SPECIFICATIONS

ENGINE:

Cylinders	Six in line
Carburettors	2 twin-choke Solex 35/4 INAT
Bore	86·0 mm
Stroke	80·0 mm
Cubic capacity	2 788 cm³
Compression ratio	9·0 to 1
Valve gear	Ohv, single OHC
Main bearings	Seven
Aircleaners	Paper elements
Fuel rating	95-octane
Cooling	Water
Electrics	12-volt AC

ENGINE OUTPUT:

Max. power SAE (kW)	143·4 (192 bhp)
Max. power net (kW)	122·0
Peak rpm	6 000
Max. torque (N.m) at rpm	234/3 700

TRANSMISSION:

Forward speeds	Four
Synchromesh	All
Gearshift	Console
Low gear	3·85 to 1
2nd gear	2·12 to 1
3rd gear	1·375 to 1
Top gear	Direct
Reverse gear	4·13 to 1
Final drive	3·54 to 1, limited slip
Drive wheels	Rear
Tyre size	175 HR 14

BRAKES:

Front	272 mm discs
Rear	272 mm discs

Boosting	Vacuum servo
Handbrake position	Between seats

STEERING:

Type	ZF Gemmer worm and roller
Lock to lock	4·2 turns
Turning circle	9·6 m

MEASUREMENTS:

Length overall	4·70 m
Width overall	1·75 m
Height overall	1·45 m
Wheelbase	2·69 m
Front track	1·45 m
Rear track	1·46 m
Ground clearance	N/S
Licensing mass	1 340 kg

SUSPENSION:

Front	Independent
Type	Coils, anti-roll bar
Rear	Independent
Type	Nivowat units, anti-roll bar

CAPACITIES:

Seating	Five
Fuel tank	75·0 litres
Luggage trunk	0·6 m³

SERVICE DATA:

Sump capacity	N/S
Change interval	6 000 km
Oil filter capacity	N/S
Change interval	12 000 km
Gearbox capacity	N/S
Change interval	25 000 km
Diff capacity	N/S

Change interval	Nil
Air filter change	Up to 20 000 km
Greasing points	Nil

(These basic service recommendations are given for guidance only, and may vary according to operating conditions. Inquiries should be addressed to authorised dealerships.)

TYRE PRESSURES:
Radial ply: Front. 1·8 to 2·2 bars (26/32 lb)
Rear . 1·9 to 2·4 bars (28/36 lb)

WARRANTY:
18 months or 18 000 miles.

BASIC PRICE:

National	R6 471

PROVIDED TEST CAR:
Euro-Republic Automobile Distributors, Pretoria.

STANDARD EQUIPMENT:
Reclining front seats, three-point seat belts, boosted disc brakes with anti-lock device at rear, radial-ply tyres, centre console, through-flow ventilation, heater/demister with blower, cigar lighter, headlamp flasher, door and seat pockets, wheel trims, tool/spares locker in trunk, reversing lamps, wood-rim steering wheel, wooden gear knob, rubber-faced bumper overriders, rev-counter, passenger roof handles, QI headlamps.

MAKE AND MODEL:
Make . . . . BMW
Model . . . . . . 2800 Sedan

PERFORMANCE FACTORS:
Power/mass (kg/kW) . . . . 11·0
Frontal area (m²) . . . . 2·54
km/h at 1 000 rpm (top) . . 34·4
(Calculated on licensing mass, gross frontal area, gearing and net power output.)

INTERIOR NOISE LEVELS:

	Min.
Idling	46·0
60 km/h	64·0
80 km/h	69·5
100 km/h	73·0
120 km/h	78·0
Full throttle	See graph

(Measured in decibels, "A" weighting, averaging runs both ways on a level road; "Minimum" with car closed.)

ACCELERATION FROM REST:
0–50 . . . . 3·0
0–60 . . . . 4·1
0–70 . . . . 5·2
0–80 . . . . 6·2
0–90 . . . . 7·6
0–100 . . . . 9·3
0–110 . . . . 11·4
0–120 . . . . 13·5
400 m sprint . . . . . . 16·2

OVERTAKING ACCELERATION:

	3rd	Top
40–60	3·3	5·5
60–80	3·1	5·2
80–100	3·5	5·4
100–120	3·8	6·3

(Measured in seconds, to true speeds, averaging runs both ways on a level road, car carrying test crew of two and standard test equipment.)

MAXIMUM SPEED:
True speed . . . . . . 193·3 km/h
Speedo reading 201
Calibration:
Indicated . 40 . 60 . 80 . 100 . 120
True speed 39 . 57 . 75 . 94 . 112

FUEL ECONOMY (litres/100 km in brackets):
60 km/h . . . . 12·7 (7·9)
80 km/h . . . . 12·1 (8·3)
100 km/h . . . . . . 11·0 (9·1)
120 km/h . . . . . . 8·9 (11·2)
Full throttle . . . . . See graph
(Measured in kilometres per litre, averaging runs both ways on a level road.)

BRAKING TEST:
From 80 km/h . . . . . Not tested

GRADIENTS IN GEARS:
Low gear . . . . . . 1 in 2·3
2nd gear . . . . . . 1 in 3·4
3rd gear . . . . . . 1 in 5·4
Top gear . . . . . . 1 in 8·1
(Tabulated from Tapley (x gravity) readings, car carrying text crew of two and standard test equipment.)

GEARED SPEEDS (km/h):
Low gear . . . . 53·8
2nd gear . . . . 99·2
3rd gear . . . . 150·7
Top gear . . . . 206·2
(Calculated to true speeds, at engine peak rpm — 6 000.)

TEST CONDITIONS:
Altitude . . . . . . At sea level
Weather . . . . Fine and warm
Fuel used 93-octane
Test car's odometer . . . . 3 785 km

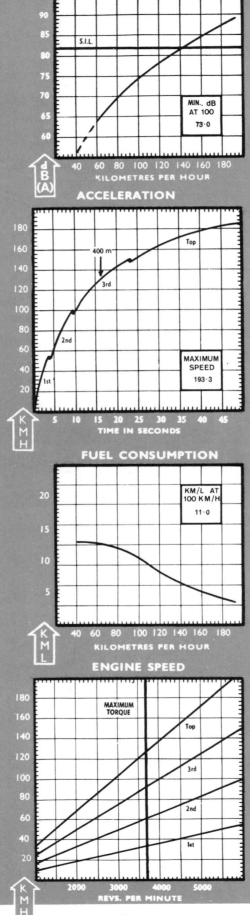

ACCELERATION

S.I.L.

MIN.. dB
AT 100
73·0

KILOMETRES PER HOUR

MAXIMUM SPEED
193·3

TIME IN SECONDS

400 m
Top
3rd
2nd
1st

FUEL CONSUMPTION

KM/L AT
100 K M/H
11·0

KILOMETRES PER HOUR

ENGINE SPEED

MAXIMUM TORQUE
Top
3rd
2nd
1st

REVS. PER MINUTE

SILENCE LEVELS:
Mechanical . . . . . Very Good
Idling . . . . Very Good
Transmission . . . . . Very Good
Wind . . . . Good
Road . . . . Very Good
Coachwork . . . . . . Good
Average . . . . . . Good

ENGINE:
Starting . . . . . . Very Good
Response . . . . . . Excellent
Smoothness . . . . . Excellent
Accessibility . . . . . . Fair

STEERING:
Accuracy . . . . . Very Good
Stability at speed . . . . Excellent
Stability in wind . . . . Very Good
Steering effort . . . . Very Good
Roughness . . . . . Very Good
Road feel . . . . . Very Good
Centring action . . . . Very Good
Turning circle . . . . . Good

BRAKING:
Pedal pressure . . . . Very Good
Response . . . . . Very Good
Fade resistance . Very Good (see text)
Directional stability . . . Very Good
Handbrake position . . Very Good
Handbrake action . . . Very Good

TRANSMISSION:
Clutch action . . . . Excellent
Pedal pressure . . . . Very Good
Gearbox ratios . . . . Very Good
Final drive ratio . . . . Good
Gearshift position . . . Very Good
Gearshift action . . . Very Good
Synchromesh . . . . Very Good

SUSPENSION:
Firmness rating . . . . Very Good
Progressive action . . . Very Good
Roadholding . . . . Very Good
Roll control . . . . . Good
Tracking control . . . Very Good
Pitching control . . . Very Good
Load ability . . . . Very Good

DRIVER CONTROLS:
Hand control location . . . Good
Pedal location . . . . Good
Wiper action . . . . Very Good
Washer action . . . . Very Good
Instrumentation . . . Very Good

INTERIOR COMFORT:
Seat design . . . . Very Good
Headroom front . . . . Good
Legroom front . . . Very Good
Headroom rear . . . . Good
Legroom rear . . . . Good
Door access . . . . Very Good
Lighting . . . . . Very Good
Accessories fitted . . . Very Good
Accessories potential . . . Fair

DRIVING COMFORT:
Steering wheel position . . . Good
Steering wheel reach . . . Good
Visibility . . . . . Very Good
Directional feel . . . . Fair
Ventilation . . . . Very Good
Heating . . . . . Very Good

COACHWORK:
Appearance . . . . Very Good
Finish . . . . . . Very Good
Space utilization . . . . Good
Trunk capacity . . . Very Good
Trunk access . . . . Fair

swirl action to ensure effective use of fuel.

On the road, at cruising speeds, this gives the car remarkable fuel economy: 11·0 km/l at 100 km/h, and 8·9 at 120 km/h, so that owners can reckon on using about 10 litres per 100 km on average — that would be something close to 28 mpg — with reasonable restraint.

STOPPING ABILITY

A formal set of brake tests was not conducted on this occasion, but after using the brakes liberally in performance tests, and timing a stop from 120 km/h, we can testify that these brakes are fully up to the car's performance ability.

There was no trace of fade in repeated stops, and the pedal remained gentle and sensitive. An anti-lock device is used at rear to balance braking effort and prevent rear-wheel locking, making an important contribution to overall safety.

VENTILATION AND NOISE

The through-flow ventilation system on the 2800 is above-average in effectiveness, and is coupled with a blower for low-speed work, and heater for cold weather.

Noise levels throughout are commendably low, with little wind flutter and road noise muted by the radials.

HANDLING AND RIDE

The BMW 2800 has a sophisticated all-independent suspension with strong progressive action and self-levelling units at rear. This makes it thoroughly load-capable and, combined with the solid weight of the car itself, makes for an outstandingly-smooth ride over bad surfaces.

The car can be pushed hard with safety, and body roll is difficult to provoke, even in throwing the car into a tight corner.

Controls are light and responsive: the driver feels at home in the car, and does not have any eccentric handling tendencies to contend with. Its directional stability is notable, making this a thoroughly-safe car under most road conditions.

CONTROLS AND LIGHTS

This new super-BMW has the finest headlights we have encountered on any car: the four quartz-iodine beams bathe the roadway ahead in the equivalent of full daylight on the darkest night, yet dip cleanly so as not to offend oncoming traffic. This penetrative brillance is

combined with fine side-spread to give magnificent road coverage.

Controls generally are well placed and easy to use: it is quite remarkable to have a car of this performance capability which is so easy to handle and drive.

SUMMARY

The BMW 2800 is one of the truly great cars: it is obvious that meticulous care has gone into its design and engineering, and we could find no flaws in the South African assembly of the test car.

This is the kind of car that is so good, that we would like to have it with a top-notch automatic transmission for town use, plus an electrically-operated overdrive ratio (by-passing the automatic transmission) for the open-road!

But wishful thinking aside, this is a prestige car which retains the common touch: it has glamour and refinement, yet can win the heart of an enthusiast driver for its sheer roadability. ●

DATA AT 120	
Min. noise level	78·0 dBA
0–120 through gears	13·5 sec
km/l at 120 9·9 km/l (10·1 litres/100 km)	
Braking from 120	4·1 sec
Reserve acceleration	0·094 x gravity
Max. gradient (top)	1 in 10·6
Speedo error	6·5% over
Speedo at true 120	128
Rpm (top)	3 495

IMPERIAL DATA

Major performance features of this Road Test are summarised below in Imperial measures:

PERFORMANCE FACTORS:	
Power/mass (lb/bhp)	18·1
Mph/1 000 rpm (top)	21·4

ACCELERATION FROM REST (in seconds):	
0–30	2·8
0–40	4·4
0–50	6·3
0–60	8·5
0–70	11·5
¼ Mile	16·2

MAXIMUM SPEED:	
True speed	120·2

FUEL CONSUMPTION (mpg):	
30	33·6
45	35·2
60	31·5
75	24·3

GEARED SPEEDS (mph):	
1st gear	33·5
2nd gear	61·8
3rd gear	93·7
Top gear	128·4

Pushed to the point of tyre distortion in a corner, the BMW 2800 leans a bit but retains true handling.

Clear instrumentation includes a rev-counter. Steering wheel and gear knob are in polished wood.

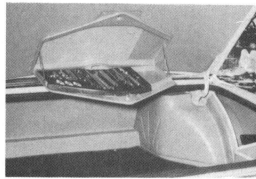

Luggage trunk measures 0·6 m³, with medium sill and tool locker in the lid.

Silenced aircleaner system dominates the engine compartment. Bonnet is front-hinged.

DRIVING IMPRESSIONS
BMW 2500

Photos by John Plow
Report by David Lamb

I didn't think I would ever see the day when I would turn my nose up at the prospects of testing a BMW 2500, and yet there I was, wishing I could postpone the whole thing. The big problem was convincing the editor that this model, a standard (four-speed) transmission 2500, really warranted another road test so soon after the automatic version (May, 1970). Consequently, we found ourselves making feeble excuses to the BMW representative, while he was insisting we take the car for at least three weeks. The average enthusiast drools at the thought of having such a car for almost a month. I too found the temptation too much and after three short minutes of struggling, gave in. Hell, I couldn't resist the thought of blasting all over the country in a vehicle that consistently gets rave reviews from the motoring press. Let someone else worry about the editor's ulcers; an opportunity such as this does not come along every day.

As mentioned before, the car was virtually the same as the one tested previously, the exceptions being the standard transmission, Michelin XAS Radials and power steering. Though this may sound like heresy, my first impressions were not all good. The

seating position felt totally foreign, probably due to the long periods of time my backside has spent cradled in one of Detroit's buckets. Though the BMW seats are fully adjustable, I still could not get myself into a comfortable position. Try as I may, I could not get away from the sensation of sitting in an armchair, perched high above the floor. Likewise, the steering wheel made me feel uncomfortable. Its large diameter (over 16 inches) felt far too big, especially since this particular model was equipped with power steering. Not only was it large, but it also tilted at a bus-like angle which dictated that the seating position be just right in order to reach the top of the rim. Adding to the general strangeness of the interior was a set of particularly aggravating seat belts. One strap crossed the lap while three others hung diagonally across the chest. Both came together in a common buckle at the right side of the driver's seat. The big headache was deciding which belt would tighten which, a recurring problem, as the belts tended to loosen with continued use. One last complaint was a loose gear selector. BMW encased the lever with a wooden knob. Unfortunately this did not fit properly and would

come off during quick shifts, especially from first to second.

Well there you have it, a complete list of complaints, most of which are a result of habits shaped by lengthy periods spent in Detroit automobiles. Certainly a small and rather picky list at best, but this is the very nature of BMW cars. In this age of lousy quality control and never-ending compliance with the whims of stylists it's a distinct pleasure to drive a vehicle that is not only well designed but put together with unbelievable care. This fastidiousness in design and construction certainly came to the fore when used for our biannual foray to St. Jovite during the weekend of the Player's Grand Prix of Canada.

Right from the start of the trip we were amazed at the speeds the car was capable of attaining. It was not until we had passed a series of vehicles, all appearing to be travelling at 50 mph that we realized we were travelling from 80 to 90 mph. Immediately, we assumed the speedometer was quite inaccurate, and though we were speeding, the actual rate was probably well below the indicated velocity. After carefully checking the time required to pass through those measured mile markers and working out the actual speed, we found that 90 mph on the speedometer was in fact 87 mph. That works out to a fine of approximately $60.00, and from that moment on made every effort to stay at least within 10 mph of the 70 mph limit.

This was not to be. The car had a mind of its own. There just wasn't any way I could keep it at "legal" speeds. Within a matter of minutes, I would have the beast back up to 85 not realizing it, until I passed another car, apparently crawling along. Everything was so effortless, speeds such as 80-plus were accomplished without any white knuckles or worried nagging from passengers. The only reminders of speed were a constant singing from the radials and a pleasant mechanical buzz from the engine compartment.

Okay, the car was a great highway cruiser but the true test was to be those wild roads in Quebec. From Calumet to St. Jovite there are approximately 40 miles of the most exhilarating stretch of road this side of Europe. The surface is patched and the crown quite high. There are virtually no straights and you pray that you don't get stuck behind a farmer or a trailer as this normally short trip will suddenly take hours. Over the years we have taken many different cars through this test of man and machine but candidly admit that none of them have travelled this route with such class. Speeds that we had not thought possible were once again popping up on the speedometer. Flashing up a small hillock not knowing which way the road would turn, or how sharply, was no problem at all. In fact, at this stage of the game we began to see the rationale behind the odd seating arrangement. BMW engineers thoughtfully slanted the six cylinder engine to one side in order to slope the hood away from your line of vision. Then, they placed the seats quite high in order to take full advantage of the already excellent visibility. Getting back to that hill, as we crested the summit you could quickly see where the road did in fact lead. The odd time, the rate of speed would be so quick our reflexes couldn't catch up. Then it simply became a matter of stabbing the brake pedal and feeling the eyeballs surge to the front of the skull as those four wheel disc brakes hauled the car down to a sane speed. Slight lean was felt in very tight corners but once again we believe this has been done deliberately to allow those great radials to get a better bite on the road surface.

I can recall one point in time zapping around a blind corner to find a train of assorted sports and pseudo sports cars flogging themselves to death in an attempt to outdo each other on these 40 miles of curves. Bearing in mind that this road has very few if any straight sections I was (continued overleaf)

One of the most carefully built Sixes in the world.

Interior is designed so that everything is exactly where it should be for maximum driver comfort.

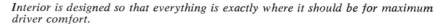

How to package the ideal four-door sedan.

Such niceties as this are standard on the 2500.

still able to slip by them one by one, until the way was clear again. I might add that those other cars were really trying since more than one tail was hung out or brake lights were flashed in panic. As the road got closer to St. Jovite it changed from patched asphalt to dusty gravel and this was where the car and I really came to know each other. In the mountains of literature that came with the car it mentioned that the rear wheel travel was 7.9 inches, which is staggering when you consider the average domestic sedan might have all of five inches. Anyway, there I was blasting along the road when it suddenly dropped off into a dismal pile of loose stones and assorted ruts. Inside the car the road noise changed in pitch but nothing really translated back to the steering wheel. Granted, the car bucked and pitched a bit, but at no

time did it become unmanageable or give any anxious moments. Then, the car was singing along on a paved section once again. Up ahead was a Volkswagen travelling at a reasonable speed but we passed him nevertheless. However, as is the case with many Volkswagen drivers, he decided to show me the superiority of his car by passing me. Feeling quite comfortable, we decided to follow him for a while in order to see how his car handled in comparison to the BMW. After a number of miles we both careened around a sharp corner to find the road had quickly deteriorated into another section of gravelly ruts. As the Volkswagen dropped off the pavement its tail wagged slightly but maintained its speed. Then, suddenly, we entered a particularly bad curve that had become very rutted. In a flash, the car ahead shuddered and bounced drunkenly off to the extreme apex of the curve. During all these dramatics the BMW remained rock steady and we slipped by the VW in almost a sedate manner. The last time I saw that car it was fading rapidly in the rear view mirror, no doubt the washboard road had not totally agreed with the car's rear suspension.

As of that moment we were convinced the BMW has a suspension far better than many of those cars reputed to be great handlers. We had pushed the car unmercifully over some of the worst roads imaginable and it had taken it in its stride without so much as a rattle. We had flogged it at 85-90

mph for hundreds of miles and the temperature gauge had not moved the slightest from its normal position. All in all, we had put approximately 1500 miles on the car through gravel, cities and throughways and never once did it falter. Quite frankly, we're at a loss to know just what it takes to make a BMW 2500 reveal something other than perfect manners.

After giving the matter some thought we have come to the conclusion that the BMW 2500 is a car that does everything extremely well with a minimum of fuss. It may not be the flashiest of cars and your next door neighbour might feel $6250 far too steep for a "little foreign car" but then he wouldn't appreciate what true handling and class are all about anyway. Frankly, the only way he will ever would be to push the car as we did on the way to St. Jovite.

In all fairness, this is not a car that can be approached with hairy arms and construction boots. You don't force or manhandle it as you would your own. On the contrary, once you adapt yourself, much the same as we finally did with respect to the seating position, everything becomes natural and right. Sample its silky gearbox, listen to the whirr of that well-balanced engine, and above all, try to drive it hard, and experience those superb brakes and all-round harmony of all its parts. Once you do we're sure you too will become a BMW convert.

Your one remaining problem will be managing that $6250 price tag. ●

AUTO TEST

BMW 3.0 CS

Performance, refinement and excellent economy

AT-A-GLANCE: Revised prestige coupe with enlarged engine at top of BMW range. Full four-seater, nicely finished with some luxury features. Incredibly sweet, free-revving six-cylinder engine, excellent gearbox, outstanding performance. Superb stability at speed, allied to positive power-assisted steering (optional extra). New ventilated disc brakes all round. Quiet, very comfortable express transport.

FIRST introduced at the Geneva Show this year, the 3-litre version of the BMW Coupé is being launched in Britain today, and we were able to have one of the first examples to reach this country for full Road Test ahead of the Press preview. Although time was necessarily rather short, we were able to knock up some 1,300 miles of very fast and enjoyable motoring, including a brief sortie to Holland for the maximum speed runs. We later drove the same car back from a point well south of Paris and enjoyed it so much that we have arranged to keep it in our long-term test fleet.

All who drove the car were convinced that it must have a rather "fast" speedometer, since an indicated 90 mph always felt more like about 75, but this was purely an illusion brought on by the impressively low noise level, the effortless free-running of the engine, and the wonderful ease of control. In fact, the car's speedometer proved exactly accurate right up to 100 mph, and was only 1 mph optimistic at top speed.

The extra 200 c.c. capacity has been obtained by increasing the bore diameters from 86 to 89mm, and a claimed 10 bhp power increase to 180 (DIN) bhp at 6,000 rpm has been achieved without in any way spoiling the sweetness and well-balanced feel of the unit. Carburation is by two big progressive choke downdraught Zenith carburettors. From low speeds the carburation is very clean, and the engine pulls without any snatch, but there is some very slight low-speed transmission harshness. In spite of the fairly low overall gearing, which gives only 20.7 mph per 1,000 rpm, third gear is called for once the speed has dropped below about 30 mph.

BMW engineers seem happy to let their engines rev hard, and do not go in for the high gearing which one would expect to evolve from their extensive motorway system and freedom from artificial speed restrictions. They therefore make provision for the car to cruise for long periods at close to maximum revs and we covered 50 miles in about 25 minutes with no signs of stress, strain or overheating. There is excellent response always immediately available in top gear, and although the sound heard from the engine confirms that it is revving hard at speed, it is a very sweet noise which never sounds overworked. The fan has a viscous coupling, contributing to the lack of thrash or roar at high revs.

It is said that BMW engines take up to 10,000 miles to give their best, and this might explain why the performance was not quite up to the standard claimed and expected. Yet the 3.0 CS does not hang about; when given full throttle and taken up to the start of the red sector on the rev counter at 6,200 rpm, it soars through the gears, giving a yelp from the tyres when changing into second and even third. The clutch can be let in abruptly at about 3,500 rpm and the car leaps off the line, leaving heavy black wheelspin marks on the road.

Maximum permitted engine speed of 6,200 rpm allows 60 mph to be reached in second gear, taking 8.0 sec from a standing start, and the quarter mile time is an impressive 16.2 sec. The time from rest to 100 mph is an equally impressive 22.3 sec, and the achievement of 110 mph in just under the half-minute reflects the good aerodynamic shape of the body.

The central remote-control gear change has delightfully easy and positive action, and synchromesh on all four gears is very effective.

Left: Under bonnet finish is very good and accessibility excellent. Above: Back seats are individually shaped and there is a drop-down centre armrest. Below left: The boot has a large area and a carpet on its floor. There is a handy bin on the right and a craftsman's tool-kit fitted in the lid. Below: Seatbacks tip up for access to the rear seats

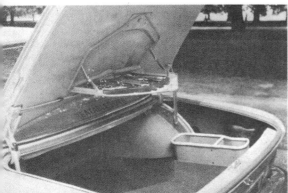

AUTOTEST
BMW 3.0 CS . . .

Although bottom gear has a maximum of 34 mph, it allows a fuss-free restart on 1 in 3 gradient. Third gear has a useful 92 mph maximum, but because of the fairly low gearing in top there is little advantage in hanging on to third, except for ultimate performance.

Choke control for cold starting is automatic, and tends to be a bit lavish for the sort of warm summery weather we had for the test, cutting in again when the car had stood for a morning although it would probably have run more

happily without it. There is a thermostatically controlled hot-spot to assist the warm-up. The engine seldom failed to start at the first attempt, though sometimes when it was really hot it was necessary to crank it over on full throttle for a second or two.

Five star super fuel is needed, otherwise the engine runs on badly. French super grade with an octane rating of only 98-99 is not good enough. The car proved exceptionally economical overall, returning nearly 24 mpg on a long run, and 18.5 mpg during performance testing including a considerable number of laps at over 110 mph on the banked circuit at MIRA. Overall consumption was 20.8 mpg after the usual allowance for mileometer error—in this case a very small percentage. The fuel tank holds 15.4 gallons and the gauge

indicates zero for some while before the tank warning light comes on. Over 300 miles can generally be covered without refuelling.

Power assisted steering is an extra, and at first it seems a little over-sensitive. The driver soon gets used to the good response and the accuracy with which the car can be placed at speed is excellent. Steering loads are pleasantly light even at low speeds, but without any excess assistance; many drivers would probably be surprised to learn that there was power assistance, so unobtrusive is it in its behaviour. The suspension absorbs most types of uneven surface very well indeed, feeling taut and well damped at all times. At high speeds the stability is quite uncanny, the car running true as a die right up to its maximum speed.

Weight distribution is fairly nose-heavy, with

56 per cent on the front wheels, but understeer is just enough for stable cornering, and the roll-free, sure-footed behaviour under power is very reassuring, making the driver feel in complete control. If the power is suddenly cut when cornering hard there is a rather abrupt but not excessive transition to tail swing.

An important change on the 3-litre is that ventilated disc brakes are used all round, with full duplication of hydraulic circuits and servos. Earlier criticisms that the brakes were too "soft" and prone to fade are completely answered—if anything the brakes are now a trifle heavy. Response goes up in steady progression with extra pedal load, to the stage where over 1g deceleration is obtained for 110lb on the pedal. Braking response at high speed is extremely good, and fade tests had no

effect after the first two stops had warmed up the pads. The handbrake operates separate small drums within the rear discs, and a strong pull on the sturdy central lever holds the car securely on 1 in 3.

Comfort and Convenience

The seats have reclining backrests adjusted by turning a knurled hand wheel on the outer lower edge of the seat. They provide good lateral support and remain much more comfortable on a long run than the initial slight firmness of the upholstery would suggest. Upholstery is in a form of velvet, no doubt warm in winter yet still comfortable in hot weather. Firm padded leather provides a very pleasant covering to the steering wheel rim. The driving position is comfortable and the

driver sits fairly high. The visibility all round is exceptionally good, especially on the rear quarters where such a body style normally has an awkward blind spot.

Immediately ahead of the driver are the diminutive but clearly marked speedometer and rev counter, and in a slightly smaller diameter dial on the right is a clock which kept good time on the test. Matching it on the left is a combined dial for warning lights plus the fuel and temperature gauges—the only other instruments provided. Wood trim backs the facia, and runs across the leading edge of what is in effect a parcels shelf, which proves useful for maps and oddments. There is a drop-down glove box in front of the passenger, but it is not locking and does not open wide enough for full advantage, also making access

BMW 3.0 CS (2,985 c.c.)

ACCELERATION

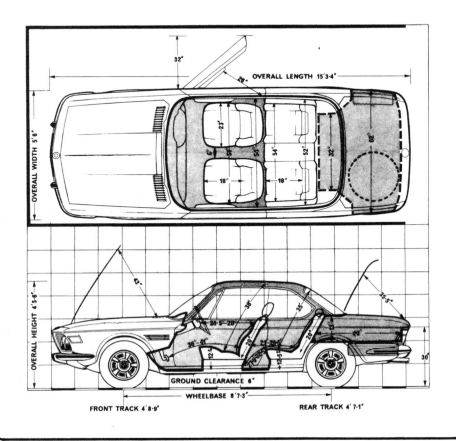

SPEED MPH TRUE INDICATED	TIME IN SECS
30	3.0
30	
40	4.6
40	
50	6.1
50	
60	8.0
60	
70	11.0
70	
80	13.9
80	
90	17.5
90	
100	22.3
101	
110	29.0
111	
120	39.8
121	

GEAR RATIOS AND TIME IN SEC

mph	Top (3.45)	3rd (4.83)	2nd (7.58)
10-30	—	6.0	3.7
20-40	8.0	5.3	3.3
30-50	7.1	5.0	3.3
40-60	7.2	5.0	3.4
50-70	7.5	5.3	—
60-80	7.6	5.3	—
70-90	8.4	6.5	—
80-100	9.6	—	—
90-110	12.6	—	—
100-120	17.5	—	—

Standing ¼-mile
16.2 sec 87 mph
Standing Kilometre
29.5 sec 111 mph
Test distance
1,736 miles
Mileage recorder
2 per cent over-reading

PERFORMANCE

MAXIMUM SPEEDS

Gear		mph	kph	rpm
Top	(mean)	131	211	6,320
	(best)	132	213	6,390
3rd		92	148	6,200
2nd		61	98	6,400
1st		34	55	6,400

BRAKES

(from 70 mph in neutral)
Pedal load for 0.5g stops in lb

1	50-40	6	42
2	40-44	7	42
3	42	8	42
4	42	9	42
5	42	10	42

RESPONSE (from 30 mph in neutral)

Load	g	Distance
20lb	0.22	137ft
40lb	0.44	68ft
60lb	0.58	50ft
80lb	0.77	39ft
100lb	0.95	31.7ft
110lb	1.01	29.8ft
Handbrake	0.25	120ft
Max. Gradient 1 in 3		

CLUTCH

Pedal 30lb and 5½in.

COMPARISONS

MAXIMUM SPEED MPH
Jensen Interceptor	(£6,138)	137
Citroen SM	(£5,500)	135
BMW 3.0 CS	**(£5,345)**	**131**
Porsche 911 T	(£3,671)	129
Triumph Stag	(£2,326)	116
Lotus Elan Plus 2S 130	(£2,710)	121

0-60 MPH, SEC
Jensen Interceptor	6.4
Lotus Plus 2S 130	7.4
BMW 3.0 CS	**8.0**
Porsche 911T	8.1
Citroen SM	9.0
Triumph Stag	9.3

STANDING ¼-MILE, SEC
Jensen Interceptor	15.0
Lotus Elan Plus 2S 130	15.4
Porsche 911T	16.0
BMW 3.0 CS	**16.2**
Triumph Stag	17.1

OVERALL MPG
Lotus Plus 2S 130	23.3
BMW 3.0 CS	**20.8**
Triumph Stag	20.7
Porsche 911T	17.9
Citroen SM	16.0
Jensen Interceptor	12.9

GEARING (with 195/70-14in. tyres)
Top 20.7 mph per 1,000 rpm
3rd 14.9 mph per 1,000 rpm
2nd 9.5 mph per 1,000 rpm
1st 5.4 mph per 1,000 rpm

CONSUMPTION

FUEL
(At constant speed—mpg)
30 mph	32.8
40 mph	34.2
50 mph	32.3
60 mph	30.1
70 mph	26.5
80 mph	22.7
90 mph	20.1
100 mph	17.3

Typical mpg . . 24 (11.8 litres/100km)
Calculated (DIN) mpg
24.1 (11.7 litres/100km)
Overall mpg . . 20.8 (13.6 litres/100km)
Grade of fuel Super, 5-star (min. 100 RM)

OIL
Consumption (SAE 30) . . . . Negligible

TEST CONDITIONS:
Weather: Fine. Wind: 0 mph: Temperature: 27 deg. C. (83 deg. F.). Barometer: 29.8 in. hg. Humidity: 50 per cent. Surfaces: Dry concrete and asphalt.

WEIGHT:
Kerb weight 27.0 cwt (3,030lb-1.373kg). (With oil, water and half full fuel tank.) Distribution, per cent F, 56.2; R, 43.8. Laden as tested: 30.9cwt (3,460lb-1570kg).

TURNING CIRCLES:
Between kerbs L, 32 ft 2 in.; R. 33 ft 9 in. Between walls L, 34 ft 6 in.; R, 36 ft 1 in. Steering wheel turns, lock to lock 4. Figures taken at 3,600 miles by our own staff at the Motor Industry Research Association proving ground at Nuneaton and on the Continent.

STANDARD GARAGE 16ft x 8ft 6in.

SPECIFICATION

FRONT ENGINE, REAR-WHEEL DRIVE

ENGINE
Cylinders	6, in line
Main bearings.	7
Cooling system	Water; pump, viscous-coupled fan and thermostat
Bore	89mm (3.5 in.)
Stroke	80mm (3.15 in.)
Displacement	2.985 c.c. (182 cu. in.)
Valve gear	Single chain-driven overhead camshaft
Compression ratio	9.0-to-1. Min. octane rating: 100
Carburettors	Two Zenith 35/40 INAT two-choke
Fuel pump	Pierburg mechanical
Oil filter	Full flow, renewable element
Max. power	180 bhp (net) at 6,000 rpm
Max. torque	188 lb. ft (net) at 3,700 rpm

TRANSMISSION
Clutch	Fichtel and Sachs, diaphragm spring
Gearbox	Four-speed, all-synchromesh
Gear ratios	Top 1.0
	Third 1.4
	Second 2.2
	First 3.86
	Reverse 4.3
Final drive	Hypoid bevel 3.45 to 1

CHASSIS and BODY
Construction	Integral with steel body

SUSPENSION
Front	Independent, MacPherson struts, lower links, coil springs, telescopic dampers, anti-roll bar
Rear	Independent, semi-trailing arms, coil springs, telescopic dampers, anti-roll bar

STEERING
Type	ZF ball and nut, with optional hydraulic power assistance
Wheel dia.	16½ in.

BRAKES
Make and type	Ventilated discs front and rear twin circuit hydraulic system Servos 2ATE vacuum
Dimensions	F 10.7 in. dia. R 10.7 in. dia.
Swept area	F 213 sq. in., R 213 sq. in. Total 426 sq. in. (276 sq. in./ton laden)

WHEELS
Type	Light alloy, five-stud fixing, 6.0 in. wide rim
Tyres—make	Michelin
—type	XVR radial ply tubed
—size	195/70–14 in.

EQUIPMENT
Battery	12 Volt 55 Ah
Alternator	630 watt
Headlamps	4 Hella quartz iodine, 220/110 watt (total)
Reversing lamps.	Standard
Electric fuses	10
Screen wipers	2-speed and intermittent
Screen washer	Standard, electric
Interior heater	Standard, air blending
Heated backlight	Standard
Safety belts	Standard, inertia reel
Interior trim	Velor or leatherette seats, PVC headlining
Floor covering	Carpet
Jack	Screw pillar, winding handle
Jacking points	4, under sills
Windscreen	Toughened
Underbody protection	Rubber underseal at wheel arches

MAINTENANCE
Fuel tank	15.4 Imp. gallons (no reserve) (70 litres)
Cooling system	21 pints (including heater)
Engine sump	8.8 pints (5 litres) SAE 30. Change oil every 4,000 miles. Change filter element every 4,000 miles
Gearbox	2.1 pints SAE 80. Change oil every 16,000 miles
Final drive	2.6 pints SAE 90EP. Check oil level 8,000 miles
Grease	None required
Tyre pressures	F 29; R 29 psi (normal and fast driving); F 32; R 32 psi (full load)
Max. payload	3,858 lb (1,750 kg)

PERFORMANCE DATA
Top gear mph per 1,000 rpm	20.7
Mean piston speed at max. power	3,150 ft./min.
Bhp per ton laden	116

Cloth seats are available and there is unpolished wood on the facia and along the door trims below the cappings. The steering wheel has a leather rim

AUTOTEST
BMW 3.0 CS . . .

to the bonnet release and locking lever at the side of the glove compartment rather difficult.

Provision is made in the wooden facia for a radio loudspeaker, but surprisingly the car's price does not include a radio. Ventilation is very comprehensive and includes adjustable central vanes ahead of the gear lever from which a welcome supply of cool air is available in summer. A separate lever controls the main air inlet and as it is moved beyond the full position it brings on the three speed fan. At its minimum speed, the fan is inaudible, yet still effective. The heater is an air-blending unit giving immediate responsive temperature variation as the regulating lever is moved, simple red and blue marking showing its function. Rear extraction allows a good through-flow.

Minor controls are governed mainly by two steering column-mounted levers, the right hand one being moved up or down for the indicators, and pulled towards the driver to turn on the windscreen washers. At the same time the wipers operate, going on for three or four strokes after the water flow ceases. The lever is pressed in to work the wipers without the washers, operation then being determined by the position of a pull-up switch to the left of the gear lever. When the switch is down, the wipers work through a pause control, once every five or six seconds. Pulled up, the knob gives slow and fast wiper speeds as well. The left lever is a combined dipswitch and headlamps flasher switch. Four Hella headlamps are fitted; they have tungsten-halogen bulbs and should give good range, but on the test car they were set too low.

On the console around the gear lever are switches for the electric windows. The glasses

do not go completely down when lowered, but the pillarless design allows the car to be pleasantly open and airy in hot weather, while the sealing between front and rear windows effectively eliminates wind whistle at speed. The electric operation of the big door windows is too slow, and it is a nuisance that they function only when the ignition is switched on. Separate rear window switches are fitted in the back armrests. A catch on the side of the front seat squabs allows the backrests to tip forward for access to the rear compartment. Provided front seat occupants move their seats fairly well forward, rear legroom is acceptable and to travel there is extremely comfortable.

Inspection under the bonnet gives an impression of the excellent engineering that has gone into the mechanical side of the car; and the coachwork is also finished to a high, but not quite equivalent, standard, the BMW 3.0 CS scores over some of its competitors in being more compact and practical as a town car, while still very fast and manageable as a main road express. We thoroughly enjoyed driving it, and its appearance aroused admiration wherever we went with it.

MANUFACTURER: Bayerische Motoren Werke AG, 8 München 13, Lercheroner Strasse 76, West Germany.

UK CONCESSIONAIRES: BMW Concessionaires (GB) Ltd., 361-365 Chiswick High Road, London, W.4.

PRICES
Basic	£4,092.67
Purchase Tax	£1,252.33
Seat belts (standard)	
Total (in G.B.)	£5,345.00

EXTRAS (inc. P.T.)
Power-assisted steering	£119.00
Automatic transmission	£220.00
Air-conditioning	£485.00

*Fitted to test car

PRICE AS TESTED	**£5,464.00**

Meanwhile, Munich has been at it too . . .

THE POWER RACE...BMW STYLE!

Capturing the older, richer man who is currently infatuated with Mercedes is the name of the latest BMW game—and the weapon is a new 180 bhp, 187 lb/ft 2885cc engine in a car called the 3.0 S. . . . From Gordon Wilkins.

THE BATTLE ROYAL between BMW and Mercedes-Benz for the international quality market is now so lively they're beginning to steal each others' trousers.

Mercedes, with the prestige image — world's oldest car manufacturer and all that — is deliberately excluding references to past history from its publicity. In fact, the recent British-organised veteran car run to Stuttgart was a minor embarrassment to it in Germany.

So now it wants to build a more youthful image — but a 350 SL sports at $12,000 isn't going to provide practical experience for many of the young.

Meanwhile, BMW on the other hand has made a hit with the young and successful with the 1600 and 2002 and now is trying to reinforce *its* appeal to the older, richer man. In this light, the 3-litre coupe introduced in March has now been followed up — at last — by a new 3-litre saloon: the 3.0 S.

It's based on the 2800, both in

body and engine. The engine is raised from the old 2788 cc capacity by increasing the bore 3 mm to 89 mm for a capacity of 2885 cc so it's not really 3-litres. The output goes up from 170 bhp at 6000 rpm to 180 bhp (and remember, with BMW they're very real horses indeed) and the torque jumps from 173 lb/ft at 3700 rpm to 187 lb/ft.

To back all this up, there are new ventilated disc brakes (all round) and light alloy wheels. First-rate power steering and a heated rear window are standard of course, along with headrests on all four seats, and electric windows are optional.

Extra bright metal has been added, too, along with Mercedes-style round screen pillars, rear window and boot lid, but the radiator grille and headlamp casings are matt black.

Even more than the 2800, this is a real executive express on the motorways. It snaps from 0 to 60 mph in eight seconds (8.9 in the 2800) and covers the standing quarter mile in 16.2 (16.7). It cruises easily at 115 mph and then winds up to a maximum of 127 (124). In short it is opulent, luxurious and bloody fast; and the one I tried had the optional automatic transmission that works very well and will probably appeal to its many buyers.

But off the autobahn and rushing along the winding woodland roads of Bavaria, I was less enthusiastic. The ride is very good; softer and quieter than on the 2800, but I felt it had been bought at the cost of reduced nippiness and lower cornering power. Anti-roll bars are now relied upon more to control body sway rather than the level-adjusting dampers, but even so there was more roll than one associates with BMWs. And a quick slalom test soon got the big radial tyres squealing loudly.

But then, the man this car is aimed at probably has forgotten about sports car driving (even if he ever knew) and the BMW range still offers many models that combine high performance with exceptional chuckability. And if you do want to corner as fast as then you were young, heavy duty springs and dampers are optional.

Following the dazzling series of new models already introduced this year — the 2000 TII Touring, the 2002 convertible, the 3-litre coupe and now 3-litre saloon — other four-cylinder models have been improved in detail. And there is a new 2-door 1802 that has the 2-litre block with the 1600 crankshaft, 1766 cc and a very useful 90 bhp DIN at 5250 rpm with lots of torque.

Now I'm just waiting for the new 2-litre four-door cars due next year.

New, racy look of BMW's biggest express: subtle rich businessman-type dress-up gear includes matt black grille, headlight surrounds.

Making sure everyone knows what's under the bonnet . . . big badge-work squats on the boot lip.

The 3.0 CS coupe has also been slightly upgraded. It now has ventilated discs on all four wheels.

AUTO TEST

BMW 3.0S

Five seats; 127 mph; 0 to 60 mph in 8 sec and 21.3 mpg

AT-A-GLANCE: Latest version of BMW six-cylinder saloon with larger engine and more performance. Excellent refinement bestowed by superbly sweet power unit and light manual gearbox. Much improved brakes, better handling, but slightly more choppy ride. Same remarkable fuel consumption as before. Well finished throughout. Very satisfying car at all times.

IT was at the Geneva Show this year, after a successful racing programme using a prototype 3-litre engine, that BMW introduced the first of their new models using an enlarged six-cylinder power unit. That was the 3.0 CS coupé and we published a full test of the right-hand-drive version on 15 July last.

This week the saloon powered by the same engine is launched in the UK, so once again our Autotest is very topical. As well as an additional 10 bhp and 15 lb. ft. more torque, the 3.0S has ventilated disc brakes on all four wheels (with duplicated hydraulic lines to the front callipers), improved front suspension geometry, intermittent as well as two-speed wiper action, revised seats with rear headrests in addition to those in front and some detail changes to the ventilation system and exterior trim. The limited-slip differential and self-levelling rear suspension have been deleted from the specification and the price goes up by £191 compared with the 2800 saloon which is discontinued.

Changes to the engine comprise little more than a 3mm increase in bore size, the same camshaft and twin progressive-choke Solex carburettors being retained. This is enough to push the DIN output up from 170 to 180 mph and peak torque up from 173 to 188 lb. ft.

Top speed therefore goes up from 124 to 127 mph (the overall gearing remains the same) and acceleration is improved by similar substantial margins. From 0 to 60 mph, for example, comes down from 8.9sec to 8 sec dead, and the 0 to 100 mph time is down from 27.8 to 23.9sec. The standing quarter-mile time is now just under 16sec.

Compared with other high performance cars in the same class, like the Jaguar XJ6 4.2, the BMW is substantially quicker. In general terms the XJ6 we tested in May this year worked out

Above: The six-cylinder engine is inclined to the right and accessibility once the air cleaner is removed is excellent. The bonnet lid is self-supporting

Below: The 3.0S is distinguished from the 2800 by its matt black grille and bright metal side rubbing strips

Above: By deleting two noughts from the type number, BMW have been able to enlarge the size of the figures substantially

Left: Instrument layout is superb, four dials and a row of warning lamps being behind a single glass. The wood of the steering wheel feels real, but the facia and door sill strips are synthetic

BMW 3.0S (2,985 c.c.)

ACCELERATION

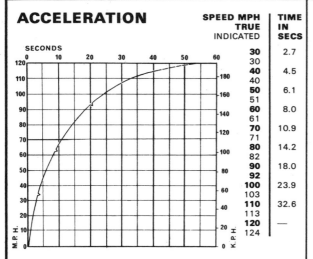

SPEED MPH TRUE	INDICATED	TIME IN SECS
30	30	2.7
40	40	4.5
50	51	6.1
60	61	8.0
70	71	10.9
80	82	14.2
90	92	18.0
100	103	23.9
110	113	32.6
120	124	—

GEAR RATIOS AND TIME IN SEC

mph	Top (3.45)	3rd (4.83)	2nd (7.58)
10-30	—	6.3	3.8
20-40	—	5.6	3.4
30-50	8.3	5.2	3.1
40-60	7.7	5.1	3.7
50-70	8.3	5.5	—
60-80	9.9	6.1	—
70-90	10.1	7.5	—
80-100	11.9	—	—

Standing ¼-mile
15.9 sec 86 mph
Standing Kilometre
29.5 sec 108 mph
Test distance
1,611 miles
Mileage recorder
0.7 per cent over-reading

PERFORMANCE

MAXIMUM SPEEDS

Gear	mph	kph	rpm
Top (mean)	127	204	6,150
(best)	128	206	6,200
3rd	93	150	6,250
2nd	62	100	6,500
1st	35	56	6,500

BRAKES

FADE
(from 70 mph in neutral)
Pedal load for 0.5g stops in lb.

1	30	6	46-40
2	40-30-40	7	47-40
3	40-35-30	8	47-40
4	47-42	9	47-40
5	47-32	10	47-40

RESPONSE (from 30 mph in neutral)

Load	g	Distance
20lb	0.16	188ft
40lb	0.40	75ft
60lb	0.63	48ft
80lb	0.78	39ft
100lb	0.88	34ft
120lb	0.98	30.7ft
Handbrake	0.33	91ft
Max. Gradient 1 in 3		

CLUTCH

Pedal 38lb and 5in.

COMPARISONS

MAXIMUM SPEED MPH
Aston Martin DBS (£5,946) 140
BMW 3.0S (£3,538) **127**
Jaguar XJ6 4.2 (£2,863) 123
Chevrolet Impala (£3,299) 116
Rover 3.5 (£2,548) 108

0-60 MPH, SEC
BMW 3.0S **8.0**
Aston Martin DBS 8.6
Jaguar XJ6 . . . . 8.7
Chevrolet Impala 9.0
Rover 3.5 . . . . 12.4

STANDING ¼-MILE, SEC
BMW 3.0S **15.9**
Aston Martin DBS 16.3
Jaguar XJ6 . . . . 16.5
Chevrolet Impala 16.8
Rover 3.5 . . . . 18.3

OVERALL MPG
BMW 3.0S **23.6**
Rover 3.5 . . . . 19.2
Jaguar XJ6 . . . . 16.0
Aston Martin DBS 12.7
Chevrolet Impala 10.3

GEARING
(with 195/70-14in. tyres)

Top . . . . . 20.7 mph per 1,000 rpm
3rd . . . . . 14.9 mph per 1,000 rpm
2nd . . . . . 9.5 mph per 1,000 rpm
1st . . . . . 5.4 mph per 1,000 rpm

CONSUMPTION

FUEL
(At constant speed—mpg)

30 mph 40.0
40 mph 37.4
50 mph 34.1
60 mph 28.5
70 mph 26.3
80 mph 22.3
90 mph 18.9
100 mph 16.6
Typical mpg . . 24 (11.8 litres/100km)
Calculated (DIN)
mpg 23.9 (11.8 litres/100km)
Overall mpg . . 21.3 (13.2 litres/100km)
Grade of fuel Super, 5-star (min. 100 RM)

OIL
Consumption (SAE 10W/40)   Negligible

TEST CONDITIONS:
Weather: Fine. Wind: 5-10 mph.
Temperature: 18 deg.C. (64 deg.F).
Barometer: 29.1 in. hg. Humidity: 52 per cent
Surfaces: Dry concrete and asphalt.

WEIGHT:
Kerb Weight 27.8 cwt (3,114lb-1,415 kg).
(with oil, water and half full fuel tank).
Distribution, per cent F, 54.5; R, 45.5.
Laden as tested 31.0 cwt (3,474 lb-1,580 kg).

TURNING CIRCLES:
Between kerbs L, 34 ft 5 in.; R, 33 ft 1 in.
Between walls L, 36 ft 5 in.; R, 35 ft 0 in.
Steering wheel turns, lock to lock 4.
Figures taken at 3,500 miles by our own
staff at the Motor Industry Research
Association proving ground at Nuneaton
and on the Continent.

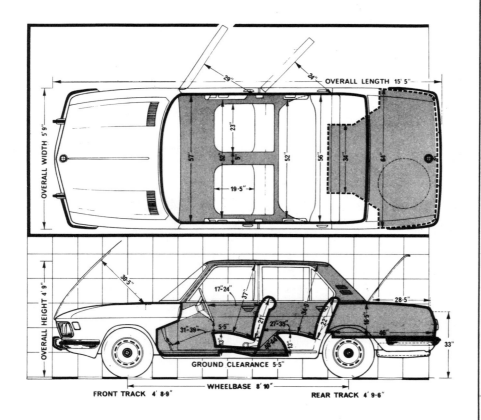

STANDARD GARAGE 16ft x 8ft 6in.

SPECIFICATION

FRONT ENGINE, REAR-WHEEL DRIVE

ENGINE
Cylinders	6, in-line
Main bearings	7
Cooling system	Water; pump, viscous-coupled fan and thermostat
Bore	89mm (3.5in.)
Stroke	80mm (3.15in.)
Displacement	2,985 c.c. (182 cu.in.)
Valve gear	Single chain-driven overhead camshaft
Compression ratio	9.0-to-1 Min. octane rating: 99RM
Carburettors	Two twin-choke Solex 35/40 INAT
Fuel pump	Pierburg mechanical
Oil filter	Full-flow, renewable element
Max. power	180 bhp (DIN) at 6,000 rpm
Max. torque	188 lb.ft. (DIN) at 3,700 rpm

TRANSMISSION
Clutch	Fichtel and Sachs, diaphragm spring
Gearbox	Four-speed, all-synchromesh
Gear ratios	Top 1.0
	Third 1.40
	Second 2.20
	First 3.86
	Reverse 4.30
Final drive	Hypoid bevel, 3.45 to 1

CHASSIS and BODY
Construction	Integral with steel body

SUSPENSION
Front	Independent, MacPherson struts, coil springs, lower links, telescopic dampers, anti-roll bar
Rear	Independent, semi-trailing arms, coil springs, telescopic dampers

STEERING
Type	ZF ball and nut with optional power assistance
Wheel dia.	16.5 in.

BRAKES
Type	Ventilated disc front and rear with dual hydraulic lines to the front
Servos	2 ATE vacuum type
Dimensions	F 10.7 in. dia.
	R 10.7 in. dia.
Swept area	F 213 sq. in., R 213 sq. in.
	Total 426 sq. in. (275 sq. in./ton laden)

WHEELS
Type	Pressed steel, 5-stud fixing. 6 in. wide rim
Tyres—make	Various, Veith-Pirelli on test car
—type	70-series radial-ply tubed
—size	DR 70HR (195)–14 in.

EQUIPMENT
Battery	12 Volt 55 Ah.
Alternator	630 watt
Headlamps	Bosch Tungsten Halogen 220/110 watt (total)
Reversing lamp	Standard
Electric fuses	12
Screen wipers	2-speed and intermittent (5 sec delay)
Screen washer	Standard electric
Interior heater	Standard air blending
Heated backlight	Standard
Safety belts	Standard/Extra
Interior trim	Pvc or cloth seats, pvc headlining
Floor covering	Woven carpet
Jack	Screw pillar
Jacking points	4, under sills
Windscreen	Toughened
Underbody protection	Rubber compound under wheel arches

MAINTENANCE
Fuel tank	16.5 Imp. gallons (75 litres) (no reserve)
Cooling system	21 pints (including heater)
Engine sump	10 pints (5.5 litres) SAE 10W/40 Change oil every 4,000 miles. Change filter element every 4,000 miles
Gearbox	2.1 pints SAE 80. Change oil every 16,000 miles
Final drive	2.6 pints Hypoy 90. Change oil every 8,000 miles
Grease	No points
Tyre pressures	F 28; R 28 psi (normal driving) F 30; R 30 psi (fast driving)
Max payload	1,035 lb (470 kg)

PERFORMANCE DATA
Top gear mph per 1,000 rpm	20.7
Mean piston speed at max. power	3,150 ft/min.
Bhp per ton laden	116

AUTOTEST
BMW 3.0S . . .

very close on performance with the BMW 2800, so the differences are about the same as those already quoted. In making comparisons though it is all too easy to forget that the BMW has only a 3-litre engine, and despite its five-seater bulk and 27cwt kerb weight, its acceleration is not much slower than that of the E-type 2 + 2 4.2 (0 to 60 mph 7.4sec, 0 to 100 mph 19.4sec) and from rest to 30 mph it is the equal.

To be truly fair this remarkable BMW performance should be compared with that of cars with a similar engine size. It is only when we look at the figures for the Broadspeed Bullitt (0 to 60 mph 8.1sec, 0 to 100 mph 24.5sec, top speed 124 mph) and the Uren Comanche (0 to 60 mph 8.4sec, 0 to 100 mph 24.6sec, top speed 132 mph), both cars being based on the Ford Capri 3000 with power output increased to 185-190 bhp, that the true mettle of the BMW starts to show up.

It is exactly true to the BMW tradition that the figures we measured on a car imported new and run-in here with no special preparation came precisely within the factory performance specification with very little effort on our part and virtually no recourse to special techniques other than two practice starts.

Getting the 3.0S away from rest quickly was easy. With about 4,000 rpm showing on the dead accurate rev counter, we dropped the clutch and shot away with several yards of wheelspin, reaching 30 mph in only 2.7sec. The tyres yelped with the snatch change into second, but not into third and top. There is a red warning on the rev counter from about 6,200 to 8,000 rpm but the engine revved up to it so freely that we ran slightly over to about 6,500 before changing up.

The gearbox has the same ratios as on the 2800 but a change to stronger synchromesh makes the action slightly more notchy and a trifle rubbery when going into bottom at rest. It is still an ultra-light and tremendously precise shift, one which must surely be the envy of all other manufacturers. The clutch is both light and progressive with plenty of bite, a truly remarkable achievement for a car this heavy with so much torque. To be honest we did not notice the effect of not having a limited-slip differential (it had only a 50 per cent locking action in any case) and on decent tyres there is no shortage of traction even in the wet. Unfortunately the test car was shod with

German-made Veith-Pirelli radials which were miserably lacking in wet road grip and seemed very prone to squeal in the dry. We know from our experience with the 3.0 CS coupe that Michelin XVR radials transform the car in this respect and it seems a pity that all BMW 3-litres delivered to this country cannot come with them fitted.

If any aspect of the 2800 could be criticized, it was the brakes which did not seem to take kindly to hard use and became rather rough and rumbly when used hard from high speed. This characteristic has now been completely eliminated by changing to ventilated discs all round, backed up twin vacuum servos and duplicated hydraulic lines to the front callipers. Thus, if one circuit fails 75 per cent of the braking effect remains acting on all four wheels and if the other circuit fails, 60 per cent remains on the front wheels only. There is also the mechanical handbrake which recorded 0.33g from 30 mph with ease.

The brakes on the test car were a little lacking in initial bite (like many dual systems), and it took as much as 120lb effort to record an ultimate of 0.98g, which was the best possible on the Veith-Pirelli tyres. When checked out for fade, there was some initial fluctuation before the system settled down to give repeated stabilized readings which decreased as the car's speed dropped. This speed sensitivity was reversed with the brakes cold, 0.5g from 30 mph requiring as much as 50lb effort compared with only 30lb from 70 mph. The net result is that the brakes feel better the faster you travel, which is a nice way to have things in a car with this kind of performance.

Power steering is still an optional extra and it was fitted to the test car. It seems to have more feel than on the 2800. Slight front-end geometry changes give more negative camber to the outside wheel on a bend and the whole car feels better balanced as a result. Before there was initial understeer which gradually gave way to slight roll oversteer, but now the characteristic is virtually neutral, with immediate steering response at all times. It is probably because of this change that self-levelling rear suspension is now felt to be unnecessary.

Most of the time the ride is the same smooth and very refined affair it was on the 2800, but occasionally there seems to be some conflict between front and rear spring rates which sets up rather too much pitching on roads like French *chaussée déformée*, especially when the car is well laden. As well as the 1,600 miles we drove the 3.0S in this country we drove a similar model through France for another 200 miles or so mostly on lesser grade roads. It was here that we spent several hours in the back and tried the optional cloth seat trim.

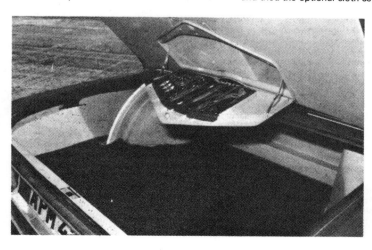

There is a carpet on the floor of the boot, which has the spare wheel under it, and a very comprehensive toolkit in the lid

AUTOTEST
BMW 3.0S . . .

Fittings and furniture

The driver sits quite high in the 3.0S with a commanding view over the large flat-deck bonnet and through the low-silled side windows. Pedal angles and operating arcs are good, provided you sit well up to them, but the throttle is a bit awkward in the latter part of its travel. The short stubby gearlever is exactly where it should be and the long-handled handbrake is well-placed between the seats. The 16.5in. dia. steering wheel feels too large and it is set just a shade too high.

Upholstery on the test car shown here was a kind of plaited pvc which despite its breathing capabilities was hot and sticky to sit on in warm weather. We much preferred the optional cloth which had the added advantage of softening the padding, or so it seemed, and giving a much more suitable air of luxury to the interior.

Front seats have reclining backrests and detachable headrests (as on the 2800) and similar headrests are now mounted also on the rear shelf for those in the back. They tended to get slightly in the way, of vision through the rear-view mirror, even when folded as far down as possible.

There is at least 40in. of total rear legroom even with the front seats right back, and enough headroom for 6ft passengers. In the middle of the back seat is a folding armrest which tucks away to give ample three-abreast seating (56in. of hip room). Front seats feel slightly short in the cushion and much too firm for real comfort when covered in pvc.

Directly in front of the driver is just about the best integrated instrument panel we have ever seen. Under a single glass are set a huge matching speedometer and rev counter, with the fuel gauge and a temperature gauge between them. Below in the centre is a strip containing all the warning lamps for ignition, oil pressure, main beam, low fuel level, handbrake on and low brake fluid level.

Under the right-hand side of the wheel rim is a stalk for the indicators (and left or right hand parking lamps with the ignition off), screen washers and wipers. The washers squirt when this lever is pulled up towards the wheel and at the same time the wipers start up and continue for several wipes after the water stops. Pushing in the end starts and stops the wipers alternately, their speed selector switch being right across the car in its original position to the left of the ashtray. As well at two continuous speeds there is an intermittent action with 5sec. delay between double sweeps.

A similar stalk under the left of the wheel is the dipswitch and headlamp flasher. Side and headlamps are operated by a push-pull knob on the facia to the right of the instrument cluster. Headlamps extinguish automatically when the ignition is switched off.

Under the facia are three coloured push-buttons which light up when in use. One (amber) is for the heated back window, another (red) for the four-way hazard-warning flashers and the third (green) for fog lamps when fitted. The horn is sounded by push bars in each of the three steering wheel spokes.

The main interior mirror can be dipped at night and the standard outside one on the driver's door is fitted with smoked glass.

Heater controls are grouped in the centre of the facia, with a progressive air-blending temperature selector, an air intake lever which also operates the three-speed booster fan, a distribution control and an air-flow regulator for the very effective ventilation system. Extractors in the rear quarters are now hidden under flush panels which replace the 2800's painted grilles.

In front of the passenger seat is a deep drop-down glove box behind which is concealed the bonnet release and fuse box. In the centre ahead of the gearlever is a big hollow console, ideal for maps, guide books, camera or handbag. In each front door there is a pocket and two more in the backs of the front seats.

It is hard to think of a car less likely to need spanners, but with every BMW 3-litre there comes the kind of tool-kit most mechanics would guard with their life. It is almost hidden in a padded compartment in the boot lid and contains spare bulbs, fuses, spanners, three new spark plugs, Allen keys, feeler gauges and even a spare wheel nut. Unfortunately the ring spanners do not have cranked ends, which makes them much less useful.

The spare wheel is under the floor of the boot, so virtually all the luggage must come out in the event of a puncture. On the right inside the boot is a very useful stowage box where odds and ends can be packed away to prevent them rattling.

The BMW six cylinder cars were the first to use flat smooth sided "computer" keys which operate the lock tumblers by means of recesses drilled to different depths. The keys are therefore smooth in the pocket and much stronger. Two are provided in the form of a master key for all locks and a sub key for the doors and ignition only.

Accessibility under the bonnet is good, especially after the large flat air cleaner has been removed. The lid is self-supporting and it has a positive lock.

Four tungsten halogen headlamps give a tremendous blaze of light on main beam, but not much spread in contrast when dipped. Adjustment is critical but easily taken care of by means of plastic knurled screws under the bonnet on the backs of the light units.

It is very hard indeed to think of any car which makes even a fair showing against the BMW 3.0S when all its considerable appeal, in terms of performance, economy, refinement and carrying power, is taken into account. Some models are more luxuriously trimmed inside (especially in the opinion of those who put great score by such things as real wood veneer and genuine leather), some are a little quieter to ride in and others perhaps more comfortable over undulating roads. But when it comes down to the real crux of how much fun there is in driving, how much verve the car naturally wants to display and how much satisfaction it gives the driver, the BMW 3.0S in our opinion is unmatched in the saloon car class. □

MANUFACTURER: Bayerische Motoren Werke AG, 8 München 13, Lercheroner Strasse 76, W. Germany.

UK CONCESSIONAIRES: BMW Concessionaires (GB) Ltd., 361-365 Chiswick High Road, London, W.4.

PRICES

Basic	£2,828.84
Purchase Tax	£709.16
Seat belts (approx.)	£17.00
Total (in G.B.)	£3,555.00

EXTRAS (inc. P.T.)

Power steering	£114.00

* Fitted to test car

PRICE AS TESTED £3,669.00

Left: There is a locking glove box in front of the passenger, a large cubby in the centre console and roomy pockets in each front door

Right: Adjustable rear headrests are standard on the 3.0S and there is a drop-down centre armrest

BMW FOR '72

Displacement is up, models are fewer and power goes up <u>and</u> down

BY RON WAKEFIELD

1972 IS A mixed year for BMW, as far as the U.S. is concerned. First, it's a year of model attrition. The 1.6-liter 2-door is off the market, as are the original 6-cyl models 2500 and 2800. Four models are left: 2002, 2002tii (new, and tested by R&T two months ago), Bavaria sedan and 3.0CS (Coupe Sport).

Second, it's a year of power increases *and* decreases. The 2002tii with fuel injection by Kugelfischer and 140 bhp SAE gross, is the most powerful 4-cyl model ever offered by BMW here. The regular 2002 stays at 113 bhp, despite a decrease in compression ratio from 8.5:1 to 8.3:1 to let it run on the sacred 91-octane fuel, and suffers the indignity of exhaust-gas recirculation for oxides-of-nitrogen control at low speeds. Both these 4-cyl models are face-lifted mildly and have minor functional improvements as described in the October test; the hatchback "Touring" models won't be available here for a while yet.

The 6-cyl Bavaria and CS both get the 3-liter engine; its bore is up to 89.0 from 86.0 mm to give a useful displacement increase over the former 2.8-liter unit. The 3.0's torque curve is fatter, 213 lb-ft SAE gross peaking at 3500 rpm, vs 200 @ 3700 for the 2.8. BMW engineers have stuck with the 3.64:1 final drive (in Europe this is used on the 2500, a 3.45:1 on 2.8s and 3.0s) for better acceleration at the expense of top speed on the Bavaria and extended it to the CS. Peak power, however, is down—from 192 bhp at 6000

rpm to 190 at 5800—because of the predictable decrease in compression ratio, again to 8.3:1 from 9.0:1. Top speed, therefore, is limited to 122 mph for both models by the engine's rev range and acceleration through the gears should be materially improved on both models. And fuel consumption will go up a bit with an accompanying decrease in per-gallon cost. The 6-cyl BMWs, by the way, don't require exhaust recycling for NO_x control and generally require less drastic alterations to carburetion and spark timing for emission control than most current engines.

There's a surprise behind the engine—a new gearbox, built by Getrag, a part of the ZF organization which is now more than half owned by Borg-Warner. The 2.5-2.8 gearbox, also a ZF unit with B-W synchronizers, wasn't quite up to the 3.0's torque and had exhibited weak synchro action on 2nd gear in many 2.8s. Ratios are virtually the same in the new box. For the optional automatic transmission the story is similar: gone is the old ZF, whose mushy shifts spoiled the car's character, replaced by the well-known Borg-Warner Model 12 automatic which is built in England and is, like the ZF, a 3-speed affair with torque converter.

The Bavaria gets a front anti-roll bar as standard equip-ment and we hope this clears up that question once and for all. It also gets recalibrated rear springs and shocks to smooth its slightly pitchy ride, ventilated rotors for its disc brakes, improved front seats, and a third muffler between the original two.

The 2800CS coupe, one of the most handsome and refined GTs available, was nevertheless a strange bird, sharing its body aft of the windshield, rear suspension and drum rear brakes with the old 4-cyl 2000CS despite a $2000 price premium over the fully disc-braked Bavaria/2500/2800. Also a bit crab-tracked with 1.7 in. less in the rear, the CS in 3-liter form remains so but gets proper brakes with internally vented rotors like the 3.0 Bavaria's all around. But the coupe doesn't get the recalibrated rear suspension. It shares the Bavaria's new transmissions.

Driving Impressions

WE TRIED the Bavaria and CS in Germany and found them to utterly match the expectations generated by their alterations. Through the gears they are noticeably quicker than their predecessors at first but run out of breath a bit sooner; the 3-liter is also a little quieter with less open-throttle power

BMW FOR '72

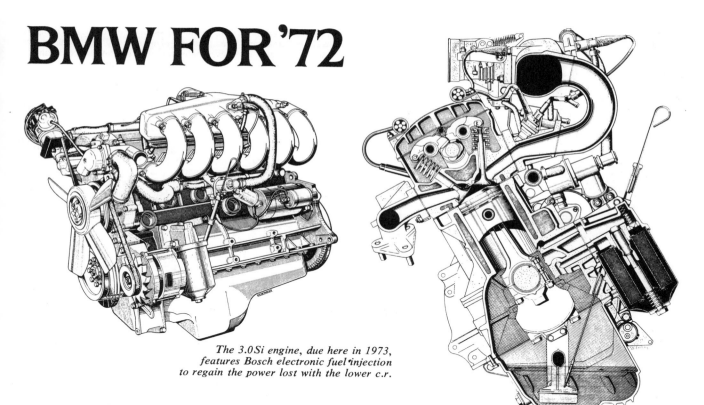

*The 3.0Si engine, due here in 1973,
features Bosch electronic fuel injection
to regain the power lost with the lower c.r.*

throb than the 2.8. The exhaust note is different—a bit less resonant, slightly lower in pitch and not quite so sporty.

In the Bavaria the ride is a little better, the pitch is gone and the seats really are nicer. Both models still carry 175-14 tires, rather small for their weight and, on the coupe's narrow rear track, looking absolutely tiny. They handle decently, at least in the dry, but at the coupe's price one is entitled to more cornering power and better appearance.

Fuel-Injection Sixes

THE BEST news lies in two additional models that won't find their way to the U.S. market until 1973; the 3.0Si and 3.0CSi, whose little "i"s are, as on the 2002tii, for fuel injection. But here it is the real wave of the future, Bosch electronic injection, giving these *Flagschiff* models an impressive 200 DIN bhp @ only 5500 rpm with the help of more radical valve timing. That's about 230 SAE gross bhp, but these ratings will be out of use by the time these cars appear over here. Figure 190 DIN for the U.S. version and you've still got a 15 percent increase over the 1972 carburetor engine. The 3.0Si will be offered in addition to the Bavaria at a higher price and has more luxurious trim and more extensive equipment including automatic rear suspension leveling; most likely the 3.0CSi will replace the CS and carry a higher price too. After all, who'd buy the carbureted version when the fuel injection is available?

One last item: Karmann, who builds the CS bodies, is also producing a limited series of lightweight, high-output coupes to homologate the lighter variant as a touring car in Group 2 and keep the CS in serious competition with the racing version of that Capri 2600 (p. 57) that's giving it such fits on the European sedan-racing circuit.

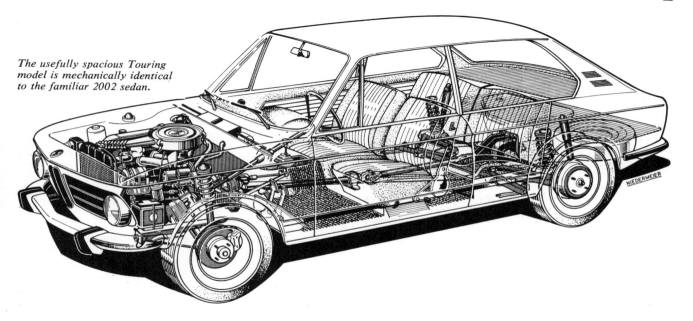

*The usefully spacious Touring
model is mechanically identical
to the familiar 2002 sedan.*

2 CAR TEST

BMW 3.0S
JAGUAR XJ6 4.2-LITRE OVERDRIVE

At first sight, comparatively testing a 3-litre high performance saloon against a 4.2-litre one may not seem a good idea. But the BMW 3.0S is highly competitive with the Jaguar XJ6 4.2-litre, in spite of a price tag inflated heavily by duties on the German car. In Britain the Jaguar with manual gearbox and overdrive as tested costs £2,926; total price of the BMW test car here is £3,652, which includes £114 for the optional power steering. In other countries however the price tables are turned, making the Jaguar the expensive foreigner.

Whatever the financial differences, the smaller-engined car from Munich more than matches the bigger capacity one from Coventry in straight-line performance. In some other equally important respects the other is dominant, or the two are closely matched. Both tend to appeal to the same sort of buyer who is looking for a four-five seater car, comfortable, refined, and of higher than usual performance from both engine and chassis.

Specification—BMW

Top saloon from this famous Bavarian manufacturer, the BMW 3.0S is a development of the highly-successful 2800. Apart from revised air-extraction vents and a little more embellishment, the spacious four-door body remains unchanged. Interior trim is also much as before, the most noticeable change being the provision of head restraints for rear seat passengers (fitted to front seats only on 2800 models). Also new are the intermittent-wipe facility (in addition to the usual two-speed

action) and courtesy switches for the rear doors.

Much of the BMW's success can be attributed to its superb power unit. An in-line six, it features a cast-iron block with light-alloy head. The robust crankshaft runs in seven main bearings and drives a single overhead-camshaft via a duplex chain. Valves are opposed at an included angle of 50 deg and are actuated by rocker followers. Two Solex twin-choke (two-stage) carburettors take care of breathing.

The 3.0S unit differs from the 2800 only in terms of bore size. This has been enlarged by 3 mm, resulting in a displacement of 2,985 c.c. (compared with the former 2,788 c.c.) and a *pro-rata* increase in power.

Of greater significance are the changes made to the braking system. Although disc diameter remains unchanged, all four are now of internally-ventilated design. Instead of a single direct-acting servo, each of the two hydraulic systems has its own ''in-line'' unit. As in the 2800 (and other models in the BMW range), the use of four-piston callipers has enabled the front brakes to be included in both systems—a valuable safety feature.

Apart from detail changes to the synchromesh units, the gearbox is the same as that used in the 2800. No overdrive is available, but ZF automatic transmission is listed as an extra (£239.00).

Like the 2800, the 3.0S has a limited-slip differential as standard.

Apart from detail geometry changes, the MacPherson-type front suspension is the same as that of the 2800. At the rear, the later car differs in not having self-levelling struts for control of the splayed trailing arms.

Steering is by ZF-Gemmer cam-and-roller mechanism, with power-assistance an optional extra (£114.00).

In basic form, the 3.0S sells for £3,538 (excluding seat belts).

Specification—Jaguar

Sensation of the 1968 Earls Court Motor Show, the XJ6 still ranks as one of the world's most coveted cars.

Rumour has it that the XJ6 was designed around Jaguar's new vee-12 power unit. When this fell foul of the ever-increasing demands of the US anti-emission laws, it became necessary to adapt the design to suit the faithful XK engine. So raptuous was its reception in this form that it has continued virtually unchanged.

There are three basic versions—the ''standard'' 2.8-litre, the de luxe 2.8-litre and the 4.2-litre model. Those seeking even greater luxury are catered for by the Daimler Sovereign variants, listed in 2.8-litre and 4.2-litre forms.

Like the BMW, the Jaguar has a cast-iron block and light-alloy head. The latter is of classic design, featuring a pair of direct-acting overhead camshafts and hemispherical combustion chambers. Drive to the camshafts is by duplex chain, in two stages. There are seven main bearings.

In 4.2-litre form, the unit has a bore of 92 mm and a stroke of 106 mm (same stroke as the XK 120), giving a displacement of 4,235 c.c. Breathing through a pair of SU HD8 carburettors, it develops 245 bhp (gross) at 5,500 rpm.

Disc brakes are employed on all four wheels, the rears being mounted inboard. Separate hydraulic circuits are provided for front and rear, power-assistance being provided by a single direct-acting servo.

An all-synchromesh four-speed gearbox is employed, with Laycock overdrive available as an extra (£64). Also listed is Borg-Warner type 12 automatic transmission (£149). Standard and automatic models have 3.31-to-1 final drives, whereas overdrive cars have a 3.54-to-1 ratio (4.2-litre models in each case).

The front suspension (employing double

wishbones, coil springs and telescopic dampers) features anti-dive geometry. The whole assembly, including the steering mechanism, is mounted on an insulated subframe.

At the rear, each universally-jointed half-shaft serves as the upper member of a pair of transverse-link systems, each controlled by two coil spring damper units. Again, the whole assembly (including the final drive) is mounted on an insulated subframe.

Adwest power-assisted rack-and-pinion steering is standard on 4.2-litre models. Tyres are Dunlop SP Sport E70 VR 15, specially developed for this model.

In its least expensive form the 4.2-litre XJ6 is listed at £2,862 (excluding seat belts). The test car, an overdrive model, represents an outlay of £2,926.

Performance

Both cars are remarkably quick for their size but there is a tremendous difference in the character of each one's performance. Used to the full, the BMW goes, feels and sounds like a sports saloon with a refined but unmistakably sporting engine. Drive the Jaguar flat out and, in spite of some most skilful and almost totally successful disguise, you are aware of a power unit that, for all its complete smoothness and great flexibility at up to three-quarters of its range, sounds somewhat unhappy towards its peak.

The BMW engine while very flexible and producing a lot of torque (188 lb ft DIN at 3,700 rpm), is at its best at middling to high revs. It will pull satisfactorily in any gear from 1,000 rpm but really gets going at around 3,000 rpm. From that speed, past 5,000 rpm – which is where the under-square Jaguar six is red-lined —and right up to the 6,200 rpm limit the over-square BMW engine is most impressive.

Except that the car really needs an overdrive 5th for less fussy high speed cruising—top gear is a shade too low as on its predecessor the 2800—the gear ratios are well chosen for maximum acceleration. Changing up at 6,200 rpm gives speeds in each intermediate gear of 33, 59 and 92 mph, the revs dropping down to 3,500 from 1st to 2nd, 4,000 from 2nd to 3rd, and 4,450 from 3rd to 4th. The gearchange itself is a delight; the small gearlever comes readily to hand, is extraordinarily light and sweet to move, and is backed up by excellent synchromesh, and a clutch that needs an average amount of pedal effort (38lb).

Such a combination of engine and gearbox installed in an average weight chassis (for the capacity class) makes exciting standing start figures. 60 mph comes up in exactly 8 sec—which is better than a number of supposedly more exciting cars—the ¼-mile in 15.9 sec and 100 mph in 23.9 sec. The mean top speed is a notable 127 mph.

The much bigger-capacity Jaguar engine has better ''lugging-power'' at low-to-medium speeds, when it is also very refined, both within the engine itself and in the insulation of engine from chassis. As a result, the car feels nowhere near as fast as it really is. Gross maximum torque is 283 lb. ft. at near-enough the same speed as on the BMW, 3,750 rpm; that, plus the spread of power over the rev range

Two classic six-cylinder engines, the BMW (left) and the Jaguar (right). 21 years younger than the 24 years-old Jaguar design, the BMW unit is tolerably accessible once the air cleaner has been removed; the only awkward items are adjustment of power-steering and fan belts. Accessibility on the Jaguar is much better than it at first appears

is what makes this Jaguar leap so smoothly. There is little evidence of much work being done up to 4,000 rpm—apart from the result of that work—but over the last 1,000 rpm a harsh note creeps in, not encouraging one to push the engine to that extent habitually. The XK unit's flexibility is as superb as ever; the car will pull away from well below 1,000 rpm without the slightest hesitation.

Gear ratios are well chosen and evenly spaced. Changing up at 5,000 rpm, which corresponds to 37 mph in 1st, 57 in 2nd, 78 in 3rd and 110 in top (4th) the revs drop to 3,250 (1st-2nd) 3,700 (2nd-3rd), 3,650 (3rd-4th) and 3,900 rpm (4th-overdrive). The Laycock de Normanville overdrive acts only on top gear and is effectively the true top gear. Its high overall gearing suits the character of the engine perfectly, requiring only 3,600 rpm to drive it at a very restful and relaxed 100 mph. One tends, in fact, to drive the car at under 4,000 rpm at all times, since that gives one more than enough performance for nearly every occasion.

The gear-change is a little sticky and noticeably notchy. Synchromesh on the test car, which at the time of this test had done over 16,000 miles, was not unbeatable in fast changes from 3rd to 4th. The clutch is tiring in traffic, needing nearly 50 lb. pedal pressure to release. But its action and the overall smoothness of the drive line makes the job of driving smoothly very easy.

The XJ6 is not a light car, being, at 32.6 cwt, 17 per cent heavier than the BMW. The extra capacity compensates for this. From a standstill the car accelerates to 60 mph in 8.7 sec, the ¼-mile in 16.5 and 100 in 27.5 sec, good figures all, but not quite as good as the BMW's. Interestingly, if one compares the acceleration in the nearly identically geared 4th ratios in each car (BMW 20.7, XJ6 21.5 mph per 1,000 rpm), the Jaguar comfortably holds off the BMW until the final 80-100 mph increment, when the BMW draws away. Therein lies one key to the fascinating differences between these two.

The BMW has great flexibility but if you're in any sort of hurry you use that delightful gearbox, whereas the Jaguar's effortless mid range power and mechanical refinement—and the not so pleasant gearchange and heavy clutch—encourage one to stay in the high gears.

Fuel consumption

In this respect the advantage is without doubt the BMW's. Previous experience of both cars had prepared us for a difference, but a confirming test was carried out. We filled both cars, then drove in convoy along a 130-mile route which included all sorts of road—fast main road, open and not so open country lanes, motorway and town. At the next filling station the BMW needed 6 gallons to fill it (22.0 mpg) and the Jaguar 7.2 gallons (18.3 mpg). That agrees well with the findings of Road Tests on both cars. If money doesn't matter, then the extra range allowed by the Jaguar's 24 gallon twin tanks (430 miles) against the BMW's 16½ gallon one (300 miles) is a useful compensation for the XJ6 owner.

Noise

Inside the BMW, the faint rustle of valve gear is audible at low speeds (up to 50 mph). Further up the rev-range, all mechanical noise is swamped by the delightfully crisp exhaust note, which, although purposeful, is effectively muted.

There is a suggestion of clutch-thrash (torsional drive-line resonance) when the engine is made to pull at around 1,500 rpm in top. This is a characteristic inherited from the 2800.

Nobbly surfaces cause a certain amount of bump-thumping, whereas smooth tarmac results in a surprising amount of hum from the Veith-Pirelli tyres. Nevertheless, we consider the car acceptable on this score.

The same cannot be said of wind noise, which is disappointing at air speeds in excess of 80 mph. In fairness, the BMW compares favourably with the majority of cars, but is not in the same league as the XJ6.

With one exception, the XJ6 is an exceptionally smooth and quiet vehicle. As already indicated, there is very little wind noise. Road-noise insulation is also very effective, although muffled bump-thumping occurs over very nobbly going.

Comprehensive sound deadening effectively deals with engine noises at speeds below 4,000 rpm. Above this, the noise level rises rapidly. In fairness, there is seldom any need to exceed these revs, which represent 110 mph in overdrive.

Ride, handling and brakes—BMW

Ride in the BMW is quite good in most circumstances but not exceptional. No bump of any sharpness jars the occupants, but one does notice quite a lot of movement of the body on an uneven country road. To use one tester's phrase, the ride is a little "nobbly"; the sensation of body movement is not helped by the character of the seats which some lighter-weight drivers find hard, a little bouncy and lacking in support; one seems to be bobbing about in the car. Pitching is noticeable, and on the test car, a suggestion of not quite even damping at all four corners of the car gives a slight "screwing" motion.

The optional power steering works well without any squelching noises. Effort needed is not as low as in some other cases (like the Jaguar's), which at first makes it seem more positive. There is enough accuracy of control and a fair amount of feel. On a bumpy road there is a small but evident degree of bump-steer and reaction at the steering wheel rim, together with not the best of straight stability. Confirming that this is derived from suspension movement is the fact that on smooth roads straight stability is excellent. Four turns are needed from lock-to-lock, and the mean turning

circle is 33 ft. 11 in. dia.—quite compact for a big-ish car. The car's relatively short nose and its shape combine with this to make it easy to handle in tight spaces.

Roll is kept down for all ordinary driving. There is little understeer, which makes the car very responsive to a touch on the helm. In the wet, especially with the German-made Veith-Pirelli radials fitted to the test car, one must take care not to put on too much power. Traction, despite the help of the limited slip differential (still fitted, contrary to what we had earlier understood), is not very good. Really fast cornering will eventually send the tail out, abruptly so and wide if one lifts off the accelerator. Roadholding is good.

Brakes need a lot of effort for this sort of car for the best possible stop (120 lb.), but at normal rates of slowing down pedal effort is acceptable. Fade performance is up to our usual Road Test treatment, though anyone who drives the car consistently hard—particularly in mountainous regions—may prefer to fit harder friction materials than those fitted to our example; these will fade to a noticeable degree on any long stop from high speed.

Ride, handling and brakes—Jaguar

There is just a trace of initial firmness to the ride of the XJ6 on any sharp bump, after which it seems to soak up disturbances in a remarkable way. Part of the pleasure one derives from this aspect of the Jaguar is the quietness of the ride, which is of an exceptionally high order. Damping is an extraordinarily successful compromise too.

As steering is very light, one at first tends to "over" steer the car; with only a little time one gets used to this thereupon finding the steering accurate and precise. Self centreing is adequate, and there is a delightful amount of feel, with just a trace of kickback over abrupt bumps. Straight stability is very good on all sorts of road. There are 3.3 turns lock-to-lock. The Jaguar is only 4½ in. longer than the BMW and near-enough the same in width, but its 38 ft. 8 in. turning circle and lack of visibility of its ends makes it more difficult to park.

Roadholding on the Dunlop E70VR15 tyres is of the highest order. There is some understeer of course, but not too much, and the car's behaviour even when pressed to most abnormal limits remains impeccable. Its balance and poise is equable under all circumstances. Roll is low. Lifting off in the middle of the same test bend taken very fast merely produced a tightening of the car's line, but no sign of abrupt breakaway.

The brakes are light (only 50 lb. pedal effort for maximum retardation), progressive, firm and resist fade well. The handbrake is not very powerful but is adequate.

Fittings and Furniture—BMW

Although 5 in. higher and 4.5 in. shorter than the XJ6, the BMW's clean lines look good in any company. It is deceptively spacious, and the wide-opening doors make getting in and out particularly easy.

Standard upholstery material is either deep-embossed plastic or ribbed cloth, to customer's choice. All four seats have head restraints as standard, the fronts being adjustable for height and the rears for angle.

Loop-pile carpet is used for the floor and cowl side-panels, pvc being used for the head-lining.

With the exception of a small electric clock, all the instruments are grouped in a binnacle ahead of the driver, the whole assembly being covered with a single lens. This arrangement completely eliminates reflection problems. Instrumentation consists of a large speedo-meter and matching tachometer (red-lined at 6,200 rpm), between which are located temperature and fuel gauges. Beneath the latter is a group of warning lamps which monitor charging, oil pressure, main beams, indicators, low fuel and brakes (fluid level and parking lever). Beneath the binnacle, to the left of the steering column, are push-buttons (with built-in warning lamps) controlling hazard warning and the heated rear window (a standard fitting). On the right is a similar switch for the rear (red) fog lamp, which is built into the right-hand lamp cluster.

Moving the stalk towards the wheel-rim actuates the screen washer and sets the wipers in motion for a pre-determined period. This stalk also controls the indicators. The stalk on the left controls headlamp dipping and flashing. All this sounds complicated, but the 3.0S is a car in which unfamiliar drivers soon feel completely at home.

The 3.0S employs an air-blending heater. The quiet three-speed blower is arranged to boost flow through the cold air vents, which consist of an eyeball at each end of the facia and an adjustable louvred outlet at the centre. Redesigned vents in the rear quarter pillars take care of extraction.

Although of modest depth, the boot is deceptively spacious. The spare wheel is under a false floor on the left, rendering removal of a considerable amount of luggage necessary in the event of a puncture. Beneath another false floor on the right is the 16.5 gal fuel tank. Luggage has to be hoisted over a sizeable sill. An attractive feature is the superb toolkit, which lives beneath the boot lid.

The front-hinged bonnet gives good access to the engine bay. Dip-stick, distributor, battery and fuel pump are easily reached. Spark plug access is also tolerably good, as is access to the oil filter. However, both the alternator and the power-steering pump seem difficult to reach. A good point is accessible finger-tip adjustment for the quartz-halogen headlamps.

Among the extras listed for the 3.0S are leather upholstery (£240), manually operated sunshine roof (£114), electrically operated sunshine roof (£161.25), a laminated wind-screen (£19), tinted glass (£56), air-con-ditioning with tinted glass (£464), ZF automatic transmission (£239) and alloy wheels.

Fittings and Furniture—Jaguar

The XJ6 has undergone only minor changes since its 1968 debut. Its unusually low build makes it seem longer and wider than it rea... is. Overall length, in fact, is 4.5 in. more than that of the BMW, but the Jaguar is a mere 0.6 in. wider.

Despite its low build and quite bulky sills, front seat access is quite good. That to the rear is less so, with relatively little room in which to manoeuvre large-sized feet. Once in, however, there is ample space.

Leather upholstery is standard on 4.2-litre models. Seating comfort is outstandingly good.

Front seats are ideally shaped and have reclining backrests.

Luxurious cut-pile carpet covers the floor, cloth being used for the headlining. Wood is used for door cappings and much of the facia.

Instrumentation is comprehensive and attrac-rively arranged. Ahead of the driver, flanking the steering column, is a large tachometer (red-lined at 5,000 rpm) and matching speedometer. In the centre of the facia is a group of five smaller instruments, comprising a voltmeter, an oil pressure gauge, a clock, a temperature indicator and a fuel gauge. The latter serves both the 12 gal fuel tanks, a change-over switch controlling it and the two fuel pumps. All 10 rocker switches are placed in a row—an arrangement which requires a little learning.

A thermostatic water valve regulates the heater output. Hot air is ducted to front and rear footwells. Each front outlet has its own control, with a third regulating the flow to the rear compartment. The two-speed fan is unob-trusive and is arranged to boost flow through the cold air vents. These comprise an eyeball outlet at each end of the facia, with a third one on the rear of the centre console (for rear passengers). There is also a ram-fed vent on each side of the scuttle. Stale air is extracted via a vent in the centre of the rear parcel shelf, thence flowing to atmosphere via the boot lid opening.

Although the boot is long, it is surprisingly shallow. Its width is also restricted by the twin fuel tanks. The spare wheel lives beneath the false floor, requiring the removal of all luggage in the event of a puncture. On the credit side, the boot is very superbly trimmed and has no awkward sill.

The front-hinged bonnet and grill assembly gives good access to the engine bay. Dip-stick, plugs, carburettors, distributor, oil filter and alternator are all fairly accessible. A surprising feature is the inclusion of no fewer than 19 greasing points, 15 of them requiring attention at 6,000-mile intervals.

An electrically heated rear window is fitted as standard to 4.2-litre models. Among the many extras listed are electrically operated windows (£56.25), air-conditioning (£241.25), a lam-inated windscreen (£13.75), chromium-plated wheels (£50.00), a pair of foglamps (£21.00) and a Philips stereo cassette player-cum-recorder (£146.25).

Personal opinion

Two-car tests are always interesting, but to be able to compare these two great motor cars side by side was more interesting than usual, and a little alarming; in most respects they are each so good.

The question of which to settle on was how-ever not as difficult as I had imagined it would be.

Driven *in extremis* down a long straight road the performance of the BMW's superb engine and the pleasure of using that gearchange would tell. It is a most wonderfully willing sophisticated tiger of a machine which jumps to your command yet remains beautifully smooth. And it is very economical, surprisingly so. It is distinctly audible from inside the car, but the noise is a very nice one, so that probably wouldn't matter. I also like the tidiness of BMW engineering, so neat even in detail; take a look at the windscreen wiper linkage, a quite

TWO CAR TEST...

accessible connecting rod arrangement instead of one of those cable things.

Things I do not care for on the BMW are its poor seats—for a middle-to-lightweight person like myself they are far too hard, unyielding and non-holding—its brakes and, its ultimate handling behaviour, though not bad, is not in my opinion in the same class as that of the XJ6.

Corresponding items which I do not care for on the Jaguar are its gearchange—adequate but not as good as one would like—that irritatingly heavy clutch and the sounds from the engine at its top end.

However, one does not often need to drive the XJ6 really hard—unless you meet a BMW 3.0S—and the almost eerie quiet of the car at middle range speeds when not accelerating is a tremendous attraction. I vastly prefer the Jaguar's handling and its better roadholding and ride. The driving seat is one of the most comfortable production ones of any car. It looks better, inside and out, for me anyway. And if I was in the fortunate position of being able to buy such a car, the fuel bill would not bother me too much. One XJ6 please.

Michael Scarlett

Personal Opinion

In the UK, there is a price differential of £726 between these two cars in the forms tested. Is the BMW worth the extra outlay? In my opinion, the answer is a categoric "no".

If the question of price is discounted, the issue is much more interesting. The Jaguar has a substantial advantage in terms of seating comfort. It also has the better ride and virtual freedom from wind- and road-noise problems. Its higher gearing (with overdrive) makes for more relaxed high-speed cruising. More responsive braking is yet another of its advantages. Most people also agree that it is trimmed and upholstered to a much higher standard.

On the debit side, its long-stroke power unit is obtrusively harsh at much over 4,000 rpm. The clutch is heavy, has too long a travel and tends to judder.

If anything, the BMW's engine is marginally the noisier at low and medium speeds. On the other hand, it is delightfully responsive and unbelievably smooth. Without doubt, this is one of the best "sixes" ever.

Although notchy by 2800 standards, the BMW's gear-change is quick and certain. Clutch effort and travel are modest and the unit well up to its job. All this adds up to exceptionally brisk performance. Even so, fuel economy is surprisingly good.

Other points I like about the BMW are the well-planned instrument and control layout, the spacious boot, the excellent visibility and the quartz-halogen lighting.

In contrast, I find the wind-noise level disappointingly high and the seats much too hard. People of slighter build are even more critical of the latter point. My experience with our long-term 2800 suggests that it is the optional cloth trim would be a much better proposition.

Which would I choose? Not without misgivings, it would be the BMW. My wife, on the other hand, says she would disown me if I failed to choose the Jaguar. There, I think, you have the crux of the matter. The Jaguar is undoubtedly the quieter and more comfortable car, but the BMW is more fun to drive.

David Thomas

Performance Comparison

Maximum speeds	BMW 3.0S £3,538 MPH	RPM	JAGUAR XJ6 £2,927 MPH	RPM
O.D. Top (mean)			123	4,470
(best)			123	4,470
Top (mean)	127	6,150	108	5,000
(best)	128	6,200	108	5,000
3rd	93	6,250	78	5,000
2nd	62	6,500	57	5,000
1st	35	6,500	37	5,000

Acceleration MPH	sec	Ind. mph	sec	Ind. mph
0–30	2.7	30	3.0	31
0–40	4.5	40	4.5	41
0–50	6.1	51	6.5	51
0–60	8.0	61	8.7	61
0–70	10.9	71	11.8	71
0–80	14.2	82	15.3	82
0–90	18.0	92	20.5	93
0–100	23.9	103	27.5	103
Standing ¼-mile	15.9		16.5	
Standing kilometre	29.5		30.4	

MPH	3rd	Top	3rd	Top
20–40	5·6	—	5.2	6.9
30–50	5.2	8.3	4.7	6.9
40–60	5.1	7.7	4.6	7.0
50–70	5.5	8.3	4.9	7.3
60–80	6.1	9.9	5.5	7.6
70–90	7.5	10.1	—	9.1
80–100	—	11.9	—	12.2

Fuel consumption				
Overall mpg	21.3		16.0	
Typical mpg	24.0		18.0	

Brief Specification

Engine	6-cyl, in line	6-cyl, in line
Valve gear	Single chain-driven overhead camshaft	Twin chain-driven overhead camshafts
Capacity, c.c.	2,994	4,235
Bore and stroke, mm(in.)	89 × 80 (3.5 × 3.15)	92.07 × 106 (3.625 × 4.173)
Compression ratio	9.0 to 1	9.0 to 1
Max. power, bhp/rpm	180(DIN)/6,000	245(Gross)/5,500
Max. torque, lb ft/rpm	188(DIN)/3,700	283 (Gross)/3,750
Gearbox	4-speed, all-synchromesh	4-speed, all-synchromesh overdrive on top
Ratios	1.0/1.40/2.20/3.86	0.78/1.0/1.39/1.91/2.93
Final drive ratio	3.45	3.54
Mph/1,000 rpm in top (O.D.)	20.7	21.5 (27.5)
Front suspension	Independent Coil springs MacPherson struts Lower links Telescopic dampers Anti-roll bar	Independent Coil springs Double wishbones Telescopic dampers Anti-roll bar
Rear suspension	Independent Coil springs Semi-trailing arms Telescopic dampers	Independent Four coil spring/dampers Transverse links Radius arms Half-shaft upper links
Steering	Power-assisted cam-and-roller	Power-assisted rack and pinion
Brakes	Ventilated disc all round, servo	Disc all round, servo
Tyres	Veith-Pirelli, DR70HR14in	Dunlop, ER70VR15in.
Weight, cwt	27.8	32.6
Length overall	15ft. 5in.	15ft. 9½in.
Width overall	5ft. 9in.	5ft. 9.6in.
Wheelbase	8ft. 10in.	9ft. 0.8in.

Driving the BMW 3.0 C S

ROAD TEST recently had the opportunity to test the BMW 3 Litre Coupe on its home ground. In Germany there are many opportunities to drive a car to the limit of its potential. There are no speed limits plus the fact that the typical German driver has good road manners and yields to a fast overtaking car typified by the new BMW 3.0 CS. It takes a bit of acclimatization to get used to German touring conditions. In the case

of the coupe we were able to cruise quite comfortably at an indicated 125 mph. It is a rather peculiar feeling at this speed to have no fear of the police and to have a police car cruising at 100 mph give way to allow us to overtake it at 120 or 125 mph.

The autobahn allows such speeds in relative safety, and even though the typical autobahn is only two lanes wide, German drivers are well mannered. An

average speed of well over 100 mph may be maintained during conditions of light to moderate traffic. There are now strong voices being raised in Germany to impose speed limits, and such ideas are not without merit. Even the best drivers are not always able to cope with the speed differential between a VW pulling out to overtake at 70 mph and another car overtaking at plus 100 mph.

The BMW coupe at high speeds feels stable beyond all comparison to any domestic vehicles. There are many American cars capable of speeds equal to the BMW 3 Litre, but no car including Corvette offers the combination of road holding, accelerarion, braking and overall comfort of the BMW. At 125 mph a light application of the brakes gives a feeling of unlimited braking ability, and braking down to 80 and then accelerating back to 120 mph can be accomplished with a minimum of fuss. This is normal procedure in Germany, and the BMW excels under such conditions.

ment. As previously mentioned, the handling is excellent, and high cornering speeds are achieved with little or no squeal from the Michelin radial tires. Wet weather behavior is also excellent, and driving in heavy rains at high speed the car feels stable and secure. This holds true even when braking or accelerating heavily. The brakes are capable of pulling the car down from very high speeds with 100% directional control. Under severe conditions there was never a hint of fade or wheel lock up. These are of course four-wheel ventilated discs, and it would take brutal treatment to achieve any loss of braking efficiency. We deliberately worked the brakes hard while descending the Austrian Alps, and there was never any question that the brakes were every bit the equal of the rest of the car's good behavior.

The seat belts and shoulder harness in our test car were really difficult to adjust properly, and in the end we reverted to using the seat belt only. The

The real achievement with this car is that it returns excellent fuel economy under high-speed driving, and 18 mpg is not unusual on long hard trips. When the next updated version of the coupe comes along with fuel injection, the performance and mileage will be even more improved. The finish of the car is absolutely above reproach, achieving standards beyond any car in its price class. The seats are comfortable and adjust to positions suitable for drivers well over six feet. Long hours at the wheel are taken in stride, and the adjustment for back angle is achieved by turning a knob to the driver's left. This is a laborious process and can best be accomplished with the door open and the car at rest. The cheaper BMW sedans have a quick action lever that allows adjustment easily with the car in motion. The electric windows are much too slow in operation, and oddly enough the front windows do not fully retract when lowered. The back seat is adequate but not ample for two six-foot passengers.

The BMW 6-cylinder engine has to be among the best in the world. At very high rpm it has a minimum of mechanical sound. The soundproofing is excellent, not to the extent, say, of the Jaguar XJ-6, but still very good indeed. The final axle ratio is 3.64, up slightly from the previous 2800 engine series. This ratio allows improved acceleration but a slightly busier feeling at high speeds. The gearbox is among the best in the world, and even die-hard automatic enthusiasts would be impressed. The car

pulls well from 1000 rpm in top gear with little or no hesitation. In fact, the lack of stumbling and bucking feels very much like fuel injection. There is some rattle from the transmission when pulling hard.

The seating position is good, and visibility through the high windshield is excellent unlike other cars in this price bracket. The steering wheel is fixed, an adjustable wheel would be an improve-

shoulder harness was awkward and poorly placed to the extent of being uncomfortable. The car we had was still quite new with less than 1500 miles on the odometer. There were absolutely no rattles, squeeks or imperfections anywhere.

In conclusion, this BMW 3.0 CS stacks up as just about the best high-speed touring car available in the under $10,000 price bracket.

ONCE upon a time Jaguar held a tight rein on the prestige sporting saloon market in England with virtually no opposition in terms of performance/price ratio. At the top end of the selective scale there were the ultra-expensive and hardly sporting Rolls-Royce/Bentley and Mercedes Benz ranges, and at the adverse end were Rovers and the like. The advent of BMW's 2500 and 2800 saloons started a trend that has spread, and in 1972 BMW, with their 3-litre range, must be giving the Coventry men a few headaches. For although both the carburetted and fuel-injected 3-litres from Munich are appreciably more expensive than the 4.2-litre XJ6 in England, they have the sales edge in Europe, and in this country where their prestige tag counts for a lot, the few hundred pounds difference is hardly likely to be a deterrent to a potential buyer of either marque.

Road testers and motoring journalists tend to get very *blase* as we all know with their incessant variety of automobiles and when they are reluctant to part with a test model, the manufacturers can take their reticence as pure compliment. Such was the case when BMW GB Ltd recently gave us several thousands of miles trying out all three of the big Bavarian machines.

Range of appeal

In fact, mechanically identical as they are save for induction arrangements, the three models do span quite an appeal range at this expensive end of the market. The 3.0S, with twin Zenith carburation, is the direct competitor to the XJ6, albeit with more performance. The fuel-injected Si is a truly remarkable car in that it is mere tenths of a second

slower than the £8,500 Mercedes 300SEL 6.3, while the so-called *flagschiffe,* the CS, is likely to appeal to a completely different buyer, a man looking for exclusivity.

What all three models have in common besides their excellent propulsion is a teutonic simplicity in design which abandons the unnecessary and the unfunctional and concentrates on producing a luxurious and efficient car to cope with all the conditions of motoring.

The engine common to the trio is derived from the utterly reliable and successful four-cylinder 2-litre single ohc mill, and is in effect one and a half four-cylinder engines which come out appre-

CS coupe frontal styling.

ciably lighter than the vintage XK unit.

With its single overhead camshaft, the carburettor version churns out a very respectable 180 bhp at a high 6,000 rpm, while the fuel-injection version peaks at 5,500 rpm, by which time it is producing 200 very real horses. In both stages of tune the six is a silky smooth engine, inherently perfectly balanced, and even under stress remains completely impeturbed.

Flexible power

Starting from cold is absolutely instant. On the S unit there is an automatic choke with warm water and electric heating device, while the Si

BMW'S BIG TRIO

Bòsch electronic computer brain works it all out for the fuel-injection. There-after, phenomenal smoothness is achieved with the ample torque (188 ft/3,700 rpm) and (199 ft/lbs at 4,300 rpm) almost obviating the need for use of the gearbox for anything apart from very determined motoring. Flexibility is certainly the keynote to the BMW's power-plant, but it is the fuel-injected engine which really is superlative in absolute terms. From idling, at around 750 rpm, right up to around 3,500 rpm there is little to differentiate the two engines. But after the 3,500 mark the fuel-injection engine really does send the rev counter needle hurtling round the dial, so that twith 5,800 rpm show-

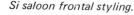

Si saloon frontal styling.

ing on the Si's dial in top gear, a genuine 132 mph can be achieved! Both the CS and the S were noticeably slower in these absolute terms — the CS will manage 130 mph on a long run, while the S is well out of breath at a mite short of 128 mph. But these are absolute terms indeed, and even the XJ6 will be left steaming in the wake of any of the BMWs . . . .

100 plus averages

But it is not so much the top speed of these machines which is the great advantage, but rather the pheno-menal cruising speeds and the com-fortable ease with which 110-125 mph

averages can be put up. None of the cars make any intolerable noise. Mech-anically they are supremely quiet, the subdued engine note picking up to a pleasingly subtle power roar at 100 mph plus, where the wind is making the greatest sound, particularly on the pillarless CS.

The 2800 series was oft-criticised for its handling at high speed, but the advent of the 3-litre range has hushed the critics. The basic ride of all the models is firm, but without the earlier 2-litre's proneness to lurch uncom-fortably.

Steering on all three cars tried was of the ZF power-assisted variety, light and precise with just over four turns lock to lock. Just how good this set-up is was brought home to us during the middle of our CS trial, when a Pon-tiac GTO with nil steering feel was experienced. For a relatively big car, the BMWs have little body-roll and list, all of them being equipped with anti-roll bars front and rear.

Roadholding ability

While the handling is very reward-ing, the roadholding performance is very much subject to the tyres fitted. Our initial car — the CS — came equipped with German Metzler Monza radials which, while being adequate in the dry, send the hard-trying wet weather driver into ecstasies of light-fingered opposite-locking and really do restrict average journeys speeds in the wet. However, a completely different picture is obtained when the high-speed Michelin XVRs are fitted. In the dry these are utterly beyond praise, while wet weather conditions are hardly noticed.

The basic tendency of the big B is to understeer, but this hardly ever manifests itself, so light and effortlessly controllable is the steering. Oversteer can be induced in certain circumstances with hefty stabs of the right foot, but for even high-speed driving the net result is a neutrality of direction, the car going where it is pointed and on the right piece of road at that.

With big ventilated disc brakes replacing on the three-litre range the old and oft-criticised disc/drum arrangement of the 2800s, stopping never causes any problems. A servo makes the effort light, and although we did get some fade after a very strenuous series of hard stops on the CS, the brakes are superlative. Whether the light-alloy cast wheels of the CS help cooling in extreme conditions we do not know, but at least they look nice!

On a concluding mechanical note, the new Getrag (a ZF/Borg Warner-owned make) four-speed box with short remote control is excellent with unbeatable synchromesh, although the Sachs & Fitchel clutch does require precision in being completely depressed.

Elegant coachwork

Of course, the major distinguishing features between the C and S models is the bodywork. In the case of the CS coupe, the extra £1000 or so pays for a Karmann hand-built pillarless two-door body with origins in the old 2000C. With agressive twin-headlamp frontal treatment, the CS coachwork draws admiring looks from the cognescenti, being simple and remarkably elegant. The same theme dominates the four-door saloon, the lines being distinguished yet uncluttered. Recessed safety door handles are used.

BMW use smooth-edged door keys with perforations, and whether connected or not, we had some troubles with all three test cars at one stage or other with stiff door locks, the worst offender being the CS which needed a real wrench to open the driver's door.

The interior of the coupe and saloons differ somewhat. On the CS the sumptous front seats, with headrests more for safety rather than comfort purposes, were finished in lovely cloth. On both the saloons the trim was in rather out-of-place plastics, of good quality, but never the equal of leather. However, adjustment of the reclining seats is superb for both travel and rake, and with its very high cruising speeds long journeys are covered without ad-

Carburetted engine of CS and S.

verse effects on travellers.

Instrumentation for the saloons is composed of two large round dials — three on the CS — 140 mph speedometer with odometer and trip recorder and 8,000 rpm rev counter. Fuel gauges and engine temperature gauges also appear on both varieties, although the lack of an oil pressure gauge is probably not understood by enthusiastic owners — perhaps a sign of BMW's confidence in their own engine?

Heating and ventilation is quite superb. An almost infinite range of hot/

warm/cold variations can be worked out with hot/cold air blowers, and so on. Otherwise, the interior equipment is very much up to luxury car standards, but functional rather than adornative. Electric windows with central console controls come as standard on the CS, and surely are an obvious optional buy for the S/Si owners. There is an automatic wash/wipe button, very useful at high-speed, and also an automatic stop-start-stop wiper selector, while there are two wiper speeds. Childproof locks

Si's fuel-injected engine.

are, of course, fitted at the rear of the saloons, while there is plenty of storage space, in a flat glove compartment above the passenger's knees and in a central console. To add music to our harmonious time with the Si, a radio was fitted to the fuel-injection car along with casette stereo player, another item which will feature in most buyers' lists of options.

New standards

With virtually identical performance between the CS/S and even more from the Si, the BMWs really set standards of their own in terms of luxurious effortless high-speed motoring. However, the Si is a truly remarkable car. When drafting out the editorial policy of this magazine, we decided to make sure that we adopted an objective critical road test programme. That the BMWs were so impressive worried us in that our praise might be taken for euphemism! But believe us, a spell at the wheel of both the carburetted three-litres is an experience which alters one's perspectives of motoring. The Si? This car is simply amazing. It has the tractability of a limousine and the performance of an astonishingly quick sports/GT machine. After that's been said, who needs a 6.3 Mercedes 300SEL at nearly twice the price?

Coupe interior

Saloon interior

ENGINE:	6-cylinder 4-stroke in-line; three-sphere turbulent combustion chamber, single overhead camshaft; overhead valves in Vee-configuration; seven-bearing crankshaft with 12 balance weights; water cooled; force-feed lubrication with rotor pump, full flow oil filter.
Stroke/Bore:	80 mm / 89 mm.
Capacity:	2985 cc (152.2 cu. ins.).
Power output:	S: 180 bhp DIN at 6000 rpm; Si: 200 bhp DIN at 5500 rpm.
Torque:	S: 118 ft/lbs at 3700 rpm; 199.2 ft/lbs at 4300 rpm.
Compression ratio:	S: 9:1; Si: 9.5:1.
Induction:	S: Twin Zenith 35/40 INAT carburetors, automatic starting device with warm water and electric heating; accelerator pump. Si: Bosch fuel-injection with electronic regulator.
Ignition:	S: Distributor with engine speed governor, centrifugal and vacuum adjustment. Si: Centrifugal adjustment.
TRANSMISSION:	Four-speed Getrag ZF gearbox with synchromesh. Ratios: 1st; 3.855:1; 2nd: 2.203:1; 3rd: 1.402:1; 4th: 1.0:1; Reverse: 4.3:1.
Final drive:	3.45:1. 20.7 mph per 1000 rpm in 4th gear. Limited slip-differential.
Clutch:	Fitchel & Sachs diaphragm single-plate.
SUSPENSION:	
Front:	Independent by wishbones, traction struts and spring struts; coil springs and telescopic shock absorbers, anti-roll bar.
Rear:	Independent by semi-trailing arms mounted in rubber. Anti-roll bar.
STEERING:	ZF hydraulic power-assisted; overall ratio 18.05:1; three-piece track rod.
Tyres:	Metzler Monza radial DR 70 HR 14 or Michelin XVR radial 195/70 VR 14.
Wheels:	CS: Light-alloy cast 6J 14 ins diameter; S/Si: Steel disc 6J x 14 ins diameter.

BRAKES:	
Front/rear:	272 mm ventilated discs with servo assistance; dual-circuit braking system.
Handbrake:	Mechanically-operated drum brake with self-centering shoes acting on rear wheels.
ELECTRICAL SYSTEM:	12-volt; alternator; Varta battery; 4 halogen headlamps; rear fog lights; reversing lights; hazard indicators; heated rear window.
CHASSIS:	CS: 2 doors; S/Si: 4 doors. Crash resistant passenger compartment.
Boot:	Flat floor, fully carpeted. 22.8 cu.ft.
Heating/Ventilation:	Twin-circuit fresh-air heating system, infinitely adjustable for hot/warm/cool air and variations of hot/cold. Fresh air output up to 100 litres per second; heating efficiency independent of road speed.
Fuel capacity:	16.5 IMP gallons with 1.8 IMP gallon reserve and warning light.
EQUIPMENT:	Speedometer with odometer and trip recorder, calibrated to 140 mph. Rev counter to 8000 rpm; fuel gauge, clock; engine temperature indicator; luggage compartment light; interior light; automatic screen washer/wiper; two-speed windscreen wipers; cigar lighter; warning lights for battery charge, oil pressure, indicators, fuel level, handbrake, braking system, headlight main beam, hazard indicators, fog lights, heated rear window. Steering lock. Inertia reel safety belts at front; ashtrays.
DIMENSIONS:	
Length:	S/Si: 185 ins (4700 mm). CS: (4660 mm).
Width:	S/Si: 68.9 ins (1770 mm). CS: (1670 mm).
Wheelbase:	S/Si: 116.6 ins (2692 mm). CS: (2625 mm).
Track:	
Front/rear:	S/Si: 56.9/57.6 ins (1446/1464 mm). CS: (1446/1402 mm).
Unladen weight:	3046 lb. (1380 kgs).

PERFORMANCE FIGURES

	CS	S	Si
Price with P/Tax (inc Power steering)	£5413	£3813	£4113
Fuel consumption (overall average)	20.5mpg	21mpg	22mpg
Acceleration 0-60 mph	8.5secs	8.0secs	7.4secs
Approx speeds in gears			
1st	32mph	30mph	30mph
2nd	60mph	60mph	65mph
3rd	90mph	90mph	90mph
Maximum speed	131mph	128mph	133mph
Turning circle	34.5ft	34.5ft	34.5ft

BMW 3·0S

FOR
Outstanding performance; good gearbox; excellent instrumentation; high standard of finish

AGAINST
Transmission judder; heavy fuel consumption; heavy brakes

Judging by the number of BMWs sold in Britain, there's no lack of awareness about the unusually high standard to which these German cars are manufactured. It's hard to believe that just 13 years ago BMW were on the verge of bankruptcy. Yet by 1968, so rapid was their recovery, they felt ready to challenge pillars of the establishment like Mercedes and Jaguar on their own ground with two new six-cylinder cars, the 2500 and the 2800. They shared a new low-line body and a straight six engine which, although also entirely new, was similar in concept to the smaller four-cylinder engines, with a single overhead camshaft operating inclined valves through rockers. The larger version was made by increasing the stroke of the 2500 from 71.7-80.0 mm.

Both cars offered outstanding performance for their capacity together with a high degree of comfort and accommodation. But BMW didn't rest on their laurels. Last summer the 2800 was superseded by a more potent 3 litre version (now there is even a fuel-injected version, the SI, which we hope to test soon), the increase in capacity being achieved by enlarging the bores from 86-89 mm. The optional Boge-Nivomat self-levelling dampers of the 2800 were dropped and the ratios for second and third gear slightly lowered. Finally, the new car was given an even bigger set of boots in the form of 195 HR 14 Michelin XVRs; otherwise the only obvious distinction was in the exterior badges.

Although some £760 more, the 3.0S is perhaps the only true rival to the 4.2 litre XJ6 in this country and, despite a smaller engine, its performance is actually superior.

The ride, however, is not in the same class and the handling, although very good, is perhaps not so forgiving because of the rather vague and low geared power steering.

An extra 197 cc for a car that already goes remarkably quickly may not seem very significant. However, it's sufficient to bump up the output from 170 to 180 bhp and to increase the already massive torque from 174 to 189 lb ft. You can certainly feel the extra urge which is substantiated by our performance figures — the acceleration times are reduced throughout the range, culminating in a 0-100 time of just 23.5 secs, some 2½ sec better than the 2800 can do. Maximum torque is produced at 3700 rpm, which corresponds to approximately 50 mph in top gear. Interestingly, below this speed top gear acceleration of the 3 litre is inferior to that of the 2800 and fierce transmission judder encourages one to change down; above it, however, the new car pulls away, 60-80 mph taking 8.5 secs instead of 9.9 secs. At 126.4 mph, the outstanding top speed is just under BMW's claim but 2.4 mph up on that of the previous model.

You usually have to pay for an increase in performance so it's not surprising that the consumption of the 3.0S is noticeably higher — the touring consumption deteriorated from 25.6 to a rather poor 18.8 mpg, and the overall from 17.5 to 15.4 mpg. Although the automatic choke assured first-time starting, it remained in operation unnecessarily long, causing lumpy idling and probably contributing a little to the high

petrol consumption.

An excellent gearbox encourages use of all the available performance. The stubby lever can be moved as fast as the hand can go and is largely free from any baulking or grating. The ratios for 2nd and 3rd gear are slightly lower than those of the 2800, maximum speeds in the lower gears now being 34 mph, 59 mph, and 92 mph. These correspond to an engine speed of 6200 rpm at which speed there is an automatic ignition cut out.

Steering on the 3 litre is by the same worm and roller system as on the 2800, but with power assistance as standard. It does not have the straight-line feel of a rack and pinion system and its low gearing is emphasised by the large diameter steering wheel inherited from the old car. Once accustomed to the steering — some drivers didn't like it at first — the car feels quite sporting and agile for a large saloon. Even with only a single anti-roll bar at the front (the Coupe has one at each end), the car corners hard with little body roll.

The adhesion of the 2800 was good; on the 3.0S it has been improved still further by means of wider rim wheels and 195/70 tyres instead of 175/70. Our test car was fitted with Michelin XVRs which give high cornering powers in the wet and dry, although there is always sufficient torque available to break away the semi-trailing rear end when cornering hard in the wet. Under most circumstances the car remains very controllable, but continuously bumpy surfaces can induce some diagonal pitching,

Left: At speed in the wet, the
very stable 3.0S

Above: massive ducting and a huge air cleaner obscure the two Zenith carbs. The engine
compartment layout is good

Left: very comfortable seats and an excellent
driving position are a hallmark of the large BMWs

Maximum speed mph

		100	105	110	115	120	125	130
BMW 3.0S	£3699							
Jaguar XJ6 4.2	£2937							
Rover 3.5S	£1977							
Audi—NSU Ro80	£2683							
Volvo 164 o/d	£2337							
Mercedes 250	£3066							

Acceleration sec

	0	2	4	6	8	10	12
BMW 3.0S	0-50 / 30-50 in top						
Jaguar XJ6 4.2							
Rover 3.5S							
Volvo 164 o/d							
Mercedes 250							
Audi—NSU Ro80							

Fuel consumption mpg

	0	5	10	15	20	25	30
Volvo 164 o/d	Overall / Touring						
Rover 3.5S							
Audi—NSU Ro80							
Jaguar XJ6 4.2							
BMW 3.0S							
Mercedes 250							

Make: BMW.
Model: 3.0S.
Makers: BMW AG, Munich, West Germany.
Concessionaires: BMW Concessionaires (GB) Ltd, 361-365 Chiswick High Road, London W.4.
Price: £2,957.70 plus £741.30 equals £3,699.00.

Conditions
Weather: Dry, Sunny: Wind SW changing to SE 0-10mph
Temperature: 40-43°F
Barometer: 29.05 in. Hg.
Surface: Dry tarmac
Fuel: 101 octane (RM) 5 Star rating.

Maximum Speeds

	mph	kph
Mean of opposite runs	126.4	203.2
Best one way run	127.2	204.5
3rd gear } All	92	149
2nd gear } at	59	95
1st gear } 6200 rpm	34	54

Acceleration Times

mph		sec
0-30		2.8
0-40		4.4
0-50		6.1
0-60		8.0
0-70		11.0
0-80		13.9
0-90		17.7
0-100		23.5
Standing quarter mile		16.2
Standing Kilometre		29.9

mph	Top sec	3rd sec
10-30	—	6.3
20-40	9.6	5.8
30-50	9.0	5.1
40-60	8.2	4.9
50-70	8.2	5.3
60-80	8.5	5.9
70-90	9.2	6.9
80-100	10.7	—
90-110	14.7	—

Speedometer

Indicated	20	30	40	50	60
True	18	28	39	49	59.5
Indicated	70	80	90	100	
True	69.5	79.5	90	100	

Distance recorder accurate

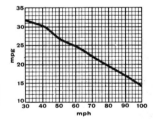

Fuel Consumption
Touring (consumption midway between 30 mph and maximum less 5 per cent allowance for acceleration) . . 18.8 mpg
Overall . . . . 15.4 mpg
Fuel tank capacity
(= 18.4 litres/100km)
Total test distance . . . 1326 miles

Engine

Block material	Cast iron
Head material	Light alloy
Cylinders	6 in line
Cooling system	Water
Bore and stroke	89mm (3.505in.) 80mm (3.150in.)
Cubic capacity	2985cc. (182 cu.in.)
Main bearings	7
Valves	ohc
Compression ratio	9.0:1
Carburettor(s)	2 Zenith 35/40 INAT
Fuel pump	Mechanical
Oil Filter	Full flow
Max. power (net)	180 bhp at 6000 rpm
Max. torque (net)	189 lb.ft. at 3700 rpm

Transmission

Clutch	Hydraulic diaphragm, self adjusting
Internal gear box ratios	
Top gear	1.0:1
3rd gear	1.402:1
2nd gear	2.203:1
1st gear	3.855:1
Reverse	4.3:1
Synchromesh	All forward ratios

Final drive 3.45:1 with limited slip diff
Mph at 1000 rpm in:—

top gear	20.9
third gear	14.9
second gear	9.5
first gear	5.4

Chassis and body
Construction . Unitary body/chassis

Brakes
Type Servo assisted ventilated discs with tandem master cylinder and dual circuits
Dimensions . . 10.7in. front discs, 10.7in. rear

Suspension and steering
Front . . . Independent by inclined MacPherson struts, lower wishbones, trailing links and coil spring/damper units. Anti-roll bar
Rear . Independent by semi-trailing arms and coil springs
Shock absorbers
Front . . . Double acting telescopic
Rear . . . Double acting telescopic
Steering type . . 2F worm & roller with power assistance
Tyres . . . . Michelin XVR 195/70
Wheels . . Steel disc 6J x 14 well based rims

Weight
Kerb weight (unladen with fuel for approximately 50 miles) . . 27.9 cwt
Front/rear distribution . . . 56/44
Weight laden as tested . 31.6 cwt

PERFORMANCE
Performance tests carried out by *Motor's* staff at the Motor Industry Research Association proving ground, Lindley.
Test Data: World copyright reserved; no unauthorised reproduction in whole or in part.

---

as on the Coupe.

The brakes of the new car have also been modified to cope with the extra power, ventilated discs all round being operated by a dual circuit system. Despite servo-assistance the brakes are really quite heavy, and demand considerable pressure to pull the car up quickly from speed. However, they are never lacking in feel, and once you are acclimatised to the pressures required, they inspire plenty of confidence.

New seats and improved damping make the 3.0S more comfortable than its predecessor, though the ride is still inferior to that of the cheaper XJ6. The seats will probably appeal most to large people as they provide little lateral support for a medium-sized back and bottom. They are very comfortable, however, and they have ample adjustment, although the rake knob is difficult to operate with the door closed. The rear seats are also comfortable and like the front ones have built-in head restraints which can be folded down when not in use. Slim pillars and one-piece side windows afford the driver excellent vision, and the corners of the car can be clearly seen when manoeuvring, making the car feel smaller than it is.

The switchgear and instruments are like those of the previous model, and very good they are too. The indicators, washers and wipers are controlled by one column-mounted stalk, the headlight dip and flash by another. The horn is sounded by one of three slab switches on the steering wheel spokes. Our only criticism here lies with the auxiliary wiper switch, on the far side of the dash. We feel it could be usefully swapped for the cigar lighter, thus bringing it within easy reach of the steering wheel. The switch has three settings, low, high and delay. The wipers themselves are excellent, as are the powerful electrically operated washers.

Four dials make up the instrument cluster, which is a model to other manufacturers. Their precise graduations are clearly visible through the steering wheel and important points, like the red line on the rev-counter, are highlighted by red lights at night. The two smaller, centrally mounted gauges register water temperature and petrol. A rectangular clock is mounted on the lip of the facia on the passenger's side.

The big BMW is fairly well insulated from noise, though on occasions a rather harsh though expensive-sounding exhaust note penetrates the interior, and some wind noise is excited by the windscreen pillars, although this is little worse at 120 mph than at 100 mph. The transmission is inaudible and road noise is well subdued apart from a certain amount of radial thump.

Four controls allow fine adjustment of the heating and ventilating and, as on previous BMWs, we found the rheostat-operated fan switch to be far superior to a normal two or three-speed set-up. A heated rear window, automatic reversing lights and hazard warning lights are all standard equipment on the 3 litre. Oddment space is well catered for with a large ribbed tray on top of the dashboard, a deep one in the console, door pockets, and a large parcel shelf at the rear.

The 3.0S is undeniably expensive in this country, but a short drive is sufficient to demonstrate its quality and outstanding performance. It's a car we greatly admire.

3-Liter BMW Technical Features

by John Ethridge

BMW has always made technically interesting cars, and the new 3-liter models, slated for future introduction in the United States, are no exception. A larger, more powerful pair of 3-liter sixes, that are further developments of the 2.5- and 2.8-liter engines, enhance the sporting flavor that BMW designs into even its 4-door sedans. Two basic body styles, a 4-door sedan and a 2-door pillarless coupe, make up BMW's top-of-the-line offerings. The engine is made in both a carbureted and fuel injected version. Models with the fuel injected engine carry a lower case "i" at the nameplate designation.

Engine

The 30-degree slant 6 ohc engine has a robust 12-counterweight crankshaft turning in 7 main bearings set deeply into the heavily webbed crankcase, a combination of design features that made it possible to stretch the displacement and power through several model changes. This latest version has a bore of 3.50 inches and a stroke of 3.15 inches, bringing the displacement up to 182 cubic inches or 2985cc. The carbureted engine breathes through a pair of 2-barrel Zenith 35/40 INAT carbs with automatic enrichment devices and both warm water heating for normal operation and electric heating for cold starts and warm-up. The top end, for those that need refreshing on the subject, is a single overhead cam running in 4 bearings and actuating the valves by rocker arms. The combustion chamber is referred to by BMW as a "three sphere turbulent." Actually it's very near a hemi design, which is ideal to keep the pace of breathing up with the latest displacement increase. Power output is 200 bhp SAE — better than 1 hp per cubic inch displacement — and torque is 185 pounds-feet. Power peak comes at 5800 rpm and maximum torque is at 3500 rpm. (Actually, the torque curve is fairly flat with output hovering near the maximum from about 2700 to approximately 4800 rpm.)

The Germans have at last discovered thermostatic cooling fans which are par-

3.0 CS coupe stretches nearly as long as 4-door sedan, features full-size rear seats. Light metal wheels, radial-ply tires, standard equipment, make BMW's latest look and feel as sporting as it is.

ticularly beneficial on high revving engines like these, permitting the carbureted engine to push the sedan 0 to 60 in 9.4 seconds and to a top speed of 121 mph. These figures are a shade better in the coupe.

The fuel injected engine uses the low-pressure Bosch electronic system (not to be confused with the Kugelfischer system on the 2002 tii) and thumps out a solid 200 bhp DIN at 5500 rpm and 27.5 meter-kilograms torque which — BMW hadn't officially translated it when this was written — figures out on our slide rule as 226 bhp and 200 pounds-feet SAE. Acceleration for this engine in sedan and coupe respectively to 100 kilometers per hour (about 62 mph) is a brisk 7.8 and 7.7 seconds. Top speeds for the two are 131 and 137 mph — never to be realized for most owners.

Transmission and Drive Line

A standard 4-speed, Borg Warner system synchromesh transmission is offered in all models with an automatic transmission optional. The drive shaft is 2-piece with maintenance-free joints. The final drive ratio is currently listed as 3.64 to 1, which may change before the

Thin pillars, many square feet of glass afford occupants panoramic view from new BMW 3.0 CS coupe.

cars actually reach this shore. (Some European models use 3.45 and 3.27 ratios.) Limited slip differential is standard on the coupe and optional on the sedan.

Chassis and Suspension

The 4-wheel independently sprung suspension system is basically similar to that used on previous models with some

important revisions to the front-end geometry. The spring strut has been tilted backward at the top and the lower pivot relocated so that when cornered, the outside wheel increases negative camber (the top of the wheel leans inward) to improve lateral traction and thus cornering force. Also effected by these changes are reduced steering effort and tendency to dive under heavy braking. The spring strut is tilted back farther in the coupe than in the sedan for greater effect. Presently, power steering is standard on the coupe and optional on the sedan.

3-liter overhead camshaft 6 leans 30 degrees away from driver's side of car to make room for massive induction system. Bosch electronic fuel injection system operates with 28-psi fuel pressure, magnetic injector valves, puts out 200 hp DIN at 5500 rpm.

Air cleaner, fule injection air collector pipe almost hide engine when rear-opening hood is popped.

The double dual-circuit brake system is one of the best and most fail-safe ever put on an automobile. The brake fluid pressure acts simultaneously through twin brake lines on two separate pairs of wheel cylinders on each front brake disc and on the disc brakes at the rear wheels. Should the circuit acting on one of the front pairs of brake cylinders fail, over 75 percent of braking efficiency is still maintained on all 4 wheels. If the circuit acting on all 4 wheels fails, approximately 60 percent braking efficiency is still maintained on the second pair of front brake cylinders. Rear wheel locking is prevented by a pressure regulating valve in the circuit.

The handbrake acts on duo-servo (same efficiency forward and reverse) drum system combined with the rear brake discs. Brake discs are now ventilated, which promises to be a definite improvement over the previously non-ventilated ones.

The springs and shocks have been retuned on the sedan to respond more softly to high frequency as well as low frequency road irregularities than before without losing road contact.

Body

Unitized construction is used with the body welded to the floor pan to form a rigid structure. Flow-through ventilation is incorporated with an infinitely variable blower capable of delivering up to 3.5 cubic feet of air per second. Air is extracted by slots above and underneath the rear window and exhausted at the rear corner posts. The heating system is a 2-circuit design with cold and warm air mixture, and finely adjustable temperature control. Heat is immediately available anytime the engine is warm and running because water circulates through the heater core at all times. An electrically heated rear window is standard on both the coupe and sedan. Electric window lofts are standard on the coupe, and front electric windows are optional.

DIMENSIONS

	SEDAN	COUPE
Length	185 in.	183.5 in.
Width	68.9 in.	65.7 in.
Height (empty)	57.1 in.	53.9 in.
Wheelbase	106 in.	103.3 in.
Front track	56.9 in.	56.9 in.
Rear track	57.6 in.	55.2 in.
Turning circle (curb to curb)	31.5 ft.	31.5 ft.
Weight	3043 lb.	3043 lb.

FIRST IMPRESSIONS OF THE
BMW 2500

HAVING MISSED various road-test BMWs last year, Mr. Anton Hille, Marketing Director of BMW Concessionaires (GB) Ltd., suggested that I might like to assess one of the fine cars he sells, over a bigger mileage than usual. I readily concurred—who wouldn't?—but when asked which BMW I would like to test, left the matter in his hands. The car eventually submitted turned out to be a Bristol grey 2500 with manual gearbox, upholstered in skai p.v.c. because, said Mr. Raymond Playfoot, who was looking after the transaction, "I know the Motoring Dog(s) travel with you." (As a matter of fact they don't ride in many road-test cars these days, because their degree of moult defeats most vacuum-cleaners, but Mr. Playfoot's thoughtfulness was nevertheless appreciated . . . .)

This elegant and spacious BMW arrived at an opportune moment in my motoring life, inasmuch as the faithful and much-liked leather-upholstered Editorial Rover 2000 TC, in which both dogs did ride, had become somewhat long-in-the-tooth, sluggish, with a boot-lid all too ready to fly open even when locked, a loose hand-brake grip, undependable starting, and front suspension which all too rapidly wore illegal flats on the outer extremities of the front tyres. It was due for replacement anyway and I favoured a Rover 3500 V8 but due to the inability of Solihull to let me try a manual-transmission version, either for road-test or as a potential customer, over a period of five months, the matter is in abeyance. So I was all set to become BMW-minded . . .

I think Mr. Playfoot suggested a 2500 for appraisal because this BMW has the merit of putting a six-cylinder car from the famous Bavarian Motor Works within reach of those who (or whose companies) have £3,000 to spend. It costs, in fact, one pound-sterling under this sum, in round figures, although in the case of "my" BMW the price would be £3,037.50, due to extras comprising power steering and front-seat headrests. Anyone contemplating a Mercedes-Benz at this price-ceiling is restricted to a plain 250 saloon, and even this costs £67 more than the BMW 2500. I have suggested previously that the V8 Mercedes-Benz 280SE 3.5 is a superior car, but so it should be, for it exceeds the cost of a BMW 2500 by no less than £2,159.

So the purchaser of a BMW 2500 is likely to compare this car with the Jaguar XJ6 (£2,937 in 4.2 de luxe form), the Rover 3500S (£2,096) or the Rover 3½-litre (£2,627). Unless absolute economy were the watchword, I would refuse the Jaguar, in spite of its larger engine, because I cannot abide its clutch and gearbox and do not want an automatic, although, to be fair, an Automatic XJ6 is available for £90 more than the BMW in question—on the performance front, however, the Jaguar with 1.7 more litres is not a noticeable advance on the BMW, but its fuel bill would be appreciably higher. The V8 Rover with 2000-type gearbox I haven't driven and both XJ6 and Rover 3½-litre I would eschew anyway as likely soon to be obsolescent—the XJ6 supplemented or replaced by an XJ12, the big Rover probably quietly faded-out.

Thus, all in all, the BMW 2500 seems an excellent proposition for those buying the lower echelon of luxury motor car—a Rolls-Royce Silver Shadow, which I readily admit is in a most worthy niche of its own, is £6,878 *more costly,* just to provide a sense of proportion . . .

There is, of course, the BMW 2800, and if you want to know how very highly I rate this car, I can but refer you to what I wrote about it in Motor Sport for October 1969. It is, however, at £3,347, well outside the convenient £3,000 spending price, and the spendthrift 2500 owner is, in fact, sacrificing only 12 (SAE) b.h.p., which represents a loss of only about 3 m.p.h. in top speed and about half-a-second on that telling 0-60 m.p.h. acceleration. There are also the magnificent BMW 3.0 S and 3.0 CS models, but these lift the customer into the £3,700 and £5,300 cost brackets, respectively. Let us look, then, at the more practical proposition of a £3,000 BMW 2500.

I put this 2500 to an immediate test for restful motoring, inasmuch as I drove to the office from Wales for the last time in the Rover 2000 TC (rather sad, after its 54,000 miles of service!), did half-a-day's work in the half-light and chill dictated by the Miners' Union, and, never having sat in it previously, drove 180 miles home in the new German car—and it was all most comfortable and effortless.

The BMW had just 143 miles on its total odometer, having presumably been driven up from the Brighton depot, and for a short distance by the receiving member of our staff, who enthusiastically reported a nice gear-change and much urge. The Managing Director of MOTOR SPORT, who knows about BMWs, although his present allegiance is to a V8 Mercedes-Benz and an Alfa Romeo 2000GTV, reminded me about running-in the new machine from Munchen. This is no hardship, involving as it does not exceeding (in round figures, converting from k.p.h. to m.p.h.) 56 in third, 78 in top for the initial 625 miles, 66 and 90 respectively, for the next 625—what you might call academic loosening-up, in this speed-limit-ridden land.

Remembering Parry Thomas' edict that it is better to break-in a stiff engine by letting it run freely but never labour, I kept the five-bearing six, which, incidentally, has the old-fangled dimensions of a stroke longer than its bore, 71.6 x 86 mm., at between 2,000 and 4,000 r.p.m., whereas its peak-power pace is 6,000 r.p.m., and launched myself into the stop-start of London commuter traffic, made worse because offices were closing early due to the blackout. While intermittent rain was falling I revelled in the effective intermittent five-seconds screen wiping obtainable by pressing a button on the extremity of the right-hand stalk control, which also serves for turn-signalling, washers and parking lights, the horn being sounded by depressing controls set conveniently in the steering-wheel spokes. As the rain became heavier I was defeated in getting continuous wiper action until I discovered an unlabelled knob, farther away than the cigarette-lighter, which brought in the two-speed wipers. But the overall system is excellent, because when this knob is used it is possible to stop or start the wipers from the aforesaid button; when the knob is set to "off" this stalk-button reverts to intermittent wiper action and pulling up the stalk powerfully washes the screen at all times.

The lamps are set to side or head from another, well-placed knob and dipped by moving downwards the precision left-hand stalk, which also works the flasher. I was disappointed in the illumination given by the Hella headlamps—the four mean-looking little Lucas lamps of the Rover, although I have heard them criticised, always gave me an excellent light, even when dipped, whereas the BMW's dipped beams are pathetic. The facia lighting dims or can be extinguished by turning the lamps' knob and the fuel-filler lives beneath the hinged rear number-plate, which seems like borrowing ideas from General Motors. The heater is adequate if the quiet fan is used in winter conditions. The gears are notably unobtrusive.

I had not gone far in "my" fine new 150-b.h.p. motor-car, enjoying the hard but extremely comfortable driving seat, easily adjustable for squab angle and with adjustable head-rest, when the gear-lever grip came off in my hand. It is a long rubber sleeve like a bicycle handlebar grip, which ever since has resolutely refused to stay on the threaded end of the gear-lever. Normally, a wooden gear-lever knob is fitted, this sleeve grip being by way of a luxury, which BMW have promised to glue on properly. This set-back marred the pleasure of using what is normally a very nice gearbox, although with long lever movements compared to the Rover, reverse quite easily engaged by poking the lever outboard of first gear. The central hand-brake, which operates sepa-

Continued on page 113

UNBEATABLE BMW

An Interim Report

THE APRIL issue of MOTOR SPORT contained initial impressions of a BMW 2500 118-m.p.h. £3,000 saloon submitted to me for a prolonged test. I think perhaps I was rather free with the criticism, in this early assessment of what I have since found to be a quite irresistible motor car. To continue the story, the overdue 600-mile free inspection was undertaken by MLG of Chiswick, W4, at 1,642 miles, during which the rubber sleeve was properly stuck onto the gear lever, the demister for the large expanse of back window was made to function efficiently, and the four Hella headlamps were re-adjusted to provide reasonable illumination on the dipped setting. Nor did the neat BMW Kangol safety-belt anchorages any longer foul the hand-brake, and the bonnet is now pulled shut by the release lever, inside the n/s stowage well, without the need to press on the lid.

Before I took the 2500 over again it had done more than 1,100 additional miles in someone else's hands, whose I never discovered, and when the Managing Director was bringing it up to the office for me it acquired a scrape along its near-side and a small dent in its n/s rear wing. It had previously been savaged on its opposite flank by a jealous Rolls-Royce Silver Shadow. Very promptly and efficiently BMW's London Service Depot erradicated the new blemishes but, on the very day that it was returned to me, parked temporarily in the road while another vehicle was let out of the Standard House car-park, it was seen to rock on its springs—a lorry had nuzzled it, fortunately only marking a tyre. I hope it isn't going to prove an unlucky BMW, because it is a car I like very much, on longer acquaintance.

I like the way its superbly-smooth 2,494-c.c. engine, in what I have come to regard as my BMW "small-six" (and, let's get it right this time, it has a bore and stroke of 86 × 71.6 mm.), will pull away in top gear from below 1,000 r.p.m. if need be, smoothing out before 2,000 r.p.m. is reached, and accelerate, at first with a typical subdued hard-note conveying a sense of hidden power, then impressively silently, to its indicated peak-speed of 6,400 r.p.m. I like the interior spaciousness of what is not, outwardly, an over-big car, so that there is great passenger (and driver) freedom, plenty of stowage space and a really commodious boot. I like the facia layout, with two big Vdo dials, speedometer and tachometer, calibrated with white numerals, their steady-reading needles sweeping round the black dials in the same plane, a sort of Derby-Bentley refinement, although one transparent sheet serves to cover these and the subsidiary fuel and heat gauges, below which, very neatly arranged, are the windows of the warning lights, for "gener", "oil", "beam", "flasher", "fuel" and "brake". I like the two substantial keys, either of which works the ignition, easily distinguishable by their grips, and front-seat head-rests which are more a safety-protection than a relaxation when driving. I admire the plain stolid appearance of the BMW 2500, so nicely off-set by the traditional blue-and-white badges and those big wheel nave-plates that almost obviate any suggestion of spoked wheels—nothing "boy-racer" about a BMW! Particularly do I like the very quiet, effortless fast cruising, the engine running at 3,500 r.p.m. at 70 m.p.h., of this essentially safe and comfortable car and the pleasant action of the gear-change, faintly reminiscent of that of a Lancia Aprilia, in the manner that the cogs can almost be felt into mesh. I like the car's ability to corner deceptively fast, without too much roll. Running at upwards of 100 m.p.h. the BMW is splendidly quiet apart from some wind noise round the rear quarters of the body. The Michelin XAS tyres display a reassuring tread pattern which is fully justified by their wet-road grip and muted cornering, on a car the inner rear wheel of which will spin on corners if it is sufficiently provoked.

I am becoming used to what is really good but low-geared power steering, which feels over-sensitive only when the 2500 is being hurled at difficult corners, transmits no road shocks and has a gentle castor-return action. The ride is acceptable, too, if just a shade unexpectedly lively for a big car on some surfaces. The all-disc brakes are reasonably progressive from ordinary speeds, but sometimes a bit sudden; when the car came back to me after that additional 1,100 miles on its odometer I thought it had been driven hard, gecause the brakes snatched in uncertain fashion; after the service session this had been cured, but they now squeal.

It is too early, after 5,000 miles, troublefree so far, to report on the long-duration performance of this delightful car, but I am already

"hooked" on BMW motoring. A fuel consumption check after it was fully run-in showed 22.1 m.p.g. of 4-star in general driving conditions. Starting is fairly quick, on the automatic choke, and the fuel range is better than 330 miles on a tankful. I had about the fastest journey yet to Mid-Wales from London, in spite of long delays getting clear of town due to the rail go-slow road congestion, in recording this useful fuel range. A long run such as this brings out the best in the car, which is a pleasure to be in, whether crawling in the quiet lower gears, accelerating purposely through the box, or devouring the miles in top gear. The fuel gauge registers zero eventually and the low-level warning light then comes on (it does not dazzle at night, nor does the full-beam light, but it *could* be overlooked in bright sunlight) and the car will then do about 35 miles before running out.

In running the fuel tank almost dry a garage-hand remarked that the filler-cap seemed to be venting reluctantly, so I may have one of the faulty yellow filler-caps fitted to early 2500s, although I would have expected this to be spotted at the 600-mile free inspection. I did not get the English instruction book I requested but they did thoughtfully pop a standard wooden gear-lever knob in the facia stowage well, in case the rubber grip sheds itself again. A small point—BMW spelling is a thought unusual—the aforesaid filler cap is called a "cab" in a special instruction relating to it, but I assume "UPM × 100" on the tachometer face refers to *units* × 100. Another thoughtful accessory is a Compact Mk. II emergency windscreen, which I found in the smartly-carpeted flat-floored boot, with its useful parcels' box (or bottle rack) on the o/s. I also commend the honesty of the BMW mechanics, who did not help themselves to a chocolate bar and apple I had inadvertently left in the facia well, which, by the way, will remain shut under the weight of the Rolleiflex. . . . The red band of the heater control does not unwind as far as the blue band but ample heat is emitted, nevertheless.

Other excellent aspects are the very small turning circle, the nice action when the doors are shut, the precision adjustment of the front-seat squabs, although the knobs are somewhat difficult to get at, the hard but comfortable seats, and the well-placed door grips and internal handles. The interior arrangements, and *decor*, with just a hint of woodwork along the facia, Mercedes-fashion, are almost all to my liking, and an excellent example of the tidy and efficient Teutonic mind is found in the under-facia n/s location of the ten electrical fuses (with spares) and junction boxes, etc., although the stowage-well does somewhat impede their accessibility. The Berga battery is accessible when the bonnet is opened and the yellow-painted dip-stick easy to find, but I would not care to have to change sparking plugs Nos. 1, 5 or 6 in the inclined engine. Otherwise, the entire car is very much my idea of what a sporting medium-sized saloon should be and I am not at all surprised to learn that last March 1,268 BMWs were sold to British dealers, a record which exceeded by 392 cars that of the January UK sales. The slogan in the back window of HML 931K simply says "Unbeatable BMW" —and with that I can find nothing wrong.—W.B.

ANY PROBLEMS WITH YOUR BMW ?

IF we do have any trouble with the BMW 2500, we are informed that BMW Concessionaires GB Ltd. have appointed a "Problem Puncher" to run a new Customer Relations Department. He is 34-year-old John Markey, a BMW engineer. The job is to handle any problems of BMW owners. "Because we are always willing to meet owners' problems, regardless of the age or mileage of the car, we have appointed a qualified engineer, and not an apologist, to handle our Customer Relations Department", said Mr. A. L. Jones, Joint Managing Director of BMW Concessionaires GB. "If a fault develops in any BMW car, we always investigate", he said. "If we are certain the fault is not due to normal wear, but to some flaw in manufacture or assembly, we are always prepared to replace the faulty part. We cannot, of course, guarantee to replace high-mileage parts free of charge, but we claim we go further than any other manufacturer in doing our best for owners." Which sounds fair enough.

Taylor in the Broadspeed developed lightweight 3.0 CS.

The G1 and G2 BMWs

By SIMON TAYLOR

To show that BMW really mean business with their Group 1 and Group 2 plans, *rennfaher* John Markey invited me to Brands Hatch on a damp Wednesday morning recently to sample a lightweight 3.0 CS and also the fearsome full-race Group 2 car that Broadspeed have been developing.

BMW Concessionaires GB took delivery earlier in the year of three prototype lightweight 3-litre coupés, which differ from the normal all-steel production cars in that they have uprated suspension, Bilstein gas-filled dampers and wider alloy wheels, as well as aluminium doors, bonnet and boot lid, Perspex rear window, and a lack of some of the CS's normal creature comforts like electric windows and sound-deadening trim. They retain the standard engine, with its twin Zenith carburetters.

These lightweights are in fact development forerunners of a new car which will be homologated next year and with which BMW hope to be unbeatable in Group 1. This will be the 3.0 CSLI, the last two letters indicating lightweight and fuel injection—a Bosch electronic system which will boost the power output to over 200 bhp DIN. It will be homologated with lightweight panels, 7-inch rims and competition suspension, but an optional extra will be a "softening" package, including steel panels, electric windows and sound-deadening, and in this form BMW will sell it as their ultimate road car.

The car I drove is in fact Markey's current road car, and was thus fully silenced and running on road tyres. In this form it felt rather strange on a circuit, but there was no denying the smooth, quiet surge of flexible power from the big six, nor the beautifully efficient, undramatic brakes—big ventilated discs boosted by twin servos. Wearing a crash helmet the silenced car felt quite leisurely, and I had to look at the speedometer to realise how rapidly it rushed up to 150 kph on the top straight after a cautious exit from the slippery Clearways before braking for Paddock. The steering felt precise but rather low-geared, and the car understeered slightly but steadily in a reassuring manner. Frankly, I'd hate to subject such a lovely, sophisticated four-seater Gran Turismo to the rough and tumble of Group 1 racing, but I'm sure that BMW will do so with success.

If that car was a lovely, sophisticated Gran Turismo, the Group 2 machine was a lovely, sophisticated pure racing car. When

No luggage space! The boot full of fuel tanks in the G2 car.

it was started up in the pits lane the triple exhaust pipes, and with its immensely wide tyres bulging from the built-out wheel arches, it really looked the part. It started life as one of the three lightweight 3.0 CSs, and was delivered to Ralph Broad for the full Broadspeed treatment. And that treatment really is full: at Brands Ralph was commenting in his own inimitable manner on the Group 2 rules.

"The rules are written by fools, and it's my job to drive a horse and cart through them. I don't build a Group 2 car to the spirit of the rules. No one does unless they want to finish second. I design the modification I make to my cars from the ground up to comply with the word of the rules, and that's what they do. I can't help it if a rule has two meanings, and I take the interpretation that suits me best."

Broad began by stripping the BMW to the bare shell and checking the shell for torsional rigidity. He then set out to treble that rigidity: adding strengthening members is forbidden, but it is amazing what careful seam welding, an FIA roll-over

bar and legally added items like new shock absorber mounting brackets can do! Detail design and machining drawings were made for all the new components: the suspension was rethought, with replotted geometry, new pickup points as far as the regulations allow, everything Rose-jointed and special variable rate springs. Ralph went through £400 worth of springs before he got the combination he wanted. Bilstein dampers are used because, says Broad, "they're so much better than anything else."

The brakes are CanAm equipment, hefty Lockheed ventilated discs all round: the servo works on the front only, and there are special adjustable balance bars. Gearbox and diff have their own oil coolers, and the gearbox is a five-speed ZF.

The weight is just over the homologated figure for the car at 1190 kgs, and this is one of the car's problems in the current Group 2 circus, for Ford Germany have been able to homologate the RS Capri at well under 1000 kg, and also get fibreglass doors and sliding perspex windows in as a production item. The weight distribution of the big BMW is, says Broad, "bloody awful" at 60 front, 40 rear in race trim, and the next one he builds will have the engine moved back six inches.

The only part of the preparation not done in England was the engine—which on Küglfischer fuel injection is now producing around 338 bhp—but Broadspeed developed their own dry sump system, having to experiment a lot to cure frothing problems which resulted in very high oil consumption.

Those very attractive German BBS alloy wheels are used, with three-piece rims: Broad finds them "cows to assemble" and much more fragile than Minilites, but very light. At the moment the car is on 11 in front and 13 in rear rims, but when the car is raced in Group 2 it will have to come down to 10 in fronts and 11½ in rears. It will also have to lose its aluminium panels until these are homologated.

BMW plan a limited Group 2 season with the car this year: with its present power-to-weight ratio they aren't expecting any outright wins, but up their sleeves for next year is a new 24-valve head now being developed in Germany for which 430 bhp is promised. That should make the 3.0 CS a real fireball.

The track was still damp as I was strapped into the Group 2 car. And there was one problem: the throttle slides in the fuel injection had been sticking. As a safety measure the mechanics fitted a very strong extra spring, and this meant that the throttle was now so stiff, and needed such a strong prod to open it, that when it finally opened it went all the way. So it was either no horses, or 335 horses. No half measures.

What an engine! Looking out of place among the standard instruments—even to the clock—was a chronometric rev counter with its red-line beginning at 8000 rpm. I was told I could use 8500 if I wanted to, and the peak of the power curve is at 7200. From 5500 onwards there is an incredible rush of power: snapping the throttle hard open in third once out of Clearways, and through the close ratios of the ZF box into fourth and then fifth before braking for Paddock, the power felt as if it would go on and on. The noise from the big single-cam straight six would do credit to a Formula 1 car, and in fact the three stub pipes which exit under the passenger's door in this left-hand-drive machine were necessary because the original single big-bore pipe kept shattering due to the resonance. "We discovered the optimum pipe length," says Broad,

The Ralph Broad developed G2 engine stables 338 bhp with Küglfischer injection.

"which gave us another 4 bhp. But it gassed the driver and set the floor of the car on fire."

On the damp track I wanted to feed the power in gently going round long corners like Paddock and Clearways, but the throttle problem prevented it, and so I was getting the power on very late. Naturally the car wanted to understeer as a result, but when I finally did flex my leg muscles enough to get the throttle open it didn't seem to upset the car, which remained rock steady on its big hand-grooved Dunlop 338 intermediates, although I was naturally careful not to get on cam suddenly when I was going through a puddle with a lot of sideways G! The brakes were faultless, very powerful and with a firm, confident feel, and they made short work of slowing this big, heavy car.

The gearbox was rather tired, and that and the throttle problem—which made it difficult to push the revs up in a rapid downward change—meant that several times I was grappling for third going into Clearways. Druids was more fun, for I was arriving in fourth from Paddock and could go straight from fourth to second without trouble. The final drive ratio, incidentally, was a legacy from the car's only race outing so far—Salzbürgring, when Fitzpatrick was third behind the Cologne Capris—and was far too high for the Brands short circuit.

Even so, and despite the damp track and the sticky throttle, it was an experience to drive the Group 2 BMW 3.0 CS, and on a really fast circuit like Silverstone it should be electrifying. Certainly next season, with less weight and 100 more bhp, it should be a major contender.

Current plans for the go-ahead BMW GB competitions department include a pair of Mathwall-prepared 3.0 CSs in Group 1 right now to take on the 3-litre Capris (now that they're beating the 2002s!): drivers will be Roger Bell and John Bloomfield, with John Markey managing the team and having the occasional shake-down drive. By next season the CSLI will be homologated, but rumour hath it that another BMW project is a turbo-charging kit for the 2002 which could be rapidly homologated as an optional extra.

No decision has yet been taken on Group 2 for 1973, although during the rest of this year the existing car will do some Wiggins Teape rounds with probably John Fitzpatrick, Tony Lanfranchi or John Bloomfield driving. What BMW GB hope will happen is that, while the factory run three cars in the European championsip, a fourth car will be run with close factory co-operation but prepared by Broadspeed or Mathwall Engineering in the British Championship. By then it'll be the 24-valve, 430 bhp lightweight, and that'll be very interesting indeed.

One of just three lightweight 3.0 CS BMWs in this country at the moment. They will be homologated for G1 to blow off the Capris.

The BMW 3.0 Si holds an impeccable line when cornered fast.

Road test/John Bolster

Superb BMWs: the 3.0 Si saloon and CSi coupé

Time was when cars under 3 litres capacity were described as small, and machines of this size were raced as *voiturettes*. Now, some of the fastest cars on the road have only this piston swept volume and among the most potent are the BMWs of the 3.0 series.

The BMW has an engine with six cylinders in line, a configuration which has many advantages for a refined high-speed touring car. A V8 would be more compact but the six is better balanced and has a far more pleasant exhaust note. The crankshaft can be the limiting factor of a straight-six, but the seven-bearing BMW shaft is safe up to 7000 revs, though the distributor is wisely set to cut out rather lower than this. The chain-driven overhead camshaft operates the inclined valves through rockers, exactly as in the firm's four-cylinder engines.

The 3-litre BMW with carburetters is fast enough for almost anybody but now an even hotter version, with Bosch fuel injection, adds some 10% to the horsepower. This is a real ball of fire, but it remains just as quiet as the standard model and is even more flexible. It is sold as a 4-door saloon, which is merely expensive, or as a 2-door coupé, which is a prestige car for the very wealthy.

Having arranged to carry out a full road test of the Si saloon, I was invited by BMW to spend a couple of days in France with the CSi coupé. This report therefore covers both cars and though I had less opportunity to take accurate performance figures with the CSi, I was able to cover long distances at very high speeds on the autoroutes, as well as to negotiate winding country roads, to thread my way through crowded towns, and to climb Mont Ventoux.

Both cars have the same 200 bhp engine and the independent suspension of all four wheels is also similar. The CSi is some 3in

shorter in the wheelbase and has a narrower rear track, the ultra-luxurious body being by Karmann coachworks. With its lower roof-line, the coupé has a smaller frontal area and the ratio of the hypoid final drive unit is 3.25 to 1, instead of the 3.45 of the saloon. In spite of the more compact appearance of the 2-door model, there is little difference in the total weight.

The Si saloon is a marvellous car to drive, being perfectly content to potter by the hour in London traffic but having an immense performance on the open road. The engine is never noisy, but it has the glorious note of a good six in perfect tune. The performance figures speak for themselves, but a large and roomy saloon that will accelerate from a standstill to 60 mph in 7.4 s can only be

described as phenomenal. Yet, I had to start off with the engine virtually idling in order to keep the wheelspin within bounds. The car is somewhat nose-heavy and the already excellent acceleration figures could be greatly improved with a bit more weight over the driving wheels.

The gearbox is light to handle and permits rapid changes. Second gear will just reach 60 mph, which permits the 0-60 mph time to be taken with only one change. As with all cars of this make, third is an excellent gear, with a maximum in excess of 90 mph. The clutch copes easily with the power of the engine. It is interesting that although the car is outstandingly flexible on top gear, the engine suddenly seems to come alive at 4000 rpm and it is between that speed and

The Si has well-placed instruments with clear round dials.

Up in the clouds — the CSi at the top of Mont Ventoux.

6200 rpm that it does its best work. It is a virtue of a highly developed fuel-injection engine that it can combine limousine flexibility with competition-type top-end performance.

From 90 mph upwards, the saloon makes a lot of wind noise and it is inferior in this respect to the coupé. I believe that these cars vary a good deal and "my" Si had covered a large mileage in many hands, so perhaps the window sealing had suffered. The insulation of road noise is satisfactory and the transmission is quiet while, as I have already implied, such sound as the engine makes will cause the pulse of any enthusiast to beat faster.

The Si accelerates rapidly up to 132 mph, which is the maximum speed claimed by the makers, at which the rev counter has just entered the red section. The ignition cutout operates at about 133 mph, which discourages further excursions into forbidden territory. Equivalent revs on the higher-geared coupé give 138 mph, but a small variation in the distributor cutout setting allowed the car to touch 140 mph without that sudden silence. The acceleration of the two cars was almost identical, but the lower-geared saloon felt

very slightly livelier and perhaps it gained the odd tenth of a second in the middle ranges.

There was very little difference in the roadholding and handling. The initial understeer is moderate, the characteristic being substantially neutral, though the rear end begins to break away when provoked beyond its high limits. In my case, the coupé had harder suspension than the saloon, but this was probably only a question of damper variation with mileage. Similarly, the steering of the CSi had more power assistance but I preferred the slightly heavier setting with more feel. The brakes of both cars seemed immune from fading, the coupé having the lighter pedal, and the pressure limiting valve effectively prevented rear-wheel locking.

The 3-litre BMW with Bosch fuel injection is a car of dramatic performance. Smooth, quiet, and refined, it does not obtain its speed at the expense of any other quality. Whether the 2-door or 4-door version is chosen is a matter of personal preference, for both are equally practical as 4-seater touring cars with ample luggage space. Perhaps the bank manager will have the last word, for the patrician appearance of the coupé costs a

lot of money and the difference in performance is slight indeed.

Cars tested: BMW 3.0 Si 4-door saloon, price £3999. BMW 3.0 CSi 2-door coupé, price £5699, both including tax.

Engine : Six cylinders in-line 89 mm x 80 mm (2985 cc). Compression ratio 9.5 to 1. 200 bhp (net) at 5500 rpm. Chain-driven overhead camshaft. Bosch electronic fuel injection.

Transmission: Single dry plate clutch. 4-speed all-synchromesh gearbox with central lever, ratios 1.0, 1.4, 2.2, and 3.85 to 1. Hypoid final drive, ratio: Si 3.45 to 1, CSi 3.25 to 1.

Chassis: Combined steel body and chassis. Independent suspension of all four wheels with coil springs and auxiliary rubber springs, MacPherson front and semi-trailing arms rear. ZF power-assisted worm and roller steering. Servo-assisted ventilated disc brakes all round. Steel wheels on Si and light-alloy wheels on CSi fitted 195/70 VR14 radial ply tyres.

Equipment: 12-volt lighting and starting with alternator. Speedometer. Rev counter. Water temperature and fuel gauges. Clock. Heating, demisting, and ventilation system with electrically heated rear window. Electric window actuation on CSi. Variable speed windscreen wipers and washers. Flashing direction indicators with hazard warning. Reversing lights.

Dimensions: Si: Wheelbase 8ft 10in; track (front) 4ft 8.9in, (rear) 4ft 9.6in; overall length 15ft 5in; width 5ft 8.9in. CSi: Wheelbase 8ft 7in; track (front) 4ft 9in, (rear) 4ft 7.5in; overall length 15ft 3.5in; width 5ft 6in; weight (both cars) 1 ton 7 cwt.

Performance: Si: Maximum speed 132 mph. Speeds in gears: Third 93 mph; Second 62 mph; First 34 mph. Standing quarter-mile 15.3 s. Acceleration: 0-30 mph 2.8 s. 0-50 mph 5.7 s. 0-60 mph 7.4 s. 0-80 mph 13.1 s. 0-100 mph 21.0 s. 0-110 mph 27.5 s. CSi: Maximum speed 140 mph.

Fuel consumption: Si 18 to 22 mpg

The Si has tremendous performance but is a full four seater.

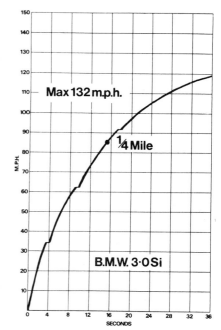

Max 132 m.p.h.

¼ Mile

B.M.W. 3·0Si

BMW v FALCON—AN IMPOSSIBLE COMPARISON? BILL TUCKEY THOUGHT SO AT FIRST, BUT FINALLY DECIDED THAT AFTER ALL IT'S ALL A MATTER OF...

More than anything else the rear suspension design typifies the concepts behind the BMW and Falcon. The German car gets four wheel vented discs and fully independent suspension, the Falcon rear drum brakes and leaf springs.

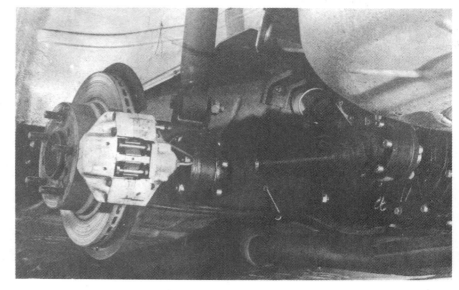

HORSES FOR COURSES

HÊ DIDN'T HAVE anything to do with it, but NSW politician Mr C. Kelly gave the point to this story.

Early in March he launched an effective and controlled attack on the Australian motor industry and the tariff policies surrounding it. Briefly, he said if the industry didn't have such high tariff protection against imported cars — brought about, he suggested, by a Government desire to protect the jobs of workers in the Australian components industry — then we would be able to buy imported cars up to $1000 cheaper.

In radio talk-back sessions subsequently, although somewhat stifled by commentators who knew little about the structure of the industry, he used Sweden's Volvo as an example. He pointed out Volvo was able to source its parts from almost anywhere in the world, but still exported nearly 70 percent of its production at very competitive prices. Yet there were no tariff barriers in Sweden to protect the two local manufacturers.

Mr Kelly (who has not been heard on the industry before but who un-doubtedly will have more to say in the future) said five car manufacturers were more than enough for Australia and the Government should not be forcing two or maybe three others to go into full local build.

He had nothing to do with it, as I said, but at the time he launched his verbal rocket I was unwinding a BMW 3.0S over Bulahdelah Mountain in NSW on the instructions of Peter Robinson, the bearded WHEELS editor whose mind works in devious ways. He asked me to try the car and look at it in the light of Australia building the wrong sort of car; that this size of car, with this size of engine, was what we should be building to give Australia not only the kind of car it should have but also the world engineering status it was capable of supporting.

He may have had in mind the WHEELS Car Of The Year award, which was conceived as a recognition of Australian design achievement and which still means far more to the industry than a small collection of

HORSES FOR COURSES

esoteric letters written by readers, most of whom may not know anyhow.

Following the XA Falcon release, I was still analysing what I now believe to be one of the milestones in the history of the Australian industry, just as was the first Holden, the first Valiant, the XR Falcon and the Morris Major/Austin Lancer Mk II. We had seen in the XA the first Australian car to show signs of European influence in ergonomical design; and it is certainly the first Australian car that from top to toe was conceived mainly in Australia with only the smallest concession to overseas design and economical control.

So I gradually evolved this into an ad hoc comparison of what the two cars represented in this market — not what they stood for in the environment for which they were originally designed. I have not put together a comparison in the traditional sense of the word; rather a cold-blooded evaluation of the design theory behind each car and how each country approaches a similar problem differently. After all, you cannot pay $10,000 for a Falcon, which is what the 3.0S BMW costs. And anyone who buys the BMW is entirely unlikely to have considered a Falcon for even a moment. So we are not denigrating the BMW or the Falcon. They are designed for different usage, different reasons, different economics, different social levels, different environment.

The key to it all lies in what the cars cost. In Germany the 3.0S BMW costs $5085.

Here, with no extras, it costs $10,165.

In a normal evaluation of a car you must establish clearly in your own mind why it was designed and for what sort of market. Most Australian motoring journalists forget this, and engage first gear of the mind without understanding that a $3000 family car does not necessarily have to lap Amaroo or Bathurst at 100 mph. But in this case I'm looking at the BMW not as a high-performance middle-range European touring car; and I'm not looking at the XA Falcon as a volume-selling, American-oriented, medium-priced Australian-conformist and Moonee-Ponds-mediocre sedan.

Any car design is inevitably the product of its environment, its environment being the market place; and the influences forming this market place, or environment, being the wants and needs of the people who buy the cars. In other words, the market gets exactly the car it wants and deserves.

So we have a $10,000 BMW. It need not necessarily be that 3.0S BMW; it could be down around the $4500 area for the 1600, although that and its warmer brother, the 2002, are performance two-door coupes and can't really be measured against a Falcon. What would a $10,000 BMW cost if it could be imported direct into Australia without paying duty? That's a hard question to answer, because duty payments run on a complicated sliding scale, and shipping charges and distributor handling charges are equally difficult to assess.

Educated guess time . . . I think that if our market were duty-free you would see this 3.0S BMW selling for about $6500.

Then comes the problem of finding an equivalent Falcon. To get equivalent bucket seats, carpeting and trim you have to select the Fairmont. That gives you a base price of $3770. But to that, to get equivalent performance, you must add $300 worth of 351 V8. Then a four-speed gearbox, disc brakes, radial ply tyres, and finally the GS pack to get full instrumentation, a good steering wheel and the other bits and pieces.

All up you finish with about $4750 worth of Falcon.

Two grand's worth of difference can be explained away in the infinitely better suspension and braking systems of the German car, which after all is a luxury touring car in the first place. So forget that and look at what else you get.

You get 106 in. of wheelbase in the BMW against 111 in. for the Falcon. Now, 106 in. is a long wheelbase for any European car, for there the optimum usable consumer average lies somewhere between 96 and 104. The Falcon is only 1½ in. longer, however, which says something about overhangs, 6 in. wider (reflecting the Australian market's styling tastes and apparent need to carry three on a front bench seat) and 3 in. lower — which can be attributed only to styling.

But both have similar tank capacities at 17.5 gals for the Falcon and 16.5 for the BMW — although the BMW's better consumption would give it a slightly longer range.

Continued on next page

And even more surprisingly, ground clearance is almost identical at 5.4 in. (Falcon) and 5.5 in. (BMW), with both on 14 in. rims and nearly the same tyres (185 Falcon against 195 BMW). But the BMW turns in 36 ft, where the Falcon takes 40.

So basically the two cars are fairly close in overall package size, except for the extra interior width demanded by the Falcon — which must also, don't forget, accommodate a much wider range of seating and body usage than the BMW.

But when you get to the nitty-gritty of what that body sits on, you start to understand why the BMW is perhaps the best sedan in the world — indeed WHEELS believes it is — ZF-Gemmer worm and roller steering against the basic ordinary recirculating ball, whose main virtue is economy; independent coil-strut front suspension with trailing links and rubber auxiliary springs, independent semi-trailing arms and coil struts and rubber auxiliary springs at rear — compared to ball-joint/coils front and good ol' 1930 semi-elliptic leaf.

Now you start to understand why the BMW will swoop around impossible corners at speed, will scream its Continentals into High C before they finally, reluctantly let go on a streaming road.

Nonetheless, I don't think the BMW optional power steering is as good as the excellent new Bishop variable-ratio system used by the Ford — but that's mere personal opinion and as such is of questionable value.

So what else? Oh, 10.7 in. ventilated discs on all four wheels with separate 6.3 in. rear drums for the handbrake. On the Ford you get 10 in. drums all round unless you pay an extra $66 for the discs (which we're doing) and that gets you ventilated front discs only. They are 11.25 in. They are bigger than the BMW because there are only two of them to stop a car that is (surprisingly) not much heavier. Base unladen weight for the BMW is 3042 lb, where the Ford goes "from" 3017 lb. This Ford figure is for the basic and spartan three-speed six-cylinder car, but even so the model we've specified would not be more than 150 lb heavier. And, of course, the basic disc brakes must be common to the whole Falcon range, for reason of economics, and thus must adequately stop the Falcon GT as well as the basic wagon loaded to the gunwales for three weeks every year.

You see? We're still no closer to our solution. The package size is similar, the suspension, steering and brakes reflect simply the extra money spent by the German engineers to build a car with the roadability demanded by the client.

Bring in engines, and what do you find? You find the delightful and unbreakable sohc BMW hemi-headed six will crank to 6200 rpm at redline and 7000 rpm without fuss, is as docile as a milkman's horse and will sit in traffic jams in 100 degree heat murmuring quietly to itself at 600 rpm. Give it at least 200 bhp by the American (Ford) method of measuring these things which is only beginning to go out of fashion across the Pacific.

It is of just 184.4 cu in. capacity, and Ford's smallest six is 200. For that they claim 130 bhp. You have to go to the 302 to get 240 bhp, but we've thrown in the 260 bhp two-barrel 351 engine. But look at the torque! The BMW has only 188 lb/ft at 3700 rpm, where the lowly 200-inch Ford six has 190 at 2000! It dies at 3700, probably delivering 20 lb/ft, but we won't go into that. The 351 hands down 355 at 2600, and there is no doubt that at 3700 it is still probably twisting the crank with around 250 lb/ft.

So. Or, Ach So. Three hundred and fifty one inches will deliver the Falcon to the end of the quarter in around mid-16s, I think, not having run figures on that particular combination.

The BMW is nearly half a second quicker and at the end of a quarter the thing is only just starting to work properly. It continues without fuss to its maximum of 125, where the Falcon (again a guess) will still at around 112-115, more because of frontal area than anything else. And the BMW is even faster over a quarter with a bend in the middle . . .

It's in the interior that your tiny brain starts desperately trying to correlate the idiomatic guide-lines of each car. You get a shock when you notice in the BMW there is no way of stowing the buckle end of the belt, something Japanese and Australian car makers long ago spent money on solving. You also notice piddling ashtrays in the rear and only one in the front — right in the centre of the dash and very close to the

crash padding, so you inevitably stub your cigarette on the padding. That's all stupid.

You notice other things on the dash are well away from you, and the carpet is a hard-wearing woven utilitarian kind, not the cut-pile style Australian cars use, which certainly won't last as well but which look and soundproof better.

You find the fresh air ventilation, while better than most, still doesn't process the volume you need for this climate. And most of all, you notice the seats.

German seats have never been good. These are among the best, but still fall short. The Germans like to sit *on* their seats, rather than *in* them, and Mercedes is probably the possessor of the unfriendliest seats around. Oh, all German seats are anatomically and orthopaedically correct, I'm sure, because they are very thorough people with an enormous patience in research and testing. But they consistently err on the firm side. They are there, no nonsense, for sit-upon, Mark One. None of this caressing and embracing baloney. They're there, you feel, to stop your bottom hitting the floor pan.

Likewise, no European manufacturer, with few exceptions, worry much about prettying up the facia. In an Australian, Japanese or British car you get used to explicit symbols and diagrams and controls you can use without referring to the handbook. The fresh air and heater controls in the BMW are, for instance, surprisingly awkward to use and slide along slots marked with chromed arrows and red and blue lines. I still haven't worked them out.

Above all, in cars like the BMW — the interior has a functional feel about it. They don't cosset the inhabitants, they don't wrap them in luxury. They put things there to work and to be used and let the driver get on with the job. They're more worried about what it does on the road than whether the windscreen wiper switch has the right satisfactory feel. They put the horn bars in each spoke; no mucking about with rims you squeeze or concealed press-tits. They don't even bother to identify the gear-lever knob with a gearshift pattern. You get the feeling that if you need to be told that then you ought not to be behind that wheel.

In that whole approach you have the essential difference between the two design philosophies. Much of the work on the new Falcon (for instance, and we are using it only as the newest *for instance* made in Australia) went into the dash. It had to be curved and angled and ergonomigimmicked so you could reach everything while in a belt. There are plenty of big ashtrays. No neat door or seat-back pockets, as in the BMW.

The carpet is lusher and the seats much more sittable. And they have coat-hooks. Coat-hooks. Do you know that the BMW doesn't have coat-hooks? Why not? Because the European businessman is simply not in the habit of driving with his coat removed. Neither climate nor custom demand you drive in shirt sleeves. Even in Britain, this is sometimes regarded as a sign of lower-middle-class decadence.

Interesting — no, fascinating. There is no direct comparison between the cars, because the BMW is a superb automobile that is marvellous on the open road and just a little frustrating around town. The Falcon is meant as an urban car, and is on the open road only a better way of getting there than Panther coach. There is no comparison at all between the cars on performance, handling, ride, steering and braking.

In the areas where the two are similar, the differences in approach are clearly defined — clearly enough to draw pictures of what market research tells each company their buyers want. And that is essentially the only difference between the two cars. Horses for courses.

So that is why it went astray, why I couldn't write what Peter Robinson wanted. You couldn't build the BMW for the Australian market because it's far too good. To me it is close to the ideal personal car — for me. But for Sandy Stone of Moonee Ponds it would be an annoying joke, with ridiculous ashtrays and no coat-hooks, by God. And a Falcon in Europe would be regarded as another example of how superficial the American/Australians are about their cars.

Finally, a postscript. I have a young and wealthy friend who owns a BMW 3.0S. He drives it rather hard. He has added Koni shockers and lowered it and added some extra rubber, because he says he doesn't get around corners fast enough.

He is quite mad.

But he loves the seats and he doesn't smoke and he drives to work with his coat on . . .   *

Aluminum Foil

BMW's new light-metal 130 mph street-racer.
Available at a dealer near you soon — maybe
By Bernard Cahier

BMW dueler gets wood-rimmed Alpina wheel

BMW has always been a sporting marque and, aside from Porsche, is the only German company that has kept a close contact with racing since that country's spectacular postwar rebirth.

While Germany's most famous racing name, Mercedes, has deliberately abandoned all forms of racing, BMW continues to have a finger in racing somewhere. With the recent change of Formula 2 rules, BMW has, temporarily we hope, pulled out from this form of competition. However, their efforts in touring car racing (particularly in Group 2 type cars) are being increased this season for two main reasons. One is that BMW does not like to be beaten by Ford, which is precisely what happened last season.

The other reason is that a well-known company director, famous for his enthusiasm for anything which goes fast on 4 or 2 wheels, has taken over the

hot seat for Herr Heineman, no longer in grace with the management.

This man, Bob Lutz, was the Sales Director of Opel in Germany. Before he left the GM-owned company, Lutz was regarded as the man behind the present success of Opel and its change of image to a smart-looking and even sport-minded product.

At BMW, Bob Lutz hired the well-known Jochen Neerpash, competition director of Ford Germany and the man responsible for the success of the Ford Capri Rs over the BMWs.

Next, Lutz activated the sport program concerning the 3-liter fuel injection coupe which was too heavy in its present production form.

When the project started, this car was called the CSL (L meaning light-weight). This car was different from the regular coupe in that it had aluminum doors, hood and trunk lid, no bumpers and plastic side and rear win-

dows. The weight savings of 300 pounds was interesting, but prior to Lutz' arrival this program suffered from at least one mistake.

The CSL was available with only the carburetor version of the ohc 6-cylinder engine, which meant that it had 180 hp (DIN) instead of 200 for the fuel injected model. The reason for this was that the technicians thought it was unnecessary to homologate it with the Bosch fuel injection system since it is unsuited for racing.

This was true, but what was forgotten was that in order to be homologated as a Group 2 touring car at least 1,000 cars must be made and that is a lot of cars for a specialized machine. Would the average customer, even the BMW type customer, be interested in paying more for a car with less smoothness and performance inferior to that of the standard fuel injection coupe! With the further consideration that the lightweight coupe has plastic windows which are easily scratched and aluminum doors which are vulnerable in everyday use.

Bob Lutz did not think so.

He reoriented the program of the CSL, which was renamed CSR. As it stands now the car is still offered, naturally, in its lightweight version, but with either carburetors or fuel injection.

It is also possible for the buyer to have what is called a street package, which is the same car but with bumpers, regular glass windows and steel doors. This makes sense since it will appeal to a larger range of buyers and as a result more sales can be expected — with the result that the quantity necessary for homologation will be reached more quickly.

We drove two cars, Bob Lutz's personal fuel injected CSR with the street package, and the standard CSR with carburetors which was the car on which our test was concentrated. With good weather conditions prevailing we were able to put the production CSR through tests on both the open road and the well-equipped BMW proving grounds.

The carbureted CSR was a splendid yellow coupe, fitted with standard 7-inch wide mag wheels. It did not have, however, the stripe on the side which will normally be on all CSR models. The standard steering wheel was replaced by a wooden, three-spoke, sport-type wheel. Without bumpers the CSR looks lower and faster than the regular CS and its sporty appearance is made even more pronounced by the aluminum fender flares designed to accommodate bigger wheels and tires. Inside, the two deep, well-designed bucket seats provide a maximum of comfort and lateral support for driver and passenger.

I would mention the back seats, however, because with those bucket seats moved back into a long-leg driving position there is no knee room left in the rear. The driving position is as good as one could wish, and the small diameter Alpina sport steering wheel is there to remind you that you are driving something different from the normal. With its black velvet lined interior and smart dash board with wood touches, the interior is all elegant and in good taste. Visibility is good and all the instruments are easy to read and use.

On the road the first pleasant thing you notice with CSR is that the aluminum hood does not seem to have increased the engine noise, which always remains, even at high speeds, at a pleasant level. I say "pleasant" because this 6-cyl ohc BMW has such a wonderful sound that it would be almost a shame if it were too quiet.

Wind noise, however, was more noticeable and I am wondering if the suppression of the quarter windows would eliminate part of this problem. The car, incidentally, has the normal heating-ventilation system which works well.

Operated by a short shift lever, the four-speed box is quick and precise; the ratios are quite good but I would have preferred a higher second gear or, even better, a five speed box. Using 6500 rpm, first gear would go to 38 mph, second to 62 mph, and third to 100. With a lightweight high performance car like the CSR coupe, one could expect a hard suspension. But this is not so, as BMW, in giving the car special Bilstein shock absorbers has succeeded in giving it a comfortable ride even on mediocre roads. It also has very little lean, even on severe corners.

The CSR has an all around independent suspension which is extremely well-tuned for fast driving.

It takes a little practice, however, especially for those who, like me, have been driving cars with a solid type axle. Indeed, when you come fast into a corner the car will understeer nicely, and there is no basic problem. On very fast bends, though, I noticed a slight wandering of the front end. I also noticed that when you are trying hard on a corner and suddenly lift your foot the normal, predictable understeer will change quickly to a surprise, pronounced oversteer. After a few times you become accustomed to that behavior which does not actually become alarming, but requires some getting used to.

The not-so-direct steering, over four turns could be improved, lock-to-lock, and we would prefer power steering (which was removed in the CSR version) which would be quicker and less tiring, especially for town driving and parking. The ventilated

》》》》

Aluminum Foil

brakes were well balanced and gave no problem, but I must say in honesty that we did not try them on a mountain road. On the open road and at maximum speed the car feels extremely stable and gives you a good feeling of confidence. The engine sounds great, the instruments work well and there is no doubt that you are driving a car which is well made to go fast comfortably.

The performances were satisfying but not as high as I had expected. Using a 6500 rpm red line, we did the quarter mile in 15.8 seconds, and the standing kilometer in 29.5 seconds. Zero to 50 mph took 5.8 seconds; 0 to 60 mph 8 seconds; 0 to 80 13 seconds; 0 to 90 16.8; and 0 to 100 22.2 seconds while maximum speed was 131.5 mph.

The engine was always remarkably willing and smooth. In fact, during our "old grandad" type test we could go nicely as low as 22 mph in 3rd gear, using only 1300 rpm, and 27 mph in 4th gear using 2000 rpm. In both cases the car would pick up speed again without fuss. On Bob Lutz's own car fitted with fuel injection we had even smoother operation at low speeds.

While talking about Lutz's car, it is a beautiful metallic grey coupe with black stripes on the sides and a front spoiler said to give an extra 3 mph in top speed. The inside was plush with all the goodies, including full stereo cassette and air conditioning. This car, which had bumpers, electrically operated glass windows and steel doors (only the hood and trunk were in aluminum) was actually a street version of the CSR, which should be on the market soon. Checking the times of this fuel injection version we discovered that it was in fact faster than the lightweight version with carburetors which had, of course, 20 hp less. The top speed was 137 mph, and acceleration was 0 to 60 in 7.4, and 0 to 100 in 18.5 seconds, while the quarter mile and standing kilometer were done respectively in 15.2 and 28.2 seconds.

This shows, I think, the advantage for the normal buyer of the fuel injection version, even with some 200 more pounds to carry in the street version. I personally would go for this version, leaving the less practical lightweight car for those who want to put in a modified engine and go racing. Naturally you can also, if you want to be different, buy the all-light version and have the fuel injection for it. In which case you would have a car faster than the street version, but which would have to remain as it is because only the carburetor version can be turned into a racing engine, in its present form. However, with the ultra-light aluminum paneling you would have a real bomb doing 0 to 60 in under 7 secs.

Following this test of the CSR we are convinced that BMW is going in the right direction in producing a high class automobile capable of satisfying a varied and demanding clientele. We are very impressed by this new CSR and just as impressed by the enthusiasm of those behind its development.

And now with a man of the caliber of Bob Lutz you can be sure that there will not be a dull moment at BMW (or a dull car) for the forseeable future. /MT

A thousand aluminum-paneled CSR coupes will be sold to homologate car for Group 2 racing. Customers will have choice of carbs or injection and a street package option, with bumpers, steel doors and glass windows.

25,000 Miles In A Bavaria

by Raleigh M. Neville

If you're interested in BMW's, you'll want to read what this owner thinks about his "magnificent compromise."

If an auto enthusiast were to list all of the qualities he wanted in an ideal, but practical road car, chances are he would come up with a package very similar to the BMW Bavaria.

Aesthetic appeal, great handling, superior brakes, fast, but delivering good gas mileage, reliable, durable, solid, well appointed, with an aura of sporting luxury and room for four or five full sized adults and all the luggage they care to carry on a coast to coast vacation . . . the BMW Bavaria has it all and then some.

Basic to its appeal is a six cylinder

overhead cam engine with hemispherical combustion chambers that has to be one of the most advanced designs on the market. Displacing only 170 cubic inches, it puts out a whopping 192 hp (SAE), and will propel this 3,000 pound sedan to 60 mph in less than nine seconds. Top speed is in the vicinity of 125 mph and it will theoretically cruise all day at 120. Are you listening Detroit?

I was one of the fortunate few who took delivery of one of these Wundercars at the factory in Munich, in June, 1971, just before a sharply devalued dollar and the imposition of a fortunately short-lived 10% import tax made many foreign cars prohibitively expensive.

I had ordered the Bavaria with standard transmission, sun roof, Michelin XAS radials, metallic blue paint and a Blaupunkt AM/FM radio (which the factory forgot to install). I discovered that

the car also contained a number of options that I had not ordered such as power steering (supposedly not available without air conditioning), tinted glass, an electric rear window defroster and a front anti sway bar which was not supposed to be available on early export models.

I spent four weeks wringing the car out in Germany, Austria, Italy, Switzerland, France and Spain, over potholed, narrow back country roads, fast autobahns, tortuous Alpine passes well over 12,000 feet and traffic choked boulevards. Initial speed during the break-in period was limited to a seemingly lazy 80 mph, but in the course of 3,000 miles of driving, I did have several opportunities to let it have its head. At 120 mph, with the speedometer still climbing and the radio tuned to a soothing FM station, there is near perfect control, no noise and little sensation of speed, other than the fact that the scenery is rushing by awfully fast and you're overtaking other cars at an alarming rate.

The first service on the car was performed as required after 600 miles, by an efficient BMW dealer in Salzburg, Austria. The $25 cost was later reimbursed by the distributor in the States. It was the only service that the car required in Europe. It was also in Salzburg, while parked at the hotel, that the Bavaria's flawless finish suffered its first dent. A butterfingered American tourist (no less), dropped a suitcase into the right side of the car while unloading his VW bus.

Driving in Europe can still be a genuine pleasure, even with main roads that are greatly overcrowded and secondary roads that are often in a terrible state of disrepair. Europeans not only know how to make fast, interesting cars, they also know how to drive them. The general absence of speed limits and the competence and courtesy of virtually all drivers, combine to give the impression of a smooth, free flowing automotive ballet.

The Bavaria ran flawlessly throughout the trip. Oil consumption was limited to about a quart, and a tank of premium gas (at $10 to $12 a tankful) would usually last through a day's driving.

It was with genuine regret and some trepidation that I turned the car over to the shipper in Paris. BMW had recommended Adolph Brauns, a large freight forwarder with head offices in Hamburg. Their manager in Paris quoted a figure of $420.00 to ship the car to Baltimore. Feeling very much at their mercy, I called another shipper (this one recommended through Europe by Car, Inc., through whom I had purchased the car), and got a similar quotation. Reluctantly, I arranged to have Adolph Brauns ship the car — COD since they would not accept a personal check. It was a good thing they didn't, for when I picked the car up in Baltimore one month later, I was pleasantly shocked to receive a bill for only $270 — including the COD charge.

With 4,500 miles showing on the odometer, I took the car to VOB Datsun in Bethesda, Maryland (one of several BMW dealers in the Washington area), for routine service. By this time it had shown itself to be a little less than perfect and there were a few items that needed repair under warranty. The synchromesh could easily be beaten when making a fast shift from 2nd to 3rd at full throttle, the left rear door would no longer lock, and water was collecting under the left front and right rear floor mats. The bill came to $40 — including $13 for retorquing the cylinder head, an item not called for at this service interval.

BMW specifies minor service at

4,000 mile intervals, with a complete tuneup called for after each 8,000 miles. Thus after 8,500 miles, with the car seemingly running perfectly, it was back to VOB Datsun for the required routine. This time the bill was a hefty $102.00, for a job that was much less than satisfactory. In the weeks that followed, the car had to be returned to this dealer at least a half dozen times to get it running properly. Items that needed attention included missing at high rpm (the distributor had not been lubricated), an improperly adjusted automatic choke, timing that was off, carburetor settings that were incorrect, and fuel lines that were not tightly connected. As if that were not enough, the garage managed to add two small dents to the car — for which they said they were sorry!

Since the warranty expired at 12,000 miles and I no longer had to worry about complying with its terms, I reverted to an 8,000 mile service interval (with the exception of course of the oil and oil filter which are changed every 4,000 miles). The Bavaria simply does not need to be tuned and inspected every 4,000 miles unless you don't mind paying someone $45 to look at your spark plugs and check your brake fluid, hoses, water, etc.

At 16,000 miles, while girl watching on the way home from work, I cruised into the back of another car that had made a sudden stop. The impact was very minor, but the damage made me appreciate the wisdom behind the Federal bumper standards. The guy I hit was driving an old, beat up '66 Plymouth commuter special. Naturally, there was no damage at all to his car. Mine suffered a slightly buckled right front fender, a broken parking light and a bent bumper. It really didn't look very bad and I was sure that repairs would not exceed my $100 deductible.

I really should not have choked when presented with a bill for a staggering $193. BMW's are not cheap to repair. True, they do cost considerably less to fix than a Mercedes or Porsche, but hit something with one and you can count on your insurance agent eyeing you nervously when you go in to renew your policy.

I had taken the Bavaria to the newest BMW dealer in the Washington area — Mt. Vernon Datsun, BMW, in Alexandria, Virginia, for repairs and the 16,000 mile service. Theirs is an impressive shop. They did a beautiful job of tuning the engine, to the point where the surging and erratic choke operation that I had chalked up to one of the penalties of cleaner air and was learning to live with, all but disappeared. I also noticed an immediate and rather striking increase in gas mileage.

Unfortunately, they did not do so well in repainting the right front fender. BMW offers some very attractive metal-

lic colors, but they are proving to be almost impossible to match. Even using the factory supplied Baikal blue metallic (at $13 a quart), the fender looked like it was painted an entirely different color from the rest of the car. Hours spent patiently compounding and rubbing it down have reduced the difference considerably, but it is still quite noticeable.

In the course of 25,000 miles of hard driving, any car is bound to exhibit some shortcomings, however minor, and the Bavaria is no exception:

• Unless the blower is operating, the flow-through ventilation is inadequate and cannot be individually controlled by driver and passenger;

• Although the seats are firm and very comfortable, particularly on long trips, the driving position is typically European, making it difficult for some drivers to get really comfortable. A smaller, adjustable steering wheel would help immensely;

• The suspension geometry is slightly off, causing an annoying weight transfer and slight bobbing motion when shifting or braking. BMW has remedied this on 1972 models;

• The gear ratios are spaced too far apart for smooth driving in heavy traffic. Shifting from 1st to 2nd and from 2nd to 3rd produces a drop of 1,500 rpm between each gear. As a result, in typical bumper to bumper traffic, the engine is either straining in 1st or lugging in 2nd. Although the standard 4-speed is positive, butter smooth, and can be snicked from gear to gear with two fingers if desired, the optional automatic would probably be more suited to this type of vehicle for general all around use. A noisy clutch throwout bearing does not add to the enjoyment;

• In spite of the fact that a dealer once spent ten minutes waxing on about the car's superior aerodynamics and how as a result, it does not need vent windows, this is just not the case. At anything over 10 mph a rear window must be partially opened to avoid the gale coming through the driver's window;

• A final criticism relates to the power steering. Although it provides excellent road feel, particularly at high speeds, it is not as quick as it could be and requires more effort to park than the typical American unit.

Most of the car's "faults" however, must be relegated to the category of nitpicking. The Bavaria simply does not have any glaring defects. In fact, the more time spent with it, the more one comes to appreciate just what an automobile should be. It is the kind of car that makes you look for an excuse to make a cross country run or a quick dash to the local supermarket. After 25,000 miles the car has lost none of its taut, crisp feel and there is still not a

Continued on next page

25,000 Miles In A Bavaria

single squeak or rattle. Driving over any road at any speed is a delightful experience that the average American motorist is totally unprepared for. The compact size, high seating position, outstanding visibility, and superb response and control, combine to produce a road car that is without equal in this country.

Handling is superb at any speed and far exceeds that which would normally be associated with a luxury sedan. The power brakes (four wheel disc of course), do a lot to contribute to the driver's confidence. They are powerful, well modulated and fade free — fully up to bringing this full size sports sedan to repeated straight line stops in a minimal distance from any speed.

The hemi six engine is a joy to behold and to listen to. It lacks the mechanical clatter of more mundane machinery and comes on strong with an almost musical whistle, and is free revving to the point where it doesn't feel like it's attached to anything. It is also astonishingly easy on gas thanks to highly efficient combustion and the car's superior aerodynamics. Several tankfuls which combined high speed 80-90 mph expressway driving with bumper to bumper city commuting, yielded 19 mpg, and in steady cruising, even when pushing the 60 to 70 mph limit on freeways, it returns 24 mpg. Around town, the low recorded was 16 mpg.

The car abounds with nice little engineering touches that aren't immediately apparent — windshield wipers with an intermittent cycle; a strange looking master ignition key that can be inserted either way and which also locks the trunk (a second key, to be left with sneaky looking garage attendants, operates the ignition only); a high quality, complete tool kit fitted in the underside of the trunk lid; seats that you don't really appreciate until you drive all day and find that you're not tired; splash panels painted with rubberized paint to protect them from corrosion; an engine compartment that is almost completely sealed to protect it from dirt and water; door locks that make it virtually impossible to lock yourself out; an enormous glove compartment on the passenger's side, a second one on the driver's side, and large storage pockets on each of the front doors and behind the front seats, and a trunk that is flat, cavernous, carpeted, and almost nice enough to live in.

From any angle, even in its remotest corners, the car exudes Quality, Craftsmanship, and Meticulous Care in assembly. It is beautifully finished and detailed, with none of the rough edges, sloppy paint, loose screws and other evidences of poor quality control that we have come to take so much for granted. And everything works — with crisp precision — even down to the VDO clock which keeps better time than my Omega watch.

The Bavaria has breezed through 25,000 miles of every type of road and weather condition imaginable and yet shows almost no signs of wear or fatigue. The Michelin XAS radials are still good for at least another 10,000 miles, maybe more. If anything, the engine feels even stronger and more flexible than it did when new, and will pull like a diesel from 1,500 rpm. The redline is 6,200 rpm and it comes very quickly and effortlessly, particularly in first and second gears. Several times I inadvertently ran it to more than 7,000 rpm (fortunately without damage), and it still wanted to rev on. The only discernible sign of weakness so far is the clutch. Although it does not slip, it has recently begun to feel a little weak and juddery.

The Bavaria quickly gives the driver the impression that he is at the wheel of a sports tank. Doors close with a solid, vault like thud, and the car can be hurtled over rough and broken pavement without so much as a squeak. It is a car that wants to run fast and it will thunder down the road all day at 100 mph plus without ever losing its poise or making you lose yours. Yet it will also tick along in bumper to bumper traffic without the stalling, overheating and fouled plugs normally associated with high performance engines producing more than a horsepower per cubic inch NET.

An unexpected but pleasant surprise has been the insurance rates on the car. Although it is by any standard an expensive luxury model that costs plenty to repair and much more to replace, and is also a sort of European muscle car with a very favorable weight to horsepower ratio and high performance potential, the Bavaria is classified by the insurance companies as a compact car, with an attractive insurance savings over, say, a Cadillac. Full coverage in Virginia costs approximately $140 per year.

The Bavaria's appeal is not that of a status symbol. Status symbols after all, have to be instantly recognizable, and most Americans have never even heard of a BMW — let alone know what it is or what it looks like. Besides, it looks like a compact car and lacks the sexy appeal of say a Pinto or a Camaro. But it should make a big hit with the performance oriented enthusiast who appreciates fine craftsmanship, a superbly competent machine, and functional understated luxury — all at a price not much more than a "loaded" Impala. Such people are not usually very attracted to a 2½ ton, 20 foot long, $10,000 domestic luxury barge anyway.

All in all, the Bavaria is a magnificent compromise that would be difficult to equal at any price. There are cars that are faster, there are a very few that handle better, and somewhere there may be one or two that are more comfortable and better finished, but there are virtually none that combine all these virtues to the degree that the Bavaria does. In any category, it is a standout in its class and the overall package adds up to much more than the sum of its parts. Cars like this should put Mercedes out of business. ●

COST OF DRIVING 25,000 MILES

Price of car as equipped at Munich (June, 1971)	$4,431.00
Registration (Europe)	63.50
Insurance (1 month Europe)	75.00
Shipping	275.00
Duty	124.00
Federal excise tax	279.00
Registration (Virginia, including 2% sales tax)	116.00
Insurance (1 year full coverage, 20/40/10, 3,000 med. pay., 100 ded. collision, comprehensive, uninsured motorists, towing & labor)	141.00
Service by dealers (including 1 wheel alignment and 1 tire rotation with balancing)	217.00
Repairs (including $8 for replacing a right rear tail lamp assembly that shorted out, $20 for replacing a transistor in the radio, and $100 collision deductible for accident)	128.00
Gas (1,315 gals of premium at 39 cents/gal & 19 mpg)	513.00
Oil (40 quarts at 58 cents/qt)	23.00
TOTAL COST TO DATE	$6,385.50
Less estimated current value	$5,000.00
NET COST OF DRIVING 25,000 MILES	$1,385.50
COST PER MILE	$.055

A SPECIAL PACKAGE, THEY SAID, exclusively for well-heeled UK customers with a taste for a bit of outer jazz and inner whizz; would we care to fly down to Naples with them and play the Walter Mitty with one for a few hours? It would be doing a sort of half-Nelson, we thought, with a glamorous car to enjoy instead of Lady Hamilton, and that only for 24 hours. But if the Admiral could only see the way we do the trip in the 1970s, at X thousand feet and in little more than the time it takes to work through a cold plastic tray by BEA, a gin and tonic and a quick drag. And we remembered the last time we were in Naples, with the ex-Prince Rainier straight-eight Daimler wedged firmly across a backstreet corner while a Blue Kangaroo was champing at the dock for us with its pouch open, ready to swallow us up and ship us to Sicily . . .

This time at least there should be no such motoring masochisms. We would be pampered in a lap of Anglo-Bavarian luxury, and wasn't ancient Sybaris only just across the way from Maratea, our goal for the night? The omens were favourable.

Vesuvius is not what it was—a non-smoker these days, and no ash to catch the wind and tip on some unsuspecting township enjoying every known form of Roman permissiveness. Naples, too, has changed, but visually only in parts and probably very little in character. Away from the main drags it still rises about you in shabby man-made gorges with the pastel-shaded stucco coming unstuck and the family washing strung out right down to street level. The buzzing Vespa is not yet dead here, ancient Appias still rub noses with modern Fulvias, and the shrieking Neapolitan *ragazzom* still teem—noisy, cheeky, and handsome as ever. Being as ho Naples is such a chaotic maelstro with so many latent opportunities losing one's way and the car's t finish, Raymond Playfoot (of BM Concessionaires GB) had decided wise to have us taken by coach to the coas town of Castellamare, a few miles sou and within two or three Olympic jave casts from Pompeii. (When we were la in Castellamare some 27 years ago t beach was a factory floor for wood fishing boats, still being whittled fro chunky timbers with the adse; now line of red-leaded steel hulls take sha in a modern shipyard). Here the silve blue BMW coops were being washed a refuelled after the last party of Guild motoring journalists had done the thing with them.

But first we must eat, and for this v

were hauled up 3000ft again, this time by long-distance cable on the *funivia* to the Grand Hotel Monte Faito where, although unaccustomed to this altitude, the squids there were as succulent as we could remember. On a clear day one can look across from that vantagepoint to the Capri that Axel Munthe and Gracie Fields had always promised themselves.

Forgive us—we nearly forgot. The Car. Well, it's a wolf in special light-weight wolfskin, being the 3.0litre six-cylinder single ohc CSi *(Coupe, S for Something, injection)*, which has been through a weight-reducing course to lave some 400lb avoirdupois, decorated with go-faster embellishment and rimmed in semi-racer style. It's really a ninly disguised homologation exercise o enable a sports-racing derivative to ualify for competitive circuitry. Let's heck the spec and see how it compares with the standard product. First you must be told that henceforth the standard coupe will be marketed in the UK only with carburettors (180bhp net), and automatic transmission, whereas hitherto one has had the additional options of either curburettors or injection with the four-speed manual box. The CSL *(Coupe, S for Something, Lightweight)* will come over only with the all-synchro box and FI; so it means, you see, that if you want the hot performance you've now got to plump willy-nilly for the rather conspicuously racy envelope.

Lightness has been added by having Messrs Karmann (who make the coupe bodies) press the bonnet, boot lid and door panels from aluminium in place of steel, and by fitting lightweight wrap-around front seats with fixed backrests. The back seat is also less thickly upholstered, which has the incidental merit of increasing *lebensraum* without losing out on riding comfort. Otherwise the interior is unchanged, and even the electric window lifts have been retained, although the prototype cars we tried had winding handles. So it's no austerity article. The engine is unchanged except for a wee increase in swept volume, from 2985 to 3003cc. We make the 18cc difference a mere 0.6percent, and understandably no extra horses are claimed above the regular 200 net; presumably the competition version is thought to stand a better chance among the over-three-litres. Then we have light alloy wheels with seven inch wide rims, shod with Michelin XWX 190/70 VR 14 tyres and nestling under extended wheel arches topped by chromium eyebrows; and stucco black stripes along the waist with '3.0CSL' stamped out.

See Naples and Drive

Should you buy a BMW CSL?
Ronald Barker goes south
to find out if a cooking foil
homologation special can
really be loved by anyone

Competition seats and sporty helm are mere cosmetics for the lightweight BMW CSL, but non-adjustable backrests are retrograde step, according to Ronald Barker

Thus any gain in performance derives solely from the weight-paring which isn't going to help the top speed any, and I doubt whether any improvement in acceleration would really be apparent except on paper—that's comparing it, of course, with the superseded CSi. The price is £6399 (are the very rich *really* beguiled by that odd pound sterling into thinking they have struck a sort of Marks and Sparks bargain?), £200 more than the CSA automatic and displaced manual CSi.

Getting in first time you're apt to bump your bum on the bucket seat's rigid frame (same both sides except that you're turning the other cheek). With cloth panels bordered by leather, they are form-fitting without being restrictive and very comfortable, although to this occupant they didn't seem to give appreciably better support than a properly-designed touring seat. Personally, we could not live with them in a £6000-plus car when lesser mortals were enjoying adjustable backrests. Imagine belting for hours down towards the Riviera with your friends, unable to alter the included angle between backbone and thighs when driving, or to let yourself right down for a zizz between spells at the wheel. These front seat frames being rigid, they hinge forward *in toto* to let in or discharge back-seat drivers, and are secured by locks with handy release triggers. The rear seat, a family two-holer divided by a rigid armrest, is comfortable enough except that one has to sit in the splits attitude. Still, we all know better now than to expect two-plus-two to equal four when we're talking motorcars.

Behind the wheel everything that should, falls nicely to hand or foot, although we should prefer a finger-tip lever for the main lighting switch.

Heeling-and-toeing comes naturally (a misnomer really as it's the instep rather than the heel). There are acres of window area, the bulkhead and bonnet are low relative to the line of sight, all of which helps to make the car feel reasonably compact.

Heigh-ho—let's go! The motor starts easily and idles with the typical FI 'hunting', the rpm rising and falling regularly. Outside, the exhaust note may remind you of the Ro80's Wankel, giving no clue as to the number of pots or strokes. Stand by the front grille and you hear a pronounced intake roar rather like an unhushed lavatory cistern taking on its next supply, but fortunately you catch none of this within the cabin. Moving off, the clutch is light to operate and feeds in smoothly—as well it should with a first gear ratio of only 12.5 to one, giving a mere 35mph or so at 6000rpm. With 200bhp and a healthy torque range we should have expected the Bavarian Motor Workers to risk something a bit higher than that. Into second, with a right and proper one-two spacing which therefore leaves second too low. Across the gate into third—a very slick and light change despite the short lever— and we have to jump a canyon from 7.15 to 4.55 overall, ratios giving about 61 and 97mph respectively at six thou.

When we branched off the famous *Autostrada del Sole* and took to the hills with their ceaseless *lacets* winding up, down and round the mountain folds, holding second kept the tachometer needle nudging at the red line with such a commotion under the bonnet, whereas changing up dropped one abruptly from the high-power range. Here we needed an upgraded second and/or lowered third to make proper use of the car's potential. That word 'commotion': granted that the engine is extremely

smooth all the way up and down, b[ut] one is not well insulated from its hig[h] pitched whine when turning fast. It's n[ot] that one has any qualms about the thin[g] suddenly reverting to a set of disunite[d] components, yet it's not relaxing.

So there it is: These days the BM[W] image has acquired such a mystiqu[e] among British pundit Nehrus that [to] criticize may seem almost as ungraciou[s] as letting off a squib under the Queen['s] horse during a colour trooping. Th[is] facet of the CSL was, frankly, a dis[-] appointment. A top speed arour[d] 145mph had been suggested, but th[e] two cars we sampled climbed sever[al] times to just over 130 (indicated) o[n] admittedly rather brief straight runs [on] *autostrada* and that's all there was roo[m] for on the somewhat Serpentine sectio[n] south of Naples. A calibration check o[f] steady speedometer readings agains[t] time elapsed between kilometre pos[ts] gave a correction factor of approx[i-] mately three percent fast, by the by[e]. Although the engines were sufficient[ly] free to be given the gun', they wou[ld] certainly perform better with a few mo[re] thousand miles behind them, but [I] should estimate 135-138 as the mo[st] likely limit. We were told later that th[e] standard undertrays were not fitted, s[o] they may mean a few extra mph.

As a motorway cruiser this BM[W] lightweight coupe has superb direc[-] tional stability on the straight, but nee[ds] stiffer damping for the front end to ove[r-] come, or at least reduce, some cork[-] screw bucking and lurching whe[n] disturbed by a poor road surfac[e] through fast bends. It behaves then lik[e] a speedboat crossing another's was[h.] Otherwise it rides very comfortably, a[nd] little road noise comes up through th[e] body structure. My notes read: *Wind Revs Drama Fuss at 100 and ove[r.]* Some of the wind roar may be excite[d] by the external mirror by the scree[n] pillar, but there remain insufferabl[e] vexations with the door window seal[s.] If you wound them down with the ca[r] moving no amount of pressure on th[e] handies could close them again withou[t] first slowing or stopping the car an[d] opening the door. Even then, in at leas[t] one case there was a visible ga[p] between the glass and the top seal. I[n] one of our two cars tried, every time th[e] car was braked fairly hard from 100 o[r] so there was a plaintive shriek fro[m] above the driver's door, just like tyr[e] squeal, as the top seal and windo[w] parted company. It might be caused b[y] distortion of the door within the bod[y] framework, but we'll be charitable an[d] put it down to the vagaries of aero[-] dynamic pressures.

The weight-saving benefits of th[e] light alloy panels seem to be question[-] able assets when set against the[ir] penalties: all the boot lids of the te[st] cars were dented where people ha[ve]

Continued on next pag[e]

See Naples and Drive

leaned on them to shut them. The trick is to push down quite gently on the BMW emblem above the lock, but who's to warn everyone who will try to shut the thing during the car's service? And at high speed the bonnet arched in the middle like a cat's back, by as much as an inch it appeared.

Now for a few compliments. On motorways one uncovers only a few aspects of a car's total roadability so, as mentioned earlier, we spent several happy hours with Michael Bowler of Motocar having a fling in the hills to discover how this one behaved when pressed as hard as most owners would attempt, and what happened when you took a few extra liberties. The roads were dry so one cannot speak of wet weather abilities, but we found it marvellously stable and well-balanced. Some of these byways were pretty rough in parts, yet it was never displaced more than a few inches from the chosen line, even when full power was turned on before completing a corner, the Michelin tyres and limited slip differential playing their parts while the

suspension saw to it that none of the wheels left *terra firma*. No over- or understeer, and the spring damping criticised for motorway use seemed well matched for this other purpose. Incidentally, it would be interesting to discover why BMW have abandoned the self-energising Boge automatic levellers used on the 2800 saloon rear suspension and also, you may remember, on the Range Rover. Was it because of unreliability—or expense?

Brakes and steering are both power-assisted, but in the European (as distinct from transAtlantic manner), neither being feather-light. Indeed, the brakes call for a little more effort than is usual with servos, probably because hard pads with strong fade resistance are fitted. They are progressive and fully responsive without the over-sensitivity that some such systems suffer at very low speeds, and we experienced none of the incidental symptoms of fade such as increased pedal load or roughness—not even a whiff of grilled friction material.

The high-speed directional stability has been mentioned already; but this is a function of the steering geometry rather than the guiding mechanism. The latter installation by ZF-Gemmer is just what one would expect of a present day top quality machine. The adjectives

already used to describe the brakes apply equally to the steering—progressive and fully responsive. You are scarcely ever aware of the oil cushion between the steering and road wheels.

We soon abandoned the inertia reel safety harness because the flexible stalk carrying the receiver end of the lock is placed just where one's left elbow strikes it when changing up from first to second or down from third.

Inevitably one applies more stringent standards of criticism to cars in the BMW's price bracket than to humbler, less pretentious products. Although it's true that that BMW lightweight coupe costs less than half the price of a Bentley Corniche, for the same money one could have a Jaguar XJ12 *and* an Alfa Romeo 2000GTV, with £88 change to put towards their insurance. In almost every respect the XJ12 is superior to both Bentley and BMW, but it will be some time before one can walk into a showroom and order one with any hope of quick delivery, and the BMW has the asset of being a rare piece. The concessionaires expect to sell 500 CSLs in 12 months. But who . . . ? It seems too specialised to appeal to that number among the successful businessmen in their fifties who we have understood to form the backbone of the clientele for exotic European coupes. ●

Continued from page 94

rate dual servo self-centring shoes in rear-wheel 160-mm. diameter drums, has an excellent action and although the dual, servo-operated, all-disc 272-mm. diameter brakes have a hard feel and at first seem unconvincing, when some Welsh sheep strayed in my path beyond New Radnor I experienced what very effective anchors they are when stamped on—this just after I had been reflecting that disc brakes, like reciprocating engines, should be run-in! Sheep are usually very sensible in avoiding cars and it is the tourists from the wens who give themselves away by getting in a flap about those they think are going to cross the road, but the couple I encountered that night were probably pre-occupied with how the Common Market vote was likely to go . . .

It is too early at this stage to write at length about the BMW 2500, except to say that I am already enamoured of its forgiving ability to corner fast without any anxieties, in spite of quite supple all-round coil-spring independent suspension, its ZF power steering, with a taxi lock, and the smooth urge, even under breaking-in limitations, which enables it to out-accelerate lesser cars out of bends, having gained yards on them by the tenacity of grip of its Michelin-shod wheels going through them. I am not sure that I quite like the balance of the car on sudden corners and I shall need time to get used to the power steering, again a distinct contrast to the Rover's not altogether distinguished manual steering gear. That gear-lever sleeve continues to come off at every gear-change, enabling me to wave it at young bloods when (and if) they go past in their Elans and Mexicos, and I was disappointed at the ineffectiveness of the rear-window demister, after I had discovered its under-facia button which flanks one for operating the panic-flashers and another which brings in an extra rear lamp (if the headlamps are on) for motoring on Motorways in fog—in this cautious age the BMW is well equipped with emergency lighting! The Vdo Kienzle clock before the front-seat passenger is commendably accurate. The release handle for the front-hinged bonnet lives inside the illuminated drop-stowage-well on the near side and as it has to be used to work the bonnet grips while someone outside shuts the lid, this is inconvenient on a r.h.d. car. There are at times too many reflections in the windscreen, as I found on the 2.8, and the safety-belt anchor-

ages are embarrassingly intimate with the hand-brake, so that one of them got caught beneath it, preventing the parking brake from releasing fully. The Blaupunkt Blue Spot radio suffered a bit from blanketing in the Brecons, in spite of the abnormally tall, tail-mounted aerial, which really requires automatic retraction to prevent it getting damaged on trees and bushes—and surely a BMW is likely to be driven through higher mountains with the radio playing Wagner, in its native country? Otherwise, no complaints in this initial 1,630 miles, apart from a tiny facia button, the purpose of which I haven't discovered, "coming off in me 'and"—the handbook, you see, appears to omit it and in any case calls for a knowledge of technical German—and rather low-geared window winders. There is already a very slight dent on the off-side rear wing, caused by the visiting chauffeur of a Silver Shadow who reversed vigorously down the office car-park approach, brushing me against the stationery BMW before rubbing the R-R along its side. Remonstrated with, he immediately paid a compliment to my virility—a sad reminder that times have changed and vulgarity comes readily to the tongue even of R-R chauffeurs, although I hope this one isn't typical of the fraternity—the car, even while being abused, was so much more dignified than its surprisingly incompetent driver . . . .

Comparing the BMW 2500 with the Rover 3500 V8 I was so keen to try, the latter has an out-dated, cramped body shell, seating four only, and over-complicated suspension, and in spite of having 1,000-c.c. more swept-volume in its Buick-crib engine than the German car, is not all that much of a better performer—equal perhaps on speed, but more accelerative by only one-fifth sec. or so in the 0-60 m.p.h. bracket, they tell me. The BMW, while not being an over-big car to park or drive in traffic, is much more spacious, with an almost unlimited amount of useful internal stowage and a very big boot. I will tell you more, as the miles mount up. (To date I have to confess that the 600-mile first-service check has been passed without an opportunity to have it carried out; indeed, the BMW became fully run-in going along Marylebone High Street *en-route* on its second round-trip of 360 miles to the office and home again in a day, a journey of which it makes very light work).—W. B.

It takes one to catch one

**On two wheels or four, only one thing compares with a BMW. Another BMW.
A powerful combination of road-shrinking acceleration, tenacious roadholding
and perfect response that stands distinguished on motorway or race circuit.**

The 132 mph BMW 3.0Si
Its 220 bhp engine retains latent reserves: in hazardous situations Apollo-like acceleration is readily on hand to speed you clear. This well-heeled three litre knows the value of wide 6J radials; controls that respond instantly to your will; safety and comfort that are integral parts of the engineering.

Unlike some luxury three litres, the new BMW 3.0Si isn't an extravagant decoration. Its a powerful Sports Saloon that earns its keep in the nuclear power age.

The 110 mph BMW R75/5 Motorcycle
Internationally renowned as the finest in the world, a BMW motorcycle offers the same engineering sophistication on two wheels as a BMW car does on four.

But it also offers what no car can: an exhilaration that only first-hand proximity to elements can bring; the excitement of close contact with wind and sun that blows free business cares and boardroom blues – awakens nostalgic memories of days when two wheels took you far and fast !

Drive a BMW car or motorcycle. After all if you can't beat them, join them.

Alpina's Ultimate BMW

A 152 mph road saloon

A driver's car in the true tradition, the BMW-Alpina combines the excitement of fantastic acceleration (0-100 m.p.h. in 13.9 sec.), 150-m.p.h.-plus top speed and superb handling, with four comfortable seats, a huge boot—and a bill for £8,000!

THE LITTLE TOWN of Buchloe, nestling deep in Bavaria an hour's drive from Munich, has nothing to commend it in the guide books, but to BMW enthusiasts across the globe it represents Mecca, home of BMW-Alpina, foremost tuners of the Munich *marque*. While Alpina have had immense success in saloon car racing and rallying, outright victory in the 1970 European Touring Car Championship marking their most notable achievement, their bread and butter is road car tuning and Alpina 2002s are among the most desirable and numerous of tuned road-burners on the Continent. However good these may be, they pale into insignificance at the side of Alpina's latest fast road car, a remarkable BMW 3.0 CSL which combines saloon car comfort and accommodation with 0-100 m.p.h. acceleration in 13.9 sec., a maximum speed of over 150 m.p.h. and sheer driving exhilaration. I came back from a recent test of this car in Germany and Austria astounded by its shattering performance, in a class with some of the most exotic sports cars. Alpina's comprehensive modifications have put this dramatic CSL into the "one of the most desirable cars in the world" bracket, and at roughly £8,000, one of the most expensive.

The firm responsible for this impressive lightweight coupé was founded and is headed by Burkard Bovensiepen, who made his fortune on the stock market before investing it in the tuning business only eight years ago. He was already a motor sport enthusiast, had done some racing, mainly in a BMW 700 and saw a lack of good tuning facilities in Germany. From early beginnings fitting carburetter kits to BMW 1500s in his father's Alpina typewriter factory at Kaufbeuren, 18 kilometres down the road from Buchloe, Bovensiepen has moulded his business into what is believed to be the largest tuning establishment in Europe. Eighty employees are involved in this almost completely self-contained small factory com-

Massive air-cleaner and cold air box channel breathe to the Alpina/Kugelfischer mechanical injection on the 260-plus-b.h.p., 3-litre, o.h.c. engine.

plex, which Bovensiepen runs on an industrial basis, designing, producing, distributing tuning equipment and accessories, modifying customers' cars in large volumes, building road, racing and rallying engines to pre-determined specifications, developing new specifications, constructing and racing their own cars and building rally engines for use by Jochen Neerpasch's BMW works competition department.

Alpina are currently pre-occupied preparing a brace of Gp 2 CSLs for their own attack on the European Touring Car Championship and a single identical car for BMW Concessionaires GB Ltd., to contest the British Saloon Car Championship and a few ETC rounds. Brian Muir has forsaken his Capri to drive for both Alpina and the Concessionaires. Initially he'll have about 340 b.h.p. under foot using slightly enlarged versions of the CSL's 3,002 c.c. six-cylinder engine, growing later to about 355 b.h.p. when Alpina complete development of a 3,300 c.c. unit. As Alpina have managed to reduce the CSL's weight from 1,165 kg. in standard form to 1,060 kg. ready for the circuit, compared with 1,250 kg. for the all-steel racing CSs which proved too heavy to be competitive last year, Bovensiepen believes that Muir will stand a good chance of out-performing the hitherto invincible Cologne Capris.

No firm could be more qualified to modify the CSL, as it was largely at Alpina's suggestion, after they'd experimented with a CS, that BMW produced the CSL in the first place. Indeed, Alpina carried out much of the development work on the production CSL for BMW and their involvement is recognised by the fitment of Alpina alloy road wheels as standard. Just to recap on W.B.'s description of the CSL in last month's issue, it's a lightweight version of the injected 3.0 CSi, introduced unashamedly specifically to homologate it for Gp 2. Bonnet, boot and doors are of aluminium, the shell is made of lighter gauge steel pressings, there's less sound damping material, engine capacity is increased from 2,985 c.c. to 3,003 c.c. to take it over the 3-litre

class limit, a limited-slip differential is standard, fuel tank capacity is increased to 17 gallons and the alloy wheels have 7J instead of 6J rims, their extra width accommodated by wheel arch extensions. Cars for the British market, like the one used by W.B. and MOTOR SPORT's Production Manager to visit 10 European capitals in four days, have glass windows all round, the side ones electrically operated, and steel bumpers, whereas the left-hand drive German market car used as the basis for this Alpina test car, had Perspex all round, apart from a laminated screen, manual winders and plastic bumpers.

The Alpina car looked more brutal than W.B.'s example, accounted for by the lack of a front bumper, altered ride heights front and rear and a striking blue and red paint scheme complete with the revealing description "BMW Alpina" on each front wing and the tail panel. Both were fitted with Alpina's glassfibre front spoiler/air dam identical to those fitted to the racing coupés, which are claimed to add three or four m.p.h. to top speed, reduce fuel consumption, improve resistance to aquaplaning and improve high speed stability.

Such fantastic performance signifies quite radical work on the o.h.c. engine, as indicated by an increase from the production output of 200 b.h.p. DIN at 5,500 r.p.m. to 260-265 b.h.p. DIN at 6,800 r.p.m. A complete engine rebuild took up a large slice of the estimated £1,800 conversion on this particular car. The block was bored out 0.5 mm. to 89.5 mm. to increase capacity from 3,003 c.c. to 3,020 c.c., using special forged pistons on polished standard con-rods and the standard flywheel was lightened. To this was attached a 240 mm. Fichtel and Sachs clutch with alloy pressure plate, 12 mm. larger than the production clutch and the same size as the racing ones, though with conventional facing material rather than the sintered bronze of the racer. The complete bottom end assembly was of course balanced.

A lot of work was put into the cylinder head, the main part of which was to convert the triple-hemisphere combustion chamber shape to fully hemispherical, together with polishing the ports and valves. The head was shaved to an extent determined by the pistons and deck height to reduce the combustion capacity after chamber work to an amount which gave a compression ratio of 10.5:1 instead of 9.5:1. A mild improvement in timing comes from the extra lift and dwell of an Alpina 300-degree sports camshaft. Alpina threw away the Bosch electronic fuel injection, replacing it with a Kugelfischer mechanical pump and their own design of injection system, using butterflies rather than the sliding throttle device used on the 3-litre racing engines. Fairly short inlet trumpets were led into a special air-cleaner and silencer fed with cold air from the grille. The production exhaust manifold was retained, leading into an enlarged system exiting in the normal place under the tail. Thermostatically controlled oil cooler and electric fan were added.

W.B. mentioned that he'd have appreciated a five-speed gearbox in place of the non-too-close ratios of the standard four-speed box; he'd have been ecstatic about the ratios in the special five-speed ZF box fitted to this tuned car: 2.99, 1.76, 1.30, 1.0 and 0.87. Fifth was technically an overdrive, but by lowering the final drive ratio from 3.45 to 3.89, Alpina enabled the CSL to pull maximum revs in this gear. The firm built this gearbox themselves using non-standard ratios, but Herr Bovensiepen doubts whether he'll make the box generally available as it has an inherent noise problem, chattering in the lower gears and howling in the higher ones, which the ZF box with normal ratios of 3.85, 2.40, 1.67, 1.26 and 1.0 doesn't have. The spread of the ratios on the latter box doesn't suit the car so well and because of its low gearing it can only be offered with the standard 3.45 final drive or a 3.27.

Speeds in the gears were staggering and made a mockery of the British 70 m.p.h. limit and the new German off-autobahn limit of 100 k.p.h.: 1st—44 m.p.h.; 2nd—75 m.p.h.; 3rd—101 m.p.h.; 4th—132 m.p.h.; 5th—152 m.p.h.

Even though the standard CSL has excellent roadholding and handling, the calibre of this car's performance made further suspension

improvements desirous. From my point of view the handling improvement I appreciated best was the basic one of replacing the power steering with a manual ZF box, instilling the steering with much more feel and precision yet remaining reasonably light by virtue of the standard 18.9:1 ratio. However, I felt that this ratio was too low and would have liked to try the car fitted with Alpina's racing box of 13.6:1 ratio, which shouldn't make things unbearably heavy on road tyres.

Modifications to the suspension included adding negative camber to the front wheels, Bilstein struts and rear dampers developed by Alpina in conjunction with the manufacturers, increased rate versions of the standard progressive coil springs which use thicker wire at the top than the bottom and are an original Alpina design, and adjustable anti-roll bars, 22 mm. thick at the front and 18 mm. at the rear. The seven × 14 in. Alpina alloy wheels were retained, but the size of the rear Pirelli CN 36 tyres was increased from 195/70 to 205/70.

Starting was usually instantaneous when hot or after being left outside in the snow all night. A Dymo tape note on the facia warned drivers to let the oil pressure build up before driving off, visible on the instrument in the three-gauge Alpina instrument panel in the middle of the facia, the other additional instruments being for oil temperature and final drive temperature, the needle on the last gauge refusing to move until cruising speeds of over 100 m.p.h. were maintained.

The clutch was heavy and abrupt, this rather than engine characteristics demanding three or four thousand r.p.m. on the rev. counter to avoid stalling on getaway. It paid to be careful with the throttle when trying to leave the mark quickly, for excessive revs. provoked violent wheelspin and squealing, burning rubber all the way through to third, the tail slewing from side to side in anguish in spite of the limited slip differential and a trace of axle judder appearing. I'm sure I don't need to qualify the resultant acceleration; the figures tell their own story. Engine and exhaust noise rose to a crescendo as the fixed backs of the Scheel bucket seats tried to push the spine through the body and the rev. counter needle darted to

Scheel seats are comfortable standard wear in the CSL, but the Alpina 4-spoke wheel and Blaupunkt stereo cassette player/radio were welcome extras.

and fro from 7,000 r.p.m. between the five gears. This same shattering acceleration continued all the way up to the end of the 240 k.p.h. speedo (149 m.p.h.), tailing off for the last three m.p.h.

Ideal cruising speeds in fifth gear were anywhere between 70 m.p.h. and 145 m.p.h., the engine showing no signs of over-exertion at the higher speed and stability remaining unimpaired, a tribute to the effectiveness of the spoiler. At the lower speed the CSL literally felt to be crawling and was deceptively slow at maximum speed, when the smooth engine's normal whirr had risen to a roar and wind noise grew around the flapping plastic side windows. At the other end of the scale, the engine was quite happy traversing heavy Munich traffic at 1,600 r.p.m. in the gears. Below that, transmission judder set in.

Much of my test was conducted in atrocious conditions of rain and snow and while moderately wet surfaces failed to disturb adhesion, heavy rain on the autobahns and studded-tyre rutted main roads showed up a serious aquaplaning problem because of the fat tyres, forcing me to curtail speed below that of narrow tyred family saloons. Rather ignominious and frustrating.

Roadholding was superb in the damp and on the occasional pieces of dry road I encountered. The limit of adhesion was so high that I never found it and I gave up trying because the impression was that it would appear very suddenly and £8,000 is a lot of motor car to drop off the edge of a mountain. After initial understeer it maintained a fairly neutral stance with very little roll and refused to budge. Unfortunately the steering lacked feel, largely because of that low gearing again, though the Alpina 15-in. four-spoke leather wheel was extremely comfortable and just the right size. The brake pedal too didn't transmit much feel, being very light with too much servo. Braking power was fantastic, however, the double-dual circuit system working calipers on four-wheel ventilated disc brakes. Alpina had removed the risk of overheated brakes and so improved resistance to fade by increasing the thickness of the 270 mm. front discs from 22 mm. to 28 mm., leaving the standard 200 mm. outboard rear discs alone.

Ride was very firm, but the size and weight of the car kept the pitch frequency at a reasonable level, the shaped Scheel seats ensuring a high degree of comfort.

In spite of the two criticisms regarding brakes and steering, the overall impression of driving this superb beast will remain with me for a long time to come. Alpina's ultimate

The business-like front view which fills the mirrors of slower vehicles and sends them scuttling for the nearside verges.

road-going BMW is genuinely race-bred, for many of the modifications have come directly from experience with circuit cars and the 260. plus-b.h.p. engine isn't far removed from those used in the early racing coupés, yet it remains a perfectly practical road machine. In many ways it's reminiscent of driving a racing Jaguar D-type or similar on the road, because sheer power makes it flexible and docile, yet when unleashed it goes like the proverbial.

Similar Alpina modifications are available for the full range of BMW six-cylinder saloons and coupés, with an alternative engine conversion for carburated cars incorporating triple 45 DCOE Webers, which restrict power output to 250 b.h.p. As mentioned below, these and all other Alpina conversions are now available through the new Sportpart organisation introduced by BMW Concessionaires GB Ltd.—C.R.

The view you'll always see, except in heavy rain when aquaplaning dangers forbid the use of the tremendous power.

PERFORMANCE

0- 40 k.p.h.	(25 m.p.h.)	..	2.3 sec.
0- 60 „	(37 „)	..	3.2 „
0- 80 „	(50 „)	..	4.8 „
0-100 „	(63 „)	..	6.4 „
0-120 „	(75 „)	..	8.4 „
0-140 „	(87 „)	..	11.0 „
0-160 „	(100 „)	..	13.9 „
0-180 „	(112 „)	..	18.5 „
0-200 „	(124 „)	..	25.0 „

Maximum speed: 152 m.p.h.

Speeds in gears: 1st—44 m.p.h.; 2nd—75 m.p.h.; 3rd—101 m.p.h.; 4th—132 m.p.h.

Fuel consumption: 16.9 litres per 100 km.

Great Minds . . .

VAUXHALL, Chrysler and BMW Concessionaires have all announced new deals for marketing conversion and tuning equipment for their respective ranges. What's more, they even took space at the Racing Car Show to display their wares, acknowledging a fresh awareness of the importance of competition and the tuning business.

For BMW Concessionaires GB Ltd., the venture into the tuning business is entirely new and coincides with the announcement of the company's 1973 involvement in Group 1 and Group 2 racing (see "Around and About"). Both the conversion and competition sides are being run by John Markey from the firm's new premises on the old Paton and Baldwin site near the Fiat headquarters at Brentford. Four- and six-cylinder BMWs are catered for and the bulk of the equipment, including engine and chassis modifications and accessories, will come from Alpina, including the parts fitted to the Alpina 3.9 CSL tested above. The Concessionaires acknowledge that Alpina parts will be expensive and for those who don't want to spend quite so much they're offering a choice of Mathwall Engineering and Mangoletsi equipment too. Mathwall, who prepared last year's Group 1 BMWs, will also build race and rally cars and customers' special engines to BMW specifications. All necessary parts for competition are available and a complete competition car build service is being offered.

Orders for conversions can be placed through local dealers, but fitting must be carried out at Brentford if the BMW warranty is not to be invalidated. Later in the year it's intended to open tuning depots in Leeds and Scotland, probably in Edinburgh. Full details of parts and prices can be obtained from John Markey or Mike Heath-Wise at the Concessionaires' old address (for the moment), 361-365, Chiswick High Road, London, W4 (01-995 4651).

Vauxhall have selected 12 dealers scattered throughout the country to sell parts and accessories under the Sportpart name. These Sport dealers stock or can obtain all the Blydenstein and Coburn Improvement parts for competition use and for improving road car performance and handling, which should encourage the widespread increase in the use of Vauxhalls for competition.

Chrysler's move is to open a Special Tuning Section at the Chrysler Competition Centre, PO Box 25, Humber Road, Coventry, CV3 IBD (Coventry 452144), to extend the activities of Des O'Dell's Competitions Department to the ordinary man in the street. The full range of Chrysler modifications can be ordered through any Chrysler dealer, who in turn will place his order through Tim Millington at the Special Tuning Section. Millington can supply anything from a carburetter kit for a standard Avenger, to a kit to convert any 1,500-c.c. Avenger to full Tiger specification, or to a full Group 6 Imp. Des O'Dell is in overall control and continues as Competitions Manager, the responsibility of his own separate department being to build cars only for the new Dealer Team Chrysler and to develop new tuning equipment for over-the-counter sales. The Special Tuning Section, now virtually a small AVO, will build competition cars for customers and also complete the assembly of Avenger Tigers, which leave the production lines without the specialist bits and pieces.—C. R.

The 2002 began as the brainchild of Max Hoffmann, BMW's US importer, who wanted a car to follow up the 1600-2, which had been very well received in the USA. The logical car for him to import would have been the hot 1600ti, but its engine could not be made to meet the new exhaust emissions regulations. So he suggested that BMW should substitute the 2-litre engine from its larger saloons, which would give excellent performance even in emissions controlled form.

The BMW engineers did as Hoffmann suggested, and the result took the motoring world by storm on its announcement in 1968. Not only did it provide the performance orientated model which Hoffmann wanted for the USA, but in European guise without the power sapping emissions control gear, it offered affordable high performance in a compact and agile package. So popular did the 2002 range become that it went on to sell just under 418,000 examples over the seven years of its production.

Today the qualities which made the 2002 range so appealing in the late 1960s and early 1970s continue to endear them to the motoring enthusiasts. The 2002 models are widely and rightly recognised as classics of their period, and enjoy a large and committed following. This book will be welcomed by enthusiasts everywhere, and will also form invaluable reference for those interested in the classic sporting saloon car.

James Taylor

AVAILABLE FROM BROOKLANDS BOOKS

According to the statisticians, the average motorist (if such a breed really exists) covers around 10–12,000 miles per year. During the 354 days our long-term BMW 3.0 Si was in our care, the car clocked up just over 22,000 miles, which is roughly double the average. It was not so much a case of driving it round the clock, more the fact that everyone wanted to take it on a long trip. With its roomy four-door body, large boot and surprising turn of speed, this car was so much in demand that it never spent a weekend parked and was hardly ever even locked up at the office overnight. And the real test for any car is how it stands up to this kind of near-endurance running; the Si never actually came to a halt on the road and required very little attention other than routine maintenance. Without ever being involved in a collision it has suffered several annoying little nicks and scrapes on the outside, but mostly has remained as smart and bright as the day it left the factory. As it now passes on to a new home, we think the next owner will find it a very durable and exceedingly rewarding car to drive. Here are the details of our experience as they occurred.

Long Term
BMW 3.0 Si

22,000 miles in less than a year

By Geoffrey Howard

LIKE its predecessor, a BMW 3.0 CS, the Si was finished in Polaris silver with dark blue cloth upholstery. It had covered just a basic delivery mileage of 108 when we collected it from MLG at Chiswick and looked superb without a mark on it anywhere. In the boot were a set of supplementary floor mats in a stout woven kind of plastic raffia and I immediately fitted these in to protect the grey-blue carpets. During the first stage of breaking in when there was a lot of friction right through the car, we logged a fuel consumption of only 16.2 mpg. As the miles built up this improved to around 17–18 mpg, but during hard driving with a fair bit of town work it never really got any better. Away on the open road we regularly managed 20 mpg, and on a long Continental trip the records actually show 22.6 mpg. The injection engine is not as economical as the carburettor one, however, a 10 per cent boost in the peak power developed being obtained only by a corresponding increase in fuel consumption.

Subjective impressions gained at the outset by stepping from the carburettor CS into the injection Si I remember most clearly. The injection car seemed smoother and more flexible and displayed none of the clutch thrash we experienced from about 30 mph in top on the CS. Except for the extra noise of the intake and a high-pitched whine from the high-pressure fuel pump, the Si was just as sweet and docile as the CS. With extended use in town there were some symptoms of plug fouling however, and it was only towards the end of the test

Handling is mostly neutral with good steering response and power oversteer available in the lower gears when required. Protection of the body with a waist-line rubbing strip and full wrap-round bumpers is good

when we switched to Champion N-8Y that this problem was finally beaten. The factory will only recommend Bosch or Beru, so owners changing to a different make do so at their own risk. We found no snags in running on the Champions, but our experience did not include any sustained running at high speed.

From inside the car the general commotion from the engine is quite subdued, unless you open the glove box for any reason, whereupon there is a lot more noise transmitted through. From outside the roar of the intake and whirr of the cooling fan are much more pronounced, the engine sounding rather like a kettle on the boil. Soon after the 4,000-mile service was carried out by MLG, the whirring noise increased to the point where it began to cause concern. At 6,360 miles we returned the car for attention and it was found that the water pump bearing had failed. This was replaced under warranty free of charge, the normal cost being £6.80 for parts and £6 labour.

About 7,500 miles later when the Si was in Greece with our company chairman, exactly the same trouble reoccurred. The BMW agents in Athens dealt with the problem very courteously and efficiently on a busy Saturday morning, charging very little more than what would have been the UK cost. From then on there has been no more water pump trouble, so we can only conclude that we have been unlucky.

During the whole of its time with us the Si needed its radiator topped up at regular intervals. It usually took about a pint each week, but we never managed to trace where this water was disappearing to. During sustained hold-ups in heavy traffic the needle of the temperature gauge would usually rise towards the red danger mark without actually reaching it. Increasing the engine speed from the regular 800–900 rpm idling to about 1,500–2,000 brought it back to the middle of the scale, so my regular practice when stationary in the rush-hour was to watch the needle and apply pressure to the accelerator as and when the temperature required it. The fan has a thermostat-controlled clutch and the difference in noise level when this engaged and drove the fan was very noticeable.

At the 4,000-mile service we complained of slight brake squeal, a squeak from the nearside front wishbone, a poor headlamp beam on the nearside when dipped and a fual tank filler cap which did not vent. The first two were rectified easily, the dipped beams were always disappointing and nowhere good enough for the speed potential of

Long Term
BMW 3.0 Si

the car and the filler cap was drilled with a small diameter hole. This hole in fact did not penetrate the inner skin of the composite cap, so there was still a rush of air as it was removed after a run. I drilled through the second skin myself, but then found the fuel had a path to atmosphere when the tank was full and fumes sometimes got pulled back into the car. A new cap was fitted instead (both were the yellow coded ones with venting which are specified for non-American market BMWs). What I had been afraid of was the tank collapsing under vacuum during a period of sustained high speed and rapid fuel consumption. By careful examination as the cap was removed I discovered that the rush of air was actually *out of* the tank and not into it, the deduction being that the evaporative losses from the fuel were pressurising the tank rather than the increasing ullage as fuel was consumed evacuating it. At any rate there was never any problem in running with the standard cap.

The 8,000-mile service was carried out normally, albeit a little late at 9,200 miles, and just before 12,000 miles the car was prepared for the long Continental trip already referred to. In the space of just three weeks Tim Priaulx covered 5,313 miles to Yugoslavia and back and despite high average speeds returned over 22 mpg—the best we ever recorded for the car. Apart from the water pump trouble, the car ran perfectly the whole time and needed only four pints of oil, which was consistent with our own recorded consumption of 1,000 miles per pint. Towards the end of the test we noticed quite a lot of blue oil smoke after a cold start and some similar emission on the over-run from high revs, but the consumption never increased.

As soon as the car got back from abroad we knew we had to do something urgently about the rear tyres. At the start of the trip there had been about 3 mm of

Above: A rear tyre after 17,000 miles compared with a new replacement. Note the way the inside shoulder has worn completely bald. Below: Fuse box and bonnet release are reached by opening the glove box and dropping it down

tread depth left on the inside shoulders, but on the return this side of the tread was completely bald. On the outside edge about 5 mm remained and had we had the foresight to have the tyres turned over on the rims at about 10,000 miles their life would probably have been doubled. Michelin make the most suitable tyre for the faster BMWs, but unfortunately their high-speed range is in short supply and usually it takes two months for replacements to come through from France. The retail price (although this is no longer fixed) is around £33 per tyre without discount, so owners need to plan

and budget ahead. The front tyres lasted slightly longer and were not replaced until 18,000 miles.

During this time when we were in need of tyres, Avon announced a new 70-series 195-14 in. HR radial, which although not quite up to the full speed rating required were perfectly adequate for all UK usage. We tried a set and found them very impressive on grip and ride, but rather lacking in lateral stability. In response to our comments on this aspect of the new tyre, Avon revised the specification by stiffening up the sidewalls and we tried a new set. There were definite improvements, but the feeling of security when making sharp steering movements was still not quite up to the Michelin standard and Avon are doing more development work on the tyre. They should soon be in production with a suitable replacement and we will publish an announcement when this happens.

One of the innovations on the injection 3-litre was ventilated discs for the front brakes. On our CS with the old pattern of solid disc we had to renew the front pads every 10,000 miles. With the new design we ran the whole of the test (22,000 miles) without changing pads and the indications were that they would continue for quite a considerable mileage beyond. On the debit side of this remarkable improvement was a particularly dead brake pedal when cold and some rumbling from high speed when hot. According to MLG, some owners can now get 35,000 miles from a set of front pads, which coupled to a drastic cut in the unit cost of replacements makes this a very frugal part of the overall picture.

At 18,500 miles we turned the car over to MLG between the normal service intervals because oil was leaking from the final drive on to the exhaust system. It was found that some sand had penetrated the pinion seal and this was replaced. At the same time the drive-shaft splines were treated with Loctite to eliminate clicking when the drive took up. Oil smoke from the exhaust when cold and on the over-run from high revs was traced to a slightly overfull sump and as soon as the level dropped to normal it became much less obvious.

Far left: Air extractors are now hidden under smooth panels in the rear quarter panels and the fuel filler is behind the rear number plate. Left: There is a carpet on the floor of the boot and a useful bin on the right. A very comprehensive tool kit is fitted in the boot trim panel and a wheel chock is also provided. The spare is under the floor. Right: Rear headrests are provided and the rear doors have child-proof latches

PERFORMANCE CHECK

Maximum speeds

Gear	mph		kph		rpm	
	R/T	Staff	R/T	Staff	R/T	Staff
Top (mean)	131	130	211	210	6,320	6,300
(best)	132	130	213	210	6,400	6,300
3rd	93	93	150	150	6,250	6,300
2nd	62	60	100	97	6,500	6,300
1st	35	34	56	55	6,500	6,300

Standing ¼-mile,	R/T:	15.7 sec	89 mph
	Staff:	15.6 sec	88 mph
Standing kilometre	R/T:	28.7 sec	111 mph
	Staff:	28.9 sec	110 mph

Acceleration,

	R/T:	2.8	4.2	5.8	7.4	10.0	12.9	15.9	20.8	27.3
	Staff:	2.6	4.1	5.6	7.3	10.0	12.9	16.3	21.4	28.1

Time in seconds 0————————————————————

True speed mph		30	40	50	60	70	80	90	100	110
Indicated speed MPH	R/T:	31	42	53	64	75	86	97	108	120
Indicated speed MPH	Staff:	31	42	52	62	73	83	94	104	115

Speed range, Gear Ratios and Time in seconds

	Top		3rd		2nd	
Mph	R/T	Staff	R/T	Staff	R/T	Staff
10–30	—	—	5.6	6.4	3.4	3.6
20–40	7.8	8.9	5.1	5.8	2.9	3.2
30–50	7.2	8.4	4.7	5.3	2.6	3.0
40–60	7.1	8.1	4.6	5.2	3.1	3.4
50–70	7.7	8.1	4.8	5.3	—	—
60–80	7.9	8.8	5.3	5.8	—	—
70–90	8.7	9.5	6.1	7.0	—	—
80–100	10.0	10.3	—	—	—	—
90–110	12.6	12.6	—	—	—	—

Fuel Consumption

Overall mpg,	R/T:	17.4 mpg	(16.2 litres/100 km)
	Staff:	17.4 mpg	(16.2 litres/100 km)

NOTE: "R/T" denotes performance figures for BMW 3.0 Si tested in *Autocar* of 9 December 1971.

Just short of 20,000 miles the speedometer cable broke and soon after the 20,000-mile service we began to experience surging at steady throttle openings. This was traced to the contact breaker points (not as I suspected the injection computer brain box) which had opened up mysteriously and over advanced the ignition. Resetting them completely cured the problem and restored the car to its former sweet self.

It was at this juncture that I took a careful look at the overall picture of the Si to see how it had endured the rigours of 12 months motoring. Mechanically there had been no problems other than the water pump failures, tyre wear and replacement difficulties and the oil leak from the final drive. In the details of the finish and trim, the paint and brightwork had lasted well, despite the car never having been garaged, with the exception of the wheel trims and hub caps which had suffered the ravages of salt corrosion quite badly. Inside, the nap of the upholstery had flattened on the driver's seat cushion and it proved the devil's own job to keep fluff off the surfaces until I

invested in one of those clever electrostatic clothes brushes being advertised on television. On the front passenger door there was now a slight "ding" where it had slipped from my fingers on a hill and caught a nasty bulging Victorian lamp post as I opened it laden with shopping, and on the offside rear three-quarter wing panel someone had left a deep zig-zag scratch from (I guess) a supermarket trolley.

When we came to make our performance check at MIRA, the Si managed to beat the original road test acceleration figures by a small margin up to 80 mph, despite (we suspect now) having over-advanced ignition. On our car the ignition cut-out operated at exactly 6,300 rpm—the start of the red mark on the rev counter—which prevented us from reaching quite the same maxima in the gears or in top.

Looking at these figures, one really sees the true appeal of the Si and the justification for the extra £269 over and above the cost of a 3.0S saloon. Here, with the Si, you have a full and roomy five-seater with performance quite outside the five-seater class. From 0 to 60 mph, for example, the Si is quicker than a Lotus Plus 2, a Jensen-Healey, an Alfa Romeo Montreal and a Citroen SM. It is only 0.4 sec slower than a V12 E-type and 0.3 sec slower than a Jensen SP. Like all the BMWs it is essentially a driver's car, one that responds well to the enthusiast's touch and gives a lot of pleasure and satisfaction all the time. Always when returning to it I marvelled at the smoothness of the straight-six engine and its lusty torque. The delightful gearbox with a low bottom and close upper ratios gave it a really quick step off the line in traffic and, as the top gear acceleration figures show so well, it pulls evenly the whole way to 100 mph. On the debit side it really needs tyres with better wet road grip and suffers from far too much wind noise from around the front screen pillars. All things considered though, this BMW more than all the rest deserves the keen following it has found among owners and we count ourselves in that enlightened band. □

COST of OWNERSHIP

Running Costs	Life in Miles	Cost per 10,000 miles
		£ p
One gallon of 5-star fuel average cost today 37p	17.4	213.00
One pint of top-up oil, average cost today 21p	1,000	1.47
Front disc brake pads (set of 4)	25,000	1.83
Rear brake pads (set of 4)	30,000	1.24
Michelin XVR tyres (front pair)	18,000	36.50
Michelin XVR tyres (rear pair)	15,000	44.00
Service (main interval and actual cost incurred)	4,000	52.00
Total		**350.04**
Running cost per mile:	3½p	
Approx. standing charges per year		
*Insurance		81.20
Tax		25.00

Depreciation		
Price when new		4,128.00
Trade in cash value (approx.)		3,000.00
Typical advertised price (current)		3,450.00
Total cost per mile (based on cash value)	18p	

*Insurance cost is for named approved drivers over 30 with £50 excess and 65 per cent no claims bonus on gross premium of £232. Excluding personal accident and medical expenses.

OUR CAMERAMAN thought this road-tunnel provided a suitable European atmosphere for Bavaria's fine road-cruiser. The road actually passes under the new multi-million dollar Penrith expressway in Sydney.

BMW 3.0 SA

essay for the enthusiast

IN WHICH we go in search of reeeel motoring . . . slicing through rain-drenched ess-bends at better than the half-ton, clambering down the edge of precipitious gorges via a tortuous strip of rock-strewn black asphalt, stealing down eerie corridors of flickering ghost gums in the late afternoon sun with the speedo quavering at one-twenty

and the tacho tell-taling at 6000, tippy-toeing down into twisty black forests on four footprint size patches of sticky rubber that hold up a ton-and-a-half of the purest-bred automotive iron you'll find. That's the magic of BMW motoring. It's yours for $11,000. Rob Luck paid nothing, got just a whiff of the real thing, and gave it back ever so reluctantly . . .

THE BMW 3.0S registered a phenomenal rise in popularity in this year's Readers'- Poll. From a relatively insignificant appearance last year, the biggest Bee-Emm took out the category for the Best Sports Sedan of unlimited price and topped that with a dazzling · performance in the class most-coveted by the quality car manufacturers and importers — the Best All-rounder. Just to prove the voting was no accident, the BMW featured strongly in the class for the Best Luxury Personal Car with a good second place.

The rapid rise of the cars that fly under the symbol of the whirling propellor is no accident. BMW Australia this year instituted a concentrated attack on its greatest rival, Mercedes, in a determined bid to abolish the aura that surrounds that marque.

Probably the greatest single contributing factor to the BMW's inroads on Mercedes territory was the substantial price rises that signalled the arrival of the 3-litre series (replacing the 2800 range completely).

I believe a major marketing mistake that BMW repeated continuously in recent years was to *undercut* the Mercedes prices. And a BMW salesman underlined the point when he told me confidentially that the hardest question he had to answer all year was also the most frequent one . . . "How can it be as good as a Mercedes if it's cheaper?"

There seems little doubt that price can outsell quality where the market is looking for a status symbol — and that is not intended as an indictment of Mercedes' undoubted quality. It merely serves as an adverse reflection on the buying motives that operate in the luxury market.

In any case, the BMW 3-litre series is now priced fairly equally with the 280 series Mercedes which it roughly parallels in specification and performance as well. I predict this pricing will lead to even greater sales success for BMW in the coming year.

The rise in popularity of the BMW in Australia duplicates the experience of most of the other major imports. Volvo has registered a remarkable market growth rate despite its local assembly (which is of a superb standard)', and Peugeot clambered on its tedious way up the charts despite a spate of overseas shipping strikes which left it almost totally unsupplied on the Australian market for five months. A sell-out of the first run of 1973 model Peugeots indicates that the car should have a record year (further backed by its promising showing in our Poll results this year).

The overall scene points-up a glaring fact to us at MODERN MOTOR — that the Australian market is showing an increasing distaste for the volume-built local product in the upper sectors and an increasing appetite for quality imported products. The Peugeot 504 and Volvo 144 represent major examples — both are rated as regular consumer family cars in their countries-of-origin, but here are regarded as the epitome of luxury and quality. This is a sad reflection on our own automobile industry and the near-sighted Federal government policies that control and regiment it.

Following its dramatic success in the Readers' Poll, we decided a revisit of the top BMW was in order as a feature road test for this month. We ran-up some 1500miles in an automatic version which is rapidly taking over as the most popular seller in the range.

In a highly varied combination of city and country mileage, the BMW was hailed by observers everywhere we stopped. But a comment that became almost invariable from pump-hands to tyre-kickers indicated that the real market position of the car is little understood by the average Australian. It seems most people still believe the BMW is a kind of Holden Premier of Germany. Most people think the BMW, Mercedes and their contemporaries are driven around Europe by Average Fred, just as Holdens and Falcons are here.

This misconception bears a little comparison with the facts. In Germany, the average family man would opt for a Ford Granada or an Opel Commodore, which roughly equate our Falcon and regular Holden anyway. These cars would cost Fred the Familyman around $2600 in the same sort of trim as the Kingswood/500, although they are almost invariably better equipped.

By comparison, a BMW 3.0S is tagged at $4666 and a 280 Mercedes runs to $4200. Even the "cheapie" 250 Merc demands $3900 and the 280SE is around the $5700 mark.

This clearly demonstrates that even in their country of origin, these luxury cars are by no means within the grasp of the average family motorist.

It's just a little sad that because of Australia's crippling import duties, these fine cars are within the reach of an even more select section of the Australian car-buying market.

The standard specifications of the BMW 3-litre are the secret of its engineering success. Power is supplied by a moderate-capacity alloy, in-line overhead camshaft six-cylinder that accepts normal super fuel by virtue of its moderate 9.0 to one compression ratio.

Carburetion via twin Zenith double-choke carburettors is sophisticated enough to extract good performance from the engine, but not so complicated it becomes a tuning nightmare. The horsepower rating at 180(DIN)bhp is impressively moderate for the engine's potential, and the large amount of available torque

(188lbs.ft) although it's produced at an unfortunately high 3700rpm, ensures the engine is more than just an enthusiast's special.

The high rev-point for the torque delivery is the only debit point in this otherwise superbly smooth engine — and it took the automatic version to demonstrate the inadequacies. While the manual model bursts with responsiveness at most speeds in any gear, the loss of a gear and the power-absorbing characteristics of the torque converter in the automatic version, are enough to produce sluggish performance off-the-mark and some unresponsiveness when caught at the lowest speed spectrum of any gear.

Otherwise the engine is remarkably smooth. This is due chiefly to the seven main-bearing design with 12 counterbalances on the crankshaft, plus an engine mounting system that ensures power delivery is transmitted fully to the driveline, with no diversions into the body as vibration.

It also offers good performance. While the automatic does not go close to equalling the performance of the manual (which further suggests that the characteristics of the engine design are more oriented to the enthusiast and manual four-speed operation) it is still a good performer in overall terms.

It beats its way up the standing quarter mile in 18.3 seconds and runs from zero to 60mph in 10.9 seconds which are just about below average for a high performance car, but it makes 100mph from a standstill in 30.1 seconds which is certainly impressive for a 3-litre towing more than 3000lbs through a three-speed automatic gearbox.

Furthermore its passing speed capacity in 20mph gaps between 20mph and 60mph never exceeds 4.5 seconds in Drive range, and at the worst end of the scale it takes only 7.4 seconds to charge from 60 to 80mph in Drive.

At the top end, 120mph-plus is possible, while 120mph is reached just over 6000rpm. The engine runs out to 46mph in first (5600rpm) and 80mph in second (5000rpm).

Fuel economy is not a strongpoint. Although the automatic tends to gobble a lot more fuel than the manual (as much as 4-6mpg under identical

THE BIG BMW provided us with our first fifth wheel failure — a tyre blow-out at 120mph! Yes, we carry a spare.

ROAD TEST DATA SHEET — SPECIFICATIONS

Manufacturer: BAYERISCHE MOTOREN WERKE AG. Munich
Make/Model: . . . . .BMW 3.0
Body type: . . . . .4-door sedan
Pricing: as tested: $11,375
basic: $11,375
Test car supplied by: . . . . Capitol Motors
Parramatta Road, Auburn.

ENGINE
Cylinders: . . . . Six, in-line
Bore x stroke: . . . . .3.404in (89mm) x 3.150in (80mm)
Capacity: . . . . .184.4 CID (2985cc)
Compression: . . . . .9.0 to 1
Aspiration: . . . . Twin Zenith two-stage carburettors
Fuel pump: . . . . .Mechanical
Fuel recommended: . . . . .98 Octane
Valve gear: . . . . .OHV
Max. power (gross): . . . . .180(DIN)bhp @ 6000rpm
Max. torque: . . . . .188lbs.ft @ 3700rpm

TRANSMISSION
Type/location: . . . . Automatic with torque-convertor — floor shift on centre console.

Gear	Direct Ratio	Overall Ratio	mph/1000rpm	(km/h)
1st	2.39	8.24	8.08	13.0
2nd	1.45	5.00	13.32	21.43
3rd	1.00	3.45	19.32	31.0
Final drive: 3.45				

Calculated Data:
Bhp/ton 247bhp/ton
Piston speed at max rpm 82.46ft/sec (25.14m/sec)

CHASSIS AND BODY
Type: . . . . .Unitary
Kerb weight: 3046lbs (1380kg)

SUSPENSION
Front: Independent with spring struts, wishbones, trailing links and coil springs.

Rear: Indpendent with boxed semi-trailing arms, spring struts springs, rubber auxiliary springs.
Shock Absorbers: . . . . .Double-acting hydraulic teles
Wheels: 6J
Tyres: . . . . .Avon 185

STEERING
Type: . . . . ZF-Gemmer hourglass worm and
Ratio: 18.05
Turns lock to lock: . . . .
Wheel diameter: . . . . .16.5in (40.
Turning circle, between kerbs: . . . . .33ft 7in (10.
between walls: . . . . .36ft (10.

BRAKES
Type: . . . Servo assisted dual circuit with ventilated discs all ro
Dimensions: 10.7in (272

DIMENSIONS
Wheelbase: . . . . .116.6in (269.
Track, front: . . . . .56.9in (144.
rear: . . . . .57.6in (146.
Overall length: . . . . .15ft 5in (470.
width: . . . . .5ft 8.9in (175.
height: . . . . .4ft 9.1in (145.
Overhang, front: 37in (9
rear: . . . . .45in (114.
Minimum Garage width
(Total width plus one door open fully) . . . . . . 103in (261.

EQUIPMENT
Battery: 12V/5
Alternator: . . . . .12V 3-phase 630 watt ou
Headlamps: . . . . .Quad quartz io
Jacking points: . . . . .4 side-p

CAPACITIES
Fuel tank: . . . . .18.3 galls (83 l
Engine sump: .11.5 pints (6.5 l
Final drive: . . . . .2.5 pints (1.5 l
Gearbox: . . . . .12.7 pints (7.23 l
Water System: . . . . .23 pints (12 l

hard-going situations) both cars are quite thirsty in flat-out motoring.

The worst figure recorded on test was 11mpg for averages that ranged upwards from 80mph to 108mph on one short section. On the other hand, the two best consumptions returned over any distance at averages ranging from 60-80mph were 15.1 and 16.4mpg.

A city average of 16mpg was typical, with a best-recorded mark at 18mpg.

The best recorded fuel consumption figure was 21mpg for a short 40-mile section covered at an average 45mph. Around 23mpg would probably be the best the average owner would record under the lowest speed conditions.

The BMW is well-specified in the road-gear department. Its long-wheelbase of 116in. straddles the roadway with near-57in. tracks either end. Overall body dimensions of 15ft 5in. (length) 5ft. 8.9in. (width) and 4ft 9.1in. (height) indicate the undergear is endowed with a fairly economic covering of sheetmetal.

When the body height is considered relative to the McPherson strut-type suspension, its conservative dimensions are impressive. Similarly, the 6in. wide wheels stretch on their tracks almost to the extremities of the flared guards, and body overhangs are restricted to the bare minimum of sheetmetal required to house engine and related components at the front, and a generous boot at the rear.

Combined with good suspension control, the small amount of body protrusion at each end means contact with the road surface under adverse conditions is extremely remote. When it does happen, it usually occurs at the front end, and contact is typically made on the towing hooks. However these serve as a type of skid-plate agent.

The rest of the mechanicals are as complete as you could ask for in the basic specifications of a car. Braking is by four power-assisted 10.7in. discs, although a pronounced fade pattern that developed on test during multiple stops, indicates BMW could pay a little more attention to brake pad materials. The car recorded consistently low g-forces under brakes, with high pedal pressures and long stopping distances.

Although fairly typical of our

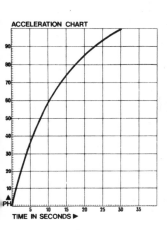

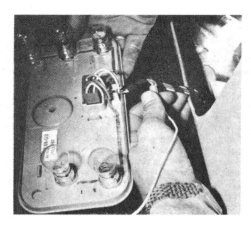

ADJUSTABLE head-rests are provided on four seats.

ALL REAR lights are located on simple screw-out plastic board. Photo shows needle-sensor for fifth wheel braking equipment being inserted in brake-light wire.

WARRANTY, INSURANCE, MAINTENANCE, RUNNING COSTS

...stration: $81.65

...rance:
...ted rates are for drivers over 25 with 60percent no-claim bonus where the car is under hire purchase. This is the minimum ...nium level — decreasing rates of experience and lower age groups have varying excesses and possible premium loadings.
...-tariff company $170
...ff company $220.85
...MA $214.90

...anty:
...months or 6000 miles. There is also a goodwill warranty which ...s outside the first six months. Warranty covers all parts and ...r charges for defective materials, components or workmanship. ...ponents from outside suppliers such as batteries, tyres etc., are ...red by their own manufacturers.

...ice:
...al service: ....free
...covers the first 1000 miles and covers lubrication and ...tenance servicing. Materials (lubricants etc.) are chargeable.

...er Service:
...rication and maintenance services every 4000 miles. Listed ...w are the manufacturer recommended labor charges.
...0 .... $16.00
...00 .... $32.00 plus $10.00 test fee
...00 .... $16.00
...00 .... $32.00 plus $10.00 test fee.

...e Parts — Recommended Cost Breakdown
...pads (set of four) $24.90
...fler (front) $31.00
...fler (rear) $40.00
...iscreen $208.00
...ck absorbers (front) $37.50
...ck absorbers (rear) $195.00
...llamp assembly $83.50
...lamp assembly $66.00

PERFORMANCE

Test conditions for performance figures: Weather: Fine; Wind: Nil; Humidity: 60percent; Max. Temp. 70deg; Surfaces: Hotmix.

Top speed, average: 120mph (192km/h)
　　　　best run: 123mph (198km/h)
Standing Quarter Mile, average .... 18.4 secs
　　　　best run: .... 18.3 secs
Speed at end of Standing Quarter: 82mph (132km/h)
0-30 mph: .... 4.6 secs
0-40 mph: .... 6.4 secs
0-50 mph: .... 8.2 secs
0-60 mph: .... 10.9 secs
0-70 mph:. .... 14.0 secs
0-80 mph: .... 18.1 secs
0-90 mph: .... 23.1 secs
0-100 mph: .... 30.1 secs

Speeds in gears:

Gear	Max. mph (km/h) Drive	Held	rpm Drive	Held
1st	46 (74)	52 (84)	5600	6000
2nd	80 (129)	86 (138)	5000	6000

Acceleration in drive:
20-40 .... 4.5 secs
30-50 .... 4.4 secs
40-60 .... 4.5 secs
50-70 .... 5.4 secs
60-80 .... 7.4 secs

Braking: Five crash stops from 60 mph

Stop	G	Pedal	Time
1	.7	60psi	3.6secs
2	.6	50psi	3.8secs
3	.6	70psi	4.2secs
4	.5	75psi	5.1secs
5	.5	75psi	5.5secs

30-0mph: ...1.8secs in 49ft (15m) with an average g-force of .743g
60-0mph: Stop 1: 3.6secs in 180ft (55.0m) average g-force of .705g.
　　　　Stop 5: 5.5secs in 243ft (74.2m) average g-force of .544g.

Speedo Corrections:

ACTUAL:	31	41	51	61	70	80	90
IND:	30	40	50	60	70	80	90

experience with this size BMW, we feel a drastically different picture would emerge with harder pads. This was further evidenced by the heavy dusting that occurred on all four wheels after any heavy work with the brakes — a fairly typical sight on BMWs if you inspect the average car closely.

On the other side of the picture, the pads produced a nice spongy feel at the start of the pedal movement with a progressively firmer response as pedal effort was increased. Very pleasant for city use, and progressive for the average sporty open road driver.

Steering is by ZF-Gemmer worm and roller on a ratio of 18.5 to one with four turns lock to lock via a 16.5in. diameter wheel. This is fairly characteristic of German steering specification, and gives a pleasant light feeling for cruising and most city work, with a fair degree of sensitivity for hard-pushing where accuracy in lining-up corners is required.

However, the steering is particularly sensitive to tyre pressures and the inexperienced driver usually takes time to adjust to the accuracy required to handle corners at speed. Once mastered, the car imparts a confident feeling.

The handling qualities of the car are by all general standards of evaluation, quite superb. The wide-track stance with wide wheels and fat rubber (in this case ultra-grippy 185HR14 Avon radials) gives a precise, sure-footed feel when pushing hard into any corner.

Steering allows completely precise positioning of the car at any stage during cornering, and it is this exactness that makes accurate cornering initially difficult to master for the average driver.

There is a natural tendency to over-use the big steering wheel, and then to over-correct when too much initial movement is supplied. With familiarity, the car can be hooked through corners at amazing speeds with little impression of speed transmitted to the cockpit occupants.

It is only at ultimate cornering levels that the suspension engineering shows any indication of its terminal deficiencies.

A real enthusiast capable of exploring the car's handling limits will find that the transition from a neutral cornering state to final oversteer is rather more rapid than is indicated by the performance of the car at lower speeds.

This is entirely predictable and the driver really should not arrive at a situation of pronounced oversteer without a full capability to handle the consequences. The suddenness of the breakaway point is determined by the combined factors of an exceptionally high cornering capacity before breakaway, and the de-cambering motion of the rear swing axles when the breakaway point is reached. According to BMW, this only occurs when sideways loadings in excess of 0.8g are reached — an exceptionally high limit.

Although the suspension is vastly more sophisticated, and the handling limits are immeasurably higher, the final reaction is comparable with a swing-axle Volkswagen. The fact that breakaway occurs at considerably higher limits (and therefore speeds) is an indication that driving to that point should only be contemplated by experts.

Certainly, the average driver would never explore those limits and most BMW drivers develop an almost child-like faith in the sure-footedness of the handling of their vehicles.

The achievement of a good ride with this sort of handling level is where the BMW engineers earn great respect. Their *modus operandi* was to employ McPherson struts to give long spring travel to offset the effects of the firmer rates required for good handling.

While the BMW certainly rides more firmly than its major competitors (its ride-handling compromise is undoubtedly tipped towards the handling side) it is not a harsh-riding car. Little suspension noise is transferred to the cockpit.

BMW claims the body and interior is engineered with one major factor in mind — functional design. Their contentions are well-supported by owner experience, although the car's appearance is typically teutonic and clinical in many respects.

But certainly the clean body lines are a delightful aspect of the application of functional engineering to aesthetics. The car presents a clean, thrusting profile to the airstream and doesn't disturb it excessively while appealing to a wide range of tastes at the same time.

The driver gets the major benefits of this thinking. Visibility from the driving seat is superb in all directions, with no major blind spots (except when the windscreen wipers are required). The exterior mirror is unnecessarily small, but the interior mirror compensates a little.

While the car appears to be aerodynamically good in most respects, there is excessive wind-noise in the cockpit above 70mph, and wind noise is noticeable above 40mph. Additionally, ventilation is poor for hot conditions, and this requires open windows. Wind noise takes a further boost when any glass is lowered.

Driving position is generally excellent with high seats offering a commanding view of the road and the well-placed steering wheel giving good control for any size and shape of driver — easy reach is assured by seats that give a wide range of adjustment.

Instrumentation is first class — possibly the best available on a sporting sedan — and is noteworthy for its absolute simplicity, the clarity of the dials, and the good positioning on the dashboard where they are clearly visible through the upper sector of the steering wheel.

There is ample evidence of intelligent approach to good design in the interior. Detail touches you notice immediately include logically located controls, good system of warning lights, simplicity in the heater/ventilation controls, sensible positioning of the switchgear, provision of the big odds-and-ends bin on the dash-top (complete with special ribbing to stop items sliding around), excellent horn tabs, "penguin" sunvisors that present a white surface to match the ceiling when in the "up" position and a black anti-glare surface when pulled down, headlights that switch to park when the ignition is killed, and so on.

Like any interior designers, the BMW engineers made their share of mistakes too. For instance, the window winders are low-geared at seven turns but are stiff in operation, and ash blows out of the ashtray when the blower-fan is operated and there is no right hand ashtray for the driver, the gearlever has a stiff movement back to second, the windscreen washers are inadequate and the armrests are a little too firm.

On the test car, the Mitsubishi tape/radio combo was poorly installed and gave an uncharacteristically bad performance. However, the clock kept immaculate time.

The seating standard is a point of major difference amongst our testers. All our drivers under 12stone complained the seats were firm and unyielding and the design was too flat, allowing lateral slippage. Women particularly complained the seats were too hard, and impossible to sleep in.

On the other hand, several 14stone members of staff regarded the seats as excellent.

It seems likely that the average German is probably heavier than the average Australian, and prefers this firmer design in seats.

The suede covers were only partially successful — they looked great, and were comfortable at most times, but they were hot and sweaty, unbearably prickly against bare skin, and easily soiled.

The BMW certainly lives up to its manufacturer's claim of a well-engineered safety package. The car excels in all areas of primary safety and the only points which mar the overall performance are inadequate lights for high speed cruising, and a poor wiper sweep for wet conditions. However BMW is certainly justified in claiming this car is less likely to get into an accident in the first place. And they have demonstrated that when a crash does occur, the engineering is also highly advanced by current standards.

The owner is presented with a product that is completely equipped for all normal use (including an incredibly comprehensive tool kit). It is functionally engineered for driveability, safety and comfort, and beautifully assembled and finished. The attention to detail extends to items like a delightfully simple and unique key design that makes for instant usability, and tow-hooks.

While we're unlikely to descend to any of the current hysterical schoolboy-annual type descriptions of the car as "The World's Best", we certainly rate it as one of the finest motor vehicles available. 🔟

BMW 3.0CS

A glorious blend of Grand Touring qualities

As a series the big BMW goes all the way back to 1966 when it was first introduced as the 4-cylinder 2000CS. Its unusual body shape, with vast glass areas, low beltline and boxy-but-rounded lines, was impressive then but it had an awkward-looking front end and its 2-liter engine just didn't give it the performance it deserved.

Then in 1969 came the new 6-cylinder engine and the big sedans BMW designed to compete head-on with Mercedes. Rather halfheartedly, it seemed, the individualistic little Bavarian carmaker also showed a facelifted coupe using the same CS body from the windshield back but with an altogether more harmonious front end just long enough to accommodate the 6-cylinder engine. Halfheartedly, we say, because the new coupe retained the old 4-cylinder's drum rear brakes and narrow rear track. It was as if BMW had said, "Okay, we have these CS bodies from Karmann, we have to do something with them."

Despite the composite nature of the car, however, it worked. The brakes weren't as good as those of the cheaper 2500 and 2800 (now Bavaria) sedans and the narrow rear track gave the car a strange crab-tracked look from the rear. But the 2800CS, as it was now called, looked good, performed like an athlete

with the brilliant BMW six, produced some of the most delicious mechanical noises known to man, and had interior and trunk accommodations that could be used to define the term *Grand Touring.*

Never intended to be a volume seller anyway, the model apparently fulfilled or exceeded BMW's market expectations for it, and when the 6-cylinder engine got its first displacement increase the coupe became the 3.0CS and got proper disc brakes for the rear—actually ventilated discs all around, whereas the 2800CS only had solid discs at the front. Strangely, the narrow track was left narrow and the car still looks crab-tracked, at least with the too-small tires fitted for the U.S. version. In Europe, and hopefully here soon too, the car comes with fat 195/70-14 V-rated tires, and on the lightweight 3.0CSL version also sold there these are fitted to 7-in. rims instead of the standard 6-inchers, so it may have been necessary to leave the track narrow to accommodate the extra width. That CSL has a 200-bhp fuel-injected engine, and there's an intermediate 3.0CSi with the injected engine but normal luxury fittings. For the U.S. market only the basic model, with its carbureted engine detuned for emission control, is available.

In any version, the CS looks right—crisp, aggressive and functional without straining to be swoopy. It's obviously not the gee-whiz exercise a De Tomaso Pantera is, for instance, but often when we parked the bright red test car a small crowd would gather around it. It looks far better with the wider tires, naturally, and it's puzzling that those small Michelin XAS you see on this car are themselves a "mandatory option"—you pay extra for them but there's no other choice. One more slight detraction from the U.S. version: to meet our safety regulations, side reflectors are added and the amber front one just behind

the standard side lighting unit looks awkward.

For 1973, to meet yet another U.S. regulation, the bumpers have been moved out a bit from the body and the front bumperguard tips redesigned. The length increase is minimal (3 in.) and the esthetic effect negligible.

The CS interior looks right too. There's not a trace of ostentation, but everything is there, tastefully and simply done. Leather upholstery is optional at a stiff price but not many CS buyers would want to forego it, we think, as it's so rich and smells so good. The front seats are superbly designed—fully supporting, generously dimensioned and adjustable through 75 degrees. The rear seats are equally good, although they lack some of the headroom and more than a little legroom, and have a fold-down center armrest between them. There's tasteful chrome trim on the seat framework and stainless steel finishing off the door jambs—the car always surprises first-time lookers with its elegant detail work.

Legible instruments, though not enough of them (no BMW production model has an ammeter or oil-pressure gauge), are set into a pod and all controls are within easy reach of a fully belted driver. To the right of the pod is a strikingly simple arrangement: a shelf with a padded edge and small wood dividers every few inches to keep things from rolling about, all faced by handsome wood veneer. The wood is picked up again in the door and side panels. There are two drop-down bins, one large and one small, plus snap-flush map pockets in each door. It's difficult to imagine a more luxurious, more comfortable or better-looking passenger compartment.

The steering wheel is large—too large for our tastes—and, on the test car, had a leather-covered, padded rim for good grip. On the steering column are two control stalks, the left

one for high beam and headlight flasher, the right one for directionals, windshield wipers and washers. Having the directionals on the right stalk creates confusion for those not accustomed to BMWs, quite naturally, and we note that BMW's latest model (the 520) now has them on the left like other cars. Our test car had the optional front window lifts—the rear ones are standard—and these are very slow in action. They also don't lower the windows entirely into the body sides, a consequence of the tall windows but seemingly a detail that could have been worked out better.

Vision out of the CS is superb—probably the best in any closed car being built today. Our federal government talks of a vision regulation; the 3.0CS, in our opinion, could be used as the basis for such a regulation.

Driven moderately, the 3.0CS is smooth and very quiet. At cruising speeds the sounds of the muffled, smooth engine and humming XAS tires blend together in an almost musical way; wind and road noise are low although one is conscious of a concentration of what wind noise there is around the windshield. The big BMW engine is without a doubt the most sophisticated inline six in the world and its sonority is very much a part of the car's character. This year's tightened limit on oxides of nitrogen in the State of California has taken its toll, to be sure; fuel economy isn't what it used to be and the exhaust-gas recirculation plus retarded spark at low engine speeds render what was once a beautifully responsive engine somewhat reluctant in around-town work. When driven hard, though, it frees up and goes almost as well as ever. Our 1973 3.0CS, at a test weight identical to that of our 1971 2.8-liter Bavaria, came quite close to matching the acceleration times posted by that more efficiently powered car. If that sounds like left-handed praise, remember that in 1973 we don't expect the current version of a car to match last year's or earlier ones.

One area where the 3.0 excels the 2.8 Bavaria and CS is in its gearbox. The one used with the 2.8 engines was delightful in everyday use, light and precise; but the synchronizers weren't always up to fast shifts. It has been redesigned for the 3-liter, and though its action is stiffer now it's still pleasant to use and the synchros now can't be beaten. A perennial problem—at least we consider it a problem—remains, in that the clutch makes a peculiar noise as it's engaged or disengaged, and on this test car the clutch also chattered a bit on uphill starts. A 3-speed automatic transmission is available on the 6-cylinder BMWs; it also has been completely changed and is now a satisfactory unit. But the manual gearbox is so good that most drivers, we're sure, will prefer it.

A true GT combines maximum performance with maximum comfort. The CS's ride is soft; good handling isn't achieved here by stiff springs and super-hard tires but rather by all-around independent suspension, anti-roll bars, radial tires and plenty of suspension travel. The ride isn't faultless; it shares the BMW family trait of an undue amount of front-rear pitch on gentle undulations—due, we think, to overly soft rear spring rates. Otherwise, though, it's satisfactory, and despite its pillarless construction the body is stiff and rattlefree, holding firm over the worst of roads.

BMW uses ZF power steering on the CS and this is almost as good as Mercedes' legendary power assist. It feels a bit light initially, but continued use of the car reveals that it has true road feel. The steering ratio is about average, not tremendously quick, but a tight turning circle and well-defined body corners make the CS a particularly maneuverable car in traffic or the parking lot—not to forget the great vision either.

The CS's brakes are greatly improved from the 2800CS's disc-drum combination. Now they breeze through our fade test as if it were nothing. They even manage decent stopping distances from freeway speed, but not without some drama.

PRICE

List price, all POE $10,720
Price as tested,
　west coast $12,599
Price as tested includes air cond
($710), leather upholstery ($650),
limited-slip diff ($163), Michelin
XAS tires ($54), elec front win-
dows ($172), prep ($130)

IMPORTER

Hoffman Motors Corp
375 Park Ave
New York, N.Y.

GENERAL

Curb weight, lb 3175
Test weight 3480
Weight distribution (with
　driver), front/rear, % 57/43
Wheelbase, in. 103.3
Track, front/rear 56.9/55.2
Length 186.5
Width 64.9
Height 53.9
Ground clearance..................... 5.9
Overhang, front/rear 40.2/43.0
Usable trunk space, cu ft........ 14.5
Fuel capacity, U.S. gal........... 18.5

ENGINE

Type .... sohc inline 6
Bore x stroke, mm ..... 89.0 x 80.0
　Equivalent in .... 3.50 x 3.15
Displacement, cc/cu in .. 2985/182
Compression ratio 8.3:1
Bhp @ rpm, net........ 170 @ 5800
　Equivalent mph 113
Torque @ rpm, lb-ft... 185 @ 3500
　Equivalent mph 68
Carburetion .. two Zenith 35/40 (2V)
Fuel requirement.... regular, 91-oct
Emissions, gram/mile:
　Hydrocarbons 2.8
　Carbon Monoxide 23.0
　Nitrogen Oxides 1.8

DRIVE TRAIN

Transmission .... 4-sp manual
Gear ratios: 4th (1.00) 3.64:1
　3rd (1.40) 5.10:1
　2nd (2.20) 8.01:1
　1st (3.85) 14.0:1
Final drive ratio.................. 3.64:1

CHASSIS & BODY

Layout ...... front engine/rear drive
Body/frame .... unit steel
Brake system............ vented disc,
10.7-in. dia front & rear; vacuum
assisted
　Swept area, sq in. 493
Wheels .... cast alloy, 14 x 6J
Tires .... Michelin XAS, 175HR-14
Steering type .... worm & roller,
　power assisted
　Overall ratio 18.9:1
　Turns, lock-to-lock 3.7
　Turning circle, ft 34.0
Front suspension: MacPherson struts,
　lower A-arms, coil springs, tube
　shocks, anti-roll bar
Rear suspension: semi-trailing arms,
　coil springs, tube shocks, anti-roll
　bar

INSTRUMENTATION

Instruments: 150-mph speedo,
8000-rpm tach, 99,999 odo, 999.9
trip odo, coolant temp, fuel level,
clock
Warning lights: oil press, alternator,
fuel level, high beam, directionals,
hazard flasher, seatbelt

ACCOMMODATION

Seating capacity, persons 4
Seat width, f/r 2x22.5/2x20.5
Head room, f/r 36.5/36.0
Seat back adjustment, deg....... 75

MAINTENANCE

Service intervals, mi:
　Oil change.......................... 4000
　Filter change 4000
　Minor tuneup 4000
　Major tuneup 8000
Warranty, mo/mi 12/12,000

CALCULATED DATA

Lb/bhp (test weight) 20.4
Mph/1000 rpm (4th gear) 19.4
Engine revs/mi (60 mph)...... 3100
Piston travel, ft/mi 1630
R&T steering index 1.26
Brake swept area, sq in./ton .. 284

RELIABILITY

From R&T Owner Surveys the average
number of trouble areas for all models surveyed is 12. As owners of
earlier-model BMW 6-cylinders reported 10 trouble areas, we expect
the reliability of the BMW 3.0CS to
be better than average.

ROAD TEST RESULTS

ACCELERATION

Time to distance, sec:
　0-100 ft...............................3.7
　0-500 ft...............................9.7
　0-1320 ft (¼ mi) 17.2
Speed at end of ¼-mi, mph....82.5
Time to speed, sec:
　0-30 mph 3.4
　0-40 mph 5.5
　0-50 mph 7.3
　0-60 mph 10.0
　0-70 mph 12.7
　0-80 mph 16.4
　0-100 mph 27.5

SPEEDS IN GEARS

4th gear (6400)......................125
3rd (6400)...............................89
2nd (6400)...............................59
1st (6400)...............................32

FUEL ECONOMY

Normal driving, mpg 17.0
Cruising range, mi (1-gal res.) .. 297

HANDLING

Speed on 100-ft radius, mph..33.3
Lateral acceleration, g 0.741

BRAKES

Minimum stopping distances, ft:
　From 60 mph 165
　From 80 mph 282
Control in panic stop ....fair
Pedal effort for 0.5g stop, lb 20
Fade: percent increase in pedal
　effort to maintain 0.5g decelera-
　tion in 6 stops from 60 mph .. nil
Parking: hold 30% grade? ....yes
Overall brake rating ....good

INTERIOR NOISE

All noise readings in dBA:
　Idle in neutral 54
　Maximum, 1st gear 81
　Constant 30 mph 65
　　50 mph 68
　　70 mph 73
　　90 mph 79

SPEEDOMETER ERROR

30 mph indicated is actually..28.5
50 mph 49.5
60 mph 59.5
70 mph 69.0
80 mph 79.0
Odometer, 10.0 mi 9.9

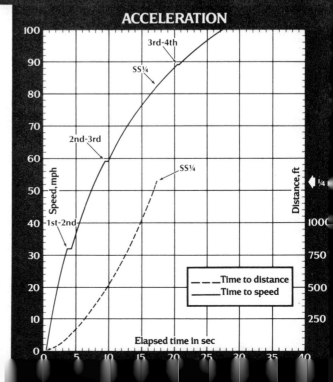

ACCELERATION

Time to distance
Time to speed

WERNER BÜHRER DRAWING

BMW 2800, BAVARIA & CS

112 owners report on the 6-cylinder BMWs

Until 1969 Mercedes had the German market for big, fast sedans pretty much to itself. That year two serious new competitors for well-heeled Germans' money were introduced, the redesigned Opel Diplomat and the 6-cylinder BMWs. Opel doesn't sell its big cars in the U.S. but BMW had the U.S. market very much in mind and the cars were introduced here shortly after appearing in Europe.

At first there were three models: the 2500 sedan, with a 2.5-liter version of the inline single-overhead-cam six and relatively plain upholstery and equipment; the 2800 sedan, bodily like the 2500 but with much fancier trim and equipment including leather upholstery and Nivomat self-leveling rear shocks; and the 2800CS, a coupe based on the earlier 4-cylinder 2000CS but with a new front end and the 2.8-liter engine of the 2800 sedan. The 2500 listed for about $5300, the 2800 for about $1000 more and the CS for yet another $1000-plus.

In 1971 an interesting marketing realignment eliminated the 2500 and 2800 as separate models and replaced both with a 2.8-engine sedan called the Bavaria. With trim like that of the 2500 and the 2800's engine, the Bavaria was offered for the bargain price of $5000, though options most customers would want put the price of a typically equipped Bavaria closer to

$6000. No matter—it was still a bargain, and sales of the 6-cylinder sedans in the U.S. took off.

For 1972 both the Bavaria and the coupe got an enlarged engine of an even 3 liters; the Bavaria's name remained the same but the coupe became 3.0CS.

Today's Bavaria and 3.0CS remain unchanged from the 1972s except as required by government regulations.

Though we had a good stock of questionnaires filled out by owners of 2500s, we decided to eliminate them and concentrate on the cars more closely related to today's BMW offerings in the U.S. This left us with a good sample of 112 owners of 2800s, Bavarias and CSs: three 1969 2800s; seven 1970 2800s and seven 2800CSs; 11 1971 2800s, 41 Bavaria 2.8s and 12 2800CSs; 29 1972 Bavaria 3.0s and two 3.0CSs.

It's not unusual for us to find a preponderance of professional people among the owners of imported cars we survey, and since the big BMWs are expensive this seems even more predictable. A car as "engineered" as these BMWs, with a certain emphasis on precision and efficiency as well as features like overhead camshaft, dual carburetors, all-around independent suspension and disc brakes, is also bound to appeal to engineers. But they also appeal to doctors, and these two professions were the ones most often mentioned. Next came managers, then businessmen who own their own companies, and then military people (most of whom are stationed overseas). The average age of our respondents was 36 years; the youngest was 16 years old and the oldest a mere 64. Sales of imported makes are always strongest at the two coasts, and the two states most frequently given as home were California and New York. Other strongholds for BMW sixes were Massachusetts and Pennsylvania. Three of our respondents live in Canada.

Optional equipment ordered by these owners for their big BMWs may surprise both other R&T readers and Hoffman Motors. Fully 79% of these R&T readers ordered air conditioning and 78% took power steering, standard on 2800s and the coupes but optional on the Bavarias. Automatic transmission was on 22% of the cars. Other options, like AM/FM radio, stereo radio or tape player, and limited-slip differential, occurred in smaller numbers. Hoffman Motors has some options that are in fact mandatory and there was some criticism of the distributor for misleading advertising on the Bavaria in that one without options (and hence available at the list price) was hard to find. But there were a few Bavarias in our survey that didn't have a single option, so they must have been available.

Nearly all these cars were purchased new, and over half of them were bought by people who own other cars—indicating to us that most people who buy expensive cars don't stretch their budgets to the limit to buy them. Our owners also use their BMWs a lot: 55% of them drive between 15,000 and 25,000 miles per year, well over the national average of annual mileage, and fully 17% of them drive more than 25,000 miles per year. The average odometer reading for all cars surveyed was 20,600 miles; the highest was 72,000 miles and we had five cars with over 50,000 on their odometers.

These owners drive their cars the natural way to drive a BMW: hard. Only Ferrari and Lotus drivers have told us they push their cars harder. There's a certain aggressive character about the way these cars perform, hard to define or describe. One owner said, "The harder I drive it, the more it seems to like it—I like to listen to the engine when it's put to work." Another, not so happy with the way his Bavaria ran at city speeds, said, "It refuses to be driven less than hard." So we had a hard-driven bunch of cars.

But they're also a well-cared-for bunch. Eighty percent of the BMW owners follow BMW's rigorous preventive maintenance schedule, which calls for a minor service every 4000 miles and a major one every 8000 (including a full engine tuneup). This sort of service is expensive but the BMW owners' adherence to the schedule has been exceeded only by Audi owners in our series of surveys. Another 8% of the owners follow the schedule "mostly" and 12% decide on their own when to have service done and how much. As religiously as they follow BMW's routine, however, 10% of the owners do complain that it's an expensive thing.

Dealers & Service

IF THEY complain of expensive service, they don't complain much about bad service. Once again—this is our second BMW owner survey—BMW dealers have come through with a remarkably good rating from their customers. An amazing 37% of our respondents rated their service excellent—the only make whose dealers approached this performance was Audi with 28%. Another 29% rated their dealers good, and adding these together we have 66% of the BMW dealers obviously satisfying what must be a demanding group of owners. (R&T readers and owners of German cars—what else?) When we surveyed BMW 1600 and 2002 owners in 1969 this figure was almost the same—65%—but then only 12% of the dealers were called excellent. On the negative end, 15% of the BMW dealers were rated poor, a low (good) reading for this category.

It's our custom to name the dealers that got excellent rating. Not all the owners gave names, but we can list these: Hyde Park Motors, Los Angeles; BMW Auto Zentrum, San Rafael, Calif.; Tulsa BMW, Tulsa; Foreign Car Clinic, Dobbs Ferry,

N.Y.; Great Neck Imports, Great Neck, N.Y.; Hafkemeyer of Kansas City; Ott & Burger, Williamstown, Mass.; Fritz's, Trenton, N.J.; Nemet Motors, Jamaica, N.Y. (an independent, not a dealer); Trans-Atlantic Motors, New York City; Jaksich of Sacramento, Calif.; Webster Motor Service, Kirkwood, Mo.; A&E Motors, London, Ontario, Canada; and O.E. Haring Inc, New Orleans.

A happy and rare situation.

Why a BMW?

IT WAS clear from what our owners told us in response to the question "What particular features influenced your choice of this make and model?" that most of them wanted a roomy sedan with sporting qualities. Only 13% of them actually said it this way, but then 47% of them said "handling," 61% said "performance" (or "engine") and 20% said "comfort." Of the 21 coupe owners a similar percentage—19%—quoted comfort as a reason for purchase. One Bavaria owner put it: "On the way to work it's a sports car. When transporting business associates it's a luxury sedan."

Other influencing factors were the assumption of high quality (quoted by 28%), styling (15% of the sedan owners and 28% of the coupe owners, logically), the BMW reputation or previous BMW ownership (13%), compact size (9%), and what they read in an R&T road test (9%). A few (6%) mentioned that the BMW was an alternate to Mercedes. And 14% of the Bavaria owners said they were attracted by its price.

Best Features

NORMALLY THE Best Features blank on the questionnaire looks pretty much like the influencing features listed above, and this was true here too. Handling came in first among the favorite qualities, 58% of the owners listing it in some form. Performance came next, 49% noting it, and a performance-related item—fuel economy—came next with 16% of the owners praising the BMW engine's remarkable fuel economy or the long cruising range these cars have on a tank of gasoline. One owner said he got 23.5 mpg with his 2800—probably a figure from a long trip—but the average for 2800s was close to our own test figure of 19 mpg for the 1970 2800CS. Unfortunately this figure is coming down steadily as the government's emission limits get tighter. Our 1971 2.8 Bavaria did 18 mpg, a 1972 3.0 Bavaria owned by a staff member is doing 17 mpg and the 1973 3.0CS we just tested managed only 16 mpg. It seems, however, that in 1973 16 mpg is just as impressive as 19 was in 1971, and we should remember that today's 3-liter runs on regular fuel whereas the 2.8s needed premium.

Other Best Features mentioned were quality, 13%; comfort, 10%; compact size, 8%; driving pleasure, 7%; reliability, 6%; and safety, 5%. One owner living in the north noted that his 3-liter Bavaria "starts instantly, even at –20 F."

Worst Features

THERE HAS to be a bad side to every car, though, and one thing came out clearly the worst in these BMWs: the air conditioning system. Everyone knows that European cars generally have been far behind the best U.S. practice, but it's paradoxical that even in such expensive cars the customer can't match a Chevrolet's air conditioning. So it is, though, and 31% of those with air conditioning complained of inadequate cooling capacity or poor air distribution. The problem is mainly one of design: there just isn't enough room in the center console of either coupe or sedan for an evaporator of adequate size, and to make up for this one has to run the A/C blower at full (read noisy) speed. It's something the BMW owner just has to put up with.

Next on the Worst list was an item mentioned by far fewer owners: brakes. And since the sedans, at least, have always had highly capable brakes we can only conclude they were unhappy with all the squeaking going on. Some said what their complaint was, others didn't, but this was what was most frequently mentioned and it is a common complaint with disc brakes designed for high-speed driving. The 2800CS had a second-rate brake system with drums at the rear, and two of the 21 owners of this model reported dissatisfaction with their brakes.

Then came hesitation, stumbles or other maladies of lean carburetion for emission control. Three more things rate mention among Worst Features: the prices of BMW replacement parts, the cost of maintenance, and wind noise (mostly on the Bavarias). Nine percent of the owners didn't think their BMWs had a worst feature.

Problem Areas and Component Life

THIS SECTION is always the nitty-gritty of our surveys. The BMWs are just above average in this respect, with 10 areas of problems afflicting 5% or more of the owners.

First was the cooling system, and the troubles were many—fully 38% of the owners had some problem. The water pump was the worst offender, failing at an average of 32,000 miles in 14% of the cars and continuing to give trouble in the newer 3-liters. Another 9% had thermostat failure, 5% had to have their electric fan clutch replaced (all of these were 3-liters) and 11% had miscellaneous cooling problems like overheating and leaks.

Instruments, commonly a trouble spot, were very much so for the BMW owners. A total of 30% mention was tallied up, the Kienzle clock being the worst offender and the fuel gauge coming next. The manual gearbox, at its best an outstanding feature of the 6-cylinders, is often not at its best and caused problems for 16% of the owners. Weak synchronizers on 2nd gear afflicted 10% of the cars, and though the box was redesigned for the 3-liters the rate of mention remained at that level for them; miscellaneous problems made up the other 6%.

There were brake troubles for 15% of the owners. Most frequent problem was pulling to one side or the other, and interestingly this occurred mainly with the all-disc brakes. Other items: untrue discs, hydraulic trouble and vacuum boosters.

If carburetion didn't rate a Worst Feature for many, it did give a large proportion of the owners trouble. In all, 20% of our respondents mentioned carburetion faults, the majority of them stumbling or hesitating upon acceleration. Faulty behavior of the choke and fast-idle system was mentioned by a few,

and it may be that they were just noting normal operation: on the 2800s the fast idle was too fast, even when everything was working right.

Air conditioning was mentioned as a problem by 16% of those who had it. Most of these had trouble with the system itself and it was unclear to us just how many were simply frustrated with its lack of capacity and how many actually needed repairs. There were only two failures of its electromagnetic cycling clutch.

Miscellaneous electrical problems affected 9% of the cars, but the incidence of trouble with electric windows was somewhat higher than this overall figure. Differential trouble, either mechanical or just lubricant leakage, affected 8% and there were 5% occurrences of starter-flywheel trouble and clutch problems—the latter not counting the clutch overhaul needed at 72,000 miles by the most-used car.

Under the heading of normal replacement items, we found the front brakes capable of just under 20,000 miles on the average before needing new pads, the rears 21,000-plus—neither particularly good. Continental tires went 20,000 miles, Michelin XAS 34,000. Front shocks did 25,000 miles before needing replacement, the regular rear shocks about 14,000; surprisingly, the Nivomat units (which have an evil word-of-mouth reputation) averaged out at nearly 19,000 miles. Sparkplug replacement was done by our owners at an average of 8400 miles, just over the official 8000-mile BMW recommendation. There weren't enough clutch jobs among the 112 cars to get a good average life, which must mean something.

Buy Another?

WITH A record of reliability that looks just above average, the big BMWs come out with a surprisingly low number of potential repeat customers: only 73%, one of the lowest percentages in our series, say they'll buy another BMW. But there was a group of 12% whose decision hangs on how the price situation looks when it's time to trade. With the prices of German cars going as they are now, these people may not be able to afford BMWs again even if they want them. Perhaps their reluctance to repeat has to do with what kind of people they are: as one satisfied sedan owner said, "Life is too short to do the same thing twice!"

SUMMARY: BMW 6-CYLINDERS

New or Used?

Bought new 92%
Bought used 8%

Driving Habits

Drivers who said they drive "moderately"........24%
Drivers who said they drive "hard" 62%
Drivers who said they drive "very hard" 14%

Would They Buy Another?

Yes 73%
No 15%
Undecided 12%

Annual Mileage

5000–10,000 .... 3%
10,000–15,000 .... 25%
15,000–25,000 .... 55%
Over 25,000 .... 17%

Problem Areas
Mentioned by more than 10% of the owners

Cooling System	Brake System
Instruments	Gearbox
Carburetion	Air Conditioning

Five Best Features

Handling
Performance
Fuel Economy
Quality
Comfort

How BMW Owners Feel About BMW Service

Rated "excellent" .. 37%
Rated "good".......... 29%
Rated "fair" 15%
Rated "poor" 18%

Mentioned by 5–10% of the owners

Electrical System	Starter-Flywheel
Differential	Clutch

Owners who reported no problems 11%

Five Worst Features

Air Conditioning
Brakes
Carburetion
Maintenance Cost
Wind Noise

BMW vs FORD

Two German firms go all-out in pursuit of the 1973 European Touring Car Championship

BY JONATHAN THOMPSON

On facing page, the Alpina BMW in which Niki Lauda and Brian Muir won the Monza 4-hour race and the Capri of Jochen Mass and Jody Scheckter. Above are the engines: at top, the factory BMW 3.3-liter inline six, and at bottom the 3-liter Ford V-6. Both have Kugelfischer mechanical fuel injection.

THE RECIPE FOR a Formula 1 car is well known: *To one slightly firm monocoque add one whole Ford Cosworth DFV (preferably fresh) and a dash of Hewland; stir vigorously. Fold in Standard British Racing Car Suspension, four Girlings (Lockheeds will do in a pinch) and four Goodyears. Top with Specialised Mouldings fiberglass body panels. Garnish with Tobacco Company paint scheme. Serves one Graded Driver.* Using different engines and components, similar recipes are available for USAC, Formula 2, Formula 5000, etc. Designers of "pure" racing cars start out with pretty much the same objectives and end up with predictably raceable machines that differ slightly in their ingredients; right now different nose shapes and radiator positions are being served up variously by individual chefs.

But the original designers of a Group 2 Special Touring Car may not even know they're creating a racing car. The project engineers, along with hundreds of detail designers, develop a road car that meets market and cost requirements laid down by management. Racing that car may only be the dream of a few development engineers. All the more remarkable, then, that the BMW 3.0CS, a luxury Grand Touring car in the 5-figure price bracket, and the Ford Capri 2600 V-6, a popular ponycar costing a third as much, should meet on the race track with only fractions of a second separating their lap times.

Those who have followed the Datsun-Alfa battle in the Trans-Am the last two years know that what you do with the ingredients is more important than what you started with. What is really remarkable about the big BMW vs Ford battle in this year's Group 2 racing is that the manufacturers themselves, both German, are meeting head-on in all the European Touring Car Championship events, with the reputation of their racing departments as much at stake as the image of their road cars. Multi-car teams have been meticulously prepared and top international drivers from Formula 1, like Jackie Stewart, Jacky Ickx and Chris Amon, have joined the regularly contracted touring-car specialists like Dieter Glemser, Hans Stuck, Jochen Mass and Dieter Quester.

The FIA's International Sporting Commission, the CSI, lays

Factory BMW is the most colorful with its white, blue and red scheme.

down the racing categories in Appendix J to the International Sporting Code. Category A is for "recognized production cars" and Group 1 is for Series Production Touring Cars of which 5000 basically identical units have been built during 12 consecutive months. Group 2 Special Touring Cars need only be built in a quantity of 1000 during the same period and can be modified in many clearly (and not so clearly) defined ways. Appendix J spells these out in seven pages of small type.

For engines, the permitted modifications include extensive machining, balancing and lightening of all parts, with changes in valve operation, induction and exhaust systems and lubrication allowed as long as the basic design features—position of the camshaft, number of valves per cylinder, etc—are unchanged. Actual series production parts must be used as raw material for the block, head(s) and crankshaft, but bearings, gaskets, pistons, valves, camshafts, fuel pumps, etc, can be replaced by a like number of parts of different design. Reboring is allowed within the limits of the capacity class to which the original homologated car belongs. Both the BMW 3.0CS and the Ford Capri 2600 normally fall in the 2500/3000-cc class.

The drive train is permitted the same scope of modification as the engine; for instance the ratios are free but the number of speeds can't be changed from a homologated option. Suspension design is almost completely free, with the basic requirement that the original *type* of spring—coils where the production car has them, or leaves, or torsion bars, or hydropneumatic units—not be changed, though *additional supplementary* springs can be used. Wheels are free of restriction other than having to be the same diameter front and back; brakes can be extensively modified within the limit of the homologated friction surface area. Fuel-tank design is open but the amount of fuel allowed for cars over 2500 cc is limited to 120 liters or about 31 U.S. gallons.

No modification to the *structure* of the body is permitted, and no exterior changes are allowed above a horizontal plane passing through the wheel centers, but new panels such as nose spoilers and fender flares can be added, and of course bumpers are not used. Lightweight panels can be used if 100 cars have been built with them. Inside the car the steering wheel and front seats can be replaced (but not by lighter ones, unless homologated with them) and the rear seat removed altogether. Interior trim such as door panels cannot be removed, yet such things as the glovebox lid and carpets can. In safety equipment

the car must conform to the general competition requirements, including the obvious internal rollbar.

After all the foregoing comes the possibility of incorporating *optional* equipment, which need only be produced in quantities of 100 and ostensibly be available for sale to the customer. The freedom granted here brings in a host of additional modifications, from the lightweight body panels to such things as 5-speed gearboxes.

Taking full advantage of the freedom of Group 2 requirements (including the commonly exercised freedom of *interpretation* of certain details), a competitive car must therefore be completely rebuilt from the shell outward, and the engineers of the original production car may not recognize a single component except for the body shell, engine block, crankshaft and a few miscellaneous parts that were doing a good enough job for racing. Looking at it that way, the BMW 3.0CS and the Ford Capri 2600 aren't as different in raw material as their marketing positions suggest (both are 6-cylinder, 4-passenger coupes in the 3-liter class, with less than a 3-in. difference in wheelbase) and their race preparation brings them to near equality. That BMW has elected to build a limited-quantity production car to high standards of quality and refinement (read weight) whereas Ford produces a high-volume good performing car with more cost compromises, has little to do with the racing potential of the two basic designs.

BMW Motorsport, Alpina & Schnitzer

BMW HAS A long history of building sports cars and motorcycles. It is hard to believe that in the mid-1950s the firm was in danger of extinction; now the progressive Bayerische Motorenwerke is the industrial backbone of Munich and solidly established in German and worldwide markets.

Pre-war BMW competition cars included the famous 328 sports car (the engine of which was developed after the war into the well-known Bristol 2-liter) and among other successes the 328 had the distinction of winning the 1940 Mille Miglia in aerodynamic coupe form. Since the war the factory has encouraged the racing of its touring cars, but its main technical achievements were in the 1600-cc Formula 2 for which various 4-valve versions of the 4-cylinder engine were raced in BMW-designed chassis. Although that formula was dominated by Ford-Cosworth, BMW obtained superior horsepower outputs in 1970 and won six events that year with cars driven by Jacky

Ickx, Josef Siffert, Dieter Quester and Hubert Hahne. In the current 2-liter Formula 2 the company's latest four may well dominate the series in a March 732 driven by Jean-Pierre Jarier.

Until this year BMW's policy toward racing the 3.0CS and the earlier 2800CS was to leave them in the capable hands of independent tuning specialists and racing teams like Burkard Bovensiepen's Alpina firm (located in Buchloe in Bavaria), the brothers Josef and Herbert Schnitzer of Freilassing, and BMW Concessionaires Ltd in England. The factory produced a limited series of the 3.0CSL (L for *leicht,* or light) model in 1972 in order to homologate an over-3000-cc engine and the equipment basic to the race preparation of the works CSL Group 2 cars for 1973. This model is lightened by 400 lb with alloy doors, hood and decklid; wider alloy wheels and lighter seats are also installed. The engine is injected as on the CSi and, negligibly increased in displacement to 3003 cc, produces the same output of 200 bhp. The factory quotes a maximum of 146 mph for the CSL, compared to 137 for the standard European CS. Naturally you can't buy a CSL in the United States.

In 1972 Touring Car races the BMWs lacked the speed and preparation of the factory Ford Capris. BMW scored one victory, in the Nürburgring 6-hour event, with a 2800CS driven by Rolf Stommelen/Hans Heyer/John Fitzpatrick outlasting the Fords, but the usual lot was 2nd and 4th places. Determined to change that in 1973, the company has formed a new division, BMW Motorsport GmbH. It is headed by Jochen Neerpasch, the very man who built up Ford's 1971–72 championship-winning Capri RS 2600 team. Under Neerpasch are Martin Braungart (also ex-Ford), chief of race engineering, development and preparation, and Herbert Staudenmeier, who provides assistance to privately-organized BMW racing teams.

Neerpasch's expectations are for a few victories but not the 1973 European Touring Car Championship and he has predicted that experienced BMW campaigners like Alpina and Schnitzer will beat the works cars in the early races. Despite this modest appraisal, the works effort cannot be described as modest: no less than five 3.3-liter CSLs have been built for the European Championship, the German Touring Car Championship and two rounds of the World Championship for Makes (basically for Group 5 Sports Cars)—the Nürburgring 1000 Km and Le Mans 24-Hour races. Drivers signed are Chris Amon, Dieter Quester, Toine Hezemans and Hans Joachim Stuck (son of the famous prewar Auto Union and BMW driver), with

Harald Menzel tackling the German Championship.

The racing 3.0CSL's bore is increased from 89.25 mm to 94 mm, giving a displacement of 3340 cc and a power output of 355–360 bhp at 7600 rpm. Kugelfischer mechanical injection is used instead of Bosch electronic and the compression ratio is 11.0:1 compared to 9.5:1 on the production CSL. A 3-plate Borg & Beck clutch replaces the stock single-plate type and the gearbox is a 5-speed in a magnesium casing. Brakes are ventilated discs of the type used on the McLaren Can-Am cars. The weight has been brought down to 2340 lb, 260 lb less than that of the production and a full 700 lb under that of the normal CS/CSi. For comparison, the weight difference between the standard Ford Capri 2600 and the racing RS 2600 is only 290 lb, so it can be appreciated how much luxury equipment and insulation BMW has built into its production models. Bodywork follows the basic lines of the production cars, with ample yet harmonious fender flares and a large fiberglass spoiler (which could better be described as a curtain) hanging from the front. Maximum speed of the racing CSL is well over 160 mph, depending on gearing.

The main private teams running CSLs are Alpina and Schnitzer, with BMW Concessionaires racing an Alpina-built car in the English Group 2 Saloon Car Championship. Alpina is just one of several firms that produce conversions for road BMWs but it is by far the best known and most successful (its racing 2800CS coupes won the 1970 European Touring Car Championship in Division 2). Many of the modifications on the production CSL were developed by Alpina, and Bovensiepen offers a road-going edition of the racer at approximately $20,000 that has 260 bhp and goes 152 mph.

That's only the Alpina that a few lucky European enthusiasts can buy. For racing, Alpina has prepared two 3.3-liter CSLs, producing 350 bhp, for drivers Niki Lauda/Brian Muir and Gerold Pankl/Jean-Pierre Jarier. While the power is slightly less than that of the works cars, the Alpina CSL is conceded to have the best set-up chassis as well as the most experience behind its race preparation. One of the working arrangements between the factory and the several tuning firms is that the technical results shall be pooled in mid-season, all the teams having the opportunity to use the best-working systems regardless of origin. This could mean that Alpina's suspension tuning, Schnitzer's engines (now giving the highest output at close to 375 bhp) and BMW Motorsport's detail engineering would result in the best possible Ford-beater.

The Schnitzer brothers' racing entry consists of two older cars (1972 chassis) which don't handle as well but benefit from the 375 bhp. The drivers for most races will be Henri Pescarolo/Jean-Pierre Jaussaud and Bob Wollek/Walter Brun, with Jacky Ickx, Rolf Stommelen and the Brambilla brothers, Ernesto and Vittorio, filling in for certain races.

With at least six CSLs in most of the events, BMW has a numerical weight that should be sufficient for the rigors of the European Championship—most of the races are for six hours, so attrition is an important factor. In pure speed the BMWs are unlikely to match the Fords before mid-season, and only then if one assumes Capri development to have leveled off. But with outputs of 60 bhp more than the Capris' and the racing knowledge that Neerpasch has brought with him from Ford, the three main BMW teams will obviously be competitive.

Ford Cologne Competitions Centre

COMPARED TO small, strictly German BMW, Ford is a huge international company with practically unlimited resources. Its racing program began seriously in 1964 with the major priorities being Indianapolis and Le Mans, and success was achieved in both types of racing. In Europe the development of Ford engines by Cosworth and other tuning firms for Formulas 1 and 2 has resulted in a continuing domination only occasionally challenged by other makers, and in the Touring Car races Ford Escorts and Capris have been equally successful in the last two years. The Capris were developed at the German

Ford facility in Cologne, under Neerpasch, and Broadspeed has run similar cars in England.

German Capris have mainly had vee engines, though presently there are 1593- and 1993-cc sohc inline fours. The range has included V-4s of 1305, 1498 and 1699 cc and V-6s of 1998, 2293, 2550 (as sold in the U.S.) and 2637 cc; the last capacity is that of the road-going RS 2600, basis of the racing car.

As sold here the 2550-cc V-6 has an 8.2:1 compression ratio, a Holley-Weber carburetor and an output of 107 bhp at 5000 rpm. The RS 2600 sold in Europe has its compression ratio raised to 10.5:1 and with Kugelfischer fuel injection the output is 150 bhp at 5600 rpm. Unlike the racing versions, the limited-production RS 2600 actually weighs *more* than the basic car (2380 lb compared to 2325,) but the additional power gives it fierce acceleration and a top speed of 130 mph. A paint scheme similar to that of the racing cars gives owners the performance image wanted.

The Capri RS 2600s that have dominated European Touring Car races since 1971 have engine components designed and made by Weslake of Britain but assembled in Germany. The displacement is 2995 cc and the current output, which would seem to be approaching the limit, is 320 bhp at 7300 rpm. For 1973, Ford (working with Kugelfischer) has concentrated on reducing the fuel consumption so that last year's limit of one hour 40 minutes between stops can be increased to two hours. Because a new 4-valve Cosworth-built engine with an output in the region of 400 bhp is expected to be homologated early in 1974, the efforts of the Ford team have turned from the current engine to the chassis, particularly to improve the road-holding to a level that will handle next year's horsepower.

The chief engineer at the Ford Cologne Competitions Centre is Thomas Ammerschlager, formerly of NSU and qualified for the Ford job by his ten years of preparing and racing an independent NSU in German touring car events. Taking over Neerpasch's former task of competition management is Michael Kranefuss.

Ammerschlager has concentrated on balancing out the front and rear handling characteristics. Using the same MacPherson-strut suspension, Ammerschlager decided on a raised front roll center to reduce the difference between front and rear—the rear roll center depends on the pivot point of the Watt linkage and can't be changed. A light-alloy rear axle tried unsuccessfully in 1971 has reappeared, now with integral brackets for the trailing arms, which should overcome previous failures of the fabricated brackets. Plastic strips are used as technical stand-ins for the usual rear semi-elliptics; since "auxiliary" springs are allowed, MacPherson struts with coils have been installed as the real rear springing medium. A special front suspension developed by Ralph Broad for the Broadspeed Capris may be used on the factory cars if it proves superior; its basic difference is the use of outboard coil spring/shock units mounted *ahead* of the wheels and connected to them by swinging links. These new units "supplement" the existing MacPherson struts, although the latter now have only token springs to meet the general conformity requirement. The brakes are ventilated discs, the only components on the car interchangeable with parts BMW uses.

Six RS 2600s have been built, three to contest the European Championship plus spares. Ford will also run in the Nüburgring and Le Mans Championship of Makes races, but the seemingly excellent chances of the BMW and Ford Group 2 cars would now seem to be much reduced by the 3-liter Porsche Carrera RSRs in Group 4. The Carreras have a competitive 330 bhp and weigh much less than the Group 2 machines at 1860 lb. Le Mans trials in April provided a comparison of lap times: the Capri RS 2600 achieved 4:19.3 (117.6 mph) ten seconds slower than the Carrera RSR on the 8.47-mi circuit and only 2.6 sec slower than the Corvette 427, but a second faster than the best Ferrari 365GTB4. Drivers of the works Capri RS 2600s include Number One Ford Driver Jackie Stewart, plus Glemser, Mass, Gerry Birrell, John Fitzpatrick and Jody Scheckter. Several private teams are running ex-works 1972 Capris but these

probably will not figure strongly in the championship series.

Confrontation at Monza

THE MONZA 4-hour race on March 25 saw the first all-out battle between BMW and Ford for the 1973 European Touring Car Championship, a 9-race series that ends at Jarama, Spain, in October. Two works 3.3-liter BMWs, sporting an overall white scheme with bright blue, purple and red stripes running all around the body, were entered for Amon/Stuck and Hezemans/Quester. Alpina's single entry for Lauda/Muir was an all-white 3-liter with a red spoiler and number panels. Schnitzer entered two beautiful silver and red 3.3-liter cars for V. Brambilla/Wollek and E. Brambilla/Brun.

All three of Ford's works Capris had the same blue and white scheme with colored bands at the tops of the windshields distinguishing them: blue for Stewart/Glemser, red for Birrell/Fitzpatrick and yellow for Mass/Scheckter. Privately entered Capris were driven by Albrecht Krebs/Hartmut Kautz, Klaus Fritzinger/Fräulein Waltraud Odenthal, and Alberto Ruiz-Gimenez/Jaime Mesia.

The new works Fords had just been completed during the week before the race and hadn't turned a wheel before arriving at Monza. Three different suspension setups were tried and none of the Capris was fast during early practice. Two of them were running on Dunlop tires while Stewart was contracted to Goodyear. The Mass/Scheckter car handled best and the Birrell/Fitzpatrick car the worst, lifting *both* inside wheels on the Parabolica curve and making the drivers guess where the inside of the corner was! This car's suspension was rebuilt to the same layout as Mass/Scheckter's, but the different characteristics of the Goodyears (the rears are a half-inch wider than the Dunlops) meant a compromise would have to do on the Stewart/Glemser car. Nevertheless Stewart justified his reputa-

Schnitzer BMWs have older chassis but started season with highest power.

tion by setting the pole time of 1 minute 38.2 seconds, just over 130 mph.

Vittorio Brambilla shocked Ford (but not the BMW works team) with a time of 1:37.7 in his Schnitzer BMW during an unofficial practice session and his best official lap of 1:38.4 put him next to Stewart on the front row; as predicted, the Schnitzer engine was easily the most powerful in the field. Mass did 1:38.8 to put his Capri behind Stewart's and Stuck put the fastest of the works BMWs next to him on the second row, at 1:39.4. Birrell was fifth fastest in the still ill-handling Capri at 1:39.9. Although immaculately prepared, the BMW Alpina of Lauda/Muir was not as fast as the works cars, qualifying 7th in 1:40.4. The best privately entered Ford (Krebs/Kautz) did 1:42.2; the second Schnitzer BMW (E. Brambilla/Brun) had troubles and started 9th with 1:42.9. The rest of the 24-car field was made up of private Capris, Escorts and 2002s, plus a lone Alfa GTAm.

Vittorio Brambilla pleased the Italian crowd by making an excellent start and leading for the first two laps. The other Schnitzer car of his brother, Ernesto, wouldn't fire up and had to be started in the pits, losing a lap and retiring on lap five with gearbox trouble. On the third lap Stewart passed V. Brambilla, to be followed later by Mass, but the BMW held to the Fords and at 10 laps the order was Ford-Ford-BMW-BMW (Stuck)-BMW (Lauda)-Ford (Krebs). The Birrell Ford was already out and the Hezemans BMW had made the first of several unscheduled tire stops, suspension problems later causing its retirement.

The initial pace slackened on lap 25 when Brambilla, who had stayed within a second of the Stewart and Mass Fords until then, pitted with a blown head gasket. At one hour the order was Ford (Stewart)-Ford (Mass)-BMW (Stuck)-BMW (Lauda), but Stuck retired soon after with a broken piston and

the head gasket gone.

At this point the two works Capris were running steadily and four of the BMWs were already out of contention, but the Lauda/Muir Alpina was hanging on, running about two seconds per lap slower than the Fords.

Glemser took over from Stewart on lap 52, with Scheckter replacing Mass the next time around. Glemser lapped Muir right in front of the pits on lap 82. At the 100-lap point came the last fuel stops with Stewart taking over the lead car again, but the second Ford was delayed, having its alternator belt replaced, so when Mass rejoined the race he was behind Lauda, now in 2nd place in the BMW Alpina and still running like a train. Stewart looked set for victory but his camshaft broke on lap 117 and the BMW was now in the lead with a minute's advantage over Mass. Although Mass reduced the difference to 21 seconds by the 4-hour mark, the Alpina's steady reliability gave it a well-earned victory as it covered 142 laps in 4 hours, 1 minute and 29.6 seconds for an average of 126.8 mph. The fastest lap of 1:38.5 was set early in the race by Brambilla's Schnitzer BMW and equaled in mid-race by Mass's Capri.

With both works teams experiencing difficulties at Monza there is no clear advantage evident for either. Ford was marginally faster but rapid development of the more potent BMW engine could reverse the positions by the next few events. Reliability is obviously the factor that Neerpasch and Kranefuss will have to worry about all season long.

The European Touring Car Championship has been ignored in the U.S. press, largely because the cars raced have had little identity to American enthusiasts. Now there are two competitors whose products have a strong following in this country and the results of the championship will be of more than routine interest to enthusiasts defending their favorites. At this point it wouldn't be wise to put any money on the outcome. ⧖

BMW 3.0S

WHY THIS SEDAN MAY BE THE BEST VALUE ON THE MARKET

BY ERIC DAHLQUIST

This is the problem: On one hand, there is the completely new 450 SE—more sophisticated, bigger, heavier, less economical to operate but handling is better and it's safer than the 280 SE 4.5 model it superceded and, nearly $4500 more expensive. A notch below is the Mercedes 280 S, the former 230-250 series that once had a list price of $8500 but now has a more powerful twin-overhead cam engine and a $10,000-plus pricetag to match.

On the other hand there is the XJ Jaguar sedan, six-and twelve-cylinder models. Wrapped with its beautifully styled body, the six is a somewhat sluggish performer. The XJ 12, by contrast, is this year's land-bound rocketship, faster than most anything else on the road —at least when it's running properly. Occasional small bugs and unreliable dealer service tarnishes the 12's brilliant design package. Cost is either $9900 or $11,425, depending on the engine you choose.

So what does that leave us with? The BMW 3.0S, that's what. Fast, nimble, powerful, it has one of the most efficient engines ever built but it's less complicated mechanically as an automobile.

The BMW, however, sells for $11,400.

In a nutshell, these are the alternatives more American buyers (more than anyone would have guessed five years ago) are facing in the luxury import sedan market. The real dilemma springs from the almost-daily price escalations caused by currency fluctuations and the fuel shortage. After all, you can't enjoy a car if you can't drive it.

Nearly four years ago in the January 1970 issue of *Motor Trend,* we surveyed the two top contenders in the field—the Mercedes 280 SE and the BMW 2800. We concluded that the BMW's lively handling, equal quality and engineering put it a bumper up on the Mercedes. In fact, many of the handling and performance improvements by Mercedes were stimulated by BMW's impressive numbers of conquest sales in the European market.

BMW is the first to agree that Mercedes-Benz builds fine automobiles. Interestingly, this respect is reciprocal. It's a more-even match in more areas than Mercedes would like to think about. For example, Mercedes benchmark in developing its new twin-cam 280s for '73 was encouraged by BMW's 3.0 six, and the BMW is still faster.

What BMW has always stressed along with agile handling was that its superb six-cylinder engines offered the best of both worlds—performance and economy. And as creators of some of the world's finest powerplants since Baron Von Richthofen's Folker D-7 Triplane, they've got as good a handle on the problem as anyone. In fact, so well does the air/fuel mixture swirl through BMW's unique triple-hemispheric combustion chamber that it not only produces a very impressive 170 SAE net horsepower from a mere 182 cubic inches of displacement, but the engine is exceedingly low on emissions as well.

Getting our hands on one of these German wonder cars to rediscover if the truths we had learned four years ago were still valid was no easy matter since everything with a BMW badge on it is sold before it rolls off the assembly line. The car that finally came into our possession was a splendidly detailed green 3.0S four-door sedan equipped standard with a three-speed automatic transmission, electric windows, power steering, air-conditioning, aluminum wheels with Michelin VR 144 tires, Becker AM/FM stereo radio with automatic antenna,

1. *The much over-worked term "turbine-like smoothness" began with descriptions of BMW engines.* 2. *And it's not hard to see why. With seven main bearings and 12 counterbalance crankshaft weights to eliminate high frequency oscillations.* 3. *MacPherson strut front suspension is inclined rearward to create superior on-center steering feel and excellent reaction to bumps.* 4. *Complementing the BMW's foreward underpinnings is an articulated, semi-trailing arm rear suspension. A whopping 7.9 inches of wheel travel can handle even America's roughest roads.* 5. *ZF-Gemmer worm and roller steering box and 3-piece track rod imparts good road feel.*

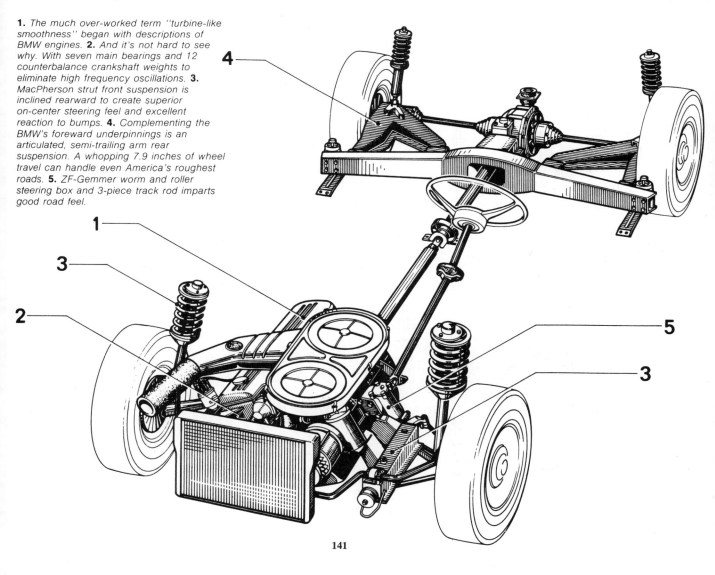

wood trim, and one of the more appealing light-tan leather interiors we've ever laid eyes on. The window-sticker base price was $11,400, or about the price of an old Mercedes 280 SE 4.5 a year and a half ago. And that Mercedes came without the leather interior.

By the time we were actually driving the 3.0S, word came from Germany that for '74, the engine's capacity will be expanded to 3.3 liters and a new, four-inch longer wheelbase (3.3L) version will be available. This follows Mercedes long-established precedent with stretched models, and lately, Jaguar. Otherwise, the '73-'74 BMWs are nearly identical except that straight-line acceleration will be improved.

While increasing the sedan's overall length from 185 inches to 189 produces a direct four-inch increase in rear seat room, the standard version has ample space. The chair height seats slide back to easily accommodate persons more than six-feet tall, and although there is no vertical movement provided, with the fully adjustable back rest, the driving position is ideal. Everything in the driver's control set—steering wheel, transmission shift handle, switches, radio, ventilation—is within easy reach with the inertia reel belt on.

And if the BMW's instrument nacelle is intelligently laid out with its great round speedometer and tachometer dials, ultra-functional looking, with white-on-black numerals, no less so is the car's engine compartment. A visual delight in these days of smog-festooned powerplants, BMW has created an antiseptically clean layout with a complete absence of helter-skelter wires, hoses, lines and linkages.

As a total engineering, styling, construction and detailing design package, the BMW car is unexcelled among the world's automobiles, the same way BMW's unique shaft-drive motorcycles are unmatched among the worlds two-wheeled manufacturers. But in the end, it is the pure, unfiltered pleasure of driving the car that makes it supreme.

For those who might not know, what BMW did, in essence, was to combine the function of a sedan with the handling, braking and acceleration properties of a sports car. Ironically, the end result was a luxury sedan that performed better than most sports cars.

The driving sensation is one of light, nimble, exquisitely refined performance. The ability to ram down roads at blurring velocity is there, and yet one retains total control, with the cockpit a calm "eye"

in the center of the hurricane. "Speed-feel" is what the Germans call it.

It is as much the product of a state of mind about building cars as the certain way the front and rear suspension pieces are aligned. Completely unsusceptible to the devilments and ailments like "freeway hop" or any other harmonic vibration, the BMW purrs along as smoothly as an electric train. On rough surfaces, the Mac-Pherson-strut front suspension and semi-trailing-arm rear with a whopping 7.9 inches of travel absorbs bumps and irregularities like a sponge blotter. You find yourself seeking out roads with long sweeping curves for no other reason than to experience that wonderful sensation of going fast around a bend with precision.

On the test track at Irwindale Raceway we found some other endearing BMW qualities. For one thing, the 3.0S four-wheel disc brakes could stop the car straight from 60 mph consistently under 125 feet, one of the shortest measures of any car we've tested in the last 23 years. Acceleration, however, wasn't as impressive, averaging some 11.4 seconds to 60 mph in the 3140-pound car. Not tortoise-like by any stretch, but certainly not in the nine-second league of the standard shift version. The addition

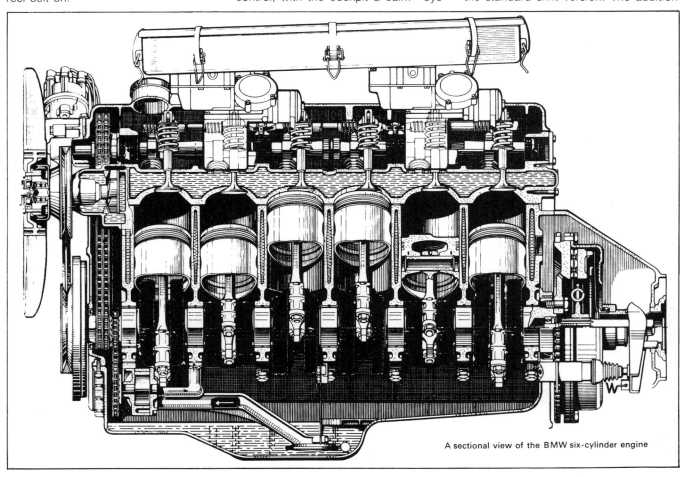

A sectional view of the BMW six-cylinder engine

of 300-cubic-centimeters of engine volume in 1974 will go a long way toward making the automatic as formidable a stop-light racer as the four-speed is.

Equally impressive with the 3.0S fantastic braking and handling was the car's totally untheatrical nature. During an intense test session, with temperature hovering around the 100-degree mark, the car never heated up beyond its normal range even with the air conditioning on. It started quickly and ran with what has become a classical BMW trait: turbine-like smoothness. Only a handful of other cars would have performed as well.

At this juncture you're probably wondering if it's even remotely possible that the 3.0S suffers from even a single flaw. It does. In the midst of a great greenhouse of visibility, the rear-view mirror is mounted too high on the windshield to be effective and needs to be repositioned lower. Also, the automatic transmission ought to have a more positive feeling between gears. It is very awkward to be up-shifting under full power only to jump from first to drive when you expected second.

Then too, the BMW's wind-noise level above 90 mph is quite high and noticeable. Finally, although all that leather upholstery looks great, it is fairly slippery and you tend to slide around on front seats that don't have a lot of lateral support to begin with.

Understandably, the one question you're asking is whether the BMW 3.0S is better than its counterparts, the Mercedes 450 SE or the Jag XJ 12. Supplying an answer poses the same problem as choosing between three fine watches; unquestionably, individual taste will bear heavily on the final decision. And yet, the BMW offers more of one particular ''luxury'' than do the other two: operation economy at no real sacrifice to performance. What other car can you name that handles, stops and goes the way the 3.0S does while still delivering 17 mpg at a steady 80 mph—with automatic yet? Under similar conditions, the stick gives an amazing 20 mpg! Added into the amalgam is fact the BMW is simply an unfussy car. It has that sort of run-forever-while-having-fun quality about it that made the original GTO Pontiac such a smash hit.

For this time and place, the BMW 3.0S (and most obviously it's lower-priced counterpart Bavaria) is probably the best value on the market. Funny, the people who can afford these fine cars seem to care about that more than the ones who don't. ■

TEST DATA

BMW 3.0S

Price	$11,400
Engine	overhead cam, inline six
Bore/stroke, in.	3.50 x 3.15
HP @ RPM	170 @ 5,800
Torque: lbs-ft. @ RPM	185 @ 3500
Compression ratio	8.3:1
Carburetion	Two Zenith, downdraft
Transmission	Automatic 3-speed
Final drive ratio	3.64:1
Type steering	Power Asst, worm & roller
Steering ratio	18.9:1
Turning diameter, curb-to-curb, ft.	31'.6''
Wheel turns, lock-to-lock	4.1
Tire size	175 HR14
Brakes	Front disc, rear drum
Front suspension	Ind. MacPh. strut,
Rear suspension	Ind. semi-trailing arm
Body/frame construction	Unit
Wheelbase, ins.	106
Overall length, ins.	185
Width, ins.	68.9
Height, ins.	57.1
Curb weight, lbs.	4140
Front track, ins.	56.9
Rear track, ins.	57.6
Fuel capacity, gals.	19.8
Trunk space, cu. ft.	23.1
Acceleration,	
0–30 mph	4.7
0–45 mph	8.2
0–60 mph	11.4
0–75 mph	15.8
Standing start, ¼-mi.; elapsed time, seconds,	18.0
Speed, mph,	79
Passing speeds	
40–60 mph	5.5
50–70 mph	6.5
Stopping distances,	
From 30 mph, ft.	26.1
From 60 mph, ft.	123.3
Gasoline mileage (91 octane or higher)	17.2

—Due to currency exchange fluctuations, exact figures could change by publication.

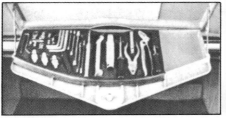

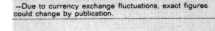

Running Report:

BMW 3.0CS AT 12,000 MILES

BY RON WAKEFIELD

PHOTO BY JOE RUSZ

IN THE DECEMBER 1973 summary of R&T's experience with test cars during the year, I mentioned that my personal BMW 3.0CS (which served as a road-test car also) had developed many problems and that Hoffman Motors had made a good effort to correct them, and left it at that. Now that a year and 12,000 miles on this car are past I want to summarize my experiences with this car briefly.

This bright red coupe with tan leather, air conditioning, electric front windows, limited-slip differential and a few minor extras was delivered to me on Feb. 5, 1973, in what seemed to be good condition. But later (within a day) I noticed an engine knock when it was cold; the left front seat was loose on its track, the right sun visor was poorly made and the rubber weatherseal on the right front turn-signal lamp was too large, bulging out around the lens. At 199 the main odometer stopped (it subsequently started and stopped repeatedly); soon afterward the engine idle speed became inconsistent, the clutch began to chatter slightly on uphill starts and there was too much wind noise around the right door. Then the vinyl on the central console started to come apart and the right windshield washer ceased to work.

So by the prescribed 600-mi service there was plenty to fix. A BMW representative listened to the engine and acknowledged the knock but said he'd like to wait and see if it might correct itself. This isn't absurd; I've had plenty of car troubles correct themselves. But we agreed it was probably a piston problem. A new speedometer was ordered, the idle was steadied and the right door was adjusted.

Our track testing was done at 1780 mi and, despite repeated use of maximum revs, didn't affect the engine knock. Convinced it wasn't going to fix itself, I returned the car to Hoffman's at 2200 mi. It wouldn't have: one piston pin was misfitted and the cylinder wall had been scored. They replaced all pistons and related parts, honed the scored cylinder and buttoned it all up. At this point the speedometer, bad visor and a broken washer connection were replaced, new parts for the failing console were ordered and I was told that the amount of clutch chatter didn't justify replacement. I wasn't happy with the fuel economy—15-16 mpg, compared with 18-19 for my 2800CS—and the solution tried was to set the carburetor floats down to the proper 21-mm level. This was a failure: fuel economy improved slightly but what had been a light surge (from carburetor leanness) below 2500 rpm became intolerable. I'd also mentioned that I thought the differential was a bit noisy. It got an adjustment, but this merely shifted the noise from acceleration to deceleration. No new one was in stock, so one was ordered.

At 2500 mi I took the car back because the engine had developed a severe stumble on acceleration where there had been only a mild hesitation before. Peter de Laat of Hoffman Motors found the float chambers, accelerator pumps and filters full of grit—apparently I'd got a bad tank of gasoline—and also applied a little alteration he had learned from experience with stumbling 1973 3-Liters. Now there's more fuel delivered by the pumps at the beginning of their strokes but less at the end; the total squirt is unaffected. I've had absolutely no trouble with stumbles since but have had the float levels raised 1 mm to bring the surge back to acceptable.

A new differential was put in at 4000 mi and was indeed quiet, though it has developed a little hum since. The bad console section had been replaced at 2500 mi; now I got a new section of carpet to replace a ripped one I'd found. I also mentioned at this point that the seatbelts' metal prongs were gouging the lower door panels when they didn't retract properly and the doors were closed, but no door panels were available.

Things have been uneventful since then. From about 5000 mi on, the engine ran too rich after a cold start, but this could be attended to at the 8000-mi service and was. I got a recall notice telling me to have a carburetor modification made; this was a little chimney over the floats to dump any overflow into the carburetor throats and avoid fire hazard.

The tiny 175-14 tires fitted to my car have been replaced by proper 195/70-14s on the 1974 cars. At about 6000 mi I fitted a set of 195/70VR-14 Pirelli CN 36 steel-belted radials, and they're terrific—adding cornering power without riding any harder than the also good-riding original Michelin XASs. With only 6000 mi on them I can't say how long they'll last, though. You'll also notice some fancy wheels: they're Mahle 14 x 7 mags for the factory lightweight version of the car (the 3.0 CSL) and increase the tracks by 0.8 in., getting rid of the funny narrow-track look at the rear. Even on the wider wheels the Pirellis ride softly, and now the handling is even better.

My overall fuel economy for the 12,000 mi has been a disappointing 15.6 mpg. Exclusively in-town driving drops it to 14 mpg; but a long, gentle run at 70 mph gives 20.5 mpg. Oil consumption runs about a quart every 1600 mi—not quite as good as for the 2800CS, but it's gradually improving. A remarkable item is that at each service the sparkplugs and points have been checked and they still didn't need replacing at 12,000 mi—in a 1973 engine without electronic ignition!

Obviously the car suffered poor workmanship at the factory; just as obviously Hoffman Motors put a lot of effort into making it right. Now it is right—running beautifully and giving me the pleasure every 3.0CS should give its owner. The only problem remaining is, how do I hold it down to 55 mph?

Lucky old Europeans. They can buy these...

Two BMW Stormers

In Germany they don't have hysterical supercar scares. That's why BMW can release these two new cars — unabashed production racers, both of them.

BMW IS OFFERING two brand new homologation specials — a turbocharged 2002 rally car and a 3-litre injected coupe, just like the works racers — in its lineup for 1974.

The three-litre coupe sells for about $A12,000 in Germany and has the spoiler in front, roof air deflector and rear tea-tray wing. Taken together the aerodynamic mods reduce air resistance by 15 percent.

The engine has been opened out to 3.2 litres and pumps out 206 bhp (DIN) and 211 lb/ft of torque. This might not equal the output of the BMW works touring cars (BMW leads the European Touring Car Championships at present) but it's enough for 135 mph and seven second 0-60 runs.

Testing the cars a month before their release (on the works test track of course) we could do only a couple of standing start acceleration runs — not easy with that kind of power.

Still, we saw 7.3 s with wheelspin before they snatched the new machinery away and can easily believe the ultimate figure.

Actually the coupe is not all that light at 2755 l, but it's 10 percent lighter than the roadgoing CSi. It is possible to order the "street pack" and go back to steel panels and a boot lid it takes two men to lift.

You get all the stripes and mag wheels, you understand, plus the bigger engine, but less vulnerability and a better platform to carry your air conditioning.

A five-speed gearbox is standard as are limited slip diff, quicker steering, longer spring travel and gas/oil shockers.

BMW has paid plenty of attention to aerodynamics on the 2002 Turbo as well — look at the full chin whiskers which clean up the airflow under the car.

The Munich factory ran works turbos in the European touring car championships back in 1969 before turbocharging was handicapped out of sight. In those days BMW kept developing the engines until it eventually saw 324 bhp from 2-litres and "the head lifted off the block — visibly".

"Detuning" to 270 bhp gave BMW a winner, so on this basis a mere 170 bhp at 5800 rpm from the 2002 Turbo should make it ultra-reliable. Torque is 177 lb/ft at 4000 rpm. The bottom end of the SOHC four has been left alone and the blower feeds through the familiar BMW mechanical injection system.

But you get more than power with the 2002 Turbo package.

Front discs are ventilated and the rear brakes are enlarged and now have a pressure limiting valve. Half shafts and rear wheel bearings are stronger. Shockers and springs are stiffer and the front roll bar is thicker (all compared with the already-hot 2002 tii).

A 3.36 final drive (the tii has 3.45) and a limited slip diff come with the turbo and so does a stronger gearbox/clutch. Camshaft timing is unchanged.

BMW plans to build 1000 of these cars for rallying by the beginning of 1974 and says it will gladly make another 4000 if the customers want them.

BMW's engine development wizard, von Falkenhausen, says the turbocharger boost on the 2002 Turbo engine has been limited, but it can be increased "a little bit".

The factory/German government puts a limit for tuned engines of 170 bhp on this chassis and that's achieved with 22.8 lbs boost. But simply by adjusting the blower, the boost can be upped to 24.3 lb and the output rises to 200 bhp. Neat.

Even with 170 bhp, the 2300 lb 2-door sedan has a top speed of 130 mph (15 mph more than the tii) and gets to 60 mph in seven seconds. Quarter miles come up in the low to mid fifteens.

Yet we found that the turbo would pull from 1500 rpm in top. When the tacho in the new redwood dash touched 3800 rpm there was a surge and the blower began to howl. Redline and rev-limited hold maximum revs to 6400 (same as the tii).

Gear speeds are 40 mph, 60 mph, and 105 mph indicated in the indirects. A five-speeder is optional.

Price in Germany — about $9000. Seems pretty unlikely that we'll see either model in Australia. We hope we're wrong.

—JERRY SLONIGER

Inside, Turbo has semi-bucket seats and sports wheel. Boost gauge is in centre of dash.

Flared guards and rear spoiler identify the 2002 Turbo outside.

Enlarged in-line six in the production racer is good for 206 bhp. The factory gets 350 bhp from 3.5 litres!

The CSL's sporting interior. Normally fairly spartan but this car has electric windows and air-conditioning. Seats are marvellous.

Flagship of the Bavarian fleet — 3-litre CSL coupe with full chin whiskers, wing-top air dams and stretched engine just like the works racers.

BRIEF TEST
BMW 3·0 Si

FOR: sparkling performance stick gearchange; comfortable driving position; unobstructed vision; superb instruments; lots of stowage space; well made and finished

AGAINST: heavy fuel consumption; expensive; wind noise; stiff throttle pedal

Since we last tested a big BMW (the 3.0S 10 months ago) a succession of increases have added £1579 to the price of the 3.0Si, raising it to the current substantial £5578 (including £178 for the mandatory power steering). That the car is in demand despite a price tag almost £1000 more than that for the Jaguar XJ12L is perhaps more an indictment of BL's inability to produce enough cars than an indication of the BMW's superiority. For a BMW is about the closest competitor the Jaguar has and it's available *now*, rather than in two or more years time, the typical waiting period for the Twelve. Faced with this sort of situation it's no wonder that the UK concessionaires for BMW sold over 5000 sixes last year.

For 1974 the big BMW is altered and improved in several ways. Importantly both the driver's seat and steering wheel positions now can be tailored to suit people of almost any size and shape; the rear seat backrest has been reset so there's more room in the back and heating ducts are provided to keep those in the back warm. The ride has also been softened with minor changes to spring rates and damper set-

Cross-country motoring is as effortless as a long motorway run in the fuel-injected 3.0Si thanks to a number of superb qualities. Below: the steering wheel is now leather covered in addition to being smaller and adjustable for reach. The throttle pedal is too upright and much too stiff though

tings, though whether this is an improvement is open to debate. Nevertheless all those who drove the car praised its numerous qualities, not least of which is its sparkling performance.

The car's Bosch electronically injected in-line six produces a healthy 200bhp (DIN) at 5500rpm and rockets the car to 60mph in 7.9sec, only half a second slower than the automatic XJ12. For a 3-litre the performance is astonishing, especially for one of its size and weight, though real gains over the carburetted car (no longer available with manual transmission here) are evident only above 60mph. The automatic choke proved faultless in operation and the engine runs smoothly without temperament, warming quickly on cold mornings. Power is transmitted in a smooth rush with a turbine-like hum that is very pleasant to the ear. The engine is also very tractable and, despite the highish gearing, will pull quite strongly from low revs in top: 30-50mph takes a brisk 7.9sec. Maximum speed is a claimed 133mph, too fast to check on MIRA's banked circuit, and we were unable to take the car abroad. However, there's lots of

performance to spare at 120mph.

Halfway through out test the 50mph speed limit was imposed so the car had several gentle runs. Even so, it returned a disappointing 15.0mpg overall, much the same as the 3.0S's 15.4 mpg. That's enough for 260 miles on the car's enlarged, 17.2 gallon fuel tank. It uses four star fuel and during the 718 mile test distance consumed one pint of oil.

The flickswitch gearchange provided by a short, stubby lever is slick and easy: ours was slightly obstructive on the lower ratios but we know from experience that this wears off with use. The sharp edge of the wooden gearlever knob emphasised any notchiness. Additionally, reverse isn't sufficiently protected and it's easy to select it instead of first.

On paper the gear ratios look ideal, giving 35, 61 and 96mph at 6400rpm in the lower gears; but on the road first feels too low, and you have to grab second very soon after a quick start. With the carburetted car we criticised the transmission snatch; petrol injection seems to have eliminated this for the 3.0Si pulls without fuss from 20mph in top.

No changes have been made to

Top left: comfortable fabric covered seats include driver's height adjuster. Left: lots of rear legroom, head restraints, seat belt anchorage points. Bottom left: excellent forward vision. Right 200 bhp lurks in Si's crowded engine bay

ZF-Gemmer worm and roller steering except that BMW now fit a slightly smaller (and hence better) leather-rim wheel which is adjustable for reach. The power assistance is just about right—light enough to make parking effortless, yet with just enough feel to enable the car to be pressed through corners with confidence. The basic trait is mild understeer, though lifting off in mid corner can make the nose tuck-in; obviously excessive power will cause the tail to slide, especially on a wet surface. Roadholding on the 195/70 VR 14 Michelin XWX tyres is excellent in the wet or dry and the car can be cornered hard with only moderate roll.

The brakes, ventilated discs all round with dual circuits, haul the car down from high speed with only slight pedal pressure, albeit to the accompaniment of slight juddering. For ordinary use, though, we felt that the brakes were slightly over-servoed as it was difficult to feather the brakes and avoid a jerk when coming to rest.

The suspension has been modified for '74 and is now less strongly damped, making the ride feel a little more resilient and less taut. The firm, comfortable fabric-covered seats now give greater lateral support. The rake of the seat is variable and the adjustment is much easier to make. The

driver's seat is also adjustable for height. With the new adjustable steering column the driving position can be tailored to suit a very wide range of shapes. There's also more room in the rear now, as BMW have reset the back of the seat. There are head restraints front and rear and those in the back fold down when not in use. All round vision is excellent: you can see every corner of the car without straining.

Switch gear and instruments are unchanged, and very good they are too. The indicators, parking light, washers and three speed wipers are controlled by one column-mounted stalk, the headlamp dip and flash by another.

The horn is sounded by one of four insets on the new steering wheel, as opposed to three on the earlier car. The wipers scythe a clear path across the screen no matter what the speed and the electrically operated screen washers are powerful.

The only complaint we have about the driving position is that the accelerator pedal of our car was too upright and stiff, so much so that after a long spell at 50mph you finish up either with an aching ankle or a numb foot.

The instruments remain unchanged for the simple reason that it would be hard to improve on them: they're a real object lesson in clean design and clarity.

PERFORMANCE

CONDITIONS
Weather	Overcast
Temperature	50°F
Barometer	298in Hg
Surface	Slightly damp

0-60	7.9	0-80	5.8	
0-70	10.5	0-100	8.5	
0-80	13.0	0-120	11.5	
0-90	16.4	0-140	15.2	
0-100	22.0	0-160	21.9	
0-110	29.7	0-180	30.7	
Stand'g ¼	15.6	Stand'g km	28.8	

Tank capacity	17.2 galls	
	79.2 litres	
Max range	260 miles	
	418 km	
Test distance	718 miles	
	1155 km	

MAXIMUM SPEEDS
	mph	kph
Banked circuit	See text	
Terminal speeds:		
at ¼ mile	74.4	119.7
at kilometre	109.0	175.0
Speed in gears (at 6400 rpm):		
1st	35	
2nd	61	
3rd	96	
4th	133 (see text)	

ACCELERATION IN TOP
mph	sec	kph	sec
30-50	7.9	40-60	5.0
40-60	8.2	60-80	4.8
50-70	7.6	80-100	4.7
60-80	7.8	100-120	4.9
70-90	9.3	120-140	5.4
80-100	10.1	140-160	6.5
90-110	12.1	160-180	8.6

SPEEDOMETER (mph)
Speedo 30 40 50 60 70 80 90 100
True mph Not recorded
Distance recorder: 2 per cent fast.

WEIGHT
	cwt	kg
Unladen weight*	28.21	1433
Weight as tested	31.91	1621

*with fuel for approx 50 miles.

ACCELERATION FROM REST
mph	sec	kph	sec
0-30	2.8	0-20	1.2
0-40	4.5	0-40	2.4
0-50	5.9	0-60	4.2

FUEL CONSUMPTION
Overall	15 mpg
	18.83 litres/100 km
Fuel grade	98 octane (RM)

4 star rating

Performance tests carried out by Motor's staff at the Motor Industry Research Association proving ground, Lindley.

GENERAL SPECIFICATION

ENGINE
Cylinders	6 in line
Capacity	2985 cc (184.4 cu in)
Bore/stroke	80 x 89 mm (3.14 x 3.5 in)
Cooling	Water
Block	Iron
Head	Light alloy
Valves	ohc
Valves-timing	
inlet opens	14° btdc
inlet closes	54° abdc
ex. opens	54° bbdc
ex. closes	14° atdc
Compression	9.5:1
Fuel injection	Bosch
Bearings	7 main
Fuel pump	Electric
Max power	200 bhp (DIN) at 5500 rpm
Max torque	199.2 lb ft (DIN) at 4300 rpm

TRANSMISSION
Type	4-speed manual Sdp, diaphragm spring
Internal ratios and mph/1000 rpm	1.0:1/20.95

	1.40:1/14.96
	2.20:1/9.52
	3.85:1/5.44
	3.45:1

BODY/CHASSIS
Construction	Unitary body/chassis
Protection	Phosphating, electrophoretic painting, underseal rust-proofed

SUSPENSION
Front	Independent by inclined MacPherson struts, lower wishbones, trailing links and coil spring/replaceable damper units. Anti-roll bar
Rear	Independent by boxed semi-trailing arms and coil springs. Replaceable shock absorber cartridges

STEERING
Type	Worm and roller

Assistance	Yes
Toe-in	0.04 ± 0.04 in
Camber	0° ± 30'
Castor	9° 30' ± 30'
King pin	6° 20'
Rear toe-in	0.04 ± 0.04 in

BRAKES
Type	4 disc
Servo	Yes
Circuits	Twin
Rear valve	Yes
Adjustment	Automatic

WHEELS
Type	Steel disc 6J x 14 H2
Tyres	Michelin 195/70 XWX with tubes
Pressures	27 F/26 R

ELECTRICAL
Battery	12V, 53A/hr
Polarity	Negative
Generator	Bosch 14V 55A 20-770W
Fuses	12
Headlights	4 halogen units

COMPARISONS

	Capacity cc	Price £	Max mph	0-60 sec	30-50* sec	Overall mpg	Touring mpg	Length ft in	Width ft in	Weight cwt	Boot cu ft
BMW 3.0Si	2985	5578	133.0†	7.9	7.9	15.0	—	15 5.5	5 8.75	28.2	12.3‡
Citroen SM	2670	6154	135.2	8.3	12.9	14.9	—	16 0.5	6 0.5	29.5	9.0
Fiat 130 Coupe	3253	5970	115.6	10.6	3.9	18.8	—	15 10	6 0	31.7	12.3
Jaguar XJ12L	5343	4702	135.7	7.4	2.6	11.5	13.5	15 9.75	5 9.25	34.8	11.8
Rover 3500S	3528	2444	119.0	9.3	8.1	19.3	23.6	15 0.5	5 7.25	26.1	10.3
Volvo 164E Fi	2979	3450	112.5	8.8	7.5	17.7	—	15 6	5 8.5	28.9	13.5‡

*in top, kickdown for automatic Fiat and Jaguar   † see text   ‡ measured with boxes, not cases
Touring fuel consumption not computed for cars with fuel injection

Make: BMW
Model: 3.0Si .
Makers: BMW AG, Munich, West Germany
Concessionaires: BMW Concessionaires (GB) Ltd, 361-365 Chiswick High Road, London W4
Price: £4530.62 plus £377.56 car tax and £490. 82 VAT plus power steering at £178 equals £5399. Extras fitted to test car: Philips radio, £80. Total as tested: £5657.

Both the speedometer and rev counter are large and clearly calibrated; between the two are smaller dials for water temperature and fuel. The instrument binnacle also contains a cluster of six warning lights. There's a clock on the facia in front of the passenger but a radio is extra.

For such an expensive luxury car the Si is only fairly well insulated from noise. At idling speed the huge air intake makes obtrusive noises and at speed above 50mph wind noise makes you turn the radio up. BMW say they usually attend to this sort of complaint by slightly bending in the top of the door window frame.

The heating and ventilation system is excellent, though you can't recirculate the air to exclude exhaust fumes. To get sufficient heat into the car you also need to use the fan. The centrally mounted air vents, perhaps a bit fiddly to adjust, push through a big volume of air. Eyeball vents each side of the facia are for side window demisting, and very effective they are.

There's ample storage space inside the car for the assorted bric-a-brac five adults can accumulate. The car's only real rival in the provision of trays, cubby holes and shin bins is the Rover 2200 which is outstanding in this respect. The boot of the BMW is huge and contains in its lid a compartment of superbly finished tools and a few important spares.

At £5578 the car is undeniably expensive and at 15mpg very thirsty. Nevertheless it's superbly engineered, very well finished and discreetly luxurious. Even if we are all reduced to travelling at 50mph, there are few more comfortable big cars in which to do it.

ROAD IMPRESSIONS
BMW's top~of~the~range COUPE

BMW INTRODUCED the 3.0 CSi coupe nearly three years ago. It was immediately apparent that the car was a tremendous improvement over its predecessor, the 2800 CS, in virtually every respect. It was quicker, obviously, and it went where the front wheels pointed on a wet road — something one could never count on with the 2800. Then, in June 1972, the CSi was introduced as the company's top model. We drove one then and thoroughly enjoyed it, and recently we tried one of the latest cars.

The 3 litre six cylinder BMW engine, particularly when equipped with fuel injection, must be one of the nicest production units manufactured anywhere. It is an extremely smooth engine, with a great deal of torque. If you feel like being lazy, you can do just that, for the engine pulls cleanly from 1000 rpm without a trace of snatch. You don't have to stir the gear lever all over the place to get from A to B. But if you're in the mood, the engine will sing all the way up to the ignition cut-out at 6500 rpm, the noise — although not at all obtrusive — reviving memories of the D-types in the mid-fifties. Our test car had covered only 1500 miles, and the engine felt a little bit tight, but nevertheless all two hundred horses were obviously working. It is a little unfair to expect such a new engine to rev as freely as one fully run-in. The gear-change is pleasant, but I prefer the slicker box of the 2002 range, frankly. Also, I feel that a car costing over seven thousand pounds really should have a five-speed gearbox as standard. The car is capable of a genuine 140 mph and will cruise forever and a day at 120, so a fifth ratio would be a big deal in these days of eleven bob a gallon.

Acceleration is very impressive. The CSi is by no means a small car, but it storms up to 60 in around seven and a half seconds, and to 100 in under twenty. If you need the power, it's there instantly; there's no real need to change down most of the time. Mind you, I still do it, but still..... The brakes are as good as you are ever likely to need. One night I was driving home in torrential rain when a small kid emerged from behind a parked car and ran straight across the road without so much as a glance. It was an extremely lucky kid, for the BMW pulled up without difficulty. There was no wheel-locking at all, nor any question of the car swapping ends. I went on my way, heart thumping, but mightily impressed. Now for the power-steering. Although I don't like power-steering per se, I'm bound to admit big cars without it are a pain in the neck at anything other than high speeds. Parking, in particular, can be a real sweat. BMW seem to have overcome the problem to a large extent. The power-assistance is sufficient to be a real boon around town without totally removing 'feel' from the driver during fast cornering — a very difficult balance to achieve. If you don't believe me, try the power steering on a Jaguar; it's great for parking with one finger, but wait till you get out of shape on a wet road at high speed..... Jaguar owners tell me it is only a matter of practice, but I m not convinced. Nothing even approaches the progressive system on the Citroen SM, of course, but that's another story. For a conventional system, the BMW's is excellent. What a pity Citroen don't fit the BMW engine to the SM instead of that rough Maserati V6......

The CSi handles extremely well, by and large, although power-off oversteer is fairly pronounced. This, of course, can be made to work for you with a little practice, particularly on a series of twisty bends. It may not be the tidiest way to drive, but it's nice to find a car these days which doesn't suffer from a surfeit of built-in understeer. The actual roadholding is of a very high order indeed, in any conditions. If the car does get out of shape, it is a relatively simple matter to get it back again, for the powerassistance allows fairly high-geared steering to be fitted.

As with every BMW the finish is excellent. It struck me that the fascia is starting to look rather old-fashioned, but still pleasing. In the latest model, there are new seats, complete with headrests, and they are excellent. The test-car was finished in bronze, with light cream seats, which looked tremendous. However, this was a very new motor car. and I can well imagine that a few months' hard wear would take its toll on such a light colour. There really is a great deal to be said for a black interior. Of course, if you want that, you can have it. I have nothing but praise for the interior and controls of the car,

with one exception. The electric windows were irritatingly slow in operation, and once or twice I seriously began to doubt that my window was going to make it back to the top of the door. It always did, mind you.

To my mind, the CSi is a thoroughly practical high-speed touring car. There is a large boot (containing a first-rate tool-kit, by the way), and the rear seats will actually take people, believe it or not, rather than the legless-pygmy-type of accommodation one normally finds in the back of this type of car. The engine is smooth and effortless, the driving position very comfortable, the roadholding reassuring, and there is a very solid, well-constructed feel about the CSi, such as one finds in every BMW. At £7400, I think it is overpriced, but that applies to the entire range, and doesn't seem to hurt sales. I really enjoyed the CSi, and I reckon it must be close to the ideal all-round road car.

Sleek Karmann lines of the CSi (top) and proof of its saloon-style accommodation (below)

TALE NO. 1

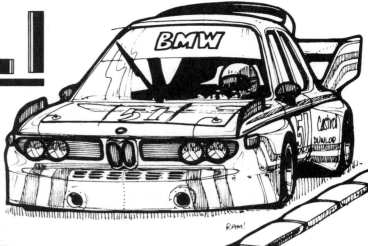

AFTER A SAFE and speedy run from Munich to Zermatt in a BMW CSL coupe (mit wings) Rob Luck says supercar/killercar tags are more ludicrous than he imagined. If only our (BH) Power-conscious politicians could get the speed/power thing in perspective sanity may influence our traffic legislation . . .

BMW'S wicked, winged, woad-wunner!

WE HIT the crest at 90k's with five thou in second slot and the road just dropped away to the left into a tight hairpin complete with offcamber, icebanks on the verges and water drifts where the snow had melted on the track — the sort of sport where a trailing throttle means doing a wall of death act, and to hit the brakes is to invite an instant exit from the roadway. Under those circumstances an extra dob of lock seemed appropriate, combined with a nudge of juice.

The tail kicked-out instantly on the slosh and the same instant I had armpits full of opposite lock as the nose came round with the rear skins howling and smoking, the exhaust screaming like a wounded lion and the tacho edging six thou. It all came out straight and a split second later we were in the triple esses and hurling from left to right with the G-forces stretching the cheek muscles and using up every last millimetre of slack in the almost too-tight racing harness with the last nasty moment well and truly forgotten in the business of getting through the next twists with no drama.

It must have been the bottom switchback that did the damage as we fought the GS round for 230degrees of camberless hotmix. It must have been the cruncher because a bare two seconds later my passenger bellowed "halt" and the big Bee-Emm fumed to a standstill in a haze of grilled Girlings. He toppled out the door, grappled at the armco and proceeded to uneat breakfast for half a minute or so.

Returning to the car disguised as a ghost he clambered into the skinfit bucket and proclaimed in perfect English . . . "Thank you I feel much better now . . . we shall continue."

"I think you'd better stay out or we'd better cut the track testing a bit short," I said.

"No, no please . . . I am enjoying myself. Please continue."

"You've got to be joking . . . You call that enjoying yourself?"

MEEP-MEEP! Editor Luck pushes BMW's road star around the snow-covered BMW test track. Yes, the wings really work. Not only that, the Continental traffic authorities will register the be-winged coupe without qualms.

TALES OF BAVARIA (CARS)

ALTHOUGH it bears 3.0CSL badges our test car is nevertheless a 3.2litre screamer. Despite its exciting performance however, the sophisticated safety qualities of the coupe cannot be underestimate. But, it sure looks like the Batmobile — right?

rather than energetic motoring.

But nothing could dampen the impact of this machine's performance. Using the full potential of the car's performance as well as that of the BMW speed loop I found that the electronic stopwatch consistently read around 30seconds for zero to 200km/h (125mph).

The Accusplit also showed the car could get from zero to 160km/h (100mph) and back to zero in around 21secs. I don't believe many drivers will do it too often either. The G-forces generated in proving-out such times is sickening.

Even more so than the cornering forces ... it must be worse, because my German escort for the track test session stood on the sidelines for the acceleration/brake tests ... I suspect he has a low threshold of pain.

Back in the towering BMW headquarters overlooking the ex-Olympic outdoor stadium, I sat in the plush velvet office bucket seats and joked about the incident with the youthful, genial boss of the BMW PR division, Michael Schimpke. "Then you need more time in the car," he said, "I think you should drive it to Geneva."

There was only one small problem — my Range Rover — but that was quickly resolved on an exchange basis.

I am still not sure whether the offer arose out of a genuine interest in my better knowledge of the great Bear-Emm-Dooblevay (as the Germans

"No, I insist. I am finding this very entertaining. I have not enjoyed the car going so fast since I drove with one of the works drivers.

I continued, but I had lost all heart. Besides I suddenly felt queasy myself. Whether it was from a personal reaction to the enormous G-forces generated by this dynamic bombshell or the sight of someone else's reactions I don't know — in any case for the rest of our laps on the closed BMW test track outside Munchen (Munich to you) it was a case of exploratory

HERE'S MCE360 on the car-train to Zermatt, high in the Swiss Alps. In winter the road is completely snowed-under and this is the only way to reach the world-famous skiing resort. Car passengers stay in their vehicles for the duration of the journey — no doubt praying their heaters continue to work effectively.

WINTERTIME in Switzerland and the road out of Geneva (en-route to Zermatt) is deserted. Under perfect touring conditions the BMW cruised sweetly and safely at the speed limit — its precise reaction to command making the trip an effortless task.

pronounce the letters BMW) or a private yearning to sample the Range Rover (half of Europe is in love with them) but the swap seemed more than reasonable.

Since I was planning to take the weekend break ski-ing at Zermatt in the Swiss alps, we agreed to rendezvous in Geneva on Press opening

day, and exchange machines and stories.

With the big wings removed from the boot decklid (Schimpke calls them his Geraniums stand) we rumbled off through Friday peak-hour traffic in Munchen in search of the hotel and an early night in the interests of an early start next morning. There is no autobahn from Munich to the South-West so I hiked the big fella along traffic-bristled minor roads relieved by stacks of three-lane passing sections until we hit Lindau on the edge of the Bodensee, almost on the Swiss border, congratulating ourselves on our good speed to that stage.

A few kilometres down the road we did a double-take at the traffic build-up on the double-borders between Germany-Austria and Austria-Switzerland. A stationary hour-and-a-half later we were cursing the gnome who advised us not to take the ferry crossing over the Bodensee at Friedrichshafen because of the delays.

But just into Switzerland we slid onto the patchy Swiss autobahn system and headed for St Gallen and Zurich. Boring on South with the BMW singing we were not surprised to find half the autobahn closed just outside of Berne with Police ushering traffic through a narrow corridor (major roadworks on autobahns supervised by Police are common all over Europe).

We were surprised to be ushered into a lorry parking lot by a Swiss police batman along with over 40 other cars and there to be informed we were exceeding the speed

limit . . . according to Swiss radar check. The operator must have been drinking because he had clocked at us at 119km/h which was over the limit and we hadn't hit over 90km/h in the preceding stretch due to a convoy of chemical trucks.

But the men in blue weren't interested in the law — just money — and since the alternative was a floorshow at the downtown bars complete with bread and water dinner we paid-up the 300 French francs (about $45).

Armed with the information that there were no further police traps we settled down to a comfortable 160km/h down to Berne and beyond. "You might as well," said Mr Moneybags, the cop, "We're lifting the speed limit in Switzerland to at least 130 or 140 next week and you're quite safe from here on down."

The autobahn lasts about 60km past Berne to Thundersee where the southern Swiss-French influence is already taking over from the northern German atmosphere and exit signs change from ausgangs to sorties when all the other signs gradually became more French than Germanic.

Peeling off the autobahn at Thundersee we rocketed around the magnificent winding lake road to Interlaken, a town that not surprisingly gets its name from its location at the point where the Thundersee joins the Brienzeree.

At this scheduled fuel point we checked maps and distances and came to the conclusion we had no hope of reaching Zermatt, high in the Alps at

TALES OF BAVARIA (CARS)

any sort of respectable time. With no advance knowledge on road conditions at high altitudes and no time-tables for the trains in Zermatt (no cars are allowed in this Alpine ski-village), we decided to backtrack along the lake to Spiez and head up the mountains for the car-train that crosses through the special tunnel at Kandersteg.

We timed our arrival perfectly with the immediate departure of a train, rolled the Bee-Emm on and settled down to the eerie 15-minute ride through the darkened tunnel under the Alps to the first station tunnel at Goppenstein, an exercise which cost a mere few dollars and sliced at least three hours and 175 kilometres off dicey alpine motoring from our trip.

With the CSL's lights stabbing holes in the pitch-black sky we raced down the fantastic stone-walled 1½-lane Alpine spaghetti road to Visp where we garaged the car just in time to make the last train up to Zermatt.

On Monday morning early we loosed the big fella again for the drive along the mountain roads to Martigny, through the endless tiny villages in the lake wine district up to Villeneueve where we picked-up the first leg of the southern Swiss autobahn that hikes down through Lausanne to Geneva.

We hit the motor show carpark on schedule to be greeted simultaneously by a glowing Michael Schimpke and newspaper banners proclaiming the speedlimit had just been raised on Swiss autobahns to 130km/h.

BORDER GATES can be time-consuming. This one is a triple variety — we are driving from Germany through Austria to Switzerland. However, the snowbound surroundings are breathtakingly beautiful.

If the epic 1500 kilometre trip proved nothing else it demonstrated that anti-supercar propaganda is nought but political clap-trap. If politicians are aghast at the danger potential of such machinery they need but follow one simple course to ease their feeble minds — graded licences and advanced driving instruction.

There is absolutely no question that a car such as the 3.2CSL is an infinitely safer vehicle than a less powerful family car, provided it is in competent hands.

In 1500 kilometres of testing, the only place we used the triple-two top speed capacity (222km/h-138mph) was on the BMW test track. At

THE GRAND HOTEL VICTORIA, on the road to Geneva, with the majestic Swiss Alps in the background. Despite heavy snowfalls the major roads are kept open and consantly patrolled.

160km/h (100mph) the car burbled along effortlessly on the autobahns, untroubled by roadsurface changes and unaffected by sidewinds.

Although better known for its total domination of the 1973 European touring car championship, this refined machine is completely compatible with the demands of everyday driving. Its acceleration is stunningly rapid — and because of this it is an exceptionally safe car in overtaking manoeuvres.

That acceleration is matched with perfectly balanced braking — and an alert driver who drives well ahead of his vehicle never need have a *moment* because of the performance and speed potential of his vehicle.

Although the car wears some of the fattest 'bags' ever fitted on a showroom floor machine, hooked up to a suspension that is pure race, this car tracks evenly and smoothly on any surface — and in Europe you can't cover 1500km without sampling broken bitumen, Belgian pave, rough-hewn stone blocks . . . in fact almost everything except dirt . . . which you rarely see.

The ride is superb for such a car — firm and controlled, but jolt and shock-free. There is no suspension reaction felt in the steering which is light, positive and direct.

Visibility in all directions is unmatched by any road car with this performance potential that I can think of — in fact it shows up the Australian GT products such as the Falcon hardtop, for the poor metalwork that we have often criticised.

AUSTRALIAN *traffic authorities please take note of the road signs. They are all in the driver's line-of-vision — above his head, not at the roadside. Continental signposting is well known for its clarity and simplicity — and standardisation.*

Sure, there are detail problems — some of the switchery could be relocated (and is being relocated), the ventilation could be a lot better and the racing buckets make rear seat entry painfully difficult for the legless midgets that you can occasionally seat there, but it is one hell of a machine for the long waiting list of buyers which queues daily on the factory order books.

The 3.2CSL is a rare thoroughbred in these times of mundane over-engineered sports cars. Well-proven on the track, it has impeccable road manners, and an image as a European status symbol that has to be experienced from the cockpit to be believed. Fortunately it doesn't need those dramatic elevators to make it stick for regular roadwork, although the downthrust this option provides was a major contributor to its Euro-champ victory. Yes, you can get them registered in Europe, but you never see a road car wearing them — there again you rarely see a road car.

Anyway, and if you do see one and you aren't driving another one, you don't get to see it for very long. ⓗ

THE EUROPEAN *road tunnels are an incredible piece of road engineering and have to be experienced in order to appreciate their contribution to road safety in all seasons.*

Bad Karmann

When Chris Jones bought his Karmann-built BMW coupé, he had little idea how bad it was underneath. A decade later it's winning prizes, as Zoë Harrison reports

Photos by **Zoë Harrison**

‘IF I did another one today, I'd make a better job of it.' That may well be a sentiment shared by many restorers, but the fact that Chris Jones's lovely BMW 3.0CSA is still winning classic car show awards nearly five years after its restoration belies his words.

The 3.0CSA is one of the 11,063 models built between 1971 and 1975 for BMW by Karmann. Today this car looks in superb condition, but at one point it was touch and go whether it was worth restoring at all. 'If the interior hadn't been as good as it was, it would have been a breaker,' reflects Chris.

As it is, the only thing to be replaced inside the car has been the carpets – with dark blue Wilton, of course. Everything else, including the upholstery, door trims and dashboard, is original.

The exterior was a different story. 'When I first saw what was under the paintwork I

BMW was finished in white with a blue vinyl roof when first bought

thought "Oh my God, what have I bought," ' Chris admits. And Chris is no amateur – he runs C J Car Body Refinishers on London Street in Worthing. He's used his skills to retain as many of the original panels as possible.

Chris acquired the CSA from a friend who

had just bought it at auction. 'I saw the back end of this car sticking out of his driveway and knew that I just had to have it.' The owner didn't want to sell and it took two weeks of negotiations, and no small amount of alcohol, before he would part with it. The CSA arrived at Chris's workshop in 1984, in rough but just about roadworthy condition.

This BMW is a 1974 model, the 'A' denoting that it is an automatic fitted with the 2985cc, 180bhp straight six. It had previously had one owner, a lady who lived in the better parts of Eastbourne, and had covered only 55,000 miles from new.

Chris ran the BMW for a couple of years without major trouble, by which time it was starting to look decidedly the worse for wear. Not only was the bodywork deteriorating, but the clutch bands in the three-speed automatic gearbox were slipping, the engine was beginning to sound noisy – and parts were disappearing from the car at a rate of knots.

Once the paint was stripped, it became clear that the car had been in an accident at some time, and a damaged front corner had been crudely repaired

restoration. The bodywork was worse than it looked and there was hardly a major panel that didn't need work of some description. Even the sunroof was shot.

'At some time it had had an almighty smash on the front corner, because someone had fitted a secondhand inner and outer wing, and a front panel,' says Chris. There was also a plate on the front corner that had been agriculturally welded in, to say the least: 'It wasn't fit for a lorry. The welding must have been as thick as my watchstrap and it had caused horrendous buckling through the wing.'

The metal around the rear lights had rotted away, as had the boot floor and rear wings. 'There's a drain tube that runs down the rear wing from the sunroof, and once that blocks up, the water runs straight into the bottom of the wing. It doesn't stand a chance,' explains Chris. 'I was dreading what I'd find when I took the roof off. It was a factory vinyl roof – they were all the rage

in the seventies – and I thought it killed the lines of the car stone dead.'

The list of corrosion seemed to include every panel: inner and outer sills, inner wings, lower sections of the front wings, rear panel, spare wheel well, boot edge, bonnet edge... But despite the extent of the rust, Chris was determined to keep the car as original as possible. In fact the only complete replacement panels fitted have been the sills. Both inner and outer sills were renewed, and Chris had mirror-finish

'I used to park it out in the street and first to go were some of the chrome trims, followed soon after by the indicators,' Chris explains. 'That's the trouble with these cars: they're so rare that once thieves have clocked one, they keep coming back and taking bits off it. It attracts them like a magnet.'

He finally decided that the coupé's time had come, and began stripping it down for

> ## 'Thieves would keep coming back and taking bits off the car'

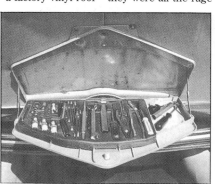

Engine rebuild was straightforward, but installing it in the car was anything but!

New light metallic blue paint was eventually done twice to rectify minor damage

stainless steel covers made up by a craftsman. You can judge the quality from the fact they were hand-beaten and yet fitted on the car first time.

The rest of the body was washed down with acid several times to kill the rust. Then Chris began making up repair sections, using cardboard templates. New steel was seam welded into position and lead loaded, then trimmed up with ordinary filler. 'People slander plastic putty,' says Chris, 'but I used it for tiny dents that I couldn't get at to knock out. It's magic for that, although you can't just stick it over rusty patches because the rust will come straight back out again.' Needless to say, there is precious little filler on this car.

For the front inner wings, Chris decided to take drastic action. He cut the rotten wings and also removed the battery tray. He then fashioned a new tray out of stainless steel and welded that in. 'You're not actually supposed to weld stainless to ordinary steel, because one feeds off the other and makes it weak, but it's the worst corrosion point of the car.' The new inner wings were painted and then covered with sheets of bitumen

sound-deadening material.

The BMW had been painted white with a blue vinyl roof when Chris bought it, but he decided to refinish it in a light metallic blue, actually a VW colour called Hellblau which is very similar to BMW's Fjord Blue.

The mechanical side of the restoration was not without its problems. 'When the car

had been painted I took the shell over to my mates to put the engine and gearbox in. You have to fit them as one unit, tilting it to slide the gearbox in first,' he describes. 'We'd just come round the front of the car with the engine and 'box on the hoist and jacked it up, when my mate turned round and accidentally hit the hoist release button.

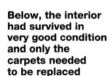

Right, Chris has kept the car fairly standard in the interests of drivability and a comfortable ride

Below, the interior had survived in very good condition and only the carpets needed to be replaced

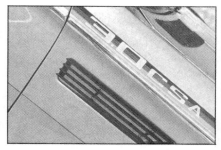

The whole engine and gearbox came crashing to the ground, smashing the pallet it had been built on to pieces and cracking the alloy sump as well. You could have cut the air with a knife.'

Fortunately nothing hit the car, and the sump was the only casualty. Chris managed to have this welded up. The engine had previously been rebuilt by a friend, with new pistons, rockers and valve guides, while the crank was also balanced. Chris cleaned the cylinder head up and took off any rough edges of the casting to give an improved airflow.

The excitement wasn't over yet, however. Starting the engine for the first time proved dramatic. 'The car was up on axle stands at the time,' recalls Chris, 'and at first it wouldn't start. The exhaust filled with petrol vapour and then a spark ran down the system into the back box, which is a huge thing, and exploded. There was a tremendous bang which lifted the car right off its stands and blew the back box wide open.' Luckily, the damage was limited!

It took another month to have the engine set up professionally, but by the time Chris got it back the BMW was starting to look slightly knocked about. 'There were scuffs around the engine bay and a jack handle had been dropped against one wing,' he recalls. 'I got the car back on the transporter, stripped the paintwork down and re-did it.'

Apart from a leaky petrol tank, there have been no more problems and Chris has taken pains to make sure things stay that way. A tendency to overheat has been cured with a thermostatically controlled Kenlowe electric fan. The wiring was also checked out thoroughly – 'it's pretty prehistoric, and these cars were prone to catching fire,' says Chris cheerfully.

The BMW's suspension uses MacPherson struts at the front and trailing

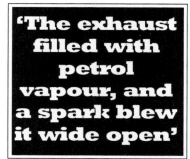

'The exhaust filled with petrol vapour, and a spark blew it wide open'

arms behind. Chris has fitted new BMW inserts into the struts, but gone for Spax adjustable dampers at the rear. 'These BMWs have always had a bit of a sorry rear end on them, and the Spax just level them up nicely,' he comments. He has tried not to stiffen up the suspension, preferring a more comfortable ride. 'It goes round corners like it's on rails in any case.'

The dual-circuit braking system has been thoroughly overhauled. The BMW has vented discs all round, and these were replaced with new parts. 'Even the handbrake works, which is rare for inboard discs,' adds Chris. The original calipers were rebuilt by Lucas in Brighton, all new pipes were run underneath the car, and the master and wheel cylinders were renewed.

Finding replacement servos was no easy task. 'The originals were no good and two secondhand ones which I got from a reputable BMW breaker also turned out to be faulty.' Finally Chris located a firm called Linwar in Southport, who rebuilt them at reasonable cost.

Apart from the bits that had been stolen, the brightwork on the BMW was generally in good condition. 'I'd still like to find some rear overriders to replace the ones that fell to pieces, and I'd really like some new bumpers, but they cost serious money,' he remarks.

Chris himself might think he could do a better job on his BMW 3.0CSA, but there's doubtless many a concours car owner who would gladly swap theirs for his, just the way it is. ∎

Mainlining...
With BMW's psychedelic CSL By Mel Nichols

THE TASK WAS SIMPLE: deliver a BMW 3.0CSL to Munich. The point, however, was a little more esoteric. The days of cars so ostentatiously aggressive, so patently spawned by the world of motor racing, so downright phallic as this winged monster CSL are over and gone. Were such machines worth the bother? Could they take two or three people across Europe any faster, more safely or any better than a less pretentious or less performance-oriented coupe or saloon? Would a standard BMW CS do the job just as satisfactorily? Moreover, do the speed limits now blanketing Europe render the coup de grace, once and for all, to such high performance cars? And do they consume expensive continental petrol at such a rate that they're a liability rather than an asset, even if you do ignore the police?

We left London on a Wednesday, threading through the cold, drizzling dreariness of the pre-dawn in order to make the first ferry out of Dover. Eighty-odd miles around London a day or two before had sucked the top from the fuel supply, but no longer did we bother to top up before

Photography: Mervyn Franklyn

162

ca-clonking onto the ferry. A quick check had shown that the 74p gallon had made British fuel the most expensive in Europe, apart from Italy's 90p rip-off. Better to fill up in Belgium, even France or Germany. Could you have expected that a year ago?

The French coast brought sunshine, the makings of a magnificent winter's day, and striking out from Dunkerque to the new autoroute that slices south of Lille and Brussels to Aachen we began to settle, easily, into the rhythm we wanted. There wasn't much traffic, but the slow and steady pace at which everyone was travelling was certain testimony to the efficiency of the enforcement agents. Take a risk? Open the BMW right up and hope to spot the traps or the pursuers? No; play it cool and ignore the car's potential, no matter how much it cried out to be used. Better to benefit from its abilities at a slow, almost dream-like 70mph and savour the day, not the law.

Indeed, our caution paid dividends. Not long after crossing into Belgium an Opel Commodore GSE flashed past. Behind him came the police, and when we saw the two parties beside the road a little further on, the gendarme's stony face showed no mercy. Only later did we learn that the instant fine for exceeding the speed limit in Belgium is now 10,000 francs for starters, with an extra 1000 on top of that for each kilometre one logs above the limit.

The CSL had been resident in Britain as part of BMW Concessionaires' test fleet. By rights, it should have been sold off months ago—it had logged a high mileage and it no longer fits the image BMW want to portray here: racing is dead; compact luxury is IN—but somehow it had evaded the hammer. Simply by being in Britain, the CSL also evaded losing its trio of spoilers. They're outlawed in Germany; BMW supply them in the boot of each CSL and it's up to the owner if he wants to defy the police and fit them. Not only the police: during the height of the fuel crisis in Germany, to drive something which looked as if it might guzzle fuel brought unsavoury reactions from other motorists. There wasn't much lure to fit the spoilers—unless, of course, you considered them essential to the CSL's performance. But more of that later.

The CSL was and is the fastest BMW road car. It is based on the CSi coupe, but the familiar six-cylinder engine is bored an extra 4mm and stroked very slightly to increase the capacity from 2985cc to 3153cc in line with homologation requirements for the 430bhp racing coupe (Ford produced the Capri RS3100 with a similar capacity for precisely the same reason). Compression is untouched at 9.5 and so is the electronically-controlled Bosch fuel injection, but the power goes up from 200 to 206DINbhp at 5600rpm and there is a more than worthwhile increase in torque (developed at slightly lower revs). The transmission and final drive ratios are as for the CSi, but the CSL is armed with a limited slip differential. There are suspension differences: the body is dropped 0.8in to lower the centre of gravity, an extra degree of negative camber has been cranked on to the front wheels to improve stability and handling, the coil springs were replaced by stronger, more progressive ones and Bilstein gas pressure shock absorbers took over from the standard dampers. This new spring/damper combination allowed the front and rear

stabiliser bars to be flung away. Fat 7in alloy wheels carrying the excellent Michelin 195/70VR14 XWX radials replace the normal 6in rims and lower specification tyres and the steering was uprated to the ZF-Gemmer worm and roller system (but with a slightly slower ratio than standard).

Part and parcel of the CSL is a lightweighting job in which alloy door skins and bonnet are substituted for the steel ones, the front bumper is tossed away to be replaced by the deep chin spoiler, the rear bumper is replaced by a black plastic imitation bumper and the windscreen is made from special Verbel laminated glass. The chin spoiler and the small one at the lip of the boot lid, along with the black rubber air guides on top of the front mudguards, are part of the basic CSL package.

The extra, outlandish spoilers—the deflector that runs across the rear of the roof and the wing that rises up from the boot—are supplied with the car so that, BMW say, the man who wants to go racing full time can bolt them on or the part-time racer can put them on for his weekend sport and take them off again to run around the streets, so appeasing the police.

Apart from running the risk of being booked in Germany, what happens when the spoilers, developed for the European Touring Car Championship racer, are used? Drag is reduced by 16percent, improving penetration as greatly as if the car had an extra 50bhp, BMW say. Fuel consumption is improved, straightline and cornering stability is improved, and so is crosswind resistance.

The Bosch injection makes the CSL fire up immediately and idle easily. Even in the cold at 5am there is no hesitation as the clutch comes out and the 2567lb coupe (that's 562lb down on the CSi) moves away. Smooth. Fuss-free. No trace of meanness, no hint of high-level tuning. Now, running along this motorway towards the German border, the thing is turning over as sweetly as ever and you're settled back comfortably in the special rally-type bucket seat. There's no squab adjustment, but the arrangement is as close to perfect as most drivers would want it: distances to the wheel, pedals and gearlever are precisely correct, vision is excellent, instruments and controls located for easy reading and reaching. The leather-covered, drilled-spoke wheel is mounted high, in an old-fashioned sort of way. But it is comfortable and, when the time comes, will permit appropriately deft applications of opposite lock . . .

Meanwhile, the fuel tank reads dangerously low and there's been no hint of a motorway service area. Playing safe, we swing off into a pleasantly sleepy town called Tournai, swap Deutsche marks for Belgian francs and fill the CSL. Calculations show the figure has been a surprising 22mpg, including the running around London. For the most part, we've been touring at 75mph, maybe 80 when the chances of being caught look remote. The next tank, taken near Frankfurt, confirms the figure—22.2mpg this time, and we've been travelling at 90mph since we've been in Germany where the 80mph limit is advisory only, occasionally logging 100mph or more. There is no doubt, then, that the aerodynamic aids fulfil this part of their promise. You will not see such figures in a CSi or an ordinary CS. No way.

The border guards, as we'd passed into

Mainlining...
With BMW's psychedelic CSL

Germany, eyed us with quizzical friendliness. The fins might have been illegal, but they still made the car look dramatic and exciting, made our journey look purposeful, and we were given the distinct impression that it was good luck to the mad Englishmen for disregarding the whole fins affair. Bolting back out onto the E5 autobahn, winding the CSL right out in first and second to slip into the traffic flow and listening to the well-mannered rumble from the OHC six and watching the tachometer needle reach to its 6400rpm red line (where it provides 38mph in first, 65 in second and precisely 100mph in third), revealed an aspect of the CSL I hadn't explored in depth before: the acceleration. It isn't earthshattering, for this is not one of the big stick supercars. It is still, however, thoroughly fast, getting to 60mph in 7secs and pushing driver and passengers deeply into the seats as the bonnet lifts and the growl from beneath it deepens. The car may, for the most part, feel refined and even docile, but it has its fair share of the mailed fist/velvet glove ingredient and when asked, it responds. Most of all, it feels especially well balanced: engine to chassis to brakes.

Although the German speed limit is advisory only, it's quite obvious from the steady 85mph progress of almost everybody that it doesn't pay to take too much advantage of the situation. Roadside radar, prowling patrol cars and predatory helicopters complete the message. So we stick to 90mph, a speed we consider will be safe enough, and the cruising is pleasant; the slightly greater speed than we'd dared use in Belgium sharpens up driver concentration, and, indeed, the car. Up to 90mph, the CSL feels pretty much as any big BMW does: supple, smooth, fairly precise but not notably so. Above 90, things begin to change and above 100mph you really know about those spoilers. From then on you almost praise them aloud.

As the speedo nears 100mph, the CSL tightens up, much as a professional athlete might suddenly turn on for a race rather than simply jogging around the park on his morning run. The steering goes rock solid, pinsharp (but not heavy). The ride stays comfortable, but seems to firm and any trace of softness is hurled away. You can really feel the thing sitting down on the road, everything clicking into place. It's one of those very special 'fingertips and seat-of-the-pants' feelings that make *real* motoring in a fine car such a high. You feel confident, but not aggressive; safe, but not shut off from the reality of the road.

And so the miles disappear with increasing ease. The top speed potential remains unexplored, save for one burst to 130mph where the rock steadiness is even more apparent. But the benefit of having such a speed and power reserve (100mph is 4500rpm, just above the torque peak) is that a quick prod on the throttle thrusts the car past trucks on the narrow two-lane autobahns, and out of harm's way.

All three of us—for I had two passengers, both travelling quite comfortably: the thin backs of the rally buckets improve rear legroom—were developing considerable respect for the CSL as the sun at last began dipping. Don't misunderstand: the car had started with no advantage. I have always disliked the big BMW coupes. They disappoint me after the 3-litre saloons. The

CS isn't just a coupe version of 3.0litre saloon: it's based on the decrepit 2000 chassis. Careful development, however, as in the CSL, can cure no end of ills.

A map showed a side road leading from the autobahn down to a series of villages on the River Main, about 40 miles past Frankfurt. We selected correctly; Marktheidenfeld, where we stopped, was a quaint and quiet little wine town on the river bank, full of very old houses, wine cellars and poky little streets as well as an enjoyable hotel called the Anker where the landlady was good enough to direct us to a restaurant called Main Blick—River View. Indeed, it looked out onto the river and the moored barges and the food was as excellent as we'd been led to believe. What's more, the bill, including a good deal of lager, totalled £2.30 each! The hotel was £3 a head so don't think you can't travel cheaply in Germany if you stay off the main routes.

We were within 200 miles of Munich by now and our plan for Thursday was to drive through the mountains into Bavaria seeking locations for Mervyn Franklyn's camera. Again, the weather was clear and bright after a night that brought very thick frost. The CSL, on the soaking and slippery backroads, was surefooted. One did not feel inhibited by its power. When we reached the high country, however, we drove into mist, icy roads and snow. I hate black ice, and I proceeded very cautiously, using only third and top. But after several miles, it was obvious that the CSL had an extraordinarily high level of roadholding, and the handling to match if the grip did break. Soon, even in those foul conditions, I was driving the car full out, snuggling back in my rally bucket, getting absolutely precise responses from the engine to the movements of the throttle and lapping up the smoothness and fluidness of the steering. We found a bend for photographs, a tight and constant uphill curve, thoroughly soaring. After a couple of exploratory runs, it was being taken at 60mph in second—that's full power, remember—and there was no hint of the tail snapping more than a few inches out of line. That bend sealed my faith in the CSL.

It was all downhill running after that: literally, because we crossed the range and figuratively, because I felt so much at ease with the car that it was pure and unbridled enjoyment without any considerations of needing to spare further time for familiarity. We completed our journey by streaking along the pleasing and almost deserted roads that snake through the hopfields close to Munich, and switched off at our hotel in the city at 6pm. We could, had we wished, have completed the trip the night before if we'd pressed on down the autobahn. But that would have been to deny ourselves a day of motoring far more excellent than anyone has a right to deserve in such conditions.

The CSL WAS worth the bother; the fins and wings may be passé now, they have done their job. They did it very well and it is not hard to feel sorry that their day is done. Is a car of the CSL's capabilities done though? No way. To eat up the miles so competently, to be given such driving pleasure even when sticking fairly closely to the speed limits and to do it at an average fuel consumption of 21.166mpg (better than a 3-litre Granada could have returned in the circumstances) is more than desirable, even now. ●

1969·1976 BMW 6·CYLINDER SEDANS

A bargain-hunter's guide to the 2500, 2800, 3.0 & Bavaria

BY PETER BOHR

DURING THE PAST decade as the BMW marque made its rapid ascent from relative obscurity to status symbol, the Bavaria and its various permutations, including the 2500, 2800, 3.0S and 3.0Si, seem to have fallen between the cracks of the used-car market. As a cult develops around the 2002, as automotive connoisseurs acknowledge the 2800/3.0CS coupes to be up-and-coming classics, and as preppy girls beg their daddies to buy them 320is, prices for these models remain strong. But the poor Bavaria, etc, languish at bargain-basement prices, which is wonderful news for driving enthusiasts with limited budgets.

Evolution of the Sixes

WHILE IT'S true that the 1600/2002 established BMW in America, the early 6-cylinder sedans were an important benchmark in BMW's history as well. These cars showed the world that the pipsqueak car company on Mercedes' home

BMW 2500.

ground was determined to become a grand marque too.

A pipsqueak car company? That might come as a shock to Americans who speak of BMW in the same breath as Rolex, Tiffany, Polo and other labels imbued with great cachet. But just 25 years ago BMW was so weak and vulnerable that American Motors flirted with the notion of buying it out.

However, in 1961 BMW staved off financial ruin and remained independent by unveiling a sensible but technically advanced family car, something altogether different from the ungainly V-8 sedans (the "Baroque Angels") and the comical Isetta (the "Bubblecars") that BMW had built during the Fifties. The new car, called the 1500, was not only the marketing success that BMW so desperately needed, but also the direct forerunner of all the models that came later and filled the company coffers with cash.

One of these was a smaller, lighter version of the 1500, the 1600 introduced in 1966. Of course, we all know the story

BMW

American enthusiasts fell in love with this sports car disguised as a boxy sedan. When Max Hoffman, the U.S. BMW importer, talked the factory into putting a larger 2.0-liter engine in the 1600 body, the enthusiasts' passion for BMW intensified.

By the late Sixties BMW was financially sound. But in America, at least, the virtues of BMW cars were still primarily known only to enthusiasts. If you asked the average American of the time about a BMW, he was likely to think it was made by the "British Motor Works" or some such thing.

Not content to rest in its cozy but narrow marketing niche as a producer of little sports sedans, the company expanded its line in 1968 with a group of new luxury models, two 6-cylinder sedans and a fancy 6-cylinder coupe. This was a gutsy move, for BMW was now trying to encroach on Mercedes territory as a maker of pricey, high quality, high performance sedans.

The two 4-door cars, called the 2500 and 2800, are nearly identical except for engine displacement and trim. They both have many of the styling cues that had come to be BMW trademarks since the 1500: a low beltline, a tall greenhouse, a relatively flat hood and trunk, a continuous fenderline and the completely distinctive grille.

Perhaps the most brilliant feature of the 2500 and 2800 is their 6-cylinder engine, with displacement of 2494 cc and 2788 cc, respectively. It was another of Alex von Falkenhausen's masterpieces. Von Falkenhausen directed BMW's racing activities before World War II and had designed the 4-cylinder engine and its variations for the 1500, 1600 and 2002. Like the 4-cylinder engines, the six had a cast iron block and an aluminum cylinder head with an overhead cam. But it had another feature as well, a trispherical turbulence-inducing combustion chamber,

with the delightfully difficult-to-pronounce German name of *Dreikugelwirbelwannenbrennraum.*

The idea of the new chamber was efficiency. It allowed more complete burning of the air/fuel mixture with a minimum of residual hydrocarbons, and in the late Sixties, as U.S. emissions regulations came into effect, that was a major concern. Von Falkenhausen's engine was clean enough that it didn't require an air pump in the U.S.

R&T's road testers called the engine a "jewel . . . with a sporting exhaust note . . . and practically no underhood noise." We added, "at low speeds it belies its modest displacement with surprisingly generous torque and flexibility." We went on to proclaim the engine the best inline 6-cylinder unit in the world.

The buyer of a 2500 or 2800 had the choice of a 4-speed manual transmission or a ZF 3-speed automatic. R&T's road testers had praise for the crisp 4-speed, but as for the automatic, the testers minced no words: "the worst we've encountered in any car." Oh, dear.

Well, at least the other important components are up to the standards of the marvelous engine. The suspension is independent at all four corners with MacPherson struts up front and semi-trailing arms in the rear, an arrangement very similar to the 1500, 1600 and 2002. It gives an excellent ride over rough surfaces, with generally neutral handling. The 2800 also came with a limited-slip differential and a novel Boge Nivomat automatic load-leveling device as standard equipment.

Both sedans have 4-wheel ATE disc brakes. Oddly enough, the more sporting 2800CS coupe has discs only in front with drum brakes in the rear. So, in this respect, the 2500/2800 sedans are more advanced.

The simple instrument panel, which contains very legible round dials with black-and-white facings, is exactly as an instrument panel should be; no digital displays or video-game gizmos here, thank goodness.

In fact, the whole interior is utterly functional. There's room enough to carry five people quite comfortably, and ingress and egress are very easy. The trunk is huge, and with all the glass, outward vision is outstanding. Yet, there's simple elegance inside, with high quality fittings and materials, including the leather upholstery that came as standard equipment on the 2800.

All the 6-cylinder cars first appeared in this country as 1969

The Bavaria's optional tool kit (right) is mounted to the deck lid for easy access. The Bavaria's interior (below) features spacious seating for five, a properly designed instrument panel and ample luxury.

The 1973 Bavaria's engine still featured twin carburetors (below), which were later replaced with fuel injection for the 3.0Si (bottom).

BMW

models. The 2500 listed for $5367, while the 2800 went for $6369. Five or six grand isn't much today, but back then it was not an inconsiderable sum—a 1969 2002 was only $3053. When you consider that upstart BMW was competing against well established Mercedes-Benz for big-buck import car buyers, in retrospect it's not surprising that sales of the 2500 and 2800 were less than robust.

But Max Hoffman came up with a clever marketing plan. He suggested that the two models be combined into one called the Bavaria. The car appeared in 1971 and was actually a 2800 minus the leather upholstery and Nivomat rear suspension. A few items that had been standard on the 2800, such as the heated rear window and the handsome tool kit attached to the underside of the trunk lid, were made optional.

However, the Bavaria's most important feature was a lower price tag. At less than $5000 ($4987 east coast POE), the car suddenly became a bargain. The name too, was clever strategy because it reinforced the Bavaria's Teutonic origin.

It worked splendidly and sales firmed up. In 1972 BMW increased engine displacement to an even 3.0 liters and decreased compression so the car could use regular gasoline. But the Bavaria name remained. That year BMW also switched from the miserable ZF automatic to a more acceptable Borg-Warner unit.

Then in 1973, BMW resurrected the idea of having two 6-cylinder 4-door models, and added the 3.0S, a car identical to the Bavaria but with every conceivable option, from leather and air conditioning to power assisted steering and stereo.

The same two models were offered in 1974, but by that time the Bavaria's base price had nearly doubled to $10,000—in just three years. The 1974 cars also received simple but not very well integrated 5-mph bumpers.

In the following year, the Bavaria nameplate was dropped. But it lived on through 1976 in the form of the 3.0Si, which was the old loaded-up Bavaria with the addition of Bosch electronic fuel injection instead of the previous twin carburetors. In fact, the 3.0Si and the new 530i shared the same engine. When emissions standards tightened in 1975, BMW chose to use thermal reactors, unlike most manufacturers who went with catalytic converters. Thus, these Bimmers are some of the few 1975 and 1976 cars that can use leaded gas.

So which model of the series should you select? Among BMW *aficionados*, there doesn't seem to be much consensus. The 2800 and the 3.0S/Si have fancier interiors with lovely leather uphol-

stery, but the 3.0Si also has the ugly "rubber baby-buggy" bumpers. And the 3.0Si's thermal reactors have proven troublesome. On the other hand, the 3.0Si's fuel injection gives better performance than the earlier carbureted cars. Fuel economy steadily declined over the years as emissions standards stiffened. However, the post-1971 models can get by on cheaper, regular gas. There are plenty of tradeoffs, to be sure, but as in most used-car purchases, what counts is finding a car that's had a life of tender loving care.

Problems, Problems—and Solutions

WHEN BMW engineers designed their cars in the Sixties and Seventies, apparently they had in mind cool breezes wafting through Bavarian forests, not the sizzling summertime temperatures of the U.S. Both the 2002 series and the early 6-cylinder cars are notorious for bursting radiator hoses and boiling coolant. Not only is such overheating annoying—who needs Old Faithful under the hood when you're creeping through rush-hour traffic?—but the aluminum heads of a BMW are extremely susceptible to warpage, and that means blown head gaskets and other expensive maladies.

Because overheating is so pervasive among these BMWs, owners have come up with a roster of cures. First is modification of the radiator. There are two ways to accomplish this. You can have the radiator recored with a thicker core, but there's a hitch: With less than an inch of clearance between the fan and the stock radiator, a thicker core, a worn engine mount, a quick step and—bingo!—the fan grinds itself up in the radiator.

Another, safer solution is to recore the old radiator entirely with a so-called "optimum core" unit. Eskimo makes one for these 6-cylinder BMWs that costs about $200. The radiator isn't any thicker, but it does contain more tubes per square inch, which effectively increases the cooling area.

Roger Moon, chairman of the board of the BMW Automobile Club of America, suggests removing the regular engine-driven fan and replacing it with two electric "pancake" fans. Both of them can be mounted behind the radiator, one in the upper left corner and one in the lower right. This modification will also cost around $200.

Locking up the temperature-controlled fan clutch is yet another trick that might help; the fan then spins continuously. Of course, it's important to remember that we're discussing 10- and 15-year-old cars with cooling systems that may be filled with rust and built-up crud. So regular radiator flushing and the use of a 50/50 mixture of coolant and water are important maintenance procedures with these BMWs.

Cracked cylinder heads are also heat-related problems. Though many early 6-cylinder BMWs develop cracked heads sooner or later, the 3.0Sis are especially plagued because of the enormous heat generated by the twin thermal reactors (at night you can see them glowing red-hot). The primary symptom is a cloud of steam from the exhaust pipe and rough running at start up. Substituting a 1980 or later cylinder head with revised water jackets is the cure.

The stainless-steel reactors are troublesome too, and expensive to replace—about $1200 for the pair. Baffles inside the reactors break and block the flow of exhaust gases. Heat shields around the reactors frequently crack and cause vibrations.

In an R&T Owner Survey of the early 6-cylinder cars, published in the July 1973 issue, we discovered that water pumps fail on a regular basis at about 40,000 miles. Fortunately at about $40, they're not too expensive. We also found considerable dissatisfaction with the performance of the air conditioners: "It's paradoxical that even such expensive cars don't have air conditioners that can match a Chevrolet's."

Ranking right up there on the gripe list with the cooling system is carburetion. The carbureted 6-cylinder cars use twin Solex/Zenith carbs, which are difficult to maintain. And even when set up properly, they're cursed for their stumbling and hesitation upon acceleration, particularly when the engine is

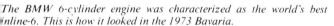

The BMW 6-cylinder engine was characterized as the world's best inline-6. This is how it looked in the 1973 Bavaria.

PHOTO BY GORDON CHITTENDEN

BMW

cold, and for surging and flat spots at moderate speeds. Many owners of 6-cylinder BMWs have switched to Weber carbs, and they're glad they did. This kind of modification poses sticky questions for owners who live in states with stringent emission-control-device inspections (like California) where non-original equipment is grounds for a failure. However, several companies are marketing "smog-legal" Weber conversion kits. JAM Engineering in Monterey, California expects to have its Weber kit for 6-cylinder BMWs certified by California state officials by the time this article appears. JAM's kit uses the stock air cleaners and costs $640.

Okay, we admit that these early 6-cylinder sedans aren't troublefree. Nor are they cheap to repair. Joe Schneider (Schneider Motors in Orange, California) gives some typical prices for jobs performed in his shop (all include parts and labor): engine overhaul with new pistons, $3000; cylinder head rebuild, $1800; brake master cylinder rebuild, $85; new clutch, $350; overhaul of manual gearbox (if the gears aren't completely shot), $400.

But once the chronic cooling and carburetion problems are cured, the 6-cylinder sedans are rugged machines. And rust doesn't appear to be a terrible problem either. Unlike their little brothers, the 2002s, and especially unlike the 2800/3.0CS coupes with their Karmann-built bodies ("Karmann invented rust and then licensed the process to the Italians," says Roger Moon), the 6-cylinder sedans are slow to corrode. When rust appears, it's likely to start in the doors at the lower back corners.

Driving Impressions

SOMETIMES A drive down memory lane seems filled with potholes. You've probably had the disconcerting experience of running into former lovers or close friends and wondering, "What the devil did I ever see in them?" And you've undoubtedly had the same thing happen with cars; you fondly remember a certain car, but when you drive one again after many years, it feels disappointingly old.

One of my treasured motoring memories is the year I shared with a 1969 BMW 2500. Together we conquered the mountain roads of the Sierra Nevadas on the way to favorite ski slopes. We challenged the twists and turns of Route 1 along the California coast. And we pretended we were on a German *Autobahn* and cruised down the empty, endlessly straight miles of Interstate 5 at 90 mph for hours.

The car was such a chameleon. When we were alone, it was a sports car. I came to love the sparkling power of the 6-cylinder engine, to revel in the feel of the communicative steering, and to delight in the bite of the disc brakes as I used them to duck the car in and out of the corners.

But when we had company, the 2500 was a luxury sedan. The engine was quiet and silky smooth. The cabin was civilized with the amenities of reclining seats, a decent stereo and air conditioning. The suspension soaked up the bumps in the road, and the trunk easily carried our guests' belongings.

So with such good memories, memories that had stayed with me through 10 years and drives in hundreds of different cars, I stepped into Dale Cassel's 1971 Bavaria with some trepidation. It was *déjà vu* all right. The big steering wheel, the upright seats and the expanse of glass were there, just as I had remembered. So too was the wonderful engine. Oh sure, there was a trace of wear in the 2nd-gear synchro, there was the old stumble on acceleration when the engine was cold (Dale still uses the original carbs in the car), and there was more wind and road noise than any modern BMW would have.

But you know what? Dale's rusty-blue (the factory called it "Riviera") Bavaria didn't seem very dated. The precision, tightness and tossibility for which BMWs have become famous were quite evident in the car, even with 159,000 miles on it.

Dale co-owns a shop that's been repairing BMWs for more than two decades (Adams Service Inc in Riverside, California). He bought the car several years ago from one of his longtime employees, Cy Franke. Both Dale and Cy are the kind of knowledgeable and dedicated mechanics in whose care every BMW should fall. Though the car is not a pampered pet—Dale uses it as an everyday car—Dale and Cy have adhered to a rigorous maintenance schedule. They change the oil every 3000 miles, perform a major service every 8000–10,000 miles and change all the cooling system hoses every two years. In return, the Bavaria has given them all those miles with little more than a chattering clutch, a couple of busted water pumps and the inevitable cracked cylinder head (at 112,000 miles).

After driving Dale's car, and considering that 2002s are selling for the same prices as Bavarias, the big 4-door sedans seem to be an incredible bargain. Fuel economy might not be as good; Dale says his car gets only 16–18 mpg around town. Otherwise the Bavaria feels like a slightly larger but vastly refined 2002.

Maybe some memories stand the test of time after all.

BRIEF SPECIFICATIONS

	2500	Bavaria	3.0Si
Curb weight, lb	3005	3170	3420
Wheelbase, in.	106.0	106.0	106.0
Track, f/r	56.9/57.6	56.9/57.6	58.3/57.9
Length	185.0	185.0	195.0
Width	68.9	68.9	68.9
Height	56.1	56.1	57.1
Engine type	sohc inline-6	sohc inline-6	sohc inline-6
Bore x stroke, mm	86.0 x 71.6	86.0 x 80.0	89.0 x 80.0
Displacement, cc	2494	2788	2985
Horsepower, bhp @ rpm	170 @ 6000	192 @ 6000	176 @ 5500
Torque, lb-ft @ rpm	176 @ 3700	200 @ 3700	185 @ 4500
Transmission	4-sp M/3-sp A	4-sp M/3-sp A	4-sp M/3-sp A
Suspension, f/r	ind/ind	ind/ind	ind/ind
Brakes, f/r	disc/disc	disc/disc	disc/disc
Steering type	worm & roller	worm & roller	worm & roller

PERFORMANCE DATA
from Contemporary Tests

	1969 2500	1971 Bavaria
0–60 mph, sec	10.0	9.3
Standing ¼ mile, sec	17.3	16.8
Avg fuel consumption, mpg	20.9	18.0
Road test date	6-69	8-71

TYPICAL ASKING PRICES*

1969–1971 2500, 2800	$2000–$4000
1971–1974 Bavaria	$2500–$5000
1973–1976 3.0S, 3.0Si	$3000–$6000

*Prices are for cars in good to excellent condition. Cars with automatic transmissions generally fall at the low end of the price ranges.

CAR CLUBS

BMW Automobile Club of America, PO Box 401, Hollywood, Calif. 90078.

BMW Car Club of America, Inc, National Office, 345 Harvard St, Cambridge, Mass. 02138.

The "Senior Six Register" is an affiliate of the BMW Car Club of America organized for older 6-cylinder BMWs. The register publishes a quarterly newsletter. Contact: Gary Apps, 3503 Kenbrooke Ct, Kalamazoo, Mich. 49007.

LEIGHTGEMETAL

In 1971 BMW needed a lightweight version of its big CS coupé to homologate for the European Touring Car Championship. The CSL was the result, a faster alloy-panelled car for real men who wore their flares tight and their sideburns long. Martin Buckley drives the 3-litre version and the winged 3.2-litre version that big coupé fans simply know, for obvious reasons, as the Batmobile

The CSL came about because BMW wanted to do this: win at Euro Touring Cars

Above: CSL has airy cabin with special hip-hugging Scheel buckets found only on lightweights

Below: 7in Alpina alloys on 3-litre CSL. Below left: rare complete drop-down tool tray a BMW trademark

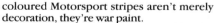

I t sounds just plain silly, the big silver BMW CSL: stridently aggressive as a low-flying Stuka when you let rip on the big organ pedal; loud enough to induce coronaries in the elderly, its bawdy war cry is best restrained if plod is on the prowl.

But then restraint never was a CSL strong point, especially if you're talking about the extravagant winged 3.2 litre car, which we are.

It was a very indiscreet price (nine grand was serious wedge in 1974) it had very indiscreet performance (quicker than a Dino) and it came with the most indiscreet spoiler ever devised, a big glassfibre bootlid construction that looked like a cross between an unfinished motorway bridge and a Black and Decker Workmate. It so offended the powers-that-be in Germany that all cars sold there had the 'racing kit' packed away in the boot for the owners to fit – or not – at their leisure.

Daft as it looked, the wing was intrinsic to the success of the coupés in the European Touring Car series, clamping the tail to the road with massive aerodynamic downforce.

It was created in a panic session in the Stuttgart wind tunnel after Jochen Neerspach and Martin Braungart of BMW Motorsport discovered a loophole in the FIA regulations that allowed 'evolutionary improvements' to be made to existing models. With the works CSL about to make a return to the ETC they were looking for a way of eliminating the aerodynamic lift at speeds over 124mph.

It worked, and the works CSLs gave the Capris a good seeing-to first time out at the Nürburgring, cutting lap times by 15 secs. For track use, the wing had to be homologated on a production car, hence the Batmobile bits, announced in the summer of 1973.

'Batmobile' was just an unofficial nickname of course, an allusion to the car used in the camped-up '60s *Batman* series. Even without the wing this big coupé – so delicate, even feminine in standard form – has did-you-spill-my-pint aggression, bumperless at the front with a big snowplough chin spoiler, chrome wheelarch extensions barely containing the plump 7in Alpina wheels. Those multi-

coloured Motorsport stripes aren't merely decoration, they're war paint.

Martin Pearce's Batmobile is one of five that came to Britain on special order during the mid-'70s out of a total production now reckoned to be 166 (see *Sorting out the CSLs, p91*). It now squats lower than standard on 16in diameter Alpina wheels, expensively shod with Dunlop G5Ds.

It's a left-hooker – all the Bats were – but otherwise the surroundings inside are familiar BMW coupé: super airy, superb vision all round with those slim pillars, plenty of width, a few slivers of wood a token nod at luxury. Drop down shin-bins and the hooded four-instrument binnacle are the same as the standard CS/CSi and date from the 1965 'Sharknose' 2000 Coupe which used the same body/chassis rear of the screen pillar.

The steering wheel, a non-period addition, seems high set because the Scheel bucket seats – as used in the 'normal' non-Bat CSLs – have low, thin cushions but otherwise the driving position, for me, is ideal.

High bucket sides mean the seats are awkward to get into at first but once you're in they are spectacularly comfortable and completely supportive. No electric windows in the Batmobile: low-geared winders operate thin weight-saving Verbel side glasses and the rear panes are fixed, denying the Bat-man (or woman) one of the great pleasures of the standard Karmann-built coupé – open plan pillarless sides.

Semi-usable rear seats are a BMW coupé feature, the electronic 'brain' for the Bosch injection safe under the left-hand seat. All CSLs have black trim – door panels, carpets, even the headlining – and the Scheel seats have no backrest adjustment, although you can alter their angle on the runners.

What's great about this coupé is its docility that goes with such hard-slugging punch. It ticks over with a gruff, round-edged burble, the Bosch injection hunting slightly at 1000rpm. It will steam away vigorously from 1500-2000rpm in top, (which is fifth gear on this car since its previous owner Brian Bradley

fitted ZF gearbox from an M535i in 1987).

Sub-3000 rpm response to the big long-travel pedal is strong but not exceptional: it hardens rapidly beyond, the power building quickly as this beautifully balanced seven-bearing SOHC 'six' shows you a flash of well-toned muscle, breathing aided by an Alpina sports camshaft fitted during the last engine rebuild. It's honest, free-revving thump-in-the-back stuff that makes overtaking child's play whether you just want to use the torque mid-range or access that wedge of solid, searing creamy thrust higher up.

This side of a four-cam exotic you'll not find a more intoxicating engine to listen to than this big 'six': let the revs climb and hear that urbane hollow burble change to deep-throated thoroughbred aggression under power. Its a real scalp-prickler, almost drowned by that blaring, strident exhaust, very non-standard and surely borderline-legal.

BMW claimed 0-60mph in 6.8 secs for this car, but it feels quicker. The only mildly limiting factor is the dog-leg first gearbox. First to

second is slow and it doesn't take kindly to a hurried downchange, say fourth to third, when the synchro' rings fight back. Otherwise it's a pleasant, quiet, lightweight change with a nice light clutch.

BMW eschewed power assistance for the pukka lightweight and with good reason because the CSL steers beautifully: it's light, precise and with perfect weight and feel for a car that feels superbly poised and confident. With just a touch of understeer and no detectable roll the car has superb front-end bite, changing direction fluidly, with no threat of the semi-trailing arm tail breaking loose in the dry. The ride is firm but comfortable.

Meaty ventilated discs all round, operated by a nice firm pedal, give the sort of strong and repeatable braking power you don't have to think about, and you can heel and toe easily between the pendant pedal and the organ-style throttle.

For comparison I drove Edward Christie's CSL, one of the 500 softer UK-spec cars imported between 1972 and '74, fresh from

Move over! Batmobile is pure aggression on the road but smooth and refined with it. Aerofoil really works, doesn't hinder vision

a long-winded, heart-rending rebuild (the original restorers nicked the engine!) that took the best part of a decade. It looks tame next to the Batmobile (but prettier to my mind) and doesn't have that car's pace, though the difference in power is officially only 6bhp.

It's still impressively quick, with sparkling upper-range pick-up: you can pass slower cars on fast A-roads simply by squeezing the throttle rather than changing down, so strong and eager is the pull. The car is limited by its four-speed gearbox, a slick-shifting Getrag unit pulling a low, 22mph-per-1000rpm top. The 'six' is spinning quite hard at 80mph and,

with added commotion caused by the badly sealed side glasses – power operated on this UK car – the CSL is a fussy cruiser.

On a more mundane level ventilation is a BMW coupé problem, with a feeble booster fan, big window areas to absorb the sun and lots of heat soak from the exhaust.

With Bilsteins all round, the 3-litre car corners almost as confidently as the Batmobile, blasting through open sweepers with superb stability. The power steering is unobtrusive, with just a touch more slop than the Bat's unassisted set-up but with still-genuine feel. The tail needs more care in this car with its taller rubber but with RHD and not too

much nose or tail to worry about the coupé feels wieldy and nimble in a way a hard-to-see-out-of, cramped mid-engined exotic can't.

After the lightweights died in 1975 BMW's big coupés got a bit fat and boring. The M6 retrieved the situation with its stunning performance but it was the little M3 and M3 Evolution cars that really recaptured the spirit of the lightweights.

Even so BMW still hasn't built a prettier car than the unwinged CSL, or a wilder-looking one that the Batmobile. Rare, fast and elegant with racing connections and bucketloads of driver appeal, the CSLs have copybook classic car credentials. I love 'em. **CLASSIC**

SORTING OUT THE CSLS

BMW built 1000 'standard' 3.0 CSLs and 39 'Batmobiles' – right? Wrong. There are many more Batmobiles than you'd think and the so-called standard CSL came in three distinct variations.

The first cars – announced May '71 – were stripped-for-action road racers: cased on the CS coupé, with the 2985cc carburetted engine giving 180bhp, they had thinner body panels, no front bumper (glassfibre rear bumper), racing latches on the bonnet, manual winding side

Special RHD Equipment for Great Britain. BMW 3.0 CSL

windows (made from Plexiglas) and of course the alloy skinned opening panels, were all in the name of weight reduction. BMW even skimped on rust protection and sound deadening.

Along with some drastically cheaper interior trim and lightweight Scheel bucket seats, 400lbs was pared off the coupé, so acceleration was decisively quicker. Suspension was stiffened by Bilstein gas shockers with progressive rate springs and the wheels were fat Alpina 7in alloys with chrome wheelarch extensions to keep them legal. Black stripes distinguished the Leightgemetal from the standard CS: 169 of these were built, all LHD.

In August 1972, a bore increase to the engine gave 3003cc, which allowed the CSL to slip into Group 2 competition. At the same time Bosch electronic injection replaced the twin Zenith carbs and power rose to 200bhp. 539 were built, including the 'Batmobiles', (see below).

The British specification RHD car (left) was introduced in the UK in October 1972 and came with a 'RHD City package' to appease fat-cat Brits who

wanted the lightweight racer cache with none of the discomfort.

The UK CSL had bumpers, standard coupé carpets, even tinted electric side windows. Power steering returned too as did softer CS suspension. The bonnet could be unlocked from inside the glovebox, although it was still manually propped rather than counterbalanced. The British importer took 500 and dropped the ordinary CSi at the same time, reckoning that buyers looking for the ultimate in BMW performance would take the lightweight, lazy drivers the automatic, carburetted CSa. But the CSL was a slow seller: prices were high – more than an Aston or Jensen – and not everybody liked the bucket seats or wanted to be bothered with the easily damaged alloy panels. So the CSi reappeared and the last of the 'British' CSLs was sold in August '74.

The 3.2 litre CSL – 'Batmobile' to you and I, although not all wore the spoiler kit – was announced in August 1973. These cars were numbered 430-539 of the run of 539 cars already mentioned, were LHD only and had a 3153cc, 206bhp engine

to homologate the 84mm stroke used on the 3.5 litre works racing coupé. They were still badged 3.0 litre.

The 3.2 used the lightweight shell (initially available only in Polaris silver or Chamonix white with optional Motorsport stripes) as before with alloy doors and bonnet but – to take the weight and downforce of the rear wing – the bootlid was steel with fittings for the spoiler. And, yes, the spoiler (or Racing kit) was packed away in the boot on cars sold in West Germany. There was a deep front spoiler, a roof hoop spoiler just above the rear window, a small lip spoiler on the edge of the bootlid and rubber 'splitters' on the front wings. Plexiglass was used and, like the previous German spec CSLs, 3.2-litre cars had fixed rear quarter windows, manual steering and Bilstein gas-pressure shockers. Not all of these 109 cars had their racing kits fitted and owners could opt for the 'Town kit' too.

There was a last batch – built in '74-'75 – of series two Batmobiles with minor differences like a three-fin rear wing and a driver's seat with an adjustable backrest. 57 were built.